Before the Religious Right

INTELLECTUAL HISTORY
OF THE MODERN AGE

Series Editors
Angus Burgin
Peter E. Gordon
Joel Isaac
Karuna Mantena
Samuel Moyn
Jennifer Ratner-Rosenhagen
Camille Robcis
Sophia Rosenfeld

BEFORE THE RELIGIOUS RIGHT

Liberal Protestants, Human Rights,
and the Polarization of the
United States

Gene Zubovich

PENN

UNIVERSITY OF PENNSYLVANIA PRESS

PHILADELPHIA

Published by
University of Pennsylvania Press
Philadelphia, Pennsylvania 19104-4112
www.upenn.edu/pennpress

Printed in the United States of America on acid-free paper
10   9   8   7   6   5   4   3   2   1

Library of Congress Cataloging-in-Publication Data
Names: Zubovich, Gene, author.
Title: Before the religious right : liberal Protestants, human rights, and
the polarization of the United States / Gene Zubovich.
Other titles: Intellectual history of the modern age.
Description: 1st edition. | Philadelphia : University of Pennsylvania
Press, [2022] | Series: Intellectual history of the modern age | Includes
bibliographical references and index.
Identifiers: LCCN 2021030566 | ISBN 9780812253689 (hardcover) |
ISBN 9780812298291 (eBook)
Subjects: LCSH: Protestant churches—United States—History—20th
century. | Protestantism—United States—History—20th century. |
Liberalism (Religion)—Protestant churches—History—20th century. |
Human rights—Religious aspects—Protestant churches—History—
20th century. | Globalization—Religious aspects—Protestant
churches. | Liberalism—United States—History—20th century. |
Polarization (Social sciences)—United States—History—20th century.
| United States—Politics and government—20th century.
Classification: LCC BR525 .Z83 2022 | DDC 280/.40973—dc23
LC record available at https://lccn.loc.gov/2021030566

For Katherine

CONTENTS

NOTE ON TRANSLATION

This book uses pinyin to romanize Chinese names and places and the Library of Congress guidelines for Russian names and locations. Exceptions were made for commonly translated names of individuals and places, and names appearing in quotations.

Before the Religious Right

Global Gospel, American Politics

In 1948, one week before the United Nations ratified the Universal Declaration of Human Rights, the Federal Council of Churches asked the American public to confront the domestic implications of the UN document. The council was the largest and most influential Protestant body in the United States, and it felt a calling to proclaim these new international human rights to Americans. It announced that respecting "the dignity of man" required acknowledging the human right "to a standard of living adequate for the welfare and security of the individual and the family." Echoing the principles of the New Deal, the council announced that every person is due an adequate living space, a good education, recreation and leisure, proper health services, and the right to join a labor union. The council's 1948 human rights statement was also a direct and public attack on racial segregation. Denouncing Jim Crow as "a violation of the gospel of love and human brotherhood," the council pledged to "work for a non-segregated church and a non-segregated society."[1]

For the Federal Council of Churches, the "denial of freedom, justice and security to others" cut across traditional boundaries between foreign and domestic. At a moment when ecumenical Protestants mobilized for a more Christian postwar international order, one that would make sure the horrors of World War II would never be repeated, they recognized that fighting injustice in the United States would be a stepping-stone to a more peaceful world. Abroad and at home, "the flagrant violation of human rights in our generation has impeded the achievement of world order," proclaimed the council.[2]

One of the most important products of ecumenical Protestants' new global outlook in the 1940s was their commitment to human rights. Ecumenical Protestants, sometimes called "liberal" or "mainline" Protestants, distinguished themselves from their evangelical and fundamentalist rivals by opposing Christian nationalism. Since the 1920s, ecumenical Protestants had engaged the world in new ways. In addition to longstanding missionary work, they began to tour the globe on study trips, built international NGOs, and created new connections with their fellow Protestants in Europe, Asia, Africa, and Latin America. As they helped build these international networks, ecumenical Protestants began to advocate for human rights. In particular, they promoted human rights as a response to the problem of nationalism, as a way of subordinating all peoples and all nations to God's will under a global government.

In the 1940s, ecumenical Protestants led the charge in bringing international human rights into the domestic politics of the United States. In doing so, they revitalized American conversations around race, the economy, and US foreign relations, and they became important supporters of mid-century liberalism. In the process, they transformed American politics by promoting ideas, policies, and popular movements that outlived the decline of ecumenicals' influence in the 1970s. They also unwittingly helped create the politically polarized nation that exists today. Their global gospel was created to change the world. In due time, it transformed the United States. In some important ways, we are living in the world ecumenical Protestants helped create.

Ecumenical Protestantism and Its Power Elite

It is hard to define any religious group with precision, and that is especially true for Protestants, who today are divided into more than 30,000 denominations.[3] Ecumenical Protestants are theologically liberal. Those who headed the Federal Council of Churches at mid-century accepted scientific and scholarly developments that led them to read the Bible critically and historically, and to make peace with doctrines like Darwinism. In this way, they differed from fundamentalists, who defined themselves in the early twentieth century against these "innovations."[4] Unlike evangelicals, ecumenical Protestants understood "evangelism" to mean more than converting others to the true faith. For ecumenical Protestants, who sent out the vast majority of American missionaries prior to the 1960s, social reform initiatives like building schools, hospitals, and agricultural stations took priority over conversion in their understanding of evangelism. But the divisions between ecumenical, fundamentalist, and evangelical Protestants were not merely theological.[5] Ecumenical Protestants distinguished themselves by promoting religious pluralism, anti-racism, the rights of labor, governmental aid to the poor, women's rights, and international organizations in the face of opposition from their religious rivals.

Ecumenical Protestants were also institution builders and cooperators. What made this group different from secular liberals who shared some of their political goals, and from other Christian communities, was their devotion to ecumenism.[6] A babel of theologies competed for Protestant attention at mid-century, including realism, modernism, pacifism, personalism, the social gospel, anti-racism, and neoorthodoxy. But ecumenism, the desire to unite Christians, towered above them all, binding together these disparate views and allowing this diverse group to withstand deep disagreements about other religious questions. They were inspired by *oikoumene*, Greek for "the whole globe," and took the biblical injunction to spread the gospel "throughout the whole globe" (Matt. 24:14) so "that they may all be one" (John 17:21) to mean that their religion demanded unity. They built organizations with the purpose of overcoming denominational and national divisions. These institutions were one of the main sources of their power in American life and in international affairs. Ecumenical Protestantism consisted of a constellation of groups that orbited around the Federal Council of Churches in the United States, and the World Council of Churches internationally.

The Federal Council of Churches—after 1950 it was called the National Council of Churches—functioned as a think-tank and a political action committee on behalf of about thirty ecumenical denominations. The most influential were the "seven sisters" of American Protestantism: Episcopalians, United Methodists, Northern Presbyterians, United Lutherans, Northern Baptists, Congregationalists, and the Disciples of Christ. These denominations were collectively much wealthier and more white than the United States as a whole. The seven sisters were joined by African American denominations, like the African Methodist Episcopal Church, which were invited to join the council as junior partners. Collectively, these denominations represented between one-quarter and one-third of the US population at mid-century. Further ensuring that ecumenical Protestantism shaped the everyday lives of millions of Americans across the country, voluntary groups like the Young Men's Christian Association, the Young Women's Christian Association, and Church Women United shared membership and staff with the council.

But numbers alone do not explain the political and cultural authority ecumenical Protestants commanded at mid-century. Their members included some of the wealthiest, most educated, and most powerful Americans. The vast majority of presidents, senators, members of Congress, Supreme Court justices, corporate executives, and university presidents were affiliated with ecumenical Protestant denominations before the 1960s. And the important role of religion for American elites ensured that ecumenical Protestants had access to the corridors of power. For example, on a single day in 1923, Methodist missionary leader John R. Mott had breakfast with Supreme Court Justice and former president William Howard Taft, followed by lunch with President Calvin Coolidge, and an afternoon visit with his good friend, the former president Woodrow Wilson.[7] From the 1920s to the 1960s, ecumenical Protestants headed a "moral establishment" deeply intertwined with American political and cultural power.[8]

Ecumenical Protestantism involved a broad swath of the American population but it was governed by a small group of leaders. They were educators, researchers, directors of missionary organizations, denominational officers, religious bureaucrats, prominent pastors, and newspaper editors. They were often joined by influential laypersons, including diplomats, politicians, labor organizers, authors, lawyers, and corporate executives. Collectively, they had multiple responsibilities in an overlapping set of heavily bureaucratized organizations that tied together local, regional, denominational, interdenominational, and international Protestant organizations. This "interlocking directorate," to borrow a phrase from the mid-century sociologist C. Wright Mills, comprised a "power elite" of American Protestantism that acted as the religion's public face.[9] Their intersecting institutional responsibilities, and their geographical concentration in a few square blocks of midtown Manhattan (before these bureaucrats moved into a single, architecturally uninspiring building in Morningside Heights nicknamed the "God Box"), make it possible to speak of a single ecumenical Protestant community in the United States at mid-century.

Protestant Globalism and Human Rights

In the middle decades of the twentieth century, American ecumenical Protestants mobilized their power and influence to implement what they called "world order." It would be one of the most ambitious and significant political mobilizations undertaken by any American religious group. Ecumenical Protestants had long been politically active. Compared with their fundamentalist and evangelical antagonists, they were more likely to take progressive positions on the issues of the day. They proudly claimed as their own the movement for the abolition of slavery and the early twentieth-century fight against the exploitation of industrial workers, known as the social gospel. They also remembered, with some embarrassment, their role in banning alcohol in 1919. Even so, during the mid-twentieth century ecumenical Protestants mobilized again, on a scale not seen since Prohibition.

This time they rallied under the new banner of globalism. Earlier in the century, it was ecumenism—the movement to unite Christians across national and denominational boundaries—that led Protestants to create new international networks. These networks presented opportunities for American Protestants to go abroad, and, beginning in the 1920s, a generation of leaders left home on study missions, toured missionary stations, and traveled to international religious conferences. Through their travel, ecumenical Protestant leaders began to see the borders between nation-states as antiquated boundaries. They reasoned that the spread of Christianity, industrial capitalism, transportation networks, education, and science was bringing the world closer together, diminishing what were once great cultural and physical distances. In the 1930s, the Protestant establishment, for the first time, saw the world of nations as a single, interconnected whole—a view this book calls "Protestant globalism."

Protestant globalism was an outlook that sought to subordinate nation-states to a world government and a universal moral code.[10] Christian nationalism, the belief in the sacredness of national boundaries and a suspicion of what lies beyond the country's borders, was a nonstarter for ecumenical Protestants.[11] Internationalism—the cooperation between distinct, autonomous nations embodied by the League of Nations—also did not satisfy ecumenical Protestants because it did not recognize forms of solidarity and connectedness that existed beyond the nation-state. The problem, as John Foster Dulles saw it in 1937, was that the international order was a "rededication of the nations to the old principles of sovereignty," of "unchanging and unchangeable compartments, the walls of which would continue as perpetual barriers to the interplay of dynamic forces."[12] In an international climate dominated by "totalitarian" states, Dulles, the Presbyterian layman and future secretary of state, was one of many Protestants who came to believe that nation-states were a problem that could only be solved through some kind of world government that would rein in their independence. Because they saw the world through the prism of globalism, ecumenical Protestants became enthusiastic supporters of the UN and the doctrine of human rights.

Ecumenical Protestants embraced globalism at a time when many of the world's peoples had liberated themselves from European empires and founded their own nation-states. This development—there were approximately fifty countries at the beginning of the twentieth century while today there are nearly two hundred—was one of the seismic shifts in world affairs in the twentieth century and something that American ecumenical Protestants could hardly ignore. Nor could they ignore the rise of American power following World War II, as the country took on the role previously played by the now-declining European empires.

Protestant globalism was a waystation between the world of empires and the world of nation-states. It helped ecumenical Protestants avoid divisive debates about decolonization even as they became more critical of imperialism. From the 1920s through the 1950s, American ecumenical Protestant thought and action were neither consistently pro-colonial nor anti-colonial. The Protestants who subscribed to globalism wanted a world government, which would simultaneously end imperialism and place restrictions on the autonomy of nation-states. Beyond that point of consensus, though, their views varied. Protestants on the left emphasized that a new world government would free oppressed peoples from empires, while those on the right insisted that a world government would force newly emergent countries to behave in accordance with Christian and Western values. For those in the middle, Protestant globalism provided a justification for many of the proximate goals that anti-colonial activists advocated, such as diminishing racism, distributing wealth more fairly, and placing limits on the behavior of empires—all without necessarily endorsing self-determination.

Similarly, globalism was compatible with conflicting views about American power. Historians have typically depicted ecumenical Protestants as either zealous cold warriors or ardent dissidents opposed to American military policies.[13] This book shows that some ecumenical Protestants, like Dulles, believed that the United States would usher in a more just world order by exporting its values, while others maintained that the United States needed to demilitarize and that it must work together with other countries—including communist ones—as a nation among nations. By focusing attention on world government instead of self-government, globalism hid deep divisions among

American ecumenical Protestants about self-determination and American power. These divisions would become public by the 1960s.

Although Protestant globalism faded away in the 1960s, it had birthed institutions, ideas, and practices that would prove more enduring. The most important product of Protestant globalism was the new doctrine of human rights. Ecumenical Protestants were central players in the invention and spread of human rights discourse and were decisive in bringing human rights to bear on American politics. If the world was an interdependent whole, as ecumenical Protestants believed, then what happens in the United States matters deeply to the whole globe. Americans are as bound to respect human rights as are others, they reasoned. Human rights discourse was therefore taken up by ecumenical Protestants to deal anew with segregation, the economy, and US foreign relations.

Thinking this way about human rights may seem counterintuitive. Today, we are accustomed to seeing human rights violations as a new and distinct realm of criminal activity, like torturing political dissidents, which takes place outside the United States. But, at mid-century, ecumenical Protestants understood human rights as a way of critically appraising social, political, and economic practices, abroad and at home, in light of what they called the God-given dignity and worth of the human person. For this reason, Christian conceptions of human rights did not displace other social justice arenas with new concerns. Instead, the rights of the "human person" reframed and reinvigorated ongoing fights over wealth inequality, poverty, militarization, war, and racism.[14]

Scholars have debated the historical origins of human rights but they have only recently begun paying attention to the important role religious groups played in their formation and dissemination.[15] Moreover, historians are only now starting to explore the role of human rights in the domestic politics of the United States.[16] Typically, historians of the United States have presented human rights as an invention of World War II, which was followed by their dramatic disappearance during the early Cold War, and their equally dramatic revival in the 1970s. Unlike other accounts, this book locates the religious roots of human rights in the ecumenical milieu, and it highlights both the institutional and theological innovations among ecumenical Protestants to help explain how human rights developed and why they became popular in the 1940s. It shows that ecumenical Protestant initiatives sometimes resonated with the US government's promotion of human rights, for example, in the 1940s. But this religious community's continued evocation of human rights into the 1950s and 1960s cuts against the standard timeline. And ecumenical Protestants' evoked human rights in arenas other than law and foreign policy, which demonstrates that the role of human rights in US history is more widespread and nuanced than is often suggested in scholarship.

This book focuses on three arenas of human rights politics that ecumenical Protestants themselves prioritized: the movements to eradicate racism, to reform the economy, and to transform America's role in world affairs. Amid the enthusiasm for world government, some ecumenical Protestants made a compelling case that a commitment to human rights necessitated desegregation. Figures like Thelma Stevens, Channing Tobias, and Benjamin Mays convinced the Federal Council of Churches in 1946 to become the first large, predominantly white religious body—in fact, the only large, predominantly white organization aside from the Communist Party—to call out Jim Crow by name and demand its immediate abolition. "We cannot hope to influence other peoples to accept the Christian way of life, or other nations to accept the democratic principles we proclaim unless we can demonstrate in our own community living that we take them seriously and are striving to translate them into effective practices," they explained.[17]

As this book shows, despite resistance within their own congregations, ecumenical Protestants mobilized politically from the 1940s to the 1960s to end segregation. They knocked on doors and asked their neighbors to stop signing restrictive covenants, they filed lawsuits against police brutality, lobbied Congress to end race-based immigration restrictions, and joined the NAACP's legal battle against Jim Crow. From the streets of Los Angeles to the Supreme Court, ecumenical Protestants mobilized to end segregation in the name of human rights.

Human rights were also intertwined with debates about economic inequality. As early as 1908, the Federal Council of Churches celebrated "the dignity of labor" and the "human brotherhood" between Christians and "the toilers of America."[18] A concern for what would later be called human rights first led the organization to advocate for an industrial democracy that would give workers a greater say over their working lives. Their ideas anticipated many of the innovations of the New Deal. Ecumenical Protestant leaders worked to ensure passage of crucial legislation, including the Wagner Act, which legalized unions, and the Social Security Act, which created a safety net for some of the most vulnerable Americans. By the 1940s, they offered a globally inspired vision of, in their words, a "Responsible Society" as a middle way between capitalism and socialism. "A responsible society is one where freedom is the freedom of men who acknowledge responsibility to justice and public order," they announced, "and where those who hold political authority or economic power are responsible for its exercise to God and the people whose welfare is affected by it."[19] They also orchestrated an ambitious mobilization to bring corporate executives and labor leaders together to agree on the ethical principles of a fair economy. Over time, they joined a growing chorus of critics worried about the poor being left behind by a thriving economy.

Ecumenical Protestants understood that segregation and the domestic economy were tied to colonial empires and the global economy. And so, they spearheaded the effort to reform international relations, especially the US role in the post–World War II world. "Many of the major preconditions of a just and durable peace require changes of national policy on the part of the United States," the Federal Council of Churches announced in 1942. "Among such may be mentioned: equal access to natural resources, economic collaboration, equitable treatment of racial minorities, international control of tariffs, limitation of armaments, participation in world government. We must be ready to subordinate immediate and particular national interests to the welfare of all."[20] On behalf of these principles they staged massive rallies, preached in tens of thousands of churches and over the airwaves, and orchestrated one of the largest letter-writing campaigns to Congress in American history. In the process, they became some of the most forceful advocates for the United Nations and the Universal Declaration of Human Rights, and they worked closely with the State Department to shape and promote these international institutions. But during the Cold War, relations with the government soured and ecumenical Protestants became more critical of US policy, especially in East Asia. When ecumenical leaders called for the diplomatic recognition of "Red" China in 1958, they signaled their opposition to American Cold War policy.

Ecumenical Protestants saw it as their responsibility to advocate for racial equality, more responsible economic policies, and a demilitarized US foreign policy in order to build a more just and Christian world. To be sure, there were many disagreements about these issues. Ecumenical Protestants on the right, like Dulles, were more likely to become Cold War hawks, to preach economic individualism, and to insist that segregation should be confronted through education rather than through legal or political initiatives. Others, like Reinhold Niebuhr, defied easy political categorization.

Despite disagreements, what remains remarkable is the extent to which globalism empowered activists seeking to combat segregation, lessen economic inequality, and undermine Cold War norms. Between the 1920s and 1960s, these separate strands of Protestant human rights activism were tied together into a single global outlook that transformed both international affairs and American politics.

Ecumenical Protestants and the Rise
and Fall of American Liberalism

American ecumenical Protestant leaders were some of the most important supporters of liberalism at mid-century—liberalism in the sense that Franklin Roosevelt used the term, to denote a greater role for government in ensuring the prosperity of its citizens and an openness to participation in international organizations. In tandem with other liberal groups, they pushed Americans to accept the New Deal and to embrace international governance. Unlike most liberals of the era, however, they strongly backed anti-racist movements. Ecumenical Protestants justified the New Deal, the UN, and the Black freedom struggle theologically, thereby endowing political liberalism with the cultural capital of Christianity. And in a country that was as devout as the United States, this was no small thing.

Ecumenical Protestant organizations also served as gateways to progressive politics for churchgoers by providing them religious sanction and institutional support for fighting injustices. For religious women, in particular, Protestant institutions were one of the few means of escaping middle-class domesticity and engaging politically in an organized fashion.[21] Ecumenical Protestants brought their concerns, rooted in theological commitments and developed in a global milieu, into the political arena. In the process, they transformed American liberalism by tying it to religious values and by making liberal leaders more attentive to religiously rooted concerns about racism, poverty, and international affairs.

The ecumenical Protestant establishment was so interconnected with the liberal political establishment in the United States that, in broad outline, their histories parallel one another. A socially conscious Protestantism and liberal social politics both began in the Progressive Era, they changed dramatically in the 1930s and consolidated during World War II, they enjoyed their peak from the 1940s through the 1960s, and they rapidly collapsed in the 1970s. Eschewing partisanship, ecumenical Protestant elites were closely tied to the liberal wings of both the Democratic and Republican parties of the mid-twentieth century, which nurtured the bipartisanship of the era. Ecumenical Protestants shared in the achievements of mid-century liberalism, including the New Deal, the founding of the United Nations, the legal challenge to segregation, civil rights legislation, and the War on Poverty. They also shared in the limits of liberalism, including its inclination toward consensus (which sometimes came at the expense of justice), its aversion to protest movements, and its elitism. Ecumenical Protestantism helped make liberalism—both its achievements and its limits—possible. When rapid secularization decimated their churches in the 1970s, it made the demise of liberalism probable.[22] Without powerful, organized backing from religious institutions, liberalism lost an important source of its political support.[23]

The decline of ecumenical power in the 1970s owed much to the growing clergy-laity gap in values. Members of the clergy, and especially those leaders in charge of Protestant institutions, had embraced political causes like the New Deal, desegregation, and demilitarization, which remained unpopular with everyday churchgoers. By the 1930s, some churchgoers mobilized against these clerics under the banner of the "laity"—a politicized identity that had as much to do with policy as with theology. The self-described laity was largely composed of wealthy churchgoers and conservative activists, who tried to wrest control of Protestant power. They raised important questions about ecclesiology—the theology of the nature and structure of Christianity—and about democracy and church-state relations. The battles between clergy and laity created new political and religious coalitions in the country, and created an opening for the rise of the religious Right. In these intramural fights, political and theological commitments blended with one another and portended the theological-political realignments that dominate today's landscape.[24]

It was through these schisms that ecumenical Protestants shaped our world most profoundly: by polarizing American politics. Just as ecumenical Protestant support bolstered the postwar liberal establishment, political divisions among Protestants cleaved the politics of the nation as a whole. When debates over Jim Crow, the welfare state, and the Cold War realigned religious communities, the new camps that emerged formed the basis of recognizably liberal and conservative coalitions. Since organizations like the Federal Council of Churches—and the council's critics—commanded the attention of such a broad swath of the American electorate, and had hands on the levers of power in the country, this division was a political shift on a national scale.

Ecumenical Protestants also helped shape what American liberalism and conservatism looked like. Ecumenical Protestant leaders bundled together ideas and values that cohered with the initiatives of liberal politicians. And evangelicals, partly in response to their ecumenical opponents, brought together ideas and formed new partnerships that increasingly marked them as conservatives. Because ecumenical Protestants undertook liberal initiatives in ways that caused them to lose support and undermine their own institutional standing, they created an opening for the rise of the religious Right. But the laws, programs, movements, and values that ecumenical Protestants promoted outlived their cultural and political hegemony. Many of the ways in which we think and speak about race, poverty, and US foreign policy today, including the very language of human rights and human dignity, were initially fostered by this community.

Histories of Ecumenical Protestants

Ecumenical Protestants transformed American life and international politics at mid-century. But historians have been slow to grasp their importance. Partly, this is because many historians agree with Richard Hofstadter's now classic contention that a defining feature of mid-century liberalism was its break with the religious outlook of the past.[25] In this book, on the other hand, I contend that religion was at the heart of mid-century liberalism. Ecumenical Protestants have also been overlooked due to the greater attention given to the rise of evangelicals. A strong collection of recent studies has reintroduced religion into the broader narratives of twentieth-century US history and, more recently, international history. Collectively, however, they create a misleading impression of the influence of evangelicals on American culture and politics, especially before the 1970s.[26] This book offers a corrective to the evangelical-centered narratives that predominate in modern American religious history. The point is not that evangelicals did not matter. Rather, in the same way that the rise of the New Right cannot be understood apart from the mobilization of evangelicals, the rise of American liberalism at mid-century cannot be understood without a historical account of the global political mobilization of American ecumenical Protestants.

The literature on the history of ecumenical Protestants has largely focused on the limits of the group's influence and on the decline of their power. Broad narratives of American religious history often stress the ways "mainline" Protestant hegemony ended in the 1960s, giving way to greater religious pluralism.[27] Others have focused on exposing the fragility of mainline Protestant power and the limits of its popular influence well before the 1960s.[28] Both of these approaches deemphasize the vibrancy of this community's political initiatives. By contrast, I contend that ecumenical Protestants were politically and intellectually vigorous at mid-century, and that their influence endured despite the demographic and financial challenges their churches faced in the late twentieth century. Ecumenical Protestants played an important role in creating institutions, legislation, and ideas that are still influential today.[29] They helped determine the landscape of American culture and politics long after the 1960s.

They also played an important role in international affairs. The traditional narrative of religion and US foreign relations focuses on the religious mobilization of the early Cold War and equates Protestantism with nationalist and anti-communist agitation.[30] But since the publication of William Inboden's path-breaking 2010 account of religion and foreign policy, historians have taken a more subtle view of ecumenical Protestants' international role. We now know that ecumenical Protestants harbored "anti-nationalist" sentiments in the interwar era and that some continued to resist militarism during the Cold War.[31] Building on these insights, this book pushes the study of ecumenical Protestant international politics in two directions. First, it resists the either/or approach to the question of religious complicity in the rise of American power. Instead, it shows that critics and boosters of American military supremacy shared a single outlook of Protestant globalism.[32] Second, by exploring the connections ecumenical Protestants made between international and domestic politics, this book places front and center this "intermestic" dimension of American history and emphasizes the links between international events, domestic political disputes, and the fracturing of American religious communities—and later, the fracturing of American politics.[33] By stressing this neglected connection, the book explores the religious roots of our present-day polarization.

From "One World" to Two

Before the Religious Right follows American ecumenical Protestants as they went abroad, developed new ideas about world order, and brought those ideas to bear on the domestic politics of the United States. Part 1, consisting of five chapters, chronicles the rise of Protestant globalism from the 1920s to 1948, when the Federal Council of Churches put forth its vision of human rights. Chapters 1 and 2 document the rise of a new generation of Protestant leaders, who went on study trips to places like India and the Soviet Union, and who came of age in the interwar years. Figures like G. Bromley Oxnam, Reinhold Niebuhr, and Henry Pitney Van Dusen were reared on ecumenism and the quest for international Protestant unity. In the interwar era, they transformed these theological commitments into the political doctrine of Protestant globalism. With this new framework as a guide, they became involved in the New Deal and in the debates over America's role in World War II.

Chapter 3 focuses on World War II, when the Protestant establishment orchestrated one of the largest political mobilizations in the history of Protestantism—the World Order movement. Enthusiasm for world government was expressed in countless books, articles, and pamphlets; in carefully choreographed rallies; in university seminar rooms and in the pews and pulpits of tens of thousands of churches; and in one of the largest outpourings of mail Congress had ever received. This chapter shows how, building on this enthusiasm, ecumenical leaders worked closely with the State Department to shape what became the United Nations.

As the enthusiasm for the United Nations and for human rights grew in the 1940s, American ecumenical Protestants confronted the place of racism in the postwar world order. Chapter 4 demonstrates that Black and white activists, under the banner of human rights, convinced fellow Protestants that racism had no place in world affairs or in the United States. Channing Tobias, Benjamin Mays, Thelma Stevens, and others persuaded the Federal Council of Churches in 1946 to become the first large, predominantly white organization to call for desegregation.[34] As Chapter 5 shows, the anti-racist mobilization of World War II shaped how human rights were understood by the American public. In the 1940s, ecumenical Protestants produced the first worldwide academic study of racism, recasting bigotry as a truly global phenomenon. When the Federal Council of Churches declared that human rights made Jim Crow immoral and illegal in 1948, it ensured that human rights became closely tied to movements against white supremacy across the world.

Part 2 of *Before the Religious Right* moves from the international arena to divisive national debates about racism, poverty, and foreign policy in the United States. Chapters 6 through 9 show that human rights were brought home and, in the process, they influenced American politics. These chapters also show how human rights activism divided American Protestants and polarized their community. Chapter 6 examines the divides among Protestants about the Cold War. Unsure at first how to respond to Truman's military doctrines, ecumenical Protestants, over time, emphasized breaking down Cold War barriers. This was especially true in Asia, where the Protestant establishment urged Americans to accept the Communist Party takeover of China and called on the US government to diplomatically recognize the new regime. In the McCarthyist atmosphere of the 1950s, it was a stance that led ecumenical Protestants to lose onetime allies, like Dulles, and to face harassment from the House Un-American Activities Committee.

Anti-racism likewise divided Protestants. As Chapter 7 shows, ecumenical Protestants transformed a commitment to human rights into concrete initiatives against segregation in the 1940s and 1950s. From going door-to-door with petitions in their local neighborhoods to filing briefs with the Supreme Court, ecumenical Protestants joined a broad coalition that attacked Jim Crow. As they made some legal headway under the banner of human rights, they encountered resistance from southern members of their own denominations, who embraced the new language of states' rights and constitutional originalism. Disappointed with the indifference and, in some cases, outright hostility to integration in their churches, the Protestant establishment turned to its youths. These young ecumenical Protestants would go on to play an important role in the civil rights movement.

As with segregation, ecumenical Protestant activism on economic matters bolstered the liberal initiatives of the era while creating new rifts in their community. Chapter 8 documents the plan in the late 1940s and early 1950s to bring labor leaders and corporate executives together to agree on what constituted a Christian economy. Ecumenical Protestant leaders had crafted the economic vision called "the Responsible Society," offering a third way between communism and capitalism. But some ecumenical Protestants resisted this economic view and had more sympathy for the Christian libertarianism of business leaders and their evangelical allies. Chapter 9 shows that under the banner of a "laymen's" movement, some ecumenical Protestants mobilized against the economic initiatives they labeled "socialistic." The laymen's movement was unable to rein in the political initiatives of the National Council of Churches. But it did create new divisions around economic issues and even led some ecumenical Protestants to organize new, breakaway denominations. These rifts facilitated alliances between business leaders and evangelicals, and created an opening for the rise of evangelicals in American politics and culture.

The final chapters collectively show how, by the 1960s, ecumenical Protestantism began to fracture along the fault lines created in the previous decades. Also by the 1960s, globalism had begun to wane. The position-paper liberalism and consensus politics of the mid-century gave way to the rise of an activist approach on both the left and the right. "Revolution" became a buzzword in ecumenical life as the universalism symbolized by the United Nations and human rights faded into the background. Ecumenical Protestants began unambiguously criticizing American power and backing decolonization movements. They protested the Vietnam War and went so far as to send aid to Marxist rebels fighting colonialism in southern Africa and apartheid in South Africa. From the perspective of the Left, the mid-century human rights politics of ecumenical Protestants had not gone far enough. From the perspective of the Right, they had gone too far.

The mobilization of American ecumenical Protestants at mid-century left their religious community—and their country—divided into recognizably liberal and conservative camps. Even so, their support for human rights, both at home and abroad, would have a long legacy in the United States. Their activism was a pillar that supported American liberalism in the twentieth century. Its legacy continues to shape our lives today.

PART I

One World

CHAPTER 1

Protestant Political Mobilization
in the Great Depression

In March 1933, the United States stood on the brink of financial ruin. Twenty-five percent of the population was unemployed, and countless Americans were without work for many years. Industrial production was cut in half from its 1929 level. The situation was even worse in large cities, where unemployment sometimes surpassed 50 percent. Yet the real worry of the era cannot be captured by statistics alone. There was a sense of fear that was palpable to those who lived in that uncertain time.[1] As the economy cratered, and as countless governments overseas collapsed, nobody was sure what would come next. This was the situation Franklin Delano Roosevelt inherited when he was inaugurated that month as the thirty-second president.

The challenge before Roosevelt was of such immensity that only the Bible captured for him, and for much of the nation, the task ahead. As he delivered his inaugural address in Washington, DC, in the cool March air under an overcast sky, he offered his listeners an account of devastation but also redemption. The economy was in tatters and hardworking men and women were destitute. "Primarily this is because the rulers of the exchange of mankind's goods have failed through their own stubbornness and their own incompetence, have admitted their failure, and have abdicated," Roosevelt told the crowd gathered in front of the East Portico of the US Capitol. "Practices of the unscrupulous money changers stand indicted in the court of public opinion, rejected by the hearts and minds of men." Like the biblical story of Jesus forcibly expelling the money changers and merchants from the temple, Roosevelt promised to restore Christian morality to the nation. "The money changers have fled from their high seats in the temple of our civilization," the new president announced. "We may now restore that temple to the ancient truths. The measure of the restoration lies in the extent to which we apply social values more noble than mere monetary profit."[2]

Roosevelt's words give us a glimpse of a nation that in many ways no longer resembles the United States today. Roosevelt spoke in Christian idiom, often hinting at antisemitic tropes, to a public he presumed to be Protestant. "This is a Protestant country, and the Catholics and Jews are here under sufferance," Roosevelt would later tell a private audience that included Jews and Catholics.[3] Roosevelt, an Episcopalian, also spoke on behalf of a Protestantism that saw science and religion as compatible, tolerance as a social good, internationalism as a Christian endeavor, and the state as an ally of Christian social work. Roosevelt spoke, in other words, on behalf of an ecumenical Protestantism that dominated the public sphere in the 1930s.

Despite appearances, Roosevelt's use of ecumenical Protestant themes at his inauguration belied a troubled relationship between Roosevelt, the spokesperson for a new political liberalism, and the Protestant leaders who spoke on behalf of theological liberalism. Between 1932, when Roosevelt won the presidential election, and 1936, when he won a landslide re-election, political liberalism and religious liberalism drew closer together through the conscious work of leaders of the Federal Council of Churches, denominational heads, missionary directors, academics and seminary heads, everyday churchgoers, labor leaders, and politicians. The coming together of the two liberalisms—political and religious—helped cement a close working relationship between ecumenical Protestant leaders and the federal government. As Roosevelt's words show, liberal Protestantism was the language through which some Americans—including the president himself—understood the reforms of the New Deal.

Historians have not fully appreciated how central ecumenical Protestants were to mid-century liberalism. Beginning with Richard Hofstadter's 1955 history of the New Deal, called *The End of Reform*, it became conventional wisdom that the New Deal shed the Protestant moralism of the Progressive Era of the early twentieth century. This wisdom held that, beginning in the 1930s, a coalition of tough-minded groups discarded the religious moralizing of the past. This "Roosevelt coalition" governed the country until it fell apart in the 1960s.[4] This view is misleading because it neglects the transformation of Protestant groups themselves. By 1932, ecumenical Protestants had moved beyond Progressive Era politics by adopting a political reform platform that prefigured many of the changes brought on by the New Deal. Influenced by developments abroad, they came to see the political arena as the best means of making Christian theology a living reality. Like Roose-velt, ecumenical Protestants experimented politically in the 1930s. As this chapter shows, ecumenical Protestantism emerged as a sophisticated politi-cal movement by the end of that decade and took its place among the groups that formed the core of American political liberalism.

The Triumph of Theological Liberals in the 1920s

The stock market crash of 1929 and the depression that followed sent shock-waves through American Protestantism. The money to pay ministers' sala-ries, to help the poor, and to build new churches dried up. More importantly, the Great Depression came as a shock to theologians and clergy who had spent the prior decade feeling confident that civilization was making steady progress toward building the Kingdom of God on earth.

The 1920s had been a good decade for Protestantism's Progressive Era causes. Prohibitionists finally won their decades-long battle in 1920, when the Volstead Act made the sale of alcohol illegal nationwide. Pacifists also had cause to celebrate. Recoiling from the horrors of World War I, peace groups sprung up from churches, and their work culminated in the Kellogg-Briand Pact of 1928, which made war illegal under international law.[5] The economy was booming in the 1920s, and it funded an ever-expanding num-ber of churches, charitable organizations, and missionary groups. It was in 1925 that Bruce Barton published his blockbuster book, *The Man Nobody Knows*, which reimagined Jesus as the world's greatest salesman and the apostles as his board of directors.[6] According to Donald Meyer, in these years, "Protestantism spoke with a degree of confidence and self-assertion befitting only men who felt themselves at the opening of a new era—and themselves responsible for that opening."[7]

A theological crisis emerged in the 1920s over the relationship of science and religion, but ecumenical leaders mostly viewed it as a yet further sign of progress. On one side were self-proclaimed modernists, who believed that science and religion went hand in hand and who argued that a critical read-ing of the Bible would yield a more enlightened religion that could withstand the demands of the modern age.[8] On the other side were fundamentalists, who saw themselves as defenders of Christian orthodoxy. They listed non-negotiable articles of faith, which were a line in the sand meant to defend what they saw as true Christianity from heresy.[9] The conflict between the two groups erupted in Dayton, Tennessee, over the teaching of evolution in public schools. Although the Scopes "Monkey" trial was substantially about majoritarian control of schools and intellectual freedom of teachers, it was popularly understood as a battle between science and fundamentalist faith.[10] Fundamentalists won the trial but lost the public, which only bolstered ecumenical confidence in the 1920s.

Confrontations between modernists and fundamentalists in the 1920s also took place within Christian institutions—churches, seminaries, and missionary organizations—and they centered on doctrine. The popular preacher Harry Emerson Fosdick became a lightning rod for these debates because of the attention he drew with his sermon "Shall the Fundamentalists Win?"[11] The sermon was printed and distributed to nearly all of the 140,000 Protestant ministers in the country, informing them that he did not believe in the Virgin Birth, the inerrancy of the scriptures, or the Second Coming of Christ. Fosdick's conservative opponents admitted his popularity. But "the question is not whether Dr. Fosdick is winning men," complained conservative Presbyterian theologian J. Gresham Machen, "but whether the thing to which he is winning them is Christianity."[12]

Fundamentalists demanded an investigation into whether Fosdick upheld the Presbyterian Confession of Faith. When an investigative body cleared him, fundamentalists demanded an investigation of the New York Presbytery for permitting heresy in its pulpits. It too was cleared of wrongdoing, thanks in part to the skillful work of their young lawyer, Presbyterian layman John Foster Dulles. Although Fosdick would indeed resign—the Baptist minister was asked to become a Presbyterian, and he refused because of his deep commitment to ecumenism—he soon took over the pulpit of Riverside Church in New York, the cathedral of ecumenical Protestantism.[13] Mobilizing their prestige, intellectual rigor, and a widespread belief in progress, advocates of a liberal theology prevailed over their fundamentalist coreligionists. By the time of the Great Depression, theological liberals, like Fosdick, had taken over much of the institutional machinery of American Protestantism.

G. Bromley Oxnam and the Internationalization of the Social Gospel

As Protestants grappled with the Great Depression, they drew on earlier traditions focused on combatting poverty. The social gospel was foremost

Figure 1. G. Bromley Oxnam was among the most influential ecumenical Protestant leaders of the twentieth century. Before he became a household name in the 1940s, he accompanied socialist evangelist Sherwood Eddy on annual trips across the world, including to India and the Soviet Union. Image courtesy of DePauw University Archives and Special Collections.

among these. Beginning in the late nineteenth century, theologians and activists came to two new insights as they recoiled at the terrible conditions that prevailed among the working class in that era. The first was that the clergy needed to minister to workers' bodies as well as to their souls. The second was that salvation was not just for individuals but that it also had a social dimension. They relegated the idea of the salvation of individuals to an agrarian past that was no longer tenable in the industrial landscape of Hell's Kitchen in New York or the railroad yards of Los Angeles.[14]

Methodist minister G. Bromley Oxnam found himself working in the Los Angeles neighborhood in the 1920s. Oxnam was part of a new generation that would take control of Protestant institutions during the Great Depression.

Like others in his cohort, he was reared on the social gospel and on international travel. In the 1940s, Oxnam would go on to lead the World Order movement, become the president of the Federal Council of Churches, and a co-founder of the World Council of Churches. Along with other members of his generation who came of age in similar circumstances and institutions in the 1920s, Oxnam would play an important role in the founding of the United Nations and the promotion of human rights.

The son of an engineer, Oxnam grew up in Los Angeles and attended the University of Southern California before studying at MIT and Harvard and finally receiving a doctorate from the Methodist-run Boston University School of Theology. Like other young Christian idealists, Oxnam was drawn back to his hometown to work in a neighborhood that was rapidly transforming from a middle-class Protestant quarter to a multi-ethnic industrial zone. The Methodist church he founded there, called the Church of All Nations, "had virtually ceased to be a church," according to a 1926 report by the Institute of Social and Religious Research, "and had become rather a Christian social center." "It has been almost three years since we had regular church services," explained Oxnam in 1927. Instead, the Church of All Nations functioned along the lines of Hull House, the famous settlement house in Chicago founded by Jane Addams. Methodists looking for a Sunday sermon were directed to a nearby church. The Church of All Peoples offered instead a medical clinic, day care center, athletics, and a meeting space for events that were conducted not just in English but also in Spanish, Japanese, and Yiddish.[15]

After World War I the social gospel became less popular among American Protestants but internationalism was on the rise. A now-classic account identifies the 1920s as a period of the "decline" of the social gospel before its dramatic "revival" during the 1930s.[16] But what such accounts miss about Oxnam's generation is how the interplay of Wilsonian internationalism and the social gospel changed their views and their politics. Like others of his generation, Oxnam's social gospel inheritance had been reshaped and sharpened during his many trips abroad. For nearly a century, American Protestants had gone abroad to proselytize as missionaries. Oxnam, however, was part of a new venture, the study mission, designed to be a dialogue rather than a lecture. Organized by the wealthy socialist evangelist Sherwood Eddy, study missions gathered bright and promising young Protestants to tour foreign nations, meeting with dignitaries in order to promote mutual understanding. In December 1918, a month following the armistice of the Great War, Oxnam took a leave of absence from his Los Angeles church and went on one of these tours as Eddy's personal secretary. Sailing from San Francisco to Japan, Oxnam was stuck inside his cabin reading forty books on Russian history and politics given to him by Eddy. Oxnam was tasked with underlining everything that was important enough for Eddy to read himself. After a brief stay in Japan, the group toured China and Southeast Asia, making their way to India, where the group would reside for six months. The journey brought Oxnam in touch with foreigners and into conversation with the latest literature on the countries and colonies he visited.[17]

In India, Oxnam toured churches, mission stations, and YMCAs, in addition to hospitals, asylums, prisons, and factories. He was left with an impression of the degradation of the lower rungs of Indian society. He felt sympathy for the poor and wrote in his diaries that the experience reaffirmed his faith in the social gospel. But Oxnam gained little appreciation for Indian culture and frequently got into altercations with locals. When a train conductor asked him to move his bags from a train compartment, he recalled in his diary, "I shouted at him, 'If you move one of those bags, you'll land on the floor so blamed fast that you won't know what hit you.'" Oxnam's impressions of the local religion were no better than those of train travel. Indian temples were filled with images "so vile that they would put the lewd Parisian post cards to shame." Hindu priests "commit every form of immorality" on "women pilgrims," he claimed.[18]

Others on this trip in 1918–19, including the famed evangelist E. Stanley Jones, gained a respect for the cultures they were encountering. Jones had been working periodically as a missionary in India for the Methodist Church since 1907. He ministered to educated Indian elites and was exposed to their criticism of Christianity. In order to promote Christianity in India, Jones started to "disentangle Christ from the accretions which the centuries had gathered around him," he would later write.[19] Jones was doing the work of inculturation—adapting Christianity to Indian culture—but he took this process further than other missionaries at the time. He became more critical of American racism and British colonialism. "The old imperialism is gone, is dead, or dying!" he explained. When he joined Eddy and Oxnam on their trip, Jones was still unknown. But, two decades later, *Time* magazine pronounced that he was "the world's greatest missionary."[20] Through popular publications, like his bestselling book *The Christ of the Indian Road* (1925), he promoted anti-racism, anti-imperialism, and interfaith dialogue to millions of Americans.[21] Eventually, Jones would win over many of his fellow ecumenical Protestants to his views.

Oxnam, on the other hand, remained sympathetic to British imperialism. Having witnessed a riot in 1919 and recoiling at the burning of several Christian churches by Hindu and Sikh nationalists, he praised the actions of the British troops at the Amritsar massacre, which left 379 unarmed protesters dead. "The Indians little realize the power of modern weapons, but I understand they were taught something of a lesson at Amritsar," he wrote in his diary. "One feels terrible over the whole situation. It means that mission work will be slowed up for years."[22]

When he returned to Los Angeles in 1919, Oxnam was hailed as an expert on East and South Asian affairs and was asked to give regular talks at his church and to civic groups. At a time when there was little academic interest in these regions, Protestant intellectuals like Oxnam and Jones served as the main interpreters of the non-European world for the US public. Protestant missionaries and travelers had been influential interpreters of events overseas since the nineteenth century, and they held on to this role until they were displaced by academic experts in area studies during the early Cold War.[23]

Oxnam's next trip with Eddy's new "American Seminar" in 1921—no longer called a "mission"—proved more transformative.[24] The group headed eastward from the United States, first arriving in London, England, where it stayed at the world's first social settlement house, Toynbee Hall. Oxnam went to work interviewing British political leaders, and his commitment to the social gospel meant he was receptive to their ideas. He began by interviewing the Labour Party leader, Ramsay MacDonald. As Oxnam took dozens of pages of careful notes of his conversations with MacDonald, as well as later talks with British social reformers and socialists, including Harold Laski, R. H. Tawney, Sydney Webb, and G. D. H. Cole, he was learning more than the minutiae of labor relations and municipal reform.[25] In these conversations Oxnam saw new political possibilities. The Labour Party was respectable, according to Oxnam's middle-class sensibilities, but it was also visionary and politically effective. The party was unlike anything back home in the United States, where one of the country's periodic Red Scares had just taken place.[26] While American officials deported socialists and anarchists, here was the Labour Party proclaiming the coming of a new economic order. "The individualist system of capitalist production, based on the private ownership and competitive administration of land and capital," had ended, the Labour Party announced. Webb and others were calling on Britain to create what would become many of the hallmark features of the New Deal in the United States, including social insurance, democratic control of industry, regulation of work, and full employment.[27] Oxnam was taking part in a transatlantic exchange of ideas, ones that would shape the New Deal.[28]

When Oxnam returned to Los Angeles in 1921, he decided to get involved in politics. He was so inspired by Christian socialism in Britain that, in 1923, he ran for a seat on the local board of education. It led him to experience the reactionary politics of Southern California firsthand. The *Los Angeles Times* ran a string of red-baiting attacks against him. It reported that the Department of Justice's chief investigator announced during a speech in Los Angeles that "soviet propaganda is being directed toward American public schools" for the purpose of "inculcating the principles of radicalism into the nation's future citizens." The *Los Angeles Times* editorialized, "As the famous criminologist spoke he emphasized his statements by bringing his right arm down before him in such a manner as to repeatedly point a seemingly accusing forefinger at the face of G. Bromley Oxnam, radical candidate for the Board of Education."[29] Unable to overcome these attacks, Oxnam lost the election. But he nonetheless remained confident in the potential of a progressive politics of the kind he had witnessed firsthand in England. International travel had given Oxnam a perspective that allowed him to see beyond the narrow valleys of the conservative politics of Los Angeles.

On Oxnam's third trip with Eddy in 1926, he visited the Soviet Union for the first time. After interviews with the British prime minister and the German president en route to the USSR, Eddy's group reached Moscow in August 1926, meeting with top officials in the country, including Stalin. In these encounters, Oxnam saw glimpses of his earlier Asian travels. "Russia is not the most Eastern of Western Nations," he wrote in a published memoir of the trip, "but rather the most Western of Eastern nations." Oxnam's experience in India was an asset in understanding Russia, he believed. "Some of the members of our party, untraveled in the Orient, found themselves judging Eastern mental attitudes and activities by Western standards, and thereby drawing incorrect conclusions. This was due to the fact that Russia is actually more Oriental than Occidental," Oxnam opined.[30]

Oxnam observed that religion had diminished in the Soviet Union but that it could not be done away with entirely. After a visit to Lenin's tomb, Oxnam left "with mixed emotions." "I noted that, along with Karl Marx, Lenin is quoted by the Communist with something of the authority with which the fundamentalist calls for proof texts. . . . Leninism seems to have become a cult, and its shrines evidence elements of religion," Oxnam wrote, concluding that religion was not going away in Russia anytime soon.[31]

Oxnam urged Americans not to rush to judgment about religion in the Soviet Union because "the situation is much more complex than such surface contacts suggest." The problem was with the Russian Orthodox Church or, as a section heading in his memoir called it, "The Degenerate Church." It "was shot through with repugnant superstition," Oxnam wrote, and had been used to enslave workers and peasants. No wonder, then, that "the destruction of religion became a part of [the Marxist's] revolutionary program, since he sought to destroy every capitalist weapon." Oxnam lamented that Protestant groups in Russia also did not live up to "the standards of the ethical and spiritual concepts of Jesus." In these denominations, "one finds a theology which out-fundamentalizes our most rigid fundamentalists."[32]

Oxnam's bitter attitude toward fundamentalism, whether Orthodox or Protestant, was shaped by personal experience. In 1923, famed Pentecostal minister Aimee Semple McPherson had sent members of her Los Angeles church to Oxnam's Church of All Nations. They occupied the church and prayed that its members would forsake their socialism and convert to true Christianity. Oxnam once again resorted to violence. As Oxnam's sympathetic biographer Robert Moats Miller put it, "the cohorts of the notorious Aimee Semple McPherson" entered All Nations to stage their protest but they soon "retreated when Oxnam gave them something they had not prayed for."[33]

The domestic and international experiences of Oxnam reinforced one another. Encounters with fundamentalists in Los Angeles shaped Oxnam's views of the Soviet Union, and his experiences in the USSR sharpened his worries that fundamentalism could lead people to abandon Christianity entirely. The problem, as Oxnam saw it, was that the communists are "men who believe themselves loyal to science, but who are in fact largely unacquainted with the religious and scientific thought of the present generation."[34] Oxnam believed that communists were opposed to religion because they were only familiar with the backward religious views of the Orthodox Church and Russian fundamentalist sects, which he also abhorred.

In the Soviet Union, as in the United States, Oxnam was optimistic that "a rising generation at home in modern science but still asking for ultimate explanation, will produce leaders who will be able to bring to the hungry souls of Russia an answer that will satisfy." Before that happens, Oxnam wrote, "I feel that the suffering [of Russian Christians] will be of value." Oxnam was perhaps thinking of his own ministry in Los Angeles when he wrote, "It will bring the priest in close touch with the poverty of the masses, it will force the churchman to face the implications of a scientific and democratic age, and out of suffering, which has ever been an asset to our Christian movement, may come a rebirth of religion that will be of significance to Christendom."[35] Oxnam was taking the fundamentalist-modernist controversy into the international arena to counter the charge that his own faith was a slippery slope toward atheism. Instead, he argued that fundamentalist Christianity could lead to no Christianity at all, as had happened in Russia.[36]

One of the starkest changes in Oxnam's outlook during his 1926 Russia trip was his about-face on imperialism. Oxnam met with Soviet foreign minister Georgii Chicherin and was very impressed. Oxnam "was struck immediately by the number of pictures of Oriental leaders," from China, Japan, and other Asian countries, that adorned the walls of Chicherin's office. "We realized immediately that he was a man at home in the state craft of yesterday, well read in history, highly cultured, and with full knowledge of where he was going." Oxnam understood that Soviet leaders "sought to guarantee to the formerly oppressed nationalities self determination or cultural freedom." Quoting Grigorii Zinoviev, Oxnam wrote that the Russian model "is naturally a shining beacon of hope for the enslaved masses of Asia." Russia was successfully breaking British imperialism in Persia, winning great sympathy from China, and making peace with Japan. This was having a remarkable effect on world politics, he reasoned. "We will have to recognize the changed status in the East, as England is already beginning to do, and be willing to sit down around the table, treat these nations as equals, and through treaty agreements work out the problems of the Pacific in the interests of the nations involved and for the good of the world." If we cling to imperialism, Oxnam now instructed, we will find that "there are lined up in the East one billion out of a total world population of one billion seven hundred or eight hundred million."[37]

Oxnam's change of heart was part of a broader reevaluation of imperialism by ecumenical Protestants. Missionary work, in particular, came under scrutiny in the 1920s and 1930s. In the early 1930s a Rockefeller-funded project sent a team of experts headed by Harvard philosopher William Ernest Hocking to assess missionary work in Asia. Hocking's 1932 report, *Re-Thinking Missions*, sent shockwaves through American Protestantism for its condemnation of the missionary project. Missionaries ought to focus more on social work than conversion and they should pay heed to nationalist movements demanding independence, Hocking argued. He also insisted that the spread of modernity—including the proliferation of technology, science, industrialization, and liberal religion—was creating commonalities among the world's peoples and religions. Buddhists, Hindus, and Muslims were becoming more and more like Christians, according to Hocking. The development of this "world culture" meant that conversion and imperialism were becoming less necessary. In fact, they were inimical to the growing unity of the world, whose promotion was the true task of Christianity. *Re-Thinking Missions* marked a broader transition among ecumenical Protestants toward religious pluralism and away from supporting imperialism.[38] It also signaled a desire to separate Christianity from the West, a move that undermined Christian nationalism. Oxnam's trajectory from supporting imperialism during his 1919 trip to India to disavowing it during his 1926 trip to the USSR was part of this pattern.

In developing his critiques of communism, fundamentalism, and imperialism, Oxnam's social gospel inheritance gained a global dimension. Like others of his generation, travel abroad helped Oxnam see beyond the American Protestant obsessions with liquor and Darwin. Through these trips he encountered, face to face, reformers and politicians whose ideas would inform the creation of the New Deal in the 1930s. Travel moved Oxnam to think about the problems of labor and poverty as universal problems demanding universal solutions. In a similar vein, the Great Depression and the New Deal would soon force ecumenical Protestants like Oxnam to position themselves in relation to global forces—fascism, communism, and social democracy—that offered competing solutions to the crisis of the era.

The Great Depression and the Revival of the Social Gospel

The Great Depression came as a shock to the Protestant establishment. Partly, ecumenical Protestant leaders responded to the poverty they saw all around them. Partly, it was the experience of having religious institutions decimated that changed their mood. By 1932, hundreds of missionaries were being recalled from Asia because of financial shortfalls. That same year, Methodists had not raised enough money to pay their bishops. The Congregationalists had planned to gather in 1932 to decide how to respond to the Depression, but they could not afford to.[39]

With the economy in free fall, the public voice of American Christianity passed from established Progressive Era moralists to the social gospelers, like Oxnam. Many social gospelers had been at work for decades, building a Protestant left on the margins of ecumenical institutions. Sherwood Eddy's American Seminar disciples were some of the most important leaders of this movement. As Michael Thompson shows, an "oppositional community of discourse" emerged among ecumenical Protestants in the interwar period. In the 1920s and 1930s, popular Protestant ministers like Kirby Page, Norman Thomas, and Reinhold Niebuhr railed against the evils of capitalism and nationalism.[40] Also active in this movement were older social gospel advocates, like Francis J. McConnell, who were closer to the center of ecumenical Protestant power. McConnell, who was Oxnam's mentor, had a decades-long track record of advocating for workers by the onset of the Great Depression.[41]

Social gospelers like McConnell and Oxnam took the reins of their denomination during the Great Depression because they had a clear explanation for the economic catastrophe and offered concrete solutions. McConnell believed that the Depression was caused by corporate greed and inequality, and that the government must take responsibility for the people's welfare. The presiding bishop at the 1932 Methodist national meeting echoed McConnell, declaring, "We know now that the Kingdom of God cannot be built upon the poverty of the many and the absurd and cruel wealth of the few." The Methodists voted to send a delegation headed by McConnell to Washington, DC, to press for immediate federal relief.[42]

The social gospel spread like wildfire from denomination to denomination during the early years of the Great Depression. The Northern Baptists gathered in 1932 to declare that "all the wealth and all labor power are intended by the Creator for the highest good of all people." Individuals were only entitled to "a normal living" and no more than that. The violation of this standard—that the individual does not have a right to be rich when others are poor—resulted from "an excessive and naïve dependence upon competitive private trading as a method of distributing goods and services." The Northern Baptist leaders declared, "The people have the natural right to hold, and can safely be entrusted with, the power of democratic control over their economic life."[43] This denomination joined a growing chorus calling for greater economic equality, support for the vulnerable, and more federal regulation of the economy.

The Federal Council of Churches gathered its leaders in 1932 to unite these denominational voices crying out for the government to do more. The synthesis took place bureaucratically in the form of the "Revised Social

Ideals of the Churches." The original Social Ideals were pioneered by Methodists, including Francis McConnell, and adopted by the Federal Council in 1908. Plans for revision of the Social Ideals had been made in 1928, when activists wanted to add planks supporting the outlawry of war. When revisions to the document were made in 1932, point 16 of the newly Revised Social Ideals now listed "repudiation of war, drastic reduction of armaments, participation in international agencies for the peaceable settlement of all controversies; the building of a co-operative world order."[44]

But it was the economic planks in the 1932 version of the Federal Council's Social Ideals that caught people's attention, including Franklin Roosevelt's. "Cooperation" was the key term tying the document together—cooperation among nations and cooperation among classes, which the ecumenists thought should express itself in democratic fashion, from the League of Nations internationally to industrial democracy in the United States. The Revised Social Ideals began with a general principle that a Christian society required "the subordination of speculation and the profit motive to the creative and co-operative spirit." The second plank called for "a wider and fairer distribution of wealth" and "a just share for the worker in the product of industry and agriculture." There were also planks that anticipated the specific reforms of the New Deal. For example, plank 5 called for "social insurance against sickness, accident, want in old age and unemployment." Plank 8 called for "the right of employees and employers alike to organize for collective bargaining and social action."[45] These economic ideas were not new—Oxnam had encountered them when traveling through Europe in the 1920s—but they were now being advocated by some of the most important religious leaders in 1932, just as Americans were electing a new Congress and a new president.

Not surprisingly, this left turn among American ecumenical Protestants began attracting attention from politicians. Among them was Franklin Roosevelt, who was running for the presidency in 1932 and began echoing the ideas swirling among ecumenical Protestants. In one of his most substantive speeches on economics, delivered in Detroit during the election season, Roosevelt felt "as if I had been preaching a sermon." He castigated the philosophy of "let things alone" and mocked the idea that "if we make the rich richer somehow they will let a part of their prosperity trickle through to the rest of us." Instead, he proposed "social justice, through social action" and called on the federal government to secure the welfare of the poorest Americans. This "ideal of social justice of which I have spoken—an idea that years ago might have been thought overly advanced—is now accepted by the moral leadership of all of the great religious groups of the country." Were his proposals radical? "Yes," he sarcastically told the audience in Detroit, "and I will show you how radical it is," quoting at length from the recent Labor Day pronouncement of the Federal Council. "The concentration of wealth carries with it a dangerous concentration of power. It leads to conflict and violence," quoted Roosevelt. "To suppress the symptoms of this inherent conflict while leaving the fundamental causes of it untouched is neither sound statesmanship nor Christian good-will." The Federal Council helped legitimize Roosevelt's proposals and shielded him from criticism. The presidential candidate claimed that he was no more radical than the spokespersons of American Protestantism.[46]

Roosevelt also acknowledged a growing sentiment that the United States was a "tri-faith," or "Judeo-Christian," nation.[47] The president quoted from Rabbi Edward L. Israel and an encyclical from Pope Pius XI, along with the Federal Council's text. After he was elected, Roosevelt maintained the loyalty of most Jewish and Catholic voters throughout his long tenure in the White House. He did so despite repeatedly airing antisemitic views in private. "You and I . . . are old English and Dutch stock," he told Senator Burton Wheeler. "We know there is no Jewish blood in our veins." But Roosevelt took care to criticize antisemitism publicly. Jewish organizations and the broader Jewish public also supported the policies of the New Deal, and about 15 percent of administration appointees were Jewish. Even when tensions between Roosevelt and Jews increased in the late 1930s over Jewish refugees, the ties remained firm.[48]

Catholics, on the other hand, had a more complicated relationship with Roosevelt. Catholic leaders were initially enthusiastic about Roosevelt, but a few years into the New Deal they began asking whether the expansion of the state threatened to undermine the work religious organizations had traditionally done, like providing relief to the poor. Catholic leaders urged Roosevelt to work through the churches instead of working around them. Meanwhile, Catholic churchgoers, many of whom were joining unions, began to vote for Roosevelt in large numbers. Roosevelt pulled many Jewish and Catholic voters into a "New Deal coalition," while alienating some of the Catholic leadership.[49]

While religious pluralism was a growing sentiment among some parts of the American public, ecumenical Protestant opinion was prized above all others in the 1930s. And politicians were not the only ones seeking approval of America's most influential religious leaders. American Federation of Labor president William Green was at ease with Bible passages and theological argument. "Trade Unions are idealistic and spiritualistic," he repeated to religious audiences ad nauseam. "Wages mean life and living, not profits. Trade Unions direct their efforts toward the elevation of living standards, toward the advancement of educational, moral and spiritual welfare of workers." Labor unions found common cause with churches because, as Green explained, "human betterment means spiritual betterment. The Church cannot make an effective appeal to those who are experiencing the pangs of poverty. It can appeal to those who enjoy decent living standards, in decent homes, in decent communities."[50]

In the 1930s, Green would invite ecumenical Protestant leaders to play a special mediating role in American politics. He argued that the church was universal, standing above class divisions. "What agency can more properly and soundly lead in the development of a national social conscience, social outlook and a sense of social responsibility than the Church? It occupies a strategic position in all the affairs and activities of human life," he declared on the occasion of the Federal Council's twenty-fifth anniversary. "For this reason, it cannot be regarded as a special pleader for a particular class."[51]

Protestantism was moving leftward, and the public was picking up on this new rhetoric. In the turmoil of the 1930s and the ascendancy of the Left, the Federal Council's Revised Social Ideals would serve as the basis for a lobbying effort that sought greater security for vulnerable Americans and the recognition of the right of labor to organize. Other ecumenical Protestant organizations followed the Federal Council's lead. Most ecumenical denominations, the YMCA, the YWCA, and the Home Missions Council adopted the Revised Social Ideals statement as their own. This gesture was a sign of what would come next: Ecumenical Protestants would play an important role in the creation of the New Deal.

Reconciling with Roosevelt

The economic views of ecumenical Protestants shifted dramatically between 1929 and 1932, but they had not yet been translated into a political program. Although they widely endorsed social democracy, ecumenical Protestant leaders who came of political age in the Progressive Era continued to stress priorities that seemed old-fashioned by the time Roosevelt came into office in March 1933. For them, social democracy was inextricably tied to the so-briety of the working class, to the moral uprightness and incorruptibility of politicians, and to a rejection of violence at home and abroad. The tension these priorities created with Roosevelt can be seen in the pages of the *Christian Century*, ecumenical Protestantism's flagship journal.

The *Christian Century* was run by Charles Clayton Morrison, a Disciples of Christ minister in Chicago. Morrison transformed the *Christian Century* from a struggling denominational journal debating the merits of immersive baptism into an influential ecumenical magazine known in academic and political circles as the place to go for Protestant debates about pressing top-ics. Morrison had grown up in Iowa and went to a small Disciples of Christ college in Des Moines before taking up a pastorate in Chicago. His church stood just west of Jane Addams's Hull House, which was a hotbed of urban reform. Further south was the University of Chicago Divinity School, a cen-ter of the historical study of the Bible and of theological liberalism. When Morrison enrolled at the University of Chicago in 1902, however, he de-clined to attend divinity school. Instead, he enrolled in the philosophy de-partment and worked with John Dewey, whose interests had strayed from the concerns of Protestantism. Morrison's choice of mentors signaled his willingness to engage with ideas beyond the Protestant milieu, something that was also reflected in his commitment to ecumenism and his coverage of politics. Morrison, a committed pacifist, prohibitionist, and reformer, was at the helm of the *Christian Century's* coverage of Roosevelt.[52]

Virtually all of the *Christian Century's* coverage of Roosevelt during the year he ran for office was critical of the candidate. Morrison focused atten-tion on Roosevelt's ties to the corrupt Tammany Hall, his foreign policy pro-posals, his opposition to Prohibition, his "subservience to the [Catholic] hierarchy," and his unwillingness to frankly discuss important issues. Miss-ing in the *Christian Century* was any mention of Roosevelt's economic pro-posals. Roosevelt was partly to blame for this, since his mercurial campaign avoided in-depth discussion of policy. He preferred to take advantage of Hoover's unpopularity.[53] For Morrison, Roosevelt was the embodiment of the corrupt machine politics that Progressive Era Protestants had worked so hard to combat. For these reasons, in February 1932 the *Christian Century* predicted Roosevelt's political death. "As the months have passed the politi-cal weakness of the New York governor has grown distressingly clear," an editorial declared. "Such a man would never have made the President that the exigencies of the present situation demand."[54]

Yet, in the same issues of the *Christian Century* were far-reaching proposals for the complete transformation of the economy, many of which
would become the hallmarks of the Roosevelt presidency. One author wrote
about an employer he knew, who was an upstanding Christian. "Not only
does he attend church every Sunday, listening with admirable tolerance to
ministerial suggestions for social progress, but he has done all within his
power to humanize conditions in his industry." But it was not enough. The
author wrote that moral suasion, a longstanding tactic of Protestant reform,
had reached its limits in this economic catastrophe. "I see no hope for improvement except in establishing within our democracy a supreme economic
council with dictatorial powers." Like the National Industrial Recovery Act
that was passed one year later, this 1932 proposal suggested that "the supreme
economic council could declare, for instance, uniform wage scale for all the
operations in the cordage factories of America."[55] These kinds of drastic
proposals appeared regularly in the pages of Protestantism's most important
magazine.

By the summer of 1932 it became clear that the *Christian Century* was
mistaken in its prediction of Roosevelt's demise. Roosevelt reached out to
Protestant leaders in a speech in Detroit, which tried to enlist them in a fight
for "social justice through social action" based on religious "fundamentals."[56] Roosevelt talked about the Fall of Man, the Flood, and other biblical
stories. He appealed to religious sentiments that had undergirded past efforts to abolish child labor, pass workingmen's insurance, and eradicate disease. These same values, Roosevelt argued, demanded an active government.
Roosevelt was picking up on the rhetoric of ecumenical Protestants, but
Morrison barely noticed. An editorial declared that Norman Thomas, the
Socialist Party candidate for the presidency and an ordained Episcopalian
minister, espoused policies and values that cohered most closely with Christianity. But Thomas was a third-party candidate with little hope of winning,
the *Christian Century's* editors wrote. Roosevelt and Hoover, the editors
concluded, offered little in terms of policy differences. But if someone had to
be entrusted with government planning, surely it should not be Roosevelt, a
crony of Tammany Hall. In the fall of 1932, the *Christian Century* endorsed
Hoover for reelection. Hoover's economic policies may have been lackluster,
but at least he embodied the values of the Progressive Era that continued to
have currency in some ecumenical Protestant circles.

That the mainstream *Christian Century* had seriously weighed endorsing a socialist for the presidency in 1932 was a sign of the rupture created by

the Great Depression—an event that opened new political possibilities for American Protestantism. In the breach, new voices emerged. Among the most important was Reinhold Niebuhr, who gained notoriety in 1932 with the publication of *Moral Man and Immoral Society*. Niebuhr's acerbic criticism of both liberals and communists, in a book full of wit and apposite observations, was designed to stoke political change. Niebuhr was running for Congress in Manhattan on the Socialist Party ticket and he was actively backing the party's presidential candidate, Norman Thomas. Electoral politics was on Niebuhr's mind as he finished the book during the summer of 1932, before devoting all of his energy to the coming fall campaign. The book came out in December 1932, a month after the Socialist Party was trounced in the election. The Democrats won large majorities, with big gains by the party's liberal, non-Southern wing. But the book was written at an earlier, more optimistic moment for Niebuhr, when the political winds were at his back. Ironically, at the moment that *Moral Man* proclaimed liberalism's impotence, it was the Socialist Party that seemed unable to make headway in conditions that favored it. Niebuhr received a disappointing 4.4 percent of the vote, while Thomas received just 2.2 percent.[57]

Ecumenical leaders, like Oxnam, emphasized cooperation as the solution to the Great Depression, but Niebuhr took a more confrontational approach. He argued that individuals were capable of living moral lives, but in social life—in the life of groups—such moral behavior was impossible. "The inevitable hypocrisy, which is associated with all of the collective activities of the human race, springs chiefly from this source: that individuals have a moral code which makes the actions of collective man an outrage to their conscience," he wrote.[58] He claimed that class prejudice and institutional imperatives make the social sphere irresponsive to moral suasion. This, he asserted, was the problem with Christian moralists and secular liberals alike: They believe that education and persuasion will solve all of our social problems. These innocents were unable to see that groups are ultimately unresponsive to moral sentiments and therefore liberals were not offering real solutions to the Great Depression. According to Niebuhr, we must recognize society's corruption and choose the least-worst route toward justice. For him, this meant going all-in for the working class.

Niebuhr's assessment of groups expressed itself most clearly in his ideas about international affairs. Like Oxnam, Niebuhr was a rising star in American Protestantism in the 1930s whose concern was increasingly global. Some of Niebuhr's newfound exuberance for dramatic social change was a result of his 1930 trip to the Soviet Union with Eddy's American Seminar. Niebuhr came away from the trip even more excited by the Soviet project than Oxnam had been four years earlier, and more willing to make generalizations about what he saw. Reinhold's brother Richard complained that "Reinie has been in Europe for a few weeks and he already thinks he knows all about it."[59]

The words "energy" and "vitality" recurred in Reinhold Niebuhr's writings about the trip to the USSR, even though he found the communist society "shot through with brutality." He universalized and brought back home in his writings what he saw abroad. The participation of average Russians in the construction of a new social order dedicated to the welfare of future generations was "not the product of communism at all, but simply the vigor of an emancipated people who are standing upright for the first time in the dignity of a new freedom." According to biographer Richard Fox, Niebuhr was "spellbound" by the Soviet experiment and "wondered if that kind of social energy could be mobilized in America." By the following year, before writing *Moral Man*, Niebuhr believed that it could be. As Fox explains, "With his Soviet visit of the previous summer firmly in mind, he asserted that religious energy was dangerous—it was closely akin to fanaticism—but necessary."[60] A year later, in *Moral Man*, Niebuhr would repeat this line: "The absolutist and fanatic is no doubt dangerous; but he is also necessary."[61]

In the Soviet Union Niebuhr also found an antidote to the nationalism emergent in that era, most dramatically in Benito Mussolini's Italian fascism. Through nationalism, the state "transmutes individual unselfishness"— the desire to be a part of something greater than oneself—"into national egotism." Niebuhr dwelled on this paradox at length: The more altruistic and selfless the individual becomes in their devotion to their national community, the more power it gives to the selfish ends of the nation. The selflessness of individuals creates big problems with no easy solutions. "What lies beyond the nation, the community of mankind, is too vague to inspire devotion," Niebuhr thought, and "the lesser communities within the nation, religious, economic, racial, and cultural, have equal difficulty in competing with the nation for the loyalty of its citizens." Even "religious missionary enterprises" were prone to patriotism and inclined toward "cultural imperialism," he worried.[62] Nothing, it seemed, was capable of restraining nationalism.

In Niebuhr's view, there were only poor candidates for taming national egotism, but support for the working class was the best among them. At a moment when much of the American Left believed that US participation in World War I was driven by financial institutions and the armaments industry, it made sense for Niebuhr to suppose that proletarian control at home would mean less crusading for markets abroad.

But at the moment *Moral Man* was published, a 4.4 percent share of the vote for Niebuhr hardly constituted an endorsement of his views. Niebuhr quickly moved away from the working class as the source of America's salvation. Making this move easier were attacks by former friends and colleagues, whose sharp rebukes appeared in the pages of the *Christian Century*. Niebuhr was frustrated with the magazine's tepid response to the 1932 election and especially Morrison's call for "disinterested citizens" to deliver votes to the party most willing to back progressive ideals. For Niebuhr, who was already annoyed about the magazine's dismissal of Norman Thomas, this was nonsense: You had to choose sides. "Disinterested politics" was an oxymoron because "all history proves the futility of expecting that men of power will divest themselves voluntarily of their power and their privilege." Morrison was not happy with this line of reasoning, and a back-and-forth ensued. But the last straw was the *Christian Century*'s review of *Moral Man*. It accused Niebuhr of endorsing violence in the name of class conflict. The reviewer concluded, "To call this book fully Christian in tone is to travesty the heart of Jesus' message to the world."[63]

The harsh reception of *Moral Man* pushed Niebuhr to focus less on attacking liberalism in general, and to focus more specifically on Protestant liberalism. "I have discovered since writing my book that the liberalism of American Protestantism has turned into a rather hard orthodoxy which turns vehemently upon every heretic who questions its assumptions," Niebuhr wrote.[64] Breaking with pacifists and those he derisively labeled "idealists," Niebuhr reinvented himself as a "realist," opposed to naive religious liberalism, which he now saw as his main enemy.

In the fall of 1933 Niebuhr was invited to take part in a group that would come to define Christian realism. The first meeting of the Theological Discussion Group included a disproportionate number of participants in Eddy's American Seminar, including Georgia Harkness, Samuel McCrea Cavert, Henry Pitney Van Dusen, and Niebuhr himself. They went back to first principles, rethinking the problems of human nature in a political world that seemed to be falling apart.[65] Their theology would become popular in Protestant circles during World War II and emerge with full force during the early Cold War.

As Niebuhr searched for a new political outlook, Morrison reevaluated his attitude toward Roosevelt after he had won the presidency decisively in November 1932. Morrison began to change his mind when Roosevelt first made public his plan for the Tennessee Valley Authority (TVA) just weeks before his inauguration in March 1933. Roosevelt proposed creating a public corporation to coordinate the construction and operation of twenty-nine dams along the Tennessee River, a massive project that would eliminate flooding in the region and bring cheap electricity to residents of seven states, many of whom had previously relied on power produced by animals and tolerated the stench of kerosene lamps. The plan's ambition caught Morrison's attention, and the emphasis on large-scale planning and uplift of rural communities matched the new economic vision of many ecumenical Protestants. The TVA was also a reaffirmation of the rational social planning Morrison had defended against Niebuhr's calls for fanaticism. "We hail it with joy as evidence that the new President is approaching his task, not merely thinking of details of local action, but realizing the necessity for planned national action on an unprecedented scale," the editors of the *Christian Century* wrote. "There is nothing impossible in Mr. Roosevelt's scheme. Let it be tried!"[66] Soon after, an assassination attempt elicited the editors' sympathy for the president-elect. But it was not until his inaugural address that the journal approved of Roosevelt's whole program.

Roosevelt's inaugural address, which hit on themes of evicting the money changers from the temple and returning to religious values, was an expression of the liberal Protestantism he had learned as a student at Groton Academy from its Episcopalian headmaster, Reverend Endicott Peabody.[67] Rather than seeing calamity in Old Testament terms—as Abraham Lincoln had done, when he evoked the notion of divine punishment in his second inaugural—Roosevelt's story emphasized human agency and social salvation that was well in line with the ecumenical Protestantism of the day. It was within the means of Americans, collectively, to restore the American economy by going back to the root values embodied by religion. Earlier presidents had evoked America's political traditions inaugurated by the Founding Fathers and enshrined in the Constitution as the means to build a good society. But in the 1930s liberalism and parliamentary democracy appeared to some observers as being too weak to withstand the Great Depression and the threats that fascism and communism posed without the aid of religion. Hoover had talked about the Constitution; Roosevelt spoke of faith.

Roosevelt's inaugural address struck all the right chords for Morrison and the *Christian Century*. "In his inaugural he looked not only *at* the emergency but *beyond* it to the construction of an order in which such emergencies will not occur," the editors wrote. The president's speech had also stressed "matters of inner renewal without which no legislative or executive policies, however cleverly devised, can get us out of the mire." Quoting Roosevelt's references to the "false money changers" approvingly, the editors recognized the broader message that they had been pushing for years. "To a great extent," the editors wrote, "we have made [the money changers] what they are, and the moral renewal must go much farther than merely putting them in jail."[68]

Almost immediately, during Roosevelt's First Hundred Days, the flurry of legislation and executive action spelled out what moral renewal would mean for the country. Amid these "revolutionary" acts, which included a bank holiday, executive powers over the budget, and departing from the gold standard, "the public has almost lost the capacity to be startled," the editors wrote. "Had a communist entered the white house on March 4, could he have set up a more vital dictatorship? Constitutional lawyers shook their heads; the nation cheered."[69]

The *Christian Century* embraced what they viewed as a revolutionary program. "His banking program is clearly headed toward socialism's government-controlled system of banking. His currency program, with its inflationary possibilities, could as easily be made to produce a redistribution of wealth as socialism's capital levy. His public works program—the Tennessee valley scheme, with its adjuncts—is as completely socialist in method and aim as any Russian five-year plan." The editors grasped the magnitude of the changes taking place during the First Hundred Days and they endorsed it wholeheartedly: "The events of the past few months have made it abundantly clear that we need a new United States."[70]

Ecumenical Protestants and the Making of the New Deal

The working relationship between the ecumenical Protestant elite and the Roosevelt administration was not only rhetorical. It also meant that they would occasionally work together in the muddy world of Washington politics. The Federal Council placed James Myers in charge of transforming the organization's pronouncements into social action. Myers's interest in the labor movement began at a moment when employers were embracing "welfare capitalism." Following the strike waves of 1919, large employers began offering perks to employees, like days off and company baseball games, and created committees that listened to employee complaints. This welfare capitalism was designed to keep employees from unionizing. Myers, a committed pacifist, had lost his pulpit at a Presbyterian church during World War I and found a job as the head of one of these committees. With this experience, he was hired by the Federal Council in 1925 to head its Industrial Relations Committee.[71]

It was Myers's middle-of-the-road approach that made him attractive to Federal Council leaders. Myers was committed to nonpartisanship and shied away from aligning himself with the fortunes of any given party. "I almost joined the Socialist Party back in Auburn Seminary days," he later recalled, "but balked at the 'Party discipline' pledge. Later I came to feel (whether rightly or wrongly) that in my work with the Federal Council and labor, I could do more effective work in my particular role without being a member of a party."[72]

That same commitment to nonpartisanship carried over to Myers's view of labor unions. Myers, like Oxnam, did not value labor unions as an end in themselves. Rather, he saw unions as a means of bringing balance to an industry dominated by too-powerful business owners. "While I do not believe in class hostility," Myers wrote to a colleague, "I do believe in democracy which means free and untrammeled organization for the workers and an opportunity to have a voice in management of industry."[73] In the 1930s, Myers became a big booster of producers' and consumers' cooperatives, which became a form of escapism for the Protestant Left. It allowed Myers to imagine a future in which Christian principles would not have to be expressed in the tense world of labor-management relations.

Nevertheless, in the here and now, Myers could not help but take sides. In 1929, he visited mill towns in North Carolina and Tennessee, where textile workers had gone on strike. He went to document events, and what he found shocked him. Managers had increased the backbreaking workloads to unbearable levels while cutting already low pay by 10 percent. He documented attacks by private security firms and, in Elizabethton, Tennessee, he discovered that a Presbyterian elder was involved in a kidnapping attempt of a union official. When strikes broke out, most of the clergy looked away or sided with employers, instructing congregants that unions were unchristian and that "servants should obey their master." During a visit Myers paid to Gastonia, North Carolina, the clergy in the town "were defensive, cold, unresponsive to a degree I have never met before in a group of ministers." In response to these conditions, Myers helped raise relief funds for striking workers, and he went to Washington to lobby Herbert Hoover, but found the experience of speaking with the president to be like "talking to empty air." He returned to DC in the spring of 1933, to a more receptive climate, and testified at congressional hearings on the textile codes of the National Recovery Administration, but to little avail.[74]

In May 1935, Myers put his years of investigating violence in the textile industry to good use. He drafted a petition on labor and civil liberties, and circulated it among hundreds of clergy. The petition asked the Senate Judiciary Committee to investigate nationwide infringements on civil liberties that aimed "to repress demands for economic change on the part of labor and to maintain special privileges and power which [employers] now enjoy." Social gospel stalwarts like Francis J. McConnell and Harry Emerson Fosdick signed the petition, along with Catholic Monsignor John A. Ryan and Rabbis Stephen Wise and Sidney Goldstein—an expression of religious cooperation in economic matters that Roosevelt had encouraged. In response to the petition, the Senate formed the La Follette Committee, named after the progressive Republican senator Robert La Follette of Wisconsin. The committee investigated attacks on the Southern Tenant Farmers Union, oversaw the unionization of the Ford Motor Company, and involved itself in both iconic and mundane labor organizing drives of the 1930s.[75]

The La Follette Committee was performing oversight work for the National Labor Relations Act, known popularly as the "Wagner Act," which was passed in 1935 with the help of Myers's lobbying efforts. The Wagner Act reestablished the right of most workers to unionize, after the Supreme Court had struck down an earlier law. Under the Wagner Act, workers had the right to hold elections by secret ballot and employers were required to bargain with unions. And an oversight board made sure that employers did not circumvent this process through unfair tactics or through employer-sponsored unions.

When the Wagner Act was being debated in Congress in early 1935, Myers went to work. First, he formed an interfaith committee of Catholic and Jewish representatives to lobby for the bill. He maintained a personal correspondence with Senator Robert F. Wagner, the sponsor of the bill. And he worked to promote coverage of the bill, writing directly to Arthur Hays Sulzberger of the New York Times, who ran the article "Three Faiths Back Wagner Labor Bill." During the Wagner Act debates, Myers served as a

Figure 2. James Myers (center), Rabbi Edward L. Israel (left), and Rev. R. A. McGowan (right) waiting to meet with Herbert Hoover to discuss economic relief in 1931. Myers frequently joined tri-faith delegations, which became increasingly common during the Roosevelt administration. Courtesy of the Library of Congress.

clearinghouse of information. He was also the last speaker during congressional testimony on the bill. Myers had connections with America's political elite, direct access to the public sphere, and a decade of investigatory reports to draw upon. His important role in the passage of the Wagner Act was one expression of the political mobilization of ecumenical Protestants on behalf of the New Deal.[76]

The same Protestant-Catholic-Jewish trio backed the "Wagner-Lewis Economic Security Bill," now known as the Social Security Act, that same year. They organized labor, business, and religious leaders to petition the Senate to pass the bill, calling on Congress to fulfill its "solemn covenant with the people."[77] For Myers, the bill would fulfill the promise of the 1932 Revised Social Ideals, which advocated for "social insurance against sickness, accident, and want in old age and unemployment." He spent less of his energy on behalf of Social Security compared with his efforts on behalf of the labor bills. He did not testify on the bill's behalf (and representatives of Protestant pension funds lobbied against it). But he could draw on a public rhetoric, developed years earlier by the Federal Council of Churches and ecumenical denominations, that identified social security as a Christian principle. Myers's ability to quickly mobilize the cultural capital of Christianity in the public sphere on behalf of the New Deal was an important part of Roosevelt's success during his first term in office.

The New Deal and the Revolt of the Laity

Convinced that Roosevelt was taking the United States in the right direction, ecumenical Protestant leaders brought their values into their churches, hoping to persuade everyday churchgoers that these big changes were socially justified and religiously sanctioned. At the United Church of Hyde Park, a uniquely cooperative venture between the Congregationalists and Northern Presbyterians in Chicago, and a tangible example of ecumenism, the minister Douglas Horton asked the congregants to personally respond to the new sense of social responsibility pervading Protestantism in 1934. Horton, who would soon head the Congregationalist denomination, encouraged his flock to write social creeds for individual professions. This largely middle-class congregation of lawyers, bankers, teachers, housewives, and doctors was asked to study, reflect upon, and respond to the Revised Social Ideals.[78]

The response Horton received from his congregants in 1934 widely endorsed the proposals of the Revised Social Ideals and backed some of the initiatives of the Roosevelt administration. "I stand . . . for publicly supported old age pension systems for the present, and the development of contributory old age insurance for the future; and for such financial and economic control as may be helpful in preventing a recurrence of the loss of savings which so tragically destroyed the security of this generation," wrote Olive H. Carpenter. Another participant declared, "I must stand for leaders who see problems as part of a whole and stand for social planning and control of the credit and economic processes for the common good," including social insurance. "I must stand for the fair distribution of money," the congregant added.[79]

Carpenter also called for greater gender equality, which resonated with the Federal Council of Churches' views on women. According to Marie

Griffith, the Federal Council "continued on a steady course in a progressive direction on birth control and sex more generally" in the 1930s.[80] Carpenter endorsed "the right of families of all social ranks to such knowledge of birth control as will assure the best home life; for social, civil and economic equality of the sexes [and for] effective public health services, and in such systems of medical group care as will make expert diagnosis and treatment available to all."[81]

The broad support given to Roosevelt's new liberalism was tied together with pacifism and family values for many congregants at Horton's United Church. For some, who called for "Aid-to-Mothers," social benefits were meant to ensure the stability of the family. They were to go hand in hand with laws that discouraged hasty marriages and that "controlled" movies, books, and radio programs that threatened to undermine family morals.[82] A congregant urged "government control and sale of alcoholic drink" and opposed "free love, lax divorce laws, and anti-marriage and anti-home sentiment," as well as "indecent movies" and "nudist colonies."[83] The churchgoer was also deeply concerned about the possibility of war and therefore backed the outlawry of war "under the sponsorship of social and religious groups for all the world."[84] The two great moral imperatives of Progressive Era Protestantism—protection of the family and the diminution of war—were understood by some of the laity to require economic stability. And economic stability required peace and good morals.

Not everyone was enthusiastic about the New Deal at Horton's church. Irene Crandall maintained that it was her duty to "fight against bureaucracy and government control of industry, education or religion, and the regimentation of our lives." Hard work was the best means of dealing with the Depression, according to Crandall. There was room for Christian charity, she wrote to Horton, but the weak must be helped in such a way that they do not unnecessarily drag down the strong.[85] Her economic views were in the minority at the ecumenical United Church—at least among those who chose to respond in writing—but she spoke for a section of churchgoers in disproportionately middle- and upper-middle-class ecumenical Protestant denominations.[86]

Chicago's United Church was one of the many sites where serious political discussions were taking place among everyday churchgoers. These spaces were important because churchgoers could experiment with new ideas within a safe community, surrounded only by like-minded Protestants. These spaces also offered women, who constituted the majority of churchgoers in Protestant denominations but were often missing in leadership positions, a place to debate and organize on behalf of political causes. And finally, Horton's church and others like it were helping constitute the kind of rational public the *Christian Century* worked to cultivate. Rather than exhortation or the chilling warnings about impending doom coming out of the fundamentalist churches, Horton's approach encouraged different affective work. It was tailored to middle-class sensibilities, telling congregants not to react too strongly, not to jump to conclusions, to be even-handed and deliberative in their analyses, and, above all, to think about today's political questions in relationship to the values of liberal theology, the social gospel, and ecumenism.

Congregants in Protestant churches were by no means passive recipients of clerical guidance, contemplating solemnly the details of the Revised Social Ideals under the supervision of clerical tutors. At times, churchgoers formed an active and organized opposition to the more radical elements in Protestant denominations.

When Congregationalist leaders appeared to be criticizing capitalism and the profit motive, the laity organized a national protest against the clergy. In 1934, the same year Douglas Horton was discussing the Revised Social Ideals with his flock, national Congregationalist leaders met for the first time in four years. Traditionally, Congregational churches had a great deal of autonomy, and their congregational polity meant that the national organization had no doctrinal authority over local churches. When they met in Oberlin, Ohio, that year church leaders decided that their denomination must change in order for it to effectively respond to the Great Depression.

The most vital of these changes was the creation of the Congregational Council for Social Action (CSA). The CSA included some young radicals, like Buell G. Gallagher and John C. Bennett, who were members of Niebuhr's Fellowship of Christian Socialists. The majority, however, were old social gospelers, like chairman Arthur Holt. At least one member joined because he wanted Congregationalists to engage in charity more effectively, but he opposed the New Deal.

Officially, the CSA was an advisory committee that would research social problems and report the facts to the churches and let each one decide what, if anything, to do about them. The new organization was tasked with investigating international affairs and peace, rural life and rural-urban conflicts, industrial relations, and race relations. Unofficially, this new group tasked itself with activism and, on occasion, lobbying. Referring to a clause in its charter that nobody gave much thought to in 1934, which read that "the Council may, upon occasion, intercede directly in specific situations," the CSA created a legislative committee in 1936 to watch over Congress.[87]

This concentration of power was all the more troubling to some church-goers because the CSA appeared to be siding with the political Left and crit-icizing the heart of capitalism. On the last day of the 1934 Oberlin conference, when many ministers had already left, the remaining conference-goers passed a resolution called "The Social Gospel and Economic Problems" by a vote of 130 to 17. The innocuous-sounding resolution had, in fact, denounced "the profit motive" and called on the denomination to abolish the "legal forms which sustain it, and the moral ideals which justify it."[88] This included abolishing private ownership when it "interferes with the social good."[89]

The protest against this "profit motive resolution" was not simply a matter of economic policy at a volatile moment in 1934, when the New Deal was being attacked from both the Left and the Right. Some asked whether their denomination still practiced its libertarian-democratic tradition. A denomination with an organized hierarchy, like the Episcopalians or Pres-byterians, could clearly say that interpreting the gospel was not up to each individual church. But for some Congregationalist churchgoers, who held fast to local autonomy, the very idea that the denomination could go on rec-ord in support of a political position—especially something that sounded Marxist—was a nonstarter.

Ecclesiology, in this case the decentralized congregational model of church governance, mattered. Congregationalist churchgoers shared a demographic profile with Episcopalians and Presbyterians. All three denominations were composed of disproportionately wealthy members. And yet, Congregation-alists expressed stronger preferences for economic individualism compared to their peers in more hierarchical denominations.[90] For many churchgoers, decentralized religious life and economic individualism went hand in hand. The objections to the profit motive resolution combined fears of a centralized government and a centralized church.

Although the creation of the CSA and the profit motive resolution were distinct measures, they were conflated in the debates that followed the 1934 Oberlin conference. Critics feared that the CSA was created to combat capi-talism. As one layman put it, "I am shocked beyond expression to learn the church I have loved and supported all my life—the church for which two centuries has carried high the banner of human freedom ... has seized the first opportunity to align itself with the most dangerous political philoso-phy yet devised."[91] Russell J. Clinchy, a dissenting member of the CSA, would later complain, "Frankly, we are Congregationalists and as such we cannot speak or act for others in social realms any more than we can in theological realms.... No minority can speak for the whole."[92] The leaders of the CSA protested, putting out a statement that declared they were followers of Jesus, not Marx or Roosevelt. But the clarification changed few minds. Protests broke out across the country as conservative activists and business leaders organized in the name of the "laity." It was men who "provided the emotional energy behind the widening controversy," writes Margaret Bendroth. These groups "became a vehicle of masculine resentment against higher forces beyond popular control."[93] As angry businessmen and well-connected laypersons—mostly men—mobilized for congregational autonomy and against the denunciation of the profit motive, they called the laity into being.

The laity was made in the 1930s in response to debates about the New Deal state. To be sure, the laity as a theological category was longstanding in Protestant thought. But as an identity, the "laity" must be treated in the same way as historian E. P. Thompson treated the "working class"—not as a transhistorical category but as a meaningful identity and solidarity that arose at a specific moment in time and whose creation was a response to specific economic, social, and political contexts. We have to ask, under what circumstances did some churchgoers come to understand themselves as members of the laity? In this sense, some churchgoers in the 1930s came to believe that they were members of the laity not only because they wanted to differentiate themselves from the clergy but because they wanted to differentiate their politics from the politics of the clergy. As this and later chapters demonstrate, the laity became a meaningful identity in the mid-twentieth century because of concerns about the New Deal, antiracist initiatives, and certain forms of internationalism. As some churchgoers started thinking of themselves as members of the laity, they were not only mobilizing a theological tradition but also taking on a political identity and staking out a position on ecclesiology.[94]

For anti-clergy activists, laity meant something more than simply non-clergy churchgoers. They argued that the wealthier, more responsible members of the church should have a louder voice in policy debates. And so, although the mobilization against the denunciation of the profit motive likely represented a broadly held belief in economic individualism among Congregationalist churchgoers, such revolts against clergy were almost always organized by very narrow segments of the denomination. The subtlety of values and political positions among everyday churchgoers expressed at Horton's church were lost in the writings and speeches of the laity.

Facing a laymen's revolt in the 1930s, the Corporation of the General Council—Congregationalism's governing body—took the unusual step of rescinding the profit motive resolution, announcing in March 1935 that it should be regarded as an "unauthoritative minority pronouncement."[95] With the resolution rescinded, Congregationalism returned to the traditional position of letting each church decide how it felt about the profit motive. The protests died down, but the laity raised broad questions about the relationship between religion, democracy, and economics that would not go away for decades and exposed a gap in values between clergy and laity. And the groups organized in the 1930s to fight the profit motive resolution would reemerge in the early Cold War with new vigor.[96] Nonetheless, the CSA remained intact and its resources would grow over the years. Congregationalism emerged out of the debates over the profit motive, like most other denominations in the 1930s, more divided and yet more critical of capitalism, more politically adept, with much of the institutional machinery in the hands of social gospel clergy.

When Douglas Horton was elected to head the Congregational denomination in 1936, there were no easy answers to the questions about ecclesiology raised during the profit motive debate. Horton acknowledged higher authorities than majority rule and expertise, although he could not entirely dismiss the demands of the churchgoers he worked so tirelessly to move leftward in the 1930s. He had little appreciation for the laity, which was attempting to seize the cultural capital of Christianity on behalf of its wealthiest members. Horton was not a socialist or even very enthusiastic about the social gospel, but he nonetheless opposed the growing threat wealthy churchgoers posed to what he viewed as Christianity's social mission.

The laity, however, was not the only threat to Horton's social politics during the Great Depression. Fundamentalist Protestants, who had been routed in the 1920s battles over denominational control, kept a watchful and wary eye on ecumenical Protestants and the political leaders they supported, especially Roosevelt. They were angered that Roosevelt helped end Prohibition and upset that his policies seemed to toe the line of groups, like socialists and labor unions, that they considered atheistic. For many fundamentalists this was enough to make them stalwart opponents of the New Deal. Others saw the New Deal in global terms, as part of the fulfilment of a prophecy about the end-times. They subscribed to dispensationalist premillennialism, which was a theory, derived from the most obscure passages of the Bible, predicting that history went through stages and that the coming of the Antichrist was imminent. Many fundamentalists saw Mussolini's attempt at restoring the Roman Empire and Hitler's antisemitism driving Jews to Palestine as a prelude to the Rapture. Roosevelt's charisma, his increasing power, and his internationalist sensibilities were seen in this global context, according to Matthew Sutton, in which "New Deal liberalism was the means by which the United States would join the legions of the antichrist." Suspicion ran high from the very beginning—at the Democratic Convention in 1932, Roosevelt had received exactly 666 votes.[97]

Four years after Roosevelt's election, national ecumenical Protestant leaders gave broad support to the New Deal, much to the chagrin of some laymen, business leaders, communist hunters, and fundamentalists. In 1936, hoping to undermine Roosevelt's chances of reelection, W. B. Riley, the founder and former head of the World's Christian Fundamentals Association, helped organize a conference in Asheville, North Carolina, in support of capitalism and religion and railing against its enemies. Riley, a rabid antisemite and future mentor to Billy Graham, was joined by professional communist hunter Elizabeth Dilling, author of *Red Network*, along with Methodist, Presbyterian, and Lutheran ministers, laymen, and educators.

Conference speakers had two targets: Reds in the churches and Reds in the White House. They saw the New Deal largely as a religious problem. Professor Theodore Graebner of the Lutheran Concordia Theological Seminary in St. Louis and editor of the *Lutheran Witness*, believed that the New Deal was based on the false theology expressed in the Revised Social Ideals. Speakers insisted that "much New Deal legislation has been enacted at radical churchmen's behest as easy steps toward Moscow." Another speaker argued that the Methodist youth "is being fed homeopathic doses of socialism and communism through Sunday school literature."[98] Although concerned about the New Deal, they saw it as a symptom of a much deeper spiritual problem: theological liberalism. Opposing bad religion and its false political prophets was their central concern.

Both Roosevelt and ecumenical Protestants kept an eye on these developments, especially during the election year of 1936. Stanley High, the former editor of the *Christian Herald*, who was then working as a political operative for Roosevelt, warned the president that the "strongest opposition" would come "not from the economic reactionaries, but from the religious reactionaries."[99] But neither Roosevelt nor the ecumenical Protestant elite were seriously worried. The attempt to rally the enemies of the New Deal and sway the election toward the Republican nominee Alf Landon—whom a Presbyterian college president called "a solid typical church-going, church supporting American"—was a failure. In November 1936 Roosevelt won 99 percent of the popular vote in the college president's home state of South Carolina. Roosevelt also won 98.5 percent of the electoral votes nationwide in one of the largest landslides in American history.[100]

One big barrier for fundamentalist politics was its religious intolerance. Fascist ministers, like Gerald B. Winrod, had shown up to the Asheville conference and "attempted to inject Nazi ideas into the convention's deliberations."[101] The attempt to include Jews and Catholics at Asheville erupted into an orgy of religious bigotry. Pastor Charles Vaughn of Los Angeles led the opposition to the very marginal Jewish participation. Defeated on the first day of the conference, he and other attendees organized a competing Protestant-only meeting at a nearby church. In a bizarre turn of events, Vaughn claimed to have been punched and knocked unconscious when returning to his hotel room, which he attributed to "sinister forces." When he came to, he found that 250 letters in his possession that had been addressed to anticommunists had disappeared. After investigating, Asheville police concluded that the whole affair had been a hoax.[102]

These theatrics only encouraged ecumenical disdain of their fundamentalist and anticommunist opponents. It also kept respectable business leaders and all but the most reactionary laypersons away and undermined alliances between anticommunist Protestants and Catholic and Jewish sympathizers. Charles Clayton Morrison delighted in listing the leaders of the American National Front and the American Nordic Folk—distributors of the antisemitic tract *The Protocols of the Elders of Zion*—alongside conservative Protestant laymen and fundamentalist preachers. The *Christian Century* blasted the "attempted alliance between the organized militaristic patrioteers, the anti-Semitic and 'Nordic' enthusiasts, some extreme fundamentalists, some economically conservative laymen, some southern republicans and some anti-Roosevelt southern democrats" for their shameful effort at "giving religious and patriotic sanction to a political program." And Morrison rightly understood that in the 1930s this was a nonstarter: "This kind of gun is much more dangerous at the butt than at the muzzle."[103]

While fundamentalists had trouble rallying their constituency against Roosevelt, ecumenical denominations appeared hard-pressed to get their churchgoers to vote for him. The sense among ecumenical leaders that their values and politics were not shared by many churchgoers was laid bare in the mid-1930s through a new technology: polling. George Gallup's survey techniques gained widespread attention during the 1936 election, when he successfully predicted the reelection of Roosevelt from only a small sample size. By 1940, 8 million Americans were reading the results of Gallup's polls in syndicated columns across the nation.[104] Protestant leaders had occasionally queried their publics before, but the advent of polling gave this technique added importance. Now it was possible for social scientists to bypass the clergy entirely and query what the "average" Protestant was thinking.

Ecumenical Protestant leaders did not like what polls told them about their religion. Horton made headway in promoting his ideals at his United Church of Hyde Park. But for the two denominations that joined together to create this church—the Congregationalists and the Northern Presbyterians—churchgoers remained resistant to the Democratic Party. While Roosevelt won in a landslide in 1936, 77 percent of Congregationalists voted for Republican Alf Landon, FDR's opponent, in that election. Landon ran on a progressive Republican platform that criticized some aspects of the New Deal while accepting others. And yet hostility toward the idea of the New Deal remained persistent among ecumenical Protestant churchgoers. A 1940s-era survey found that 72 percent of Congregationalists and 65 percent of Northern Presbyterians disapproved of the New Deal.[105]

This did not mean that Horton was not getting through to his flock but only that they did not switch their party loyalty. "Political preference is a less stable index" of values than other markers, Protestant leaders themselves observed.[106] The extent of the shift in values among ecumenical Protestant churchgoers in the 1930s is difficult to gauge. In the long term, it appears that many remained loyal to the Republican Party but gravitated toward its respectable, liberal wing. But whatever steps they took leftward, for ecumenical leaders this was hardly enough. A gap existed between the values of Protestant clergy and laity. Deciding how to deal with the clergy-laity gap would become a perennial problem for members of the Protestant establishment, who would struggle between the two great forces that shaped their politics: their faith and their congregants.

By the time of Roosevelt's reelection campaign in 1936, there was more support for him than there had been in 1932. To be sure, there was opposition among the laity and criticism of FDR among the left-leaning clergy. But by 1936 there was a sense that ecumenical Protestant leaders could work with

Roosevelt and that his major accomplishments—the Wagner Act, the Social Security Act, the Tennessee Valley Authority—were in accord with Protestant principles.

The previously hostile *Christian Century* celebrated Roosevelt's Democratic convention speech in 1936. "It moved on a plane above these matters of partisan apologetic and polemic," the editors wrote. "It was the statement of a philosophy of government based on a realization that men who are in economic bondage cannot be politically free."[107] The relationship between ecumenical Protestant clergy, the spokespersons for Protestant liberalism, and Roosevelt, the spokesperson for political liberalism, had strengthened by 1936. Initially suspicious of Roosevelt's political ties to machine politics and the Catholic Church, and critical of his opposition to Prohibition, ecumenical Protestants now celebrated Roosevelt as a prophet of a new economy rooted in Christian values.

"A Summons for Us to Stand Together"

In 1934, G. Bromley Oxnam traveled once again on Sherwood Eddy's American Seminar, now in its fourteenth year. When the party arrived in Germany, where Nazi officials had gotten wind of Eddy's antifascist remarks, Oxnam took over as the seminar's leader. On an earlier trip to Italy, Oxnam was fascinated with fascism, noting that Italians went "about their business with a new spirit," and he judged Mussolini to be "the greatest orator I have ever heard." What he witnessed in Germany in 1934, however, felt far more sinister. Two weeks after the Night of the Long Knives, Oxnam listened to a speech by Hitler defending the murder of his opposition. As Oxnam stood listening, standing near Göring, Goebbels, and a throng of SS members, he saw Hitler as "a modest person of awful dignity and compelling magnetism; a mystic, a man of purpose, a personality in repose, yet ready to deliver devastating blows for a cause, a man tender at heart but willing to become ruthless in his messianic mission." Hitler's opposition "lives in terror," Oxnam wrote in his diary. "The concentration camp, the firing squad and exile loom like specters of the night in his mind." Soon, he concluded, Germany would go to war with its neighbors.[108]

Roosevelt noted the danger as well. In 1932, Roosevelt had evoked religion on behalf of a new economic program. In 1936, he began mobilizing religion again to confront the new fascist threat. "Religion in wide areas of the earth is being confronted with irreligion; our faiths are being challenged," he told a nationwide radio audience. "The very state of the world is a summons for us to stand together."[109]

By 1936, the New Deal was largely spent.[110] Its tremendous accomplishments—the creation of the Tennessee Valley Authority, the passage of the Social Security Act, and the Wagner Act—all benefited from a Protestant Christianity that was publicly associated with liberal causes and whose institutions were largely in the hands of supporters of the New Deal. That Roosevelt began using Protestant language to describe his foreign policy lent a great deal of attention to those issues and would eventually pave the way for American involvement in World War II. The change in emphasis likewise worked against further domestic reforms, as Protestants followed Roosevelt's lead in focusing on the Nazi threat to the detriment of new economic initiatives.

Roosevelt's 1936 reelection bookended the remarkable transformation of the nation's economy and of the country's religious life. A new generation, including Oxnam, Horton, and Niebuhr, took on leading roles in Protestant institutions. In 1936, Oxnam became a bishop in the Methodist denomination. That same year, Horton became the national leader of the Congregationalists. Niebuhr became a celebrated author. With their rise, Prohibition and other Progressive Era concerns faded away. As ecumenical Protestants became more politically organized they worried about the difficulties of justifying their politics theologically to churchgoers. Nevertheless, four years into FDR's presidency, the assumption that the New Deal was an expression of Protestant values was widespread. It would be more accurate to say that during the Great Depression, the spokespersons for religious and political liberalism improvised, began speaking the same language, and finally made common cause. Whether they would do the same for the looming war was another matter.

CHAPTER 2

The Coming War and the Pacifist-Realist Split

After his 1936 reelection, Franklin Delano Roosevelt began mobilizing religious groups against the looming threat of fascism.[1] As he explained in his 1939 State of the Union address, fascism threatened the three pillars of world peace. "The first is religion," he told Congress and the American people. "It is the source of the other two—democracy and international good faith."[2] The president called on religious people to mobilize against the evils of fascism, and ecumenical Protestants answered this call enthusiastically. Like Roosevelt, who transformed himself from "Dr. New Deal" to "Dr. Win the War," American ecumenical Protestants shifted their attention from ending the Great Depression to combating what they called "world disorder." During the brief moment of international crisis, from the Japanese invasion of China in 1937 to the attack on Pearl Harbor in 1941, ecumenical Protestants formulated a new political understanding of international affairs, which this book calls "Protestant globalism." They abandoned the old imperial system and proposed new pillars of world order. The first pillar, they insisted, would be religion.

The effort to plan out a new world order was the most ambitious intellectual project among ecumenical Protestants in the years immediately before American entry into World War II. Ecumenical Protestant leaders articulated a new understanding of international affairs, one that treated the globe as an interconnected whole, which required a single political system to govern it. The interwar order of the League of Nations—of individual states that came together as sovereign units in a world parliament—had failed. As they watched Italy, Germany, and Japan go to war with their neighbors, ecumenical Protestants concluded that the unlimited sovereignty of nation-states created international anarchy and led to war.

Ecumenical Protestant leaders came to believe that a new international organization must stand over and above the nation-state. It must be a world government representing all the peoples in all the lands, with the capacity to coerce countries into behaving in accordance with Christian values. "This League-of-Nations-with-teeth," as *Time* magazine called their proposal, would be "a duly constituted world government of delegated powers: an international legislative body, an international court with adequate jurisdiction, international administrative bodies with necessary powers, and adequate international police forces and provision for enforcing its worldwide economic authority."[3] The call for a new world government was the most tangible product of the new political ideology of Protestant globalism.

American ecumenical Protestants joined intellectuals across Europe and North America in experimenting with new ideas about world order in this moment of crisis.[4] Ecumenical Protestant ideas about world government also opened up room to discuss economic reforms, racism, imperialism, and human rights. What made American ecumenical Protestants different from the myriad academic groups and think tanks delving into the same issues was their ecumenical theology and their emphasis on the interconnection between the foreign and domestic arenas. By imagining a more peaceful world, they also imagined a more democratic country that promoted justice for racial minorities and economic rights for workers. A world government, they came to believe, would also reinvigorate democracy at home.

But before they could advocate for a world government, American ecumenical Protestants had to put aside their differences about American involvement in World War II, which ran deep. As self-styled realists like Reinhold Niebuhr and Henry P. Van Dusen mobilized religious networks to get the United States to side with Great Britain, pacifists resisted tooth and nail. Realists and pacifists fought over food aid to Europe, embargoes of Japan, the role of the United States in the war, and the very meaning of Christianity. Protestant globalism emerged through heated debates about what it meant to be Christian in the face of fascism.

"The Demonic Influence of National Sovereignty"

In 1937 American ecumenical Protestants were confident that they had a special role to play in creating a new world out of the destruction they saw all around them. For nearly three decades they had labored to bind together their fellow Protestants into a global fellowship. In the spring of 1937, they boarded ships on their way to England, where they attended a conference on "Church, Community and State" at Oxford. At the conclusion of the meeting, delegates from over one hundred denominations from dozens of countries voted to merge the "Life and Work" movement with the "Faith and Order" movement, and to create the provisional World Council of Churches. "In a world in which every international structure and society has been rifted or shattered," wrote American theologian Henry Pitney Van Dusen, "it is beginning to be realized that one world fellowship has been able to maintain its reality unbroken; indeed, has actually strengthened its cohesion and structure in the very days when every other international community has been disintegrating."[5] The creation of the World Council of Churches was a momentous triumph of Christian unity. As Union Theological Seminary president Henry Sloane Coffin put it, "It was in July in the year of our Lord 1054 that the Christian Church broke at what is called 'the Great Schism' into two hostile camps" of Catholicism and Eastern Orthodoxy. "Last July, 883 years later, one could not help recalling that bitter incident when representatives of all the non-Roman churches, East and West, and churches from parts of the world unknown in 1054, gathered together in the University town of Oxford and owned themselves one in the unity of the one body of Christ."[6] The creation of the World Council of Churches was a millennial moment, whose participants felt the course of the Great Schism and the Protestant Reformation to be near its end.

The 1937 Oxford gathering projected Protestant unity at a moment of global disunity. That unity came about partly because few Orthodox Christians or Protestants from the Global South were present. American fundamentalists also stayed away. There was a definite tilt toward the concerns of Anglo-American Protestants in the proceedings. And differences were generally downplayed. For example, official publications ignored German Methodist Otto Melle's praise of Adolf Hitler at the conference.[7] Oxford represented something far less than Christian unity, but for American ecumenists it was more than enough. "At all times, in all places, let the Church be the Church—the body of Christ, an enduring, universal community in which His spirit may live and speak to the world and carry on its mighty work of individual and social redemption," American pastor Ernest Fremont Tittle exclaimed. "What a vision! Yet it is not only a vision. To an amazing extent, even now, it is a reality."[8]

The 1937 Oxford conference was a massive academic undertaking, involving research offices in Geneva, London, and New York and three years of meetings, position papers, dozens of books, and thousands of letters among theologians, economists, legal experts, and politicians. Debates raged about everything from the differing theological conceptions of the Kingdom of God to the relations of church and state (and a last-minute addition of "the Church and War").[9] Through these painstaking deliberations, ecumenical Protestants offered a new account of "world disorder."

At the close of the Oxford conference, the Protestant and Orthodox representatives diagnosed the international situation. Modernity had torn the world apart, dissolving closely knit communities into masses of atomized individuals. Without adequate resistance from the churches, peoples across the world looked to the new gods of nation, race, and class to worship. "A false sacred, a false God," announced British ecumenist and conference organizer Joseph Oldham, "prepares for mankind an even worse and wider conflict."[10] Only by restoring God to his rightful place above all material things could order be restored. It was time for the churches to wake up—"Let the Church be the Church," declared Oldham—and fight these false gods.

Americans were well-represented at Oxford but they were very aware of their distance from their European colleagues. Union Theological Seminary professor William Adams Brown, the senior statesman of ecumenism, offered a warning to his fellow Americans about the anti-secularism they should expect to find in Europe. "As representatives of a country which for more than a century and a half has had no national establishment of religion while at the same time the attitude of the government has been friendly to Christianity, we have had the opportunity to explore more fully than the Christians of Europe the possibilities of a free church in a democratic state," he wrote.[11] Indeed, the European ecumenical leaders were much more hostile to what they perceived as secular forces than were the Americans.[12] In some ways, American ecumenical Protestants held a more privileged place in public life than Europeans, who had been experiencing declining church attendance since the 1880s and had periodically clashed with governments. Americans did not share the siege mentality of their European coreligionists.[13]

American ecumenists also did not feel as threatened by the far-away Soviet Union, which loomed large over European politics in the 1930s. Many of the leading American ecumenists at Oxford, including Niebuhr and G. Bromley Oxnam, were interested in the Soviet experiment and were involved in the popular front movements of the 1930s. To them, fascism was the far bigger threat. As the American ecumenists took stock of international affairs in 1937, they carefully parsed differences in ideology. Following the sociologist Karl Mannheim, who was then working in England and was close to church groups there, American ecumenists saw the world as a battle between rival ideologies or "worldviews." "Totalitarian states are essentially churches and can be met only by churches," wrote American ecumenist John Mackay. "The new churches have become rivals of God and of the Christian Church." European Christians worried in equal measure about fascism and communism, but American ecumenists fretted most about Nazism. "While Communism regards tyranny as a transitory phenomenon in the development of a world order, Fascism regards it as a permanent expression of political life," Mackay explained. Communism offered a warped, materialist idea of the unity of mankind, but fascism rejected anything beyond the nation-state itself. For these reasons, he concluded, "The Fascist communal ideal is the most inimical to the Christian ideal of world community."[14]

In this antifascist context, ecumenical Protestants focused on what Philip Kerr, the Marquess of Lothian and soon-to-be British ambassador to the United States, called "The Demonic Influence of National Sovereignty." Kerr argued that nation-states create peace within their own boundaries by monopolizing violence and mediating disputes among rivals, but in the international arena they operate under anarchy. The League of Nations was "mankind's first recognition of the need for a world government and for a reign of law among the nations," he argued, "but because it is based upon the complete national sovereignty of its members it begins to be paralysed as soon as one or more powerful states resign membership or repudiate their obligations." There is no solution to the problem of national sovereignty except in "a common sovereignty" represented by a "world federation—a state which, in its own sphere, will command the allegiance of mankind, will be able to legislate for, judge, and tax everybody." Such an organization is the only remedy to world war. But, Kerr cautioned, "It is certainly not the duty of the Church . . . to advocate the creation of a federation of nations to-day."[15] Such an idea would be premature, destined to fall apart. He argued that it is better to spread a Christian ethos that subordinates the nation-state to God, and to lay the groundwork for a more united world in the distant future.

John Foster Dulles, the future secretary of state, was also on his way to Oxford in 1937. He agreed with Kerr about the problem of nationalism. But he was more optimistic about solutions. "It is easy to become discouraged as to the possibility of eliminating war," he cautioned, but "discouragement is premature, our abandonment of an essential objective is unjustified," Dulles warned.[16] A new world government was possible.

Dulles's call for a new international organization was personal. In 1919, when Dulles was only thirty-one years old, he had traveled to Versailles with his "uncle Bert," Secretary of State Robert Lansing. Dulles was in Paris as the League of Nations was being negotiated. Two decades later, in 1937, he had come to Geneva to witness its demise. Dulles was now a famous corporate lawyer and he looked on as the league tried to stop the Japanese invasion of China that year, but with no success. He personally witnessed the league censure Italy for its invasion of Ethiopia and watched it stand by impotently as Italy withdrew from the organization. In 1937, it seemed as if the world Dulles had helped put together was falling apart. Dulles had every reason to be pessimistic, but as he arrived in Oxford directly from Geneva, the atmosphere of the ecumenical gathering gave him hope. "At Oxford, differences were obliterated" and "an amazing unity of thought and interpretation prevailed," which Dulles credited to the "common denominator" of "a genuine belief in Christ's life and teachings as the guide to human conduct."[17] Christianity offered unity, he thought, while the League of Nations was dissolving into irrelevance.

The vision Dulles brought to Oxford was of a dynamic, ever-changing world. War, he said, "is manifestation—a violent manifestation—of human energy." "The achievement of peace involves the control of such energy." He argued that too often, countries refuse to adapt to new conditions and, in damming up the flows of human energy, they encourage war or revolution. Both the Versailles treaty and the League of Nations were "an attempt to secure peace by piling up forces to make national boundaries more durable and impenetrable." The league was a "rededication of the nations to the old principles of sovereignty," of "unchanging and unchangeable compartments, the walls of which would continue as perpetual barriers to the interplay of dynamic forces." He asserted that with sovereignty, travel and tourism are made more difficult, trade and immigration are cut off, and suspicion of all things foreign prevails. In order to create a peaceful world, "safety valves" had to "be cut through the barriers of boundaries so that human energy will diffuse itself peacefully."[18]

Dulles believed that "the early history of the United States" could serve as a model for the world in 1937. At first, "the Union was formed by states originally exercising the same sovereign rights as any other nations.... Yet through the adoption of a multilateral treaty known as the Constitution, they have found an essential basis for peace in the renunciation by each of the right to interfere with the interstate movement of people, goods, and ideas." According to Dulles, each state maintained sovereignty over "all social, educational, and religious matters"; they each had their "own courts" and their "own system of taxes"; and they varied quite drastically from one another but created "a single monetary unity" and unimpeded trade and travel. America's history of political development was not a perfect model, Dulles admitted, but it provided a viable path forward for the world.[19] At the World Council of Churches, new, radical ideas about national sovereignty and world government were being debated.

The Pacifist-Realist Split

Behind the facade of global unity, American Protestants were becoming increasingly divided over the question of American involvement in the turmoil in East Asia and Europe. Full-scale war between Japan and China broke out in 1937, and two years later Germany invaded Poland, igniting war in Europe. Debates about American involvement in the conflicts raged among Protestants, just as they did across the United States. Should the country treat all belligerent nations equally, as it had attempted during World War I? Should the United States embargo Japan and send aid to Britain? Should the United States itself wage war? No consensus emerged on any of these questions before Pearl Harbor brought the United States into World War II.

A new theological movement, known as Christian realism, gained wide attention during the late 1930s because it made a compelling argument on behalf of American involvement in a war against "totalitarianism." Among the realist theologians, Henry Pitney Van Dusen was second only to Reinhold Niebuhr in his prominence at mid-century. Known as "Pit" to his friends, he was born in 1897, a scion of a Dutch New York family and a member of the tenth generation of Van Dusens, whose roots went back to the original settlers of colonial New Amsterdam. At a religious revival led by fundamentalist preacher Billy Sunday, young Van Dusen was "twice-born." The experience led him to pursue religious studies as an undergraduate at Princeton, where his youthful religious enthusiasm matured into a more cerebral faith. Inspired by the social gospel movement then en vogue among Christians on college campuses, he volunteered his time working with the poor. He graduated Princeton in 1919, earning the title (at once laudatory and insulting) of "the best all-around man outside athletics." Van Dusen enrolled in Union Theological Seminary in 1922, where he began teaching systematic theology after graduating four years later. Like many of the young, ambitious religious figures of his generation he travelled abroad in his twenties, joining Sherwood Eddy, G. Bromley Oxnam, and Niebuhr on trips through Europe, Asia, and the Soviet Union. He later received his PhD at the University of Edinburgh, where he met his wife, Elizabeth Coghill Bartholomew. After World War II he succeeded Henry Sloane Coffin as head of Union Theological Seminary.[20]

Van Dusen was ordained in the 1920s, during a heated moment among Protestants, whose "modernist" wing clashed with the "fundamentalists." Like other wealthy and respectable Protestants, Van Dusen was committed to theological liberalism from an early age, shaped partly by his dislike of fundamentalists. He moved in the same theological direction as many Protestant seminaries were heading in the 1910s and 1920s: toward a rejection of biblical literalism, an interest in non-Christian religions, and openness to secular ideas and institutions. Van Dusen's denomination, the Northern Presbyterians, who were formally known as the Presbyterian Church of the United States of America, experienced some of the most embittered fighting over institutional control, as fundamentalists established a red line of theological absolutes they called orthodoxy. Was Jesus born to a virgin? No, said Van Dusen, knowing that saying so would result in a challenge to his ordination by conservatives. Van Dusen hired a fellow Presbyterian and a lawyer worthy of his social class—John Foster Dulles, who was then a young lawyer and layman. With Dulles's help, Van Dusen prevailed in his heresy trial.[21]

Van Dusen moved toward Christian realism in the 1930s, when he joined a small group of intellectuals led by Niebuhr, called the Theological Discussion Group. Formed in 1933, they self-consciously moved away from what they now viewed as naive conceptions of liberal theology—especially modernism, popular at the Chicago School of Divinity, which they accused of a too-optimistic view of human nature. Recoiling from the rise of fascism, their theology was pessimistic, with more attention to sin, irony, and tragedy. Christianity did not offer easy solutions, they argued, but only a fighting spirit in a dangerous and broken world. Most pressing was the need for Christian unity across denominational and national boundaries into a global communion against materialist forces that threatened to tear the world apart. In order to do this, Van Dusen concluded, Protestant intellectuals

Figure 3. Union Theological Seminary president Henry Pitney Van Dusen (right) sits with Professors Reinhold Niebuhr (center) and Paul Tillich (left) circa 1952. Photo by Gjon Mili / The LIFE Picture Collection via Getty Images.

must reexamine liberal theology and uproot all that is naive in their traditions. With this theological foundation, he set out across the world.[22]

In 1938, a year after he attended the World Council of Churches' founding, Van Dusen circumnavigated the world on a six-month tour of missionary stations that included meetings with missionaries, visits to Christian colleges, and chats with American and foreign diplomats.[23] The journey culminated in a three-week conference at Madras Christian College, in Tambaram, India, under the auspices of the International Missionary Conference. The meeting, unlike the Oxford conference of the previous year, had representatives from the Global South in equal numbers to those from the North Atlantic West. It was slated to take place in Hangzhou, China, but had to be moved to India because of the Japanese invasion the previous year. The specter of war weighed on the minds of the participants.[24]

In the same way G. Bromley Oxnam's social gospel was reshaped by international travel, so too was Van Dusen's realism. The journey revived Van Dusen's confidence in the unity of Christianity. His trip reinforced his belief in the religion's ability to resist "totalitarian" forces, and it furthered his drive to get the United States to oppose the fascist governments of Japan and Germany. In his travelogue of his 1938 trip, Van Dusen wrote that his confidence in Christian missions had been undermined by William Ernest Hocking's 1932 report *Re-thinking Missions*, which had called on missionaries to do less preaching and provide more social services.[25] Van Dusen blamed Hocking for spreading the belief that missionaries were cultural imperialists who trampled on ancient and respected cultures. Van Dusen concluded in 1938 that Christian missions played a vital role in helping the world's poor in the regions few other Westerners were willing to live in. Van Dusen gave an account of his trip that included areas of the world with "primitive" cultures, where missionaries were doing God's work and were oftentimes the only ones providing education and charity. It was Van Dusen's first time seeing missionaries in the field, and he was impressed with their work. Just as global war seemed imminent, Van Dusen revived his confidence in Christianity—and Christian missions—as a potent antifascist force.[26]

Although he praised the missionary project, Van Dusen did not entirely abandon cultural pluralism, especially the idea that God is revealed in a variety of religious traditions. At Tambaram, however, others did. Dutch neoorthodox theologian Hendrick Kraemer declared that Christianity was unique and superior to other religions. Neoorthodoxy, a largely European movement in the 1930s, went much further in abandoning liberal Protestant principles than had realists. Neoorthodoxy was a battle cry against both "secularism" and against other religious traditions.

As Kraemer announced the exceptional genius of Christianity at Tambaram, Hocking defended religious pluralism. Hocking was joined by Indian and Chinese delegates, along with theological liberals from the United

States, in making the case that Christians should recognize divinity even when it appears in the guise of Buddhism, Hinduism, or Islam. As Kraemer and Hocking sparred, it was Van Dusen who mediated between the two sides. "Among the saints of all religions are those who clearly have been touched by God and have responded to his touch," he wrote. And other world religions bear "the marks of God's revelation." "But these partial apprehensions of God," he went on, "pale before the disclosure of God in Christ."[27] As a result of his travel abroad, Van Dusen gained confidence in the political potential of his religion.

Shortly after his return to the United States in 1938, Van Dusen became the most vocal Protestant supporter of American entry into the European war. Van Dusen had long been sympathetic to Britain. He was married to a Scot and had spent years in Edinburgh. Like many Americans of a certain pedigree, he viewed Britain as a place of high culture and civilization. Writing to Joseph Oldham, shortly after Germany's invasion of Poland in September 1939, Van Dusen explained that "present prevailing attitude regarding American assumption of her share of responsibility in this tragic business is discouraging. But it is my personal conviction that sooner or later the resources of this country will have to be cast in support of Britain and France to whatever extent that may be necessary."[28] Van Dusen was ready to do his part.

Van Dusen's links to both sides of the Atlantic made him an important intermediary in the years leading up to Pearl Harbor. In the early days of World War II, transatlantic Protestant institutions suddenly became important avenues for the spread of British propaganda at a time when Congress remained skeptical of American aid to the Allies.[29] The Ministry of Information, a British wartime propaganda agency, decided in July 1940 that Van Dusen and his allies would be one of the primary conduits of British propaganda to the United States. Van Dusen agreed to the arrangement: He would sign his name to articles originating in the Ministry of Information. In addition, Britain sent religious figures to the United States to urge aid for Britain. Scottish theologian John Baille gave seventy-eight talks to large audiences during an American trip that lasted a month and a half.[30] The British wanted to use American ecumenical Protestantism to draw closer links between the two countries, which coincided with Van Dusen's own desire for America to join the war effort. And the influence flowed both ways. In late 1940, when the British ambassador Philip Kerr was about to issue a statement defending the British blockade of Europe, Van Dusen asked him to postpone it. When the ambassador finally issued a statement on the matter, it closely resembled a draft written by Van Dusen.[31]

Van Dusen's influence extended beyond his religious community to public opinion and government policy. In the immediate years before American entry into World War II, Van Dusen became an unofficial ambassador to England on behalf of an interventionist group of prominent religious leaders, businessmen, journalists, academics, lawyers, and diplomats who came to be known as the "Century Group." Francis Pickens Miller brought this group together. Miller was the long-time leader of the World Student Christian Federation, and he was working in 1940 for the National Policy Council, a foreign policy think tank. After gathering a few people at his Virginia home in June that year, Miller and others put out a statement calling for American military intervention in the European war (at a time when 71 percent of Protestants said they would stay out of war, if given the choice).[32] In 1940, several groups had called for more aid to the Allies, but Miller's group stood out because it called for outright war against Germany. After the statement made headlines across the country, Van Dusen got in touch with Miller and urged his group to continue its efforts, which led to the creation of the pro-intervention Century Group. It launched a coordinated propaganda effort on behalf of American involvement in World War II.[33]

Out of the Century Group emerged the idea of the "Bases for Destroyers" deal. The group advised Roosevelt to trade several dozen warships that Britain desperately needed in exchange for leases on British military bases in the Western Hemisphere. This approach had advantages for both cash-strapped Britain and for Roosevelt, who was prevented by Congress from selling these military supplies to belligerents. The Century Group worked in secret and convinced the weary Roosevelt administration to go along with the plan. The Century Group also reached out to Republican presidential candidate Wendell Willkie and persuaded him not to attack Roosevelt over the terms of the deal during the 1940 election cycle. It also promoted the plan among voters, and they saw General John J. Pershing's speech on behalf of the deal—which it helped write and orchestrate—as the turning point in public opinion.[34] During these efforts, it is likely that Van Dusen was actively cooperating with the British intelligence agency MI6 and receiving confidential information from the organization.[35]

Roosevelt, too, was coordinating with the British, although in more public and more dramatic ways. By 1941, the United States was actively aiding Britain. The country had sent a large military aid package to Britain through the Lend-Lease Act and was fighting an undeclared war against German submarines in the Atlantic. When Roosevelt met Churchill "somewhere at sea" in August 1941, it was to justify this alliance. The Atlantic Charter, the joint declaration of war aims by Roosevelt and Churchill, was received with a mixture of bewilderment and excitement. It was bewildering because the document carried no legal force and this statement of war aims had been co-signed by a president whose country was not at war. But it also earned the attention of many, including ecumenical Protestants, because it gave "assurance that all the men in all the lands may live out their lives in freedom from fear and want." Roosevelt and Churchill also agreed on "a wider and permanent system of general security" after the war and called on the nations of the world to abandon the use of force for "spiritual reasons," a phrase Roosevelt added into the text.[36]

Soon after the Atlantic Charter was issued, Van Dusen decided to visit Britain. On September 14, 1941, Van Dusen left for Scotland and England, where he spent four weeks conferring with government and church officials. According to Andrew Preston, "While some Europeans viewed the war as a larger and more violent version of previous wars," Van Dusen and other Americans "perceived it in millennial terms, as ushering in a totally new epoch."[37] And so Van Dusen's initial impressions of Britain were positive, giving hope that the British were moving toward a new, more Christian way of life. He was especially surprised at the healthy appearance of the British people. This was due not only to better distribution of food, Van Dusen insisted, but also resulted from the common purpose given to British citizens. "Let no one say war may not also ennoble and redeem," Van Dusen wrote to his friends. To him, the wartime temperament of the British people was a hopeful political and spiritual development. They were becoming more Christian because "community," a Christian ideal, "has come to reality in wartime Britain."[38]

Van Dusen had a singular goal: to convince the British to plan for the millennium that would follow the war. Meetings and speeches took up most of Van Dusen's time in Britain in the fall of 1941. He met with Foreign Minister Anthony Eden and Minister of Information Brendan Bracken, along with the Minister of Economic Warfare, Hugh Dalton, with whom he discussed the food blockade Britain had implemented. He also spoke with representatives of the Belgian and Norwegian governments-in-exile, whose countries were occupied by Germany. In every meeting he stressed the necessity of peace aims.

In an address carried throughout Britain, the Commonwealth, and colonies, Van Dusen stressed the need for a grand vision matching Woodrow Wilson's idealism during World War I. The support of the American government for the British war effort was assured, Van Dusen told his listeners in 1941, but the American people continue to be divided. The problem, Van Dusen argued, was that aiding Britain or defeating the Nazis was not enough to win over everyday Americans. "We have been handicapped by lack of clear, positive and compelling objectives beyond the overthrow of Nazism," he told his British listeners just months after Churchill and Roosevelt had issued the Atlantic Charter. "The lesson from the last war is clear," Van Dusen insisted. "The American people did not believe themselves entering that war to save their own security, but to secure a great possibility for the whole world, including themselves. So, today." Without bringing up Churchill's deliberate policy of withholding peace aims, Van Dusen warned, "As things are now going, you will have our formal partnership in the struggle. You will not have the all-out enlistment of our people."[39]

Van Dusen believed making idealistic postwar plans would capture the imagination of the United States and that it would encourage the country to join the war effort. He was right that planning for a new world government, which had been proposed earlier by the World Council of Churches, would appeal to many Americans, and especially to ecumenical Protestants. But the links he drew between the postwar peace and American belligerence were met with resistance. His call for war was bound to provoke a fight with his fellow believers.

The Pacifist-Realist Food Fight

Van Dusen's call for the United States to aid Britain, even if it led to war, put him on a collision course with Protestant pacifists, who counted thousands of individuals as members of their organizations and many adherents who were in positions of power in Protestant institutions. Whereas Van Dusen preached a renewed Wilsonian gospel, Protestant pacifists had formed their identity in response to Wilson's failures.[40] The Fellowship of Reconciliation was founded during the Great War, but this pacifist group experienced its greatest growth in the years that followed. Figures like Niebuhr, who had supported the war effort in 1917, recoiled when the United States failed to join the League of Nations and the war unleashed a right-wing mobilization that ended in attacks against labor unions, socialists, African Americans, and immigrants. Niebuhr became a committed pacifist soon after World War I (only to dramatically break with the pacifists in the 1930s).

The growth of pacifism among ecumenical Protestants was one reason why Christian nationalism went into decline in this community. As American ecumenical Protestants became embarrassed by their vocal support for Wilson's crusade during World War I, they began to distance the Christian religion from the state. During the 1920s leading pacifists and other leftists began attacking the idea that the United States was an elect nation destined to carry out God's work in the world. Missionary evangelist Sherwood Eddy lamented in 1928 that only a few years before, "we felt a divine call to go from our own favored 'Christian' nation to the backward 'heathen' nations lost in darkness." But he now recognized this Christian nationalism was "complacent, paternalistic, imperialistic."[41] The criticism of Christian nationalism had gone mainstream by the 1930s and rang out from pulpits, the press, and radio programs across the country. Many ecumenical Protestants viewed Protestant globalism as an alternative to Christian nationalism.

The memory of World War I sustained the pacifist movement and encouraged Protestants to abandon Christian nationalism. Popular novels like Ernest Hemingway's *A Farewell to Arms* and Erich Remarque's *All Quiet on the Western Front*, both published in 1929, dramatized the disillusionment with war that many Americans felt. In the political realm, the Nye Committee's 1936 congressional report promoted a new understanding of the causes of World War I, casting greedy industrialists and munitions makers as the villains in the plot to go to war for the sake of their bottom lines.[42]

In 1933, sociologist Ray Abrams wrote *Preachers Present Arms*, a careful study of the clergy's involvement in American propaganda campaigns during World War I. It was also a condemnation of Christian nationalism. "The rise of modern Nationalism has become a religion with its sacred scriptures, dogmas, ritual propaganda, priests and devotees," he lamented. Sadly, "the churches were consistent in the record of supporting all popular wars and proved, what had long been suspected, that Christianity has been becoming increasingly nationalistic, while the god of Nationalism is more powerful in his ability to command obedience and devotion unto death than is Jehovah himself."[43] Abrams warned against a cozy relationship between church and state, about the mistaken reporting of German atrocities, and about preachers' support for xenophobic and right-wing politics. Charles Clayton Morrison, editor of the influential *Christian Century*, believed Ray Abrams's exposé of Christian nationalism was so vital that he serialized the book in the *Christian Century* just after World War II broke out in Europe in September 1939.

With the memory of World War I very much alive, it is no wonder that the most bitter quarrels took place over a revival of Herbert Hoover's food aid plan. Hoover, the engineer-hero of the Great War, had saved thousands of starving Belgians during World War I. The former US president, whose reputation was marred by his response to the Great Depression, proposed saving Europeans from starvation once again in 1940. Hoover had a plan, like the one he put into effect during World War I. The British were skeptical. They had organized a naval blockade of Europe and barred any goods from crossing that might potentially help Germany's war effort.

Hoover, a Quaker and former vice president of the Federal Council of Churches, framed food aid as a strictly moral issue. And he believed that religious leaders were in the best position to promote this supposedly apolitical plan. Hoover asked Congregationalist minister Benjamin F. Wyland to organize religious support. The Hoover plan quickly gained widespread backing in Protestant circles as Hoover sought to arouse public opinion by mobilizing religious leaders, with the goal of pressuring the British into allowing the food aid through the blockade. Morrison and other pacifists joined the cause. So too did several Theological Discussion Group members, including Georgia Harkness and Walter Horton.[44] Hoover found an especially useful ally in one of the most popular and respected pacifists in the United States, Ernest Fremont Tittle. In November 1940, Tittle preached a sermon on behalf of Hoover's plan, which was then printed in the *Christian Century* and the Methodist journal *Zion's Herald*. Hoover's committee mailed a copy of the article, accompanied by a cover letter written by Chicago Theological Seminary president Albert W. Palmer, to sixty thousand Protestant ministers.

Feeding the hungry, once seen as an unquestionably Christian endeavor, now stirred up immense controversy. Ministers across the country replied to Tittle's article with accusations that the pacifist was aiding Hitler's war effort. Tittle defended himself by arguing that opponents of food aid were undermining the very thing they claim to defend—civilization. Christian values are "terribly imperiled by the deliberate killing of innocent aged persons and women and children, even though the killing be done slowly with a food blockage and done in the name of 'civilization,'" Tittle wrote.[45]

Van Dusen rapidly emerged as the fiercest critic of Hoover's food aid plan. For Van Dusen, moral actions were always intertwined with political problems that presented difficult choices. He argued that it would be impossible to design a plan that would deliver food to countries conquered by Germany without the possibility that the aid would wind up in Nazi hands. Even if Germany could be trusted—and he believed it could not—Van Dusen argued that feeding conquered nations would allow Germany to relocate its resources toward its war effort. A hungry Europe would become restive and more likely to rebel against the Nazis, and disease resulting from hunger might spread into Germany, thereby helping the British cause. Van Dusen believed that deliberately withholding food aid was necessary given the grave threat Nazism posed to the world.

Van Dusen waged his campaign with the cooperation of the Century Group, but not all got on board. Henry Luce, a child of American missionaries in China and the owner of a media empire that included *Time* and *Life* magazines, broke with the Century Group over this issue, believing food aid to be an exception in an otherwise all-out effort on behalf of the British. Harvard president James Conant, another member of the Century Group, thought it was inappropriate for him to oppose the plan (while Yale president Charles Seymour, a historian of World War I, sided with Van Dusen). The Hoover food aid plan created tensions among interventionist groups.[46]

Even Van Dusen privately lobbied the British to ease the blockade, pleading with them to allow some medical supplies to reach children in Europe. Van Dusen, Union Theological Seminary president Henry Sloan Coffin, and presiding bishop of the Episcopal Church Henry St. George Tucker had several dinners with the British ambassador to the United States, Philip Kerr, during which they pleaded for "the safeguarding from actual starvation of children." But Van Dusen never pushed too hard and stressed that he and the Century Group would support the blockade "if in the considered judgment of your Government that is the only safe possibility."[47] Van Dusen kept his hesitations private. In public, he remained a stalwart supporter of the British blockade.

Van Dusen's absolutist position, the one he expressed publicly, meant that there would be no compromise with Hoover or the pacifists. In response, Morrison unleashed a barrage of editorials in the *Christian Century* in 1940.[48] The editorials became more withering after October 1940, when Van Dusen helped organize a statement denouncing Hoover's plan. It was especially hurtful that Mary E. Woolley and Carrie Chapman Catt, Morrison's allies in the interwar disarmament movement, disavowed the Hoover plan.[49]

Morrison wondered whether any of the signatories had "ever heard a starving child cry for a piece of bread?" "Do American Christians still possess the capacity for compassion? Thirty million people in Europe want to know, for their lives depend upon the answer. Ten million of this number are children. Children die first in famine." A later editorial said that politics are one consideration, but the "final word on this matter is uttered by Christian compassion. Is pity dead in the world? Have we forgotten the meaning of mercy? Do we, who have never learned to love our enemies, need now to be admonished not to slaughter our friends?"[50] Van Dusen's opposition to feeding hungry children made him, according to his critics, care more about politics than about biblical commandments.

Such personal attacks led Van Dusen, Niebuhr, and other realists to launch a new journal, *Christianity and Crisis*, in February 1941. The magazine imitated the style and format of the *Christian Century*, but it was wholeheartedly dedicated to the interventionist cause.[51] "*Christianity & Crisis* is a propaganda sheet used by Van Dusen and Niebuhr for English purposes," Wyland complained.[52] This small but influential journal strove, first and foremost, to turn Christian opinion against Nazism and to push Americans to aid the Allies. In later years, it would serve as the vehicle for the development of a Protestant just war theory, a tradition largely lacking in American Protestant theology.[53]

Another prominent pacifist, John Haynes Holmes Jr., went after Van Dusen even more directly and more personally. Holmes's impatience with the realists was first made public in his 1934 review of Niebuhr's *Reflections on the End of an Era*. In that article he accused Niebuhr of sacrificing his Christianity for the sake of class war.[54] Now, in 1941, it seemed that Van Dusen was sacrificing Christianity for the sake of the British Empire. Holmes, in a letter to Van Dusen that was circulated to other Protestant leaders, accused Van Dusen of being "fixed in your determination to starve women and children in Europe." Van Dusen's determination was like Hitler's, so complete that it is "impervious either to rational argument or spiritual appeal." Holmes admitted his commitment to loving his enemies was strained with Hitler, but "it is even more strained in the case of a man like yourself, who, unlike the Nazis, has had the advantage of Christian training." "I wonder if I can find in the Nazi record anything worse than your deliberate attempt to break down the Hoover plan and thus starve the struggling populations of

Europe," Holmes wrote in January 1941. He ended the letter even less gener-
ously: "In the light of this I dare to say that Jesus would blister you as he
blistered the Pharisees, only a thousand times worse."[55]

Van Dusen countered that pacifists were so near-sighted that they were
missing the bigger picture. "Men cry for freedom and are given bread," Van
Dusen retorted. And few people got more joy from attacking pacifists than
Niebuhr, whose contempt for what he deemed naive idealism he summarized the following way: "If modern churches were to symbolize their true
faith they would take the crucifix from their altars and substitute the
three little monkeys who counsel men to 'speak no evil, hear no evil, see no
evil.'"[56]

In the absence of reliable polling data, the popular Christian press indicated that the views of churchgoers were mixed but tended to be more
sympathetic with the attitudes of the pacifists about food aid. The Federal
Council of Churches surveyed its membership and found broad support for
Hoover's plan.[57] But Van Dusen and the realists succeeded in making the
subject controversial, and the popular Christian mobilization on behalf of
food aid that Hoover prayed for never materialized. Amid the controversy,
the Hoover plan went nowhere. The British refused to let food aid through
to Europe, and the Roosevelt administration declined to pressure the British. Onetime allies—Holmes, Morrison, Van Dusen, and Niebuhr had all
participated in interwar popular front movements—found themselves on
the verge of tearing Protestantism apart over the war.

Divided by War, United by Peace

The fight over Hoover's food aid plan dramatized just how badly the war had
divided ecumenical Protestants. Because of these schisms, in the years 1940
and 1941 ecumenical Protestants refocused their attention onto something
they could agree about: the postwar peace. It was a remarkable thing to look
past the war that was engulfing the world, in the years when nothing seemed
to stop Japanese and Nazi conquests, and to imagine a postwar peace. And
yet, that is exactly what ecumenical Protestants did, and their decision
would have important consequences.

Looking forward to the postwar settlement had the advantage of minimizing the clashes between pacifists and realists. The vast numbers of clergy
and churchgoers who did not think of themselves as either pacifists or real-

ists were drawn selectively to the ideas of both groups. By early 1941 an in-creasing number of Americans, including ecumenical Protestants, were in favor of aid to Britain and supportive of Roosevelt's call for the United States to become an "Arsenal of Democracy." The Congregationalists' journal of record, *The Advance*, reported that many in the denomination were in favor of aid to Britain short of war. While Congregationalists were sympathetic to the realists' pro-British politics, they were critical of their theology. "It has seemed to us that Professor [Reinhold] Niebuhr tends to make a matter of ideology out of what may be only a matter of necessity, or of unavoidability; and that this involves a sort of militarization of Christianity, which cannot be militarized without ceasing to be Christianity," the editor wrote. Living in an "un-Christian world" requires "some adjustment," he went on to say, but "it is a dangerous and disastrous thing" if "we use casuistry to reduce Christianity to the level of current life."[58] To safeguard Christianity, non-aligned Protestants disassociated the war effort from Protestant theology. It was better to treat the war as a state of exception, divorced from Christian thought, then to leave the stamp of militarism permanently on Christian thinking. This begrudging interventionism, which combined realist politics with pacifist theology, became widespread by 1941. As a result, ecumenical Protestants who were neither realists nor pacifists were especially attracted to postwar planning as a convenient way of holding onto some of the trea-sured concepts of the pacifist version of Protestant Christianity. And they urged pacifists and realists to do the same.

The last great attempt by ecumenical Protestants to formulate a united policy on global affairs prior to American entry into World War II occurred in Philadelphia in 1940. The Federal Council of Churches brought together ecumenical leaders in the City of Brotherly Love to overcome growing divi-sions. The conference followed the basic model of international ecumenical meetings of the interwar era. It gathered prominent religious speakers and lay experts, invited broadly representative constituencies, created expert-led study groups that would work diligently to prepare position papers on con-troversial topics, discussed and amended the position papers over the course of a few days, and published a final conference statement that presented an official, usually unanimous, ecumenical Protestant position, and distributed it to churches across the country.

In 1940, ecumenical Protestant leaders did not see themselves as standing on either side of "internationalism" or "isolationism." Instead, they focused on their mutual enemy: "power politics." The Philadelphia

conference-goers agreed that the United States needed "to renounce its political and economic isolation" and participate with other nations in the
creation "of a world government." "Only then will we be freed from the
burden of power politics," they concluded.[59] Years of veneration of national sovereignty and moral apathy had led countries like Germany, Italy,
and Japan to pursue their selfish interests despite world opinion. Ecumenical Protestant leaders pointed to the economic causes of the European
conflict and decried quotas, tariffs, and other barriers to world trade that
encouraged winner-take-all contests between nations. As they saw it, each
nation had become the judge of its own cause and ignored universal moral
law in the quest for furthering its own self-interest. Echoing Dulles's earlier
ideas, ecumenical Protestants in Philadelphia announced that a "permanent
peace involves some sort of world organization to which individual states
must be willing to surrender certain aspects of sovereignty, such as was
surrendered in the formulation of the United States," they told America's
churches.[60]

The creation of a postwar peace also required doing away with imperialism,
ecumenical Protestant leaders argued. Power politics and economic competition was driven by imperial rivalries. "The principle of eventual freedom
for all peoples is not only the recognition of an essential right," ecumenical
Protestants declared in Philadelphia, "but is also a prerequisite to the creation of that sense of justice and goodwill without which we cannot hope
to rid the world of war."[61]

There were some hints of a more domestically conscious global vision at
the 1940 Philadelphia meeting that went largely unnoticed. "We . . . believe
that it is impossible wholly to divorce foreign policy from domestic policy
and that any comprehensive program for peace must contain a synthesis of
both," the conference-goers declared. "Moreover, we are convinced that a
constructive, creative foreign policy can stem only from a domestic policy
which is firmly rooted in democracy and which provides for adequate social
security." Ecumenical Protestants feared that the problem of unemployment
was being solved through militarization and they deplored the growing influence of the army and the navy in American life. They also asked for "just
and considerate treatment for members of religious, racial and political minorities," especially more tolerant attitudes toward the Jews. But the only
specific proposal endorsed at Philadelphia in 1940 was to pass antilynching
legislation, something the Federal Council of Churches had advocated for
years.[62]

Despite all the talk of postwar planning, it was hard to keep the issue of war at bay. In 1940, ecumenical Protestants still held out hope for a negotiated peace. Until the attack on Pearl Harbor on December 7, 1941, few Protestant leaders believed that aid to the Allies meant that the United States would become a belligerent. Indeed, the Philadelphia meeting took place during a pause in European fighting after the German subjugation of Poland in September 1939 but before the invasion of France in May 1940, which led Senator William Borah to describe World War II as the "phoney war." Without the benefit of hindsight, ecumenical Protestant leaders were not confronted with the many things that would later alarm them—the attacks on neutral Belgium and the Netherlands, the fall of France, the assault on Britain, and the bloodiness of the campaign on the Eastern front.

In this climate it seemed that a negotiated peace might still be possible. Tittle had called for a negotiated peace back in September 1, 1939, when Germany invaded Poland, and the pacifist did so again in 1940.[63] Ecumenical leaders agreed with Tittle, declaring that the United States ought to stay out of the war and calling for neutral nations to moderate between the belligerents. At Philadelphia in 1940, this position was approved without dissent.[64]

Ecumenical Protestant endorsement of a negotiated peace took place against the backdrop of a national discussion about the meaning of American neutrality. The Hague Convention of 1907 codified the legal right of nations to trade with and travel to belligerent nations during wartime. But in the aftermath of World War I, Americans increasingly concluded that their country's insistence on the legal form of neutrality was precisely what led the country into war in the first place. How to square the desire to remain "neutral" with the new, totalizing form of warfare became the dominant foreign policy challenge in the interwar era.[65]

The question of neutrality also played out in debates about the Pacific, and whether to issue a "moral embargo" against Japan. It was a deeply contentious issue. A moral embargo meant that American corporations would voluntarily cease sending goods to Japan that aided the country in its ongoing war in China. President Roosevelt had first called for a moral embargo against Italy after that country's invasion of Ethiopia in 1935 and later for one against Japan. In 1940, ecumenical Protestants endorsed the plan by a divided vote. They also urged the Roosevelt administration to renegotiate economic treaties with Japan and attempt to ease friction with that country, while simultaneously offering loans to China. Should this plan fail to ease tensions between the United States and Japan, and should the moral embargo prove ineffective, the Philadelphia conference recommended—again by a divided vote—that the United States government mandate an embargo that sharply limited the amount of goods American firms could sell to Japan. This scenario, some ecumenical Protestants believed, "would effectively dissociate the United States from participation in Japan's attack on China, while it would at the same time show Japan that our attitude towards her is friendly, and that our action is intended only to avoid injury to China with whom also we desire to be friendly."[66] Ecumenical Protestants wanted to maintain neutrality while coercing Japan into ceasing its attack on China. It was a muddled policy.

Ecumenical Protestants largely repeated Wilsonian ideas about neutrality and offered few viable options for the United States in 1940 in regard to the war. Their calls for a world government were novel and ambitious, while the domestic implications of the new world order they were proposing remained unexamined. Recognizing that they were at an impasse, the Federal Council of Churches announced shortly after the Philadelphia conference that they had created a "Commission on the American Churches and the Peace and War Problem," headed by John Foster Dulles. It would work independently of the group that had put on the Philadelphia conference and answer only to the highest officers of the Federal Council.[67] They hoped Dulles would put an end to Protestant infighting.

In 1940 and 1941, during the impasse over the role of the United States in the war, American ecumenical Protestants abandoned Wilsonian conceptions of "world order." They abandoned internationalism—that is, a parliamentary system of individual, sovereign nation-states—and embraced instead a global conception of world order. In doing so, they drew on earlier ideas about the interconnectedness of the world, like Hocking's "world culture," but now imagined it as a political space that provided a meaningful defense against the "power politics" of nation-states.[68] Earlier, in the 1930s, Christianity was imagined as a counterforce to the disorder of the day. Ecumenical Protestants had believed their religion would help keep nation-states in check. Christianity was also held up as a form of unity independent of the nation-state system, with its own nonstate ways of relating people to one another. By the early 1940s, drawing on earlier ideas by Dulles, Kerr, and Hocking, American ecumenical Protestants began to seriously consider the globe as a sphere of governance and imagine in detail a world government.

The second leap among American ecumenical Protestants was to connect their emerging global political vision to national and local practices. Ecumenical Protestants reimagined the scale of politics, closely tying the global and the local. What happened on a global scale had a direct relationship to what was going on in communities across the United States in ways that were unmediated by the American government. If everyday Americans wanted to shape world events, swaying government officials was not their only option. They could also take part in global affairs in their communities. Fighting racial segregation or poverty in one's hometown was not only an ethical imperative but also a way of creating the conditions under which a world government could emerge. By reimagining the scale of politics as a way out of their disagreements about food aid and moral embargoes, ecumenical Protestants finally cast away the ghosts of Woodrow Wilson and World War I. They invented a new global Christian politics premised on world government.

Methodists played a vital role in developing this conception of world order. Historians have associated the world order movement of the 1940s with a small group of realists led by Van Dusen and Niebuhr.[69] The pioneering role of Methodism has been largely ignored. The United Methodist Church was the largest American Protestant denomination in the 1940s, with about eight million members, and among them were some important thinkers on international affairs, including G. Bromley Oxnam, Georgia Harkness, Harry Emerson Fosdick, Walter W. Van Kirk, Thelma Stevens, Dorothy Tilly, Will W. Alexander, and Ernest Fremont Tittle. The denomination also devoted more resources and enthusiasm to reshaping international politics, and did so earlier, than other denominations. The commission led by Dulles, which would be the most important policy arm of American ecumenical Protestantism in the 1940s, got its start by attaching itself to the Methodist political initiatives orchestrated by Oxnam.

The United Methodist Church was also very sympathetic to pacifism. The influence of the long-standing and pacifist-leaning Methodist Commission for World Peace was felt in the uniting conference in 1939, when Northern and Southern Methodists jointly declared, "We believe that war is utterly destructive and is our greatest collective sin and a denial of the ideals of Christ. We stand upon this ground, that the Methodist Church as an Institution cannot endorse war nor support or participate in it."[70] Whereas Van Dusen and the realists saw postwar planning as a means of bringing the

United States into the war, Methodist leaders hoped to create a peace plan that would dissuade American belligerence.

When the Methodists met in Chicago in May 1941, the gathering served as a dry run for Dulles's recently renamed Commission on a Just and Durable Peace.[71] Founded in 1940 under the chairmanship of Presbyterian layman and future secretary of state Dulles, and usually referred to as the "Dulles Commission," the group was organized to plan for the postwar peace on behalf of the Federal Council of Churches. Dulles himself addressed the Methodist meeting at Chicago and worked closely with Oxnam, who had convened the meeting. Oxnam's goal was to hold Protestants together. "This Pacifist-Interventionist fight is likely to split many a church," Oxnam told the audience in Chicago. "If we can center all of them upon a discussion of what are the bases of a just peace when at last the war is over we will do something constructive."[72] For this reason, he placed a gag order on the Chicago meeting. "Discussion on pacifism, aid to Britain, and America's entry into the war are being omitted," the conference invitation warned.[73] "All of the speakers held fast to the assignment," Oxnam observed.[74]

The war issue, of course, could not be completely ignored. While the speakers focused on the peace to come, pacifists addressed the present. The phoney war was now over, and the United States was waging an undeclared war against German submarines in the North Atlantic, which troubled many Methodists because it could draw the United States into the war officially. "We deplore administrative actions that, step by step, are involving us in a shooting war, though undeclared, without giving the National Congress a chance to exercise its constitutional right in this matter and without regard for the predominant sentiment of the nation," the Methodists protested. Asking President Roosevelt "not to send our boys to war overseas," they pleaded again for a negotiated peace. "We believe that our nation can best serve mankind by abstaining from belligerent participation in present wars, by employing its immense resources for the constructive ministry of healing and rehabilitation and by associating itself with other nations, at the earliest possible moment, in an earnest effort to rebuild the world on a foundation of justice and co-operation for the good of all."[75]

In the long term, however, it was not the Methodist opposition to American entry into World War II but their ideas about postwar planning that proved to be the most enduring legacy. "After the bomber comes the builder," Oxnam told the Chicago audience. "But what kind of world will men build?"[76] Speakers asserted that the peoples of the world were becoming more and more connected. "The spiritual unity of mankind and the interrelatedness of peoples demand a political, economic, and cultural structure to encourage and sustain this emerging world consciousness," argued Earl Craston, a Methodist and historian. Declaring "unlimited national sovereignty" to be "outmoded," he contended that each country "must relinquish some of its authority and powers to the world organization" that would act "not only upon the member peoples or groups, but also, on occasion, upon individuals themselves."[77] Craston was proposing something new in Protestant thought: a world government that would not only mediate problems between countries but also have a direct relationship with people living in those countries.

"That unlimited national sovereignty as now practiced is outmoded was taken for granted" at Chicago, according to the journal *Methodist Woman*, and a world government was deemed "ultimately inevitable." The participants also contemplated regional federations, like "the United States of Europe," as a stepping-stone to an "all-inclusive world body." The "economic sovereignty" of each nation must be reduced in order to encourage "a free flow of goods between nations, equal access to necessary raw materials, [and] free access to markets." A "World Economic Congress" was needed, *Methodist Woman* explained, along with "regional economic federations or customs unions" to ensure goods would flow across borders.[78]

Linking the global to the local, the Methodists also called for big changes at home. "Within our own nation," the conference delegates declared, "economic democracy is a necessary basis for political democracy." This meant expanding the New Deal, promoting cooperatives, nationalizing key industries, and empowering labor unions. Like the Roosevelt administration, the Methodists emphasized the responsibility of the federal government to ensure full employment and economic stability and to enact unemployment insurance and compulsory health and accident insurance. Some areas of the economy, the conference report urged, ought to be placed under "social ownership," including "coal, steel, and oil, and utilities such as power, light, water, and transportation." Calling for the Congress of Industrial Organizations and the American Federation of Labor to merge, the Methodists believed that labor unions with "real social vision," along with cooperatives, would be central to these economic transformations.[79]

The Methodist leaders were repackaging and popularizing ideas that had achieved limited support in the previous decades by interweaving them with the one issue on everyone's mind: how to achieve world peace. In these subtle connections were the beginnings of a social movement that pushed for domestic reforms within a global frame of reference. Taken together, these planks of the Methodist conference reflected the social gospel ideals of cooperation, appreciation for labor unions, and the use of the regulatory power of government. They also reflected the new ideas of the Christian socialist movement that had come to prominence in the preceding decade, which envisioned a greater role for the federal government and was more willing to side with labor in economic disputes. Now these reforms had clear global implications.

Methodist leaders also chastised their churches for their apathy. They called for "the same critical scrutiny" to be applied to church life as to foreign policy and economic reform. "Justice," the Methodists declared, "must begin at home." There was a noteworthy absence of any discussion of segregation in the Methodist Church, which was practiced from top to bottom in the denomination. Instead, the churches' labor practices, real estate holdings, and funding sources were scrutinized. Methodist leaders advised local churches to form co-ops, credit unions, group medicine insurance schemes, and labor organizations. In these ways, they could contribute to world peace.[80]

Dulles was inspired by the Methodist proposals and their strategy of talking peace, not war. The Dulles Commission was created to study postwar peace, but its real challenge was to settle the rift between the realists and pacifists.[81] "Our task is a difficult and delicate one," Dulles said at the first meeting of his new commission. "The first requirement of success is that we should develop and preserve unity among ourselves."[82] To everyone's surprise, Dulles managed to do just that.

The Dulles Commission made plans for a great gathering of ecumenical Protestants in February 1942 in Delaware, Ohio, on the campus of the Ohio Wesleyan University, a Methodist school. Nobody predicted that the United States would be at war by the time the Delaware conference took place. When the nearly four hundred delegates met at Delaware, they showed surprising agreement on most issues, now that America's relationship to the war was not on the agenda. A gag order, like the one at the earlier Methodist meeting, also helped. The delegates endorsed what the *Christian Century* called "The Church's Thirteen Points," a reference to Woodrow Wilson's fourteen points, two and a half decades earlier.[83] Under the guiding hand of Dulles, the Delaware conference-goers affirmed a belief that the world is un-

Figure 4. John Foster Dulles, chairman of the Commission on a Just and Durable Peace, speaking at the Delaware conference in February 1942. Photo by William C. Shrout / The LIFE Picture Collection via Getty Images.

dergirded by moral laws that all people must obey, and which the churches had a special duty to proclaim. They called for a spirit of cooperation, the end of unrestrained national sovereignty, economic security, autonomy for all subject peoples, and freedom for people of all races and religions.

Ecumenical Protestants also fleshed out their proposal for a world government. At Delaware, they urged the creation of an international organization with the power to reduce armaments, regulate international trade, and to mediate disputes between nations.[84] This world organization was to have a police force, a legislature, and a court, and would be able to apply economic sanctions against belligerent nations in times of crises. Earlier ideas about world government that had been deemed radical now gained widespread support.

A united statement on the future of international relations would have been a remarkable accomplishment by itself. As impressive were the domestic reforms advocated at a meeting ostensibly focused on international affairs. Within this framework of Protestant globalism, the ecumenical leaders gathered at Delaware veered leftward on a number of domestic issues. William Paton, a British ecumenist and a relative of Elizabeth Van Dusen, told the Americans in attendance at Delaware that "collectivism is coming, whether we like it or not."[85] The conference delegates agreed: a "new ordering of economic life" was inevitable. The only question was whether it would take place "within the framework of democracy or through explosive political revolution." Delegates demanded an "industrial democracy" in the United States and experimentation with "various forms of ownership."[86]

The pacifist contingent, with agreement from the realists, had shepherded through the economic planks at Delaware. Pacifists also pushed through one of the most critical statements on racism produced by any predominantly white Protestant body to date. The task of preparing the statement on the "social bases for a just and durable peace" fell on pacifist A. J. Muste. The Dutch-born clergyman was a longtime leader in the labor movement, whose roles included general secretary of the Amalgamated Textile Workers of America, chairman of Brookwood Labor College, and leader of the American Workers Party. Muste ran in Marxist and Trotskyite circles in the 1920s and early 1930s, but a mystical experience in 1936 led him to a rededication to religious life and to pacifism.[87] He went on to head the Fellowship of Reconciliation, a pacifist Christian group best known for creating the Congress of Racial Equality.

For Muste, war and racism were intertwined, both rooted in a psychological tendency to stick to one's own group and dominate others. America's aggression toward nations in Latin America and in the Pacific occurred repeatedly "because we are not genuine democrats at home, but treat negroes, Orientals, 'foreigners' generally as 'Inferiors' here." He argued that likewise, when the United States goes to war against nonwhite nations, "authoritarian practices tend to develop against minorities at home," which carry over into the postwar settlement. He pointed to the Red-baiting and race riots that followed World War I. "I do not believe that the problems of peace within, and peace between nations can be isolated from each other," Muste made clear.[88]

By imagining the global sphere as a site of politics and insisting that the global and local were intertwined, ecumenical Protestants birthed new ideas at Delaware. The most important was a yet-undefined field of human rights. Whereas civil rights were the prerogatives of nation-states, human rights were a matter of God's law and would be the province of the coming world government. Some of the impetus to articulate human rights came from Leo Pasvolsky, who represented the Roosevelt administration at the Delaware meeting. He privately circulated a fifty-two-page report of the National Resources Planning Board, which he headed, and which included a new economic bill of rights that Roosevelt would make famous in his 1944 State of the Union Address. Ecumenical Protestants drew inspiration from Roosevelt's rights talk. They linked rights to the coming world government and applied them to Jim Crow, which the Roosevelt administration largely ignored. Indeed, the final proclamation of the Delaware conference only mentioned human rights in the context of anti-imperialism and antiracism. The Federal Council of Churches declared: "WE BELIEVE that the government which derives its just powers from the consent of the governed is the truest expression of the rights and dignity of man. This requires that we seek autonomy for all subject and colonial peoples. . . . WE BELIEVE that the right of all men to pursue work of their own choosing and to enjoy security from want and oppression is not limited by race, color or creed. The rights and liberties of racial and religious minorities in all lands should be recognized and safeguarded."[89] Ecumenical Protestant ideas about human rights emerged in discussions of a world government and were interconnected with debates about racism and imperialism.[90]

Linking world events to racism in America, ecumenical Protestants began to more seriously confront white supremacy. The Federal Council explained that "some local current outrages," including a lynching in Missouri and rioting in Detroit over the Sojourner Truth Housing complex, "have national significance and therefore international effects in the attitudes of other peoples." They also observed that Protestant churches remained segregated. It was important to make churches racially inclusive because "each local church will do much to create the mood out of which a just and durable peace can grow."[91] Ecumenical Protestants condemned unequal treatment of racial minorities in employment, education, business, housing, transportation, the justice system, and in elections. The conference applauded President Roosevelt for his use of executive powers to create the Fair Employment

Practices Commission. This statement criticizing racism was the Federal Council's first since 1931.

In addition to introducing new ideas about race, human rights, and world government, the 1942 Delaware conference also helped heal the pacifist-realist rift. Van Dusen, a realist, applauded calls for a new world government. And so did Charles Clayton Morrison.[92] The pacifist editor wrote that ecumenists "discovered that the areas of agreement among American Christians are very large as to what is required if a just and durable peace is to be established." For Morrison, the significance of the Delaware conference was the critical distance Christianity would maintain from the state, even in wartime. During World War I, Protestants had been duped by the government. This time, Morrison thought, the churches would lead the way. Van Dusen had a different take, emphasizing the abandonment of older, childlike liberalism. "Today [Protestantism] is as tough-minded as twenty-five years ago it was naïve," he wrote.[93] Van Dusen and Morrison continued to disagree about many things, but they found common ground on the postwar peace.

Van Dusen and Morrison also agreed that the gag order on discussing the war at Delaware was a bad idea, but for different reasons. They butted heads over a plank Morrison proposed at the conference, which stated that "the Christian Church, as such, is not at war." The statement explained that, while the state has certain necessary functions, "the church in its essential nature is an ecumenical supranational body, separate from and independent of all states, including our own national state." The idea of Protestantism transcending state loyalty was an old one, but the existence of the recently created World Council of Churches gave new relevance to the notion of Christianity as a "supranational" body. Morrison emphasized that "the Church" was a set of ideals, and these ideals were best expressed by international organizations and religious communions, not countries.

But for Van Dusen, this was all too abstract. The Christian Church was composed of real people in real churches with real responsibilities to the state. Van Dusen's realist ecclesiology—his views of the nature and structure of the Christian Church—matched his desire to mobilize American Christianity against Nazism. No nation could claim to be fully on God's side, he concluded, but some nations were closer than others. Protestants were part of a transnational community, but they were Americans, too, and had a duty to help their country when it waged a just war. The question of ecclesiology, and therefore the question of the relationship between church and state, simmered in ecumenical Protestant circles. The Methodists, for example, did not jettison their formal opposition to the war until 1944. But debates about belligerency no longer dominated Protestant attention.[94] Instead, ecumenical Protestants devoted their energy to planning for peace.

The Eclipse of the Pacifist-Realist Rivalry and the Rise of Protestant Globalism

American entry into World War II did not entirely end the infighting among ecumenical Protestants, but it did change the terms of the debate. In refocusing their attention on global (rather than merely international) politics and by self-critically debating what changes needed to take place at the level of the nation, town, and church in light of new international standards, they began to banish the ghosts of World War I. They moved on to new, creative solutions to international problems. For Morrison and for Van Dusen, the ecumenical Protestant churches had changed dramatically between the two world wars, and they agreed it was a good thing. At Delaware in 1942, America's leading Protestants pledged themselves to work for a world government and experimented with human rights. Clarifying these ideas and getting the United States government to take them seriously became one of the most important goals of American ecumenical Protestants during World War II.

In the 1920s, Protestants began viewing the world as an interconnected whole, tied ever closer together by the spread of modernity and the Christian gospel. By the late 1930s and early 1940s, they began to think through the political implications of this interconnectedness. In concert with their European coreligionists they organized a countermobilization to the forces of world disorder and, in an antifascist context, they sketched plans for a new world government. Their plan to bind nations to a world government and, by extension, to God's moral order, was their solution to the problem of nationalism and "power politics."

By imagining a world order premised on globalism, American ecumenical Protestants reinvigorated the quest for democracy at home. Ideas once relegated to the margins of Protestant life—obscure journals, socialist societies, and seminary discussion groups—enjoyed an unprecedented popularity during the debates about the postwar peace. Radical ideas about world government, economic reforms, and racial justice were repackaged by 1942 and spread to popular audiences under the guise of postwar peace planning and came, increasingly, under the new banner of human rights. In this way, ecumenical Protestants and their institutions helped popularize once-marginal ideas and made them safe for a predominantly Christian nation.[95]

The global gospel of American Protestants during World War II also facilitated a massive wartime political mobilization on behalf of their new outlook. Despite its origins as an elite and largely Anglo-American project, the mobilization would invite women, African Americans, and others to take part in the debates over the new world order. These discussions would remake American liberalism.

CHAPTER 3

_____

The World Order Movement

In 1942, American ecumenical Protestants launched the World Order movement. When this drive for a world government and human rights ended in 1946, it had become the largest and most sophisticated Protestant political mobilization since Prohibition. The World Order movement was led by future secretary of state John Foster Dulles, who ensured that millions of Americans were reached through rallies, parades, sermons, small discussion groups, school curricula, letter-writing campaigns, pamphlets, and books. The World Order movement would play an important role in shaping the postwar world, including the creation of the United Nations.[1]

But the popularity of this movement hid ongoing disagreements about what the shape of the postwar world should be.[2] While Dulles concentrated on international affairs, others were refocusing ecumenical Protestants' attention on domestic issues of long-standing concern, especially the fight against racism and poverty. Women's groups took a leading role in pushing ecumenical Protestants toward a more progressive political stance. Shut out of key positions of power in international affairs, women like Methodist activist Thelma Stevens were nonetheless empowered by the World Order movement to push an anti-racist and pro–New Deal agenda. The World Order movement reflected the broad social vision of wartime ecumenical Protestantism and it would transform domestic politics just as it had transformed international affairs.

As this chapter shows, Dulles's high-level diplomatic wrangling and Stevens's grassroots mobilization against racism and poverty became deeply intertwined. Historians have recognized the outsized role of Dulles in the plans for the United Nations. By contrast, this chapter shows that the United Nations also created enthusiasm for domestic reforms. And the domestic mobilization likewise shaped the ecumenical Protestant vision of international affairs during World War II, as demands for racial justice and economic reform were incorporated into the postwar planning process under the rubric of human rights.[3]

Human rights, which ecumenical Protestants helped articulate and popularize during the 1940s, reflected a dual desire for a peaceful world order and for domestic reforms. Christian human rights came out of discussions of the postwar settlement and were strongly influenced by the vibrant debates of the World Order movement. Dulles created a diplomatic climate in which human rights made sense, and his allies justified human rights by appealing to the theology of personalism and the importance of religious liberty. At the same time, activists like Stevens insisted that human rights stood in opposition to racism and economic injustice. Evocations of human rights combined UN-centered visions of peaceful postwar international relations and demands for justice in the United States. By 1945, the international and local spheres of activity merged together under the rubric of human rights. In other words, without ever meeting one another, Dulles the diplomat and Stevens the activist jointly shaped the meaning of human rights, international affairs, and domestic politics.[4]

The Decline of the Anglo-American Alliance

John Foster Dulles understood in 1942 that his vision for a postwar world government would be exceedingly difficult to implement unless the pressure for it was international. It was hard enough to get the United States to renounce isolationism; it would be impossible to get the great powers of the world to set aside their concerns about sovereignty without an international effort by Protestants to pressure their own governments. And no two governments would be more important to establishing the postwar peace than the United States and Great Britain.

And yet Protestant leaders from the two countries had already butted heads over postwar plans. In the fall of 1941, Henry Pitney Van Dusen met with a group of British Protestants at Oxford. Van Dusen used the Dulles Commission to coordinate American policy with the British, and he worked with his relative-by-marriage William Paton to write what he hoped would be a Protestant version of the Atlantic Charter. But disagreements, even between family members, quickly appeared. Paton believed that by coordinating the policy of the two nations the United States would more fully support the British war effort and that an Anglo-American alliance would dominate the postwar peace.[5] For Van Dusen, on the other hand, the creation of the postwar world needed to be a multilateral affair. He stressed to his British colleagues that China must have a big role after World War II. American ecumenical Protestants' commitment to an inclusive, democratic postwar peace was moving them away from some of their most stalwart allies.

In March 1942, Dulles invited British representatives to make the perilous journey across the Atlantic for face-to-face meetings in Princeton, New Jersey. Like American Protestant denominations, the British Anglican Church had recently moved leftward in 1941, with William Temple, the Archbishop of Canterbury, calling for the creation of a welfare state. Temple did not travel to Princeton himself in 1942, but many of his close associates did, including Paton. Dulles hoped that this meeting would produce an agreement on postwar peace plans on the model of the recently concluded Delaware conference.[6]

Dulles became frustrated when he found that Paton was more interested in strengthening the Anglo-American war effort than in planning for a postwar settlement. To the delegates from shell-shocked Britain, the end of the war seemed like a faraway dream. And Paton was only following the lead of Prime Minister Winston Churchill, who steadfastly avoided any talk of the postwar peace when victory was not yet assured and when the British were in a weak bargaining position. The Atlantic Charter, Paton pointed out, said nothing about a postwar association of nations. Paton called for a "world organisation, with Anglo-American leadership at its heart," echoing the views expressed by both Roosevelt and Churchill early in the war.[7]

Dulles rejected the idea of an Anglo-American alliance, especially one that would defend the British Empire. Instead, he suggested a middle ground: rather than an Anglo-American alliance or, as demanded at Delaware, that all nations be included in the new international organization, he proposed that the group of nations that composed the wartime alliance, popularly known as the "United Nations," be the basis for the eventual creation of an international organization.[8]

Dulles's compromise was enough to gain British cooperation. British ecumenist Kenneth Grubb and historian Arnold Toynbee agreed with Dulles that a world government could not be created immediately but would have to grow organically out of the close cooperation of the United Nations, which included the United States, Great Britain, the Soviet Union, and China.[9] For a fleeting moment, Dulles found a way to maintain Anglo-American cooperation. But when word got back to Britain about the Princeton meeting, key religious figures were repelled by what they viewed as American naivete about international affairs.[10]

In July 1942, just a few months after the Princeton meeting, Dulles traveled to Britain with his colleague Walter W. Van Kirk to promote Anglo-American cooperation. Van Kirk, a Methodist and a former pacifist, had been the Federal Council of Churches' most prominent spokesperson on international affairs, whose popular books and weekly radio program kept millions of Americans up to date on religion and foreign affairs.[11] In Oxford, Van Kirk was direct in his criticism of British plans, and of Dulles's appeasement. Van Kirk stuck to the official position of the Federal Council that "there should not be alliances or coalitions between any two or three countries, but some scheme which would take in the whole world; 'all nations,' not just the United Nations." Likewise, Van Kirk pulled no punches about colonialism. Earlier, Paton had conveyed the "feeling on the part of finest Christian opinion [that] what the British Empire has been at its best should be reflected in some international system."[12] But Van Kirk shot back, suggesting "that the whole area of colonial administration might hereafter assume an international character."[13]

Dulles tried to reconcile the conflicting views of American and British religious and political leaders. He outlined his evolving vision to the British churchmen and in his meetings "with most members of the British Government" during his brief visit. He argued that "there is a great opportunity in the world today to raise the moral, material and spiritual standards of life in the whole world." The productive capacity employed for wartime purposes, Dulles believed, cleared the way for unprecedented relief work in the postwar world. He "felt sure that in order to raise the level of life in the world there would have to be such a tremendous effort made that the productive capacity of everyone could be used to the full." Dulles "pointed out the necessity to increase the population of the world by better living conditions, education, and so on, and said that the increased numbers would provide markets for goods of every kind."[14] Better government planning after the war would ensure global prosperity.

Dulles believed that Christianity would play a central role in inspiring international cooperation after World War II ended. "In times past there had been slogans used which had inspired people—American Destiny, the White Man's Burden, and so on, and they stood for something and gripped the imagination," he told the Bishop of Canterbury and other listeners. Christianity calling for "a world-wide view of reconstruction and aiming at the raising of moral and cultural and spiritual standards, as well as material standards, in every country of the world" would be the next great slogan. For Dulles this global reconstruction—"something like a 'new deal' for the world"—would appeal to Americans by giving them a sense of purpose. It would also ensure continued cooperation of the Allies into the postwar period by creating a common mission that would benefit all nations involved. Britain and America were cooperating "because there was a vast practical task to be performed," Dulles believed. "But the test would come when the war was over, and it would be necessary to envisage beforehand the great concrete tasks of reconstructure [sic] so that the inspiration to cooperate would continue to be felt."[15]

Anglo-American tensions continued into the following year, 1943, when the Dulles Commission issued a document called the "Six Pillars of Peace." The statement condensed the Federal Council's earlier thirteen points and formed part of Dulles's search for simple, captivating slogans to entice Americans to embrace internationalism. Dulles presented the Six Pillars on March 18, 1943, at a press conference while he stood next to the aging philanthropist John D. Rockefeller, who had opposed the League of Nations in the aftermath of World War I. Rockefeller dramatized his conversion to internationalism and implored the religious, educational, financial, and labor leaders gathered at the event not to repeat the same mistakes: "God forbid that we should ever follow that road again!"[16]

LIST 1: The Six Pillars of Peace

In 1943 the Commission on a Just and Durable Peace of the Federal Council of Churches (known popularly as the "Dulles Commission") issued the "Six Pillars of Peace" document. It listed the following six principles to guide the postwar peace settlement.

I. Political collaboration between the United Nations and ultimately all nations.
II. Collaboration on economic and financial matters of world-wide import.
III. Adaptation of the world's treaty structure to changing conditions.
IV. Assurance, through international organization, of ultimate autonomy for subject peoples.
V. Control of armaments.
VI. Establishment of the principle of the rights of peoples everywhere to intellectual and religious liberty.

The Dulles Commission believed that its Six Pillars of Peace were essential to eliminating the conditions that had created World War II. The first pillar called for the continued collaboration of the United Nations into the postwar period under a "political framework" that would include "in due course . . . neutral and enemy nations."[17] Pillars 2 through 5 dealt directly with the perceived failures of the League of Nations and the causes of World War II. The second pillar called for international regulation of economic and financial policy. The third, responding to the inflexible system of treaties under the League of Nations, called for a regular reexamination of treaties. Arthur Hays Sulzberger, the owner and publisher of the *New York Times*, explained the importance of this pillar. The "fate of the League of Nations indicates that it might be wise not only to provide machinery for changing the peace structure, but also to make it *mandatory* that all nations reconsider the treaties at definite intervals," he wrote soon after the Six Pillars had been issued.[18] The fourth and fifth pillars called for autonomy for all subject peoples and for the control of armaments. The final pillar called for religious and intellectual freedom, which reflected the widespread belief that moral principles would be at the heart of any successful postwar peace. Protecting religious freedom was central to ensuring all other rights.[19]

To Dulles, the Six Pillars were a condensation of ideas ecumenical Protestants had endorsed, but critics charged that he was veering away from the consensus reached at the 1942 Delaware conference. The first pillar, in particular, caused a dustup. Charles F. Boss, a member of the Dulles Commission and the executive secretary of the influential Methodist Commission on World Peace, complained that it seemed to contradict the Federal Council's position that all nations must be included in the initial formation of a world government.[20] Boss passed along to Van Kirk a note of protest from a meeting of Colorado Methodists, who were upset over the abandonment of the "all-inclusiveness" message at Delaware. The letter explained that in 1942 a "sizable minority" led by Crozer Theological Seminary president James Franklin "attempted to substitute 'The United Nations' for 'all nations.' The amendment was decisively defeated."[21] Dulles had embraced the wartime alliance, known as the "United Nations," as the basis of the new world government in his talks with the British in 1942, and this new idea made its way into the Six Pillars. Dulles was subtly reshaping the ecumenical Protestant agenda on international affairs.

As early as 1943, resentment of Dulles's leadership was building, but it tended to remain in private correspondence. With the war raging, American isolationism still a threat, and the successful development of a broad Protestant agreement on the need for an international government, these disagreements remained in the background for the time being.

Dulles's position may have annoyed some Methodists, but it won the approval of the Roosevelt administration. Dulles brought the Six Pillars to the attention of Roosevelt during several face-to-face meetings in 1943. The president was understandably skeptical of Dulles, who was widely believed to be the Republican secretary-of-state-in-waiting. Yet, seven months after the Six Pillars had been published, the United States, the Soviet Union, China, and a reluctant Great Britain announced in the "Moscow Declaration" that they, the "United Nations," would continue their alliance after the war ended. These countries pledged for the first time to create a permanent international organization. It was a victory for Dulles.[22]

While Dulles found ways to cooperate with the Roosevelt administration, he could not get British ecumenists to join the Americans in their quest for a world government. At the press event for the Six Pillars in March 1943, the Harvard philosophy professor and human rights theorist William Ernest Hocking had told the audience he thought coordinating policy with the British should have a high priority. Hocking called on American and British groups to "join hands." But British ecumenists could not come to an agreement with their American counterparts.[23] Both groups had wanted to issue a united declaration on the postwar settlement, but a separate British statement in June 1943 announced, "It will not be possible to deal with the many and vast problems affecting the world through a single international organisation for world government."[24] The British leaders urged avoiding any sort of formal structure, which Van Dusen attributed to the British preference for "gradualism."[25] It was a disappointing moment for the Dulles Commission, which suddenly refocused its efforts away from transatlantic cooperation and toward America's role in the postwar world. Dulles was concluding that American leadership needed to be at the heart of postwar international relations.

The Crusade for World Order

Shortly after Dulles issued the Six Pillars in March 1943, the Federal Council of Churches organized a massive publicity campaign designed to mobilize popular support on behalf of a world government.[26] Organizers called the campaign the "Christian Mission on World Order," which they launched at New York's Cathedral of St. John the Divine in October 1943 before taking the program on the road.[27] Ecumenical leaders, senators, members of Congress, State Department officials, and business leaders composed a "flying squadron" of speakers who held large rallies in 102 cities across the country. Senators Joseph H. Ball (R-MN) and Harold Burton (R-OH), and Representatives Walter Judd (R-MN) and Jerry Voorhis (D-CA) were among those traveling from town to town urging the United States not to repeat the mistakes of the past and to call upon President Roosevelt and the Senate to embrace a new international organization. Senator Ball called these rallies "the greatest crusade since Jesus sent his twelve disciples out to preach the brotherhood of man."[28]

As the dignitaries visited cities across the country in late 1943, ecumenical leaders worked to organize long-term programs in those cities. In Johnstown, Pennsylvania, for example, churches organized a series of events that continued for half a year after the November 4, 1943, visit by the flying squadron. Local church officials gave sermons and made speeches in December, created a steering committee on international affairs in January 1944, and organized education programs during February and March, rallies and conferences in April, and a final mass meeting in May 1944.[29] In a city of about sixty thousand residents, Johnstown churches attracted nearly four thousand participants.[30]

As Walter Van Kirk explained, "The Mission did not advocate the use of the pulpit for political agitation. But it did highlight the pressing need of translating Christian principles on world order into political conduct."[31] The flying squadron encouraged Protestants at the grass roots to put pressure on politicians to create a world organization. Beginning in 1943 many local councils of churches established international affairs committees to coordinate Protestant political agitation. Noting these developments, the British Embassy in Washington, DC, reported back to London that the "influence of the crusade begun by the Protestant churches, inspired by John Foster Dulles . . . is not to be underestimated."[32]

The Federal Council's "mission" inspired denominations to launch their own "crusades" for world government. The Northern Baptists' "World Order Crusade" began in early 1944 and culminated on May 7, which the denomination designated "World Order Crusade Sunday." On that day, the denomination requested that pastors of all of their 5,500 churches ask churchgoers "to write their Senators, the Secretary of State, and the President expressing their conviction as Christian citizens 'that their nation should join with all other nations who are willing, in some broad form of world organization.'"[33]

The Congregationalists also launched their own campaign for world order in early 1944. On May 21 Congregationalists across the country were asked to sign the "World Order Compact." Nearly 1,100 Congregational churches participated in the effort, which was modeled on the "Mayflower Compact" of their denominational ancestors.[34] The compacts were delivered to the denominational meeting in the summer of 1944, where Congressman Walter Judd, a Congregationalist, spoke in support of an international organization.[35] The Congregationalists were smaller than the Northern Baptists, with about one million members compared with the Baptists' one and a half million. But among their members were six senators, three of whom sat on the Senate Committee on Foreign Relations.[36]

Denominations that were usually reticent to take a stand on political issues joined the World Order movement as well. In 1944, the United Lutherans implemented a two-month study program, several meetings and study conferences, and four summer schools.[37] The more conservative Southern Presbyterians' program included one-day study conferences in sixty communities, study groups that met for longer periods, and a *Post-Easter Period of Commitment and Action*," which emphasized political involvement.[38] Southern Baptists, who kept their distance from the ecumenical and theologically liberal Federal Council, endorsed a six-point program in 1944 remarkably similar to the Six Pillars of Peace. These six points included a world where all racial minorities were free to "exercise their God given freedom," a world organization with the power to issue economic sanctions and take police action, an end to trade barriers, and freedom of religion.[39]

None of these efforts, however, matched the vigor or scope of the Methodist "Crusade for World Order," which was conceived and organized by Bishop G. Bromley Oxnam. As the *Atlanta Constitution* explained, "The idea originated with him, was given its initial impetus by him, was largely planned by him, and more than by any other single individual, was implemented by him."[40] Oxnam overcame hesitation among Methodists by assuring them that this would not be a political movement. Convinced, the Council of Bishops poured enormous resources into the effort. Of the eight million members of the United Methodist Church, the largest denomination in the country, more than 200,000 churchgoers turned out to hear the crusade's speakers. The people were given postcards and asked to write to "men in the armed forces, telling them that the people at home stand for a new world order, that religion must dominate the peace table." Between January 30 and February 6, 1943, the Methodist leadership sent teams of two to each of the 42,000 Methodist churches in the country to discuss with churchgoers the need to write "at least once a month" to government and military officials about the need for a just and durable peace. These churchgoers were instructed not to mention the crusade or the Methodist Church but to express themselves as "Christian citizens." The vast majority of these letters were "penciled postcards and handwritten letters," which caught the attention of Congress. According to Robert Divine, during the crusade, "Washington received one of the largest outpourings of mail in history."[41]

Methodist churches were awash in reading materials. The denomination distributed two million copies of the leaflet "Your Part," 600,000 leaflets on "Christian Citizens' Opinion on World Order," and 75,000 copies of *The Primer of Action*. These materials urged churchgoers to get in touch with their political leaders and gave detailed instructions about whom to contact and how to address members of Congress, senators, and the president. These pamphlets were cultivating a foreign policy public at the moment when public opinion was taking on a more visible role in American politics.[42]

In asking churchgoers to downplay their religious affiliations and instead speak in the broad language of Christian citizenship, ecumenical leaders were expressing confidence in "Christian republicanism," which is the idea that Christianity was the key to developing a virtuous citizenry required for a democracy to thrive. They believed that Christian values undergirded democratic governance, but that those values could be expressed in civic, nonsectarian terms. In this way ecumenical Protestants could express ownership of American politics, while also creating room for other groups to take part.[43]

The Methodist crusade was a vast political mobilization that reached millions of Americans. *The Methodist Woman*, which had a circulation of 1.3 million, devoted two issues of its magazine to the crusade. *The Upper Room*, with a circulation of two million (including 200,000 GIs) devoted an issue to it. The curriculum of church schools was revised for 80,000 adult classes and 40,000 youth classes, with a total of nearly 3.5 million individuals participating in discussions of world order.[44] International affairs permeated nearly all aspects of Methodist life in the United States during the years 1943 and 1944.

"Right Here in the United States of America Are to Be Found Many Obstacles to World Peace"

The political mobilization for a world government created a groundswell of support for domestic reforms and empowered activists to focus attention on racism and poverty. Dulles and Oxnam inspired the World Order movement, but the day-to-day operation was handed over to "social action" groups that sought to advance their own agendas by linking their domestic concerns to the cause of a stable international order. For example, the Northern Baptists' "World Order Crusade" was organized by their Council on Christian Social Progress, and Congregationalist efforts were coordinated by their activist Committee for Social Action. These groups had been founded in the Progressive Era or during the New Deal as small, activist wings of their denominations, whose long-standing agendas included the expansion of New Deal programs, support for labor unions, and federal anti-lynching legislation. Suddenly, during the World Order movement these left-leaning groups were propelled to the center of religious life.

Methodist women's groups were among those that sought to mobilize the internationalist rhetoric on behalf of their own long-standing social and political concerns. The war had created new circumstances that made drastic changes possible, they believed. Foreign policy expert Vera Micheles Dean, in an essay widely circulated among women's groups, called World War II "revolutionary in character" for its introduction of economic planning in the United States. "When the war is over, we may accept similar if less drastic controls" of the economy, she suggested. Methodist activist Thelma Stevens argued that "the war has brought together various races, cultures, and religions and welded the individual representatives into a group with common experiences and purposes. *The church must stretch its muscles and be strong enough to capitalize on these enriching experiences.*"[45] For Methodist women, a new world order could only come about if they were successful in keeping alive the wartime spirit of cooperation and sacrifice after hostilities ceased.

Figure 5. During World War II, activist Thelma Stevens mobilized an
organization of two million Methodist women to lobby for a world government, while also emphasizing the need to diminish racism and poverty in the
United States. Image courtesy of the General Commission on Archives and
History of the U.M.C., Madison, New Jersey.

Stevens seized upon the human rights rhetoric of the World Order movement and used it to publicize her long-standing anti-racist agenda. Like many
other women, including Jane Addams and Lillian Smith, Stevens was drawn
to Christian social welfare institutions because they offered one of the few
life paths that allowed women to escape the demands of heterosexual marriage and domesticity. Stevens was never married. Male Protestant leaders
shunned independent women and in the 1940s moved to exert greater
control over women's groups. But denominations, ecumenical groups, and

missionary organizations relied on the labor of women like Stevens. And because such women worried about inviting scrutiny of their personal lives, they were both made invisible and made themselves invisible. Unlike most of the individuals mentioned in this chapter, Stevens has no archive.[46]

During the Great Depression Stevens had worked hard to publicize violence against African Americans and to ensure that economic aid reached poor Black people. As the director of the Methodist group representing two million women in the 1940s, Stevens was in charge of the many rallies and meetings designed to promote a world government.[47] Stevens was determined to use her new resources to focus attention on Jim Crow, an issue she believed the Dulles Commission ignored. And her anti-racism was part of a broader vision of justice. The Department of Christian Social Relations, which she led, lobbied the US government during World War II to stop the conscription of women and postwar compulsory military training, and also lobbied in support of repealing the Chinese Exclusion Act, repealing the poll tax, extending Social Security to domestic and agricultural workers, passing federal anti-lynching legislation, and ensuring racially blind distribution of government services.[48] Newly empowered by the World Order movement, Stevens set out to popularize her progressive agenda.

Just months after the 1942 Delaware conference, Stevens gathered women together to study the recommendations of the Dulles Commission.[49] By the summer of 1943, she had put together a course of action that urged participants to study issues such as postwar peace, how to overcome racism, and how to help relocate Japanese-Americans out of internment camps. She insisted that "every course should lead to some specific action."[50]

Stevens organized a study course for the years 1943–44 called "The Church and America's Peoples." "Last year, when some of us studied *Planning for Peace*," an organizer wrote, "we discovered that right here in the United States of America are to be found many obstacles to world peace." Linking world events to local practices, she explained that "we hope to discover ways by which the church may help to ease tensions here in the United States and make the probability of a just and enduring peace certain."[51] Stevens had Methodist women read Louis Adamic's *From Many Lands* and Carey McWilliams's *Brothers Under the Skin*, both of which encouraged their readers to think of America as a multicultural nation.[52]

Stevens shared the widespread belief that prejudice was an affliction that could be combatted with the right combination of empathy and social engineering. Her study groups began with all participants identifying their ethnic and racial roots and economic backgrounds. They talked about the difficulties their ancestors faced and addressed the problem of "intolerance" in the United States. Later meetings included a "dramatic presentation" of the successive waves of immigrants to the United States, with women dressing in costumes and imagining the perilous journey to America their ancestors took. The group would then study the facts and figures of America's demographic diversity and survey their local community to find out which groups lived there and what challenges they faced. Local participants were encouraged to research legislation that affected nonwhites and, most importantly, to get in touch with minority groups living in the area to start joint projects.[53]

In 1943 Methodist women also participated in the "World Community Day" organized by the United Council of Church Women. The ecumenical group worked with denominations to appoint over a thousand local chairpersons who arranged gatherings that the United Council hoped would involve a broad cross section of the ten million women it represented.[54] The event fell on November 11, then known as "Armistice Day," and was a self-conscious attempt at diverting the holiday from a patriotic celebration of America's war effort to a day dedicated to transcending nationalism in favor of global cooperation. Although less popular than the many civic and veteran-sponsored events on Armistice Day, the women's World Community Day saw the participation of nearly 100,000 women in more than 1,300 locations across the country.

The women who participated in the World Community Day shared an overwhelming desire for global cooperation and a self-sacrificial economic policy in the postwar years. Each local group voted on two questions: Are you willing to tell your representatives in government to pass legislation authorizing the United States to join a world organization? Are you willing to continue rationing into the postwar period in order to help other nations recover from the war?[55] Overwhelmingly, the participants said "yes" to both questions, by a margin of 58 to 1 and 41 to 1, respectively.[56] The results were publicized and sent to every legislator in the House and Senate.

Stevens urged Methodist women participating in World Community Day to organize in groups without boundaries of race or religion. "This means Jews and Catholics, Negroes, Mexicans, Japanese, Chinese, or any other group living in the community" should be invited to take part. She also encouraged Methodist women to embrace political action. She told Methodist women to look at "pending legislation" to see what could be done to influence Congress: "What about the Oriental Exclusion? The Anti-Poll Tax Bill?

The Federal Aid to Education Bill? The Austin-Wadsworth Bill for total conscription of manpower?"[57]

In 1944 Methodist women became more interested in human rights. The language of rights permeated the pages of the magazine the *Methodist Woman*. Stevens promoted the "nine freedoms" enumerated by the National Resource Planning Board during the year the organization was disbanded by Congress. The nine freedoms included the right to fair pay, the right to "security, with freedom from fear of old age, want, dependency, sickness, unemployment, and accident," equality before the law, the right to rest and recreation, and the right to education.[58] The increased attention to "rights" came at a moment when Methodist women became concerned about economic reconversion to a peacetime economy and wanted to make sure Americans would be guaranteed full employment and adequate housing.[59]

By 1944 Stevens's economic views were in line with the most radical aspects of the New Deal. Stevens called for a "new world economy" based on the principles of the Four Freedoms and emphasized *"Freedom from Want."*[60] A study conference led by Stevens declared that the global economy ought to distribute goods to those who need them in order to decrease the economic competition that was widely believed to be the cause of World War II. Her vision fell just short of a welfare state but endorsed "planning on a national scale with full participation of government, labor, agriculture, and management." She insisted that "democracy must be economic as well as political" and that "labor should be given an increasing share of responsibility for management of the plant."[61] Only such a system could limit economic competition and avert future wars.

Stevens differed from many of her male colleagues in her advocacy of women's integration into the workforce.[62] Both married and unmarried women had the right "to work in any occupation" and to receive "equal pay for equal work." She urged the extension of state minimum-wage laws to service industries, where women often labored, and for more protective legislation for women "along such lines as hours, weight lifting, etc." In order to accommodate women with children in the economy, Methodist women's leaders called for maternity leave "guaranteed by legislation" and nurseries and day care centers in factories, along with counseling and education on effective parenthood, in order to ensure the integrity of the family unit. To get this done, they suggested that more women needed to be on planning boards and in charge of labor unions.[63] These propositions were meant to integrate women into the workforce while accommodating their widely perceived role as the family's caretaker. Viewed as "women's issues" by Stevens's male peers, these demands were largely ignored by the Federal Council, which did not make equality for women a priority at mid-century.[64]

By 1945 Stevens's economic proposals were subsumed into a more general discussion of demobilization, the creation of the United Nations, and the need to reconstruct Europe and Asia. When the United Nations Organization was being debated in the spring of 1945, Methodist women rallied in support.[65] At this time, the focus of Methodist women's groups was on the need for America to join some sort of world organization, as it had been in 1942. In the interceding years, however, the World Order movement encouraged Protestant women to see world peace as intertwined with racial and economic justice. And Methodist women were encouraged to engage politically in support of their vision of social justice. Stevens used the resources of the World Order movement and the wartime enthusiasm for globalism to propose big changes for the United States at home.

The Creation of the Protestant Lobby

The modern form of Protestant lobbying was born during the World Order movement. At a time of widespread enthusiasm for the United Nations, there was little objection to using bureaucratic techniques and institutions to express religious principles in national and international politics. Ecumenical leaders wanted to keep watch over legislation affecting the postwar peace process because they believed that Washington politicians might repeat the mistakes of World War I, when the Senate rejected the League of Nations treaty. Lobbying offices began popping up on and around Capitol Hill in the 1940s. The Congregationalists, for example, opened theirs in 1944 despite long-standing opposition by some of their members to the denomination's involvement in politics. The Federal Council's lobbying office opened in 1945, just in time for the peace settlement. By the end of the decade, twenty offices opened in Washington, DC, which harnessed the power of the letter-writing campaigns Oxnam and Stevens had organized.[66]

The first Protestant lobbying offices were often no more than a room in a larger building, with a single person in charge of most of the work. The Methodists, Northern Presbyterians, Quakers, and Northern Baptists crowded together in a building on 11th Street. The Methodist activists who created the lobbying group avoided the Methodist House, one of the few religious lobbies to predate the 1940s. The Methodist House, an impressive building that sits across the street from the Supreme Court, was founded by prohibitionists and continued to be controlled by them in the 1940s. Oxnam and other Methodist activists had abandoned the issue and avoided this embarrassing constituency. Although the Methodists set up shop in smaller quarters and were further away from the Capitol, they pursued a more progressive agenda.

These early lobbies were improvised efforts in the 1940s, but they drew on the powerful connections religious groups had established with politicians in previous years. For the Congregationalists, Thomas Keehn and an advisory council made up of local leaders in Washington, DC, met regularly to discuss the latest legislation. Keehn was an ordained minister with one master's degree in economics from Columbia University and another in social ethics from nearby Union Theological Seminary in New York City. Later in his career he would work with secular development agencies in India, Zambia, and Zimbabwe. In the 1940s, however, he remained committed to religious work. Although his resources were limited at first, Keehn was able to tap into the broader national network of influential political players, like Dulles. These lobbying offices were quite effective in Congress.

Keehn's efforts were clumsy at first. The Congregationalists decided that a two-thirds vote of the Senate was too high of a threshold for treaty ratification. They called for a constitutional amendment to lower the margin for passage to a simple majority to ensure the ratification of the UN treaty. The move proved embarrassing. But, over time, Protestant denominations became sophisticated political animals. Budgets and staffs grew, drawing praise from some and condemnation from others.

As early as 1946, a Congregationalist minister from Pittsburgh protested at a national gathering by handing out handbills that read: "When the overwhelming majority of our Congregational Christians who hold to the free American way of life, find out how their tithes and offers for 'missions' are being misused by [the denomination] to maintain a left wing lobby in Washington and to promote state socialism, how are they going to react? Eighty thousand dollars for political action in 1945!"[67] The right-wing layman Verne P. Kaub accused Congregationalist leadership of "using missionary funds to maintain a political lobby at the national capital at a time when warnings are heard from many quarters that the church and state should remain in their separate fields." As denominational conservatives cautioned against political advocacy, liberals pressed on. "The separation of church and state cannot mean that the church must never be concerned about government actions," retorted Congregationalist leader Francis McPeek. "Thruout [sic] Protestantism there is a swiftly mounting interest in the political process."[68]

That mounting interest centered on the United Nations and the postwar settlement. But almost as soon as these lobbying groups were established, they turned their attention to areas of concern that Stevens had stressed. Keehn's very first action at the 79th Congress (1945–47) was in support of a permanent Fair Employment Practices Commission, which would mitigate racial discrimination in industry. By the end of that year he had lobbied for the approval of the United Nations Organization treaty, for the continuation of price controls, for the full employment bill, and for a national minimum wage.[69] Keehn's work expressed the broad social vision articulated by Stevens during the World Order movement.

From World Government to the United Nations

As the World Order movement mobilized millions of Protestants on behalf of a world government, events clarified the shape of that institution. In 1944 the Roosevelt administration organized the Dumbarton Oaks Conference, which took place in the historic mansion in the Georgetown neighborhood in Washington, DC. The United States, the USSR, China, and Britain met there to decide on the shape of the world body. Roosevelt had previously been cool to the idea of an international organization, preferring instead an Anglo-American alliance to police the postwar world. But public opinion and political pressure, much of it generated by Stevens and Dulles, convinced Roosevelt to embrace an international organization.

The Dumbarton Oaks Conference produced an outline of what would later become the United Nations: an assembly consisting of all members, an eleven-seat Security Council with five permanent members, an Economic and Social Council, and an international court.[70] But a few key issues were not settled. Most importantly, there were no provisions for voting or for vetoing proposals. Moreover, Dulles believed that there was too much reliance on force to the exclusion of law, moral aims, and other noncoercive measures he had advocated.[71] Van Kirk and Charles F. Boss echoed the criticism voiced by many foreign critics that the United Nations would be a continuation of the wartime great powers alliance.[72]

Dulles also worried that the Dumbarton Oaks proposal would carry on the tradition of power politics by the great powers. Mobilizing his powerful connections, he convinced New York governor Thomas Dewey to speak out against the proposal. Like Roosevelt, Dewey had supported an Anglo-American pact and remained skeptical of an international organization. But as Dewey challenged Roosevelt for the presidency in 1944, he sounded more and more like Dulles, his foreign policy advisor. When some of the Dumbarton Oaks discussions were leaked to the press, Dewey announced in a speech written by Dulles, "I have been deeply disturbed . . . that it is planned to subject the nations of the world, great and small, permanently to the coercive power of the four nations holding this conference."[73]

In a shrewd move, Roosevelt convinced Dewey to remove discussions of the United Nations from the presidential campaign, which was entering its final months in the fall of 1944. He sent Secretary of State Cordell Hull to meet with Dulles and convince him to make the issue nonpartisan for the sake of the UN's survival. Dulles, recalling that the League of Nations failed partly because of partisanship, could hardly risk seeing years of his efforts go the way of Woodrow Wilson's. Dulles agreed to Hull's demands, and Roosevelt moved a step closer toward reelection. At the same time, it was understood that Roosevelt would seek input from Republicans on Dumbarton Oaks, and Dulles had plenty of input to give.

Dulles was worried that church leaders would reject the treaty because it did not resemble the world government ecumenical Protestants had been calling for. He asked the new secretary of state Edward Stettinius for help putting "the Dumbarton proposals on international organization in a favorable light before a meeting of the Council of Churches." Stettinius reported to President Roosevelt in late 1944 that Dulles "was anxious to get a good statement from them" but "he was finding considerable opposition."[74] Hoping for consensus, the Dulles Commission quickly organized a 1945 meeting in Cleveland to take stock of Dumbarton Oaks. The city was selected because it was easily accessible by train and because they received "assurances from Cleveland that Negro delegates would not be discriminated against." Organizers decided to discourage participation of Europeans in order to focus on America's role in the world.[75]

As the Dulles Commission began planning for the Cleveland meeting, there were already signs of divisions. A preparatory group called "Commission I," which focused on the "current situation" and was chaired by Harvard philosophy professor William Ernest Hocking, revealed disagreement on whether Dumbarton Oaks was in line with the Six Pillars. Van Kirk acted as the secretary for the group and urged Hocking to be critical of Dumbarton Oaks. "I foresee a considerable raking over the Dumbarton Oaks proposal. Care will have to be exercised not 'to throw out the baby with the bath,'" Van Kirk wrote to Hocking. "I believe we would do well to embody in our statement a pretty thorough going documentation of the weak points and shortcomings of Dumbarton Oaks. The government has asked for criticism and suggestions. Let us do what we can to enlighten the Government [*sic*] in this respect."[76]

"The discussion revealed a difference of opinion about the Dumbarton Oaks proposal," the minutes of the Hocking group reported. "Although the preponderance of judgment seemed to be that these proposals should be supported but with a careful delineation of the Christian concerns not met by these proposals."[77] Broadus Mitchell soon emerged as the fiercest critic of Dumbarton Oaks in the group. Mitchell, who was then a New York University economist and historian, and whose socialist views culminated in a 1939 run for the governorship of Maryland on the Socialist Party ticket, urged Protestants to "refuse to commit" to a document that "promises new misfortunes." Instead, American Protestants should "demand embodiment in the document of the principles of democracy which are proclaimed in the Atlantic Charter, the Four Freedoms, etc." Hocking countered that the "possibilities for building and growth which the document gives us" need to be acknowledged, along with "reaffirmation of the Christian ideal in comparison with which Dumbarton Oaks is in certain respects defective."[78]

Hocking delegated the task of writing a policy statement on the Dumbarton Oaks proposal to Reinhold Niebuhr, who was usually not involved in the deliberations of the Dulles Commission. Niebuhr acknowledged that the proposal "falls short in many ways of even minimal requirements for a stable and just peace" but insisted that it "be recognized as being a step in the right direction." He dismissed criticism that Dumbarton Oaks "gives the great powers special responsibilities." For Niebuhr, the great advantage was that it "seeks to make power and responsibility commensurate," unlike the earlier League of Nations. But the arrangement went too far because it "does not give the small nations any significant position or power in the world organization." The United Nations was in danger of becoming "a mere alliance of the great powers, with only the slightest trimmings of a world organization." Moreover, Niebuhr faulted the Dumbarton Oaks proposal for only having the power to deal with military disputes and lacking provi-

sion "to deal with large scale politico-economic questions and conflicts between nations." Additionally, he signaled that its emphasis on "regional
arrangements" was "a step in the direction of 'spheres of influence,'" which
will "prevent a more completely mutual approach to world problems."[79]

Still, Niebuhr cautioned against being too critical. A recent conflict with
the Soviet Union over whether a permanent member of the Security Council should abstain from voting on matters in which they were entangled revealed that little trust had developed between the USSR, Great Britain, and
the United States. Threats to the stability of the world organization come not
only from domestic isolationists and nationalists but also from foreign
nations. He argued that Protestants should tread carefully amid this
minefield.[80]

Hocking agreed with Niebuhr that the Dumbarton Oaks proposal should
be supported first and criticized second. However, Hocking was discouraged by what he believed was Niebuhr's overemphasis on the fragility of the
United Nations. Hocking quipped to Van Kirk that "realism leads a good
man to lie down frequently when he ought to be up and kicking."[81]

Others went further than Niebuhr in their criticism, pointing out, for
example, that Dumbarton Oaks made no mention of a human rights charter, which ecumenical Protestants had called for back in 1942. Niebuhr, like
Dulles, showed little interest in human rights. In Hocking's group, O. Frederick Nolde was the most forceful advocate for "human rights and fundamental freedoms" to be enumerated as soon as the UN's Economic and
Social Council was established.[82] Nolde had been charged with elaborating
on the sixth Pillar of Peace, which called for religious liberty throughout the
world, and came to believe in earlier years that a broad statement on human
rights was the best means of defending religious liberty. Nolde had little experience in ecumenical politics prior to his attendance of the 1942 Delaware
conference at the age of forty-two.[83] But he was a quick learner, and he
pushed ecumenical Protestants to support human rights as a key part of the
postwar settlement ahead of the 1945 Cleveland conference.

Hocking supported Nolde's lobbying to make human rights part of the
mandate of the United Nations organization. Hocking was a philosophical
personalist, which meant that he emphasized the right to develop one's personality to its full capacity. He was also one of the earliest theorists of human
rights, having written a slim volume on the subject in 1926 called *Present
Status of the Philosophy of Law and of Rights*.[84] Years later, in 1947, his former
student Charles Malik asked Hocking to critique an early draft of the

Universal Declaration of Human Rights. Malik was the rapporteur of the UN Commission on Human Rights and oversaw the writing of the declaration. Looking at this draft, Hocking reminded Malik that he believed "that every human being has one 'natural' right." Hocking denied "that any human being has a plurality of unconditional and inalienable rights. And I have expressed the belief that the liberal position in politics is weakened today, as it has long been weakened in law, by staking out elaborate and plural areas of individual right without showing their relation to each other and to their own central meaning, and especially by leaving indefinite the nature of their limitations."[85]

Hocking's emphasis on personality was not his invention. At the turn of the century, Boston University's Methodist-dominated Philosophy Department had developed "personalism" into a philosophical system that placed the human personality and the dignity of the human person at the heart of ecumenical Protestant thought. The language of personality, dignity, and the human person thrived in the Methodist milieu, becoming by the 1940s "virtually the 'party line' of American Methodism."[86] Personalism also became widespread at international ecumenical Protestant gatherings in the 1920s and 1930s, and used by Africans and African Americans to condemn Jim Crow and colonialism.[87] Max Yergan, for example, convinced an international meeting in 1928 to support the right of all to hold any profession, to have freedom of movement, to receive equal treatment before the law, and to exercise citizenship rights—all irrespective of race—by appealing to "the Fatherhood of God and the sacredness of personality," which "are vital truths revealed in Christ."[88] While Dulles and Niebuhr were largely indifferent to human rights, they could not help but notice how popular the notion of the inherent dignity and worth of the human person had become within the Protestant establishment.

In its language, Protestant personalism mirrored Catholic personalism. Long a European tradition associated with radical politics, Catholic personalism became tied to human rights in the 1930s and 1940s through the work of French philosopher Jacques Maritain and popularized by the Christmas address of Pope Pius XII in 1942. The "rights of the human person" listed by Pius mostly focused on religious liberty.[89] Pius's address spurred American Catholics to action. In the United States, the Catholic Church was the only other religious organization capable of broad mobilization, and its less public efforts promoted the UN and a human rights charter. Of the Catholic leaders who spoke on behalf of human rights in the 1940s, however, most focused on their anti-communist and anti-secular implications. "Darwinism, Marxism, quantitative science, mobilization and the totalitarian state," announced popular Catholic speaker Fulton Sheen in 1938, have degraded man's "personality and his rights."[90] Catholic leaders conceived of human rights as a means of instantiating natural law principles in global governance, opposing the Soviet Union internationally, and limiting secularism domestically. Substantial theological and political differences, along with a history of mutual suspicion, prevented Catholics and ecumenical Protestants from working together in the 1940s.[91] Jewish groups joined ecumenical Protestants in actively supporting the religiously neutral and anti-racist conception of human rights, but their membership and public stature was dwarfed by organizations like the Federal Council of Churches.[92] In 1945, just before the United Nations was created, ecumenical Protestants focused on promoting human rights as a part of the postwar peace settlement.

For ecumenical Protestants, human rights were not just a top-down phenomenon. Philosophical debates were invigorated and transformed by a groundswell of enthusiasm for a new world government throughout the country. While the Hocking group focused on the proposal for the United Nations in light of ecumenical Protestant values, local discussion groups established during the World Order movement focused on other pressing issues. Their statements, which were written on "World Order Sunday" in November 1944 and sent to the Hocking group as it prepared its evaluation of Dumbarton Oaks, demonstrated Thelma Stevens's success in focusing attention on issues that were secondary to many on the Dulles Commission. Because of the participatory nature of the World Order movement, local churches had a say in how human rights would be understood. Overwhelmingly, they emphasized that human rights were incompatible with racism.

When churchgoers met in Detroit, for example, they concluded that "lifting to new levels of justice and good will the relations in Detroit between the negro [sic] and the white" should have high priority. In Saginaw, Michigan, a town of about ninety thousand, the World Order meeting focused on "the serious problems of race, color, and cultural pressures."[93] To be sure, there was a lot of attention paid to international affairs. In Kalamazoo, Michigan, local leaders declared support for the United States taking "an active part in the new world order," and they backed a "positive and creative" international organization that is "inclusive of all nations." Yet the emphasis on doing something about racism was present in virtually every document received by Hocking. And criticism also focused on Protestant churches. In the awkwardly named town of Indiana, Pennsylvania, local leaders urged Protestants to deal with racism because "Church people are guilty of prejudice and discrimination and the Church practices segregation."[94] The links between the international situation and racial tensions at home were clearly put by a gathering in Philadelphia. "In order to clear America's record abroad," they wrote, "it is necessary for us to start our race problems at home on the road to solution."[95]

The Hocking group's deliberations in 1944 brought together Stevens's criticism of racism, Nolde's emphasis on religious liberty, and Hocking's personalism under the rubric of human rights. The group affirmed "the dignity of the human person as the image of God" and urged "that the civic rights which derive from that dignity be set forth" in the UN charter. "We recognize that wherever human rights are suppressed, the seeds of disorder are sown. When minorities—racial, national, or religious—are oppressed, a threat to peace and order appear[s]."[96] Hocking's human rights rubric was officially taken up by the Federal Council of Churches in 1945.

The Dulles Commission advocated nine changes to the Dumbarton Oaks proposal, which the Federal Council also endorsed.[97] The Dulles Commission called for the UN charter to include a preamble embodying the spirit of the Atlantic Charter, a commitment to developing international law, and for the organization to issue a human rights charter. The Dulles Commission also demanded the United Nations establish a commission on colonies, that the organization eventually include all nations, and that it give a greater role to small nations. Additionally, the major powers were to abstain from voting on (and vetoing) rulings that affected them. Changes to the UN charter were to be allowed without approval of all permanent Security Council members, the Dulles Commission urged. Lastly, it called on all countries to shrink their militaries.[98]

After heated debate in Cleveland in January 1945, the Federal Council of Churches voted to unconditionally endorse the United Nations Organization, while presenting their nine amendments as working policies for the meeting in San Francisco later that spring.[99] Disappointed that "the proposed organization is certainly not a world government," ecumenical Protestant leaders continued to worry about the precariousness of the world organization despite the overwhelming support it gathered in polls.[100] Hocking acknowledged that in "the recent political campaign, traditional American isolationism certainly showed signs of recession," but "there is every reason to expect a postwar reaction of some sort." He continued to worry about isolationism. "It is hardly to be expected that a policy so deep-rooted in American history should disappear overnight," Hocking argued.[101]

The debate about the United Nations raged on in the spring of 1945. Senator James M. Tunnell (D-DE) wrote to Van Kirk to condemn what he viewed as Dulles's political partisanship.[102] Others resented the close cooperation between the Protestant establishment and the Roosevelt administration. The *Michigan Christian Advocate* editorialized, "If we had had our way a much stronger statement in criticism of the President and our government at Washington would have been formulated." The paper pulled no punches: "President Roosevelt and his opportunistic colleagues have all but sold out the peace and laid the foundation of World War III by their sins of omission."[103]

A. J. Muste echoed these points in a letter to Hocking. Muste contrasted the Dulles Commission's proposal with a "straight-forward, dignified and clearly religious statement" by the Catholic bishops, which withheld endorsing Dumbarton Oaks unless changes to the treaty were made. He blamed the tepid Protestant document on "the spell of the fear, assiduously cultivated in certain quarters, that if the Dumbarton Oaks organization bad as it is and in the worst possible setting is not adopted, then the end of the world will have come and the heavens will fall." For Muste this was a symptom of an uncritical attitude by a group that had "been a mere adjunct to the State Department's campaign to get Dumbarton Oaks adopted."[104]

Hocking sympathized with Muste's criticism. As Hocking put pen to paper, he wrote that Protestants had to fight on two fronts. The first was against an attempt to keep colonial issues out of the scope of the United Nations. The second was against the effort to keep Japan and Germany impoverished for years to come. In the final draft of the letter he sent to Muste he decided to delete mention of the colonies. By this time Dulles had temporarily resigned to advise the US delegation in San Francisco, and Hocking took over as chairman of the Dulles Commission. Hocking explained to Muste that while he agreed with Muste's criticism, he could not make any substantive changes: "I have to answer that this Commission is handicapped by the absence of its Chairman in San Francisco ... [and I do] not feel free to depart, in his absence, from the line of strategy which he proposed to us."[105] Despite his absence, Dulles continued to mute criticism of the Dumbarton Oaks proposal.

The divisions among ecumenical Protestants over Dumbarton Oaks carried over into the founding of the United Nations. Dulles came to San

Francisco in 1945 to attend the founding conference of the United Nations Organization as a State Department adviser. Unofficially, he represented the Republican Party in the deliberations over the UN charter and was closely tied to influential senator Arthur H. Vandenberg (R-MI). Hoping to build popular support, the American delegation also invited several dozen NGOs to send representatives. The Federal Council of Churches sent a three-person team, composed of Walter W. Van Kirk, Methodist bishop James C. Baker, and religious liberty expert and human rights advocate O. Frederick Nolde.[106] The divisions that would emerge between Dulles and Nolde at the UN conference dramatized ecumenical disagreements about the role of the new organization.

Nolde emerged as the Federal Council's leading spokesperson at San Francisco. As the executive secretary of the Joint Committee on Religious Liberty, he had experience dealing with both church officials and state bureaucrats, and was at ease with international law. Nolde's organization, founded jointly by the Federal Council and the Foreign Missions Conference, was established to pressure governments to grant Protestant missionaries access to Catholic and Muslim countries. By 1945, however, Nolde was ready to drop the missionary justification. According to John Nurser, Nolde came to believe that "freedom demands a broader base than can be offered by religion alone" and that human rights needed to be grounded in a "secular context."[107] The presence of a variety of religious traditions represented at the United Nations as well as the officially atheistic Soviet Union in San Francisco drove him to defend religious liberty in nonsectarian terms.[108]

When Nolde arrived in San Francisco in April 1945, he encountered a US delegation that was uninterested in pursuing a human rights commission.[109] Working feverishly, Nolde assembled an umbrella group, which met with Secretary of State Edward Stettinius just before a key vote would be taken. One by one, the leaders of American civil society pleaded for a human rights commission.[110] Judge Joseph Proskauer, the president of the American Jewish Committee, made an eloquent plea on behalf of human rights. And NAACP executive secretary Walter White urged the State Department not to forget that human rights entitled foreign peoples to self-determination. Stettinius "thought it had been an excellent meeting and he had been deeply impressed by the discussion." He told the American delegation later that evening that "Mr. Nolde, Mr. Proskauer and others had made speeches and they presented a statement signed by a considerable group" and advocated "informing the President this evening about this matter and telling him of the sincerity with which the proposals had been put forward." Stettinius "felt that the Delegation should make public its position." Dulles solidified support among his colleagues and made the human rights doctrine a bipartisan position. Vandenberg agreed a public statement "would make for better public relations all around."[111] The decision was a dramatic turnaround.

Ultimately, four of the Federal Council's nine amendments to the Dumbarton Oaks proposal made their way into the UN charter. In addition to the development of a human rights charter, Nolde successfully lobbied for a preamble that explained the United Nations' moral aims, for the creation of a body of international law, and for a Trusteeship Council to transition some colonies toward statehood.[112] Nolde's commission "was not the only body to propose such measures," writes Andrew Preston, "but it was among the most adept. Rarely had religious lobbying been so effective, or so consequential."[113]

By May 1945, however, Dulles and Nolde were working at cross-purposes on several issues. During US delegation meetings, American officials hesitated about the possibility of the United Nations intervening in domestic matters. In April 1945, Dulles told skeptical senators and State Department officials that "the trouble with international law was that it had reserved the right of any state to do as it pleased." He pushed the Federal Council's position to Senate Foreign Relations Committee chair Tom Connally (D-TX), who "was skeptical whether the Senate would approve the idea of permitting the Security Council to decide as to 'domestic jurisdiction.'" Connally's skepticism was echoed by Senator Vandenberg. Dulles tried to calm the senators' fears by assuring them that UN deliberations were "just a matter of talk," with few ramifications for the United States. But Connally thought talk "would imply responsibility and action" and Vandenberg insisted that "the Senate had always thought that the United States should decide what was within its 'domestic jurisdiction.'"[114]

Once Dulles understood the Senate would insist on explicit protection for domestic jurisdiction, he not only dropped his objection but became the foremost advocate of strengthening the domestic jurisdiction clause. His biographer Ronald Pruessen wonders, "Did Dulles find it difficult to work as an American watchdog as far as 'domestic jurisdiction' was concerned? If he did, there is no evidence of it."[115] At Dulles's initiative, the wording of the jurisdiction clause was strengthened from "solely" domestic matters to "essentially" domestic matters, weakening UN authority over the affairs of nation-states.

A similar about-face occurred with Dulles's view on the Trusteeship Council. At first, he tried to reassure American military officials that the commission would not pose a threat to US Pacific naval bases. In the face of opposition, Dulles changed his mind and emerged as an advocate of keeping the word "independence" out of the Trusteeship Council's mandate. As State Department minutes record, "Mr. Dulles added that the church groups with which he was associated were satisfied in all their statements with self-government or autonomy as objectives of the trusteeship system and had never insisted on independence."[116]

Dulles's machinations in San Francisco ended the possibility that Stevens's capacious understanding of human rights would be expressed by the United Nations. As a matter of American foreign policy, human rights were put on the back burner, despite many attempts by NGOs—especially African American groups like the NAACP—to force the State Department to take the issue seriously.[117] Yet they remained vital for ecumenical Protestants. Human rights provided the framework within which they understood and justified their political work on racism, economic reform, and foreign affairs. Ecumenical Protestants became one of the most important custodians of human rights in an era when human rights were largely ignored by the US government.

While the US government downplayed human rights, evangelicals opposed them outright. As the United Nations took shape, dissent was building among those Protestants who had only recently started calling themselves "evangelicals." Carl Henry helped form the National Association of Evangelicals (NAE) in 1942 in opposition to the theological and political liberalism of the Federal Council of Churches. He hoped to leave behind the label "fundamentalist," which many Americans associated with ignorance, racism, and antisemitism. Evangelicals, Henry hoped, would stick to the literal word of the Bible and continue to emphasize conversion and the superiority of the Christian faith, while also becoming more engaged in solving important social problems. The NAE occasionally expressed sympathy for racial minorities and workers in these early years. But when they talked about policies that the Federal Council supported, they turned sharply rightward, embracing the enemies of the Federal Council as their political allies and expressing harsh sentiments about nonwhites and labor unions. Opposing the liberalism of the Federal Council remained their top priority.

Evangelicals opposed the UN and human rights from the beginning. The official mouthpiece of the NAE, *United Evangelical Action*, called the work of the Dulles Commission an attempt "to superimpose upon the nation a great social reform without having first laid a spiritual foundation." Lamenting the priority given to political action by church leaders, the journal cautioned, "Will these leaders never realize that the first need of the nation is that Christ shall be reborn in the hearts of its people. Then, and then only, have we any proper basis of expectation that we may meet with success in campaigns for social or political betterment."[118]

This logic applied doubly to the Federal Council's support for the United Nations. "The Ten Commandments have been in the world for three thousand five hundred years and look at the world. The Sermon on the Mount has been in the world for two thousand years and look at the world," an NAE columnist cautioned. "Yet there are some people so foolish that they think that the San Francisco charter will do in six months what the Sermon on the Mount and the Ten Commandments failed to do in centuries."[119]

Evangelicals pulled no punches about the United Nations. "From the very start we hail it as godless, as a child of illegitimate alliances, born lame and due to die in the further catastrophes that come upon the earth," an NAE columnist wrote.[120] Even Carl Henry, who wrote enviously about the fervor generated by the World Order movement, chastised ecumenical Protestants for promoting "a global peace without any reference to the vicarious atonement and redemptive work of Christ."[121]

The evangelical critique of ecumenical Protestants' alleged secularism got nowhere during the war. Dulles and Nolde could safely ignore the NAE, a new and obscure organization. The Federal Council continued to work comfortably in the "secular" world of politics. That the UN charter largely avoided any explicit reference to religion did not bother Federal Council officials much. The Dulles Commission had pushed for each UN meeting to begin with a tri-faith prayer. Their attempt signaled the growing popularity of "Judeo-Christianity" in the United States in the 1940s.[122] It also signaled the limits of the Federal Council's pluralism, which attempted to impose this American idea onto the world. Secretary of State Stettinius was understandably cool to a tri-faith prayer because of opposition from the Soviet Union. Van Kirk was "inclined to think that we had better not press the matter on Mr. Stettinius further."[123]

While evangelicals would not accept a United Nations that made no mention of Jesus, ecumenical Protestants took further steps in reconciling their faith with a diverse world. When UN delegates gathered in Paris in 1947 to discuss human rights, Nolde most clearly broke with the

missionary-inspired idea of the "right to persuade" that had driven some of
the Protestant advocacy of religious liberty and human rights. He now opposed any mention of missions or conversion in the human rights charter,
and some missionary heads applauded his resolve.[124] John E. Merrill of the
Foreign Missions Conference urged Nolde not to "have the opinions of
Protestant Christians brought to the attention [of the United Nations] with
a view to their reflection in a Bill of Rights" or to seek protection for "Protestant missionaries to proselytize in Muslim and other non-Christian
countries."[125]

When article 18 of the Universal Declaration of Human Rights was finally passed in 1948, it reflected some of the nonsectarian character Nolde
advocated. "Everyone has the right to freedom of thought, conscience and
religion; this right includes freedom to change his religion or belief, and
freedom, either alone or in a community with others and in public or private, to manifest his religion or belief in teaching, practice, worship and observance," the United Nations declared.[126] The article emphasized individual
autonomy instead of the rights of missionaries. As a whole, the Universal
Declaration reflected some of the capaciousness of ecumenical Protestant
thought during the 1940s. It listed social, economic, and political rights that
appeared to indict racial and economic practices in the United States. The
Universal Declaration captured a moment in time, just before the Cold War
began, when an ambitious, universally inclined reform movement captured
the imagination of many Americans.

*   *   *

Dulles's dramatic change of heart in the spring of 1945 about "domestic jurisdiction" ensured that the UN's Human Rights Commission would have
little impact in the United States. And human rights would have virtually no
role in American foreign policy during the early Cold War. But Dulles's
machinations were only half of the story. The high-stakes negotiating by
elites like Dulles, Van Kirk, and Nolde, and the more mundane organizing
by forgotten figures like Stevens, contributed in equal parts to a robust and
permanent ecumenical Protestant presence in Congress and at the White
House. Women's groups, in particular, moved the World Order movement
institutionally and ideologically toward a fuller expression of human rights.
This point has been lost in most historical accounts of the era, which agree
with Andrew Preston that the Federal Council "became a forum for the pro-

motion of Dulles's views."[127] As this chapter has shown, so many things the Federal Council said and did about human rights, colonialism, Jim Crow, and religious liberty cannot be explained through Dulles alone. For the Federal Council, ecumenical denominations, and the twenty lobbying offices they founded during the World Order movement, human rights remained central to their work. And they understood human rights in the capacious way Thelma Stevens understood them: as an indictment of so many domestic practices that Dulles had worked to keep out of the purview of the United Nations. As a consequence of both Stevens's and Dulles's efforts, human rights became a discourse of dissent in the early Cold War, identified more closely with religious groups and nongovernmental organizations than with the US government.

The institutions created during the World Order movement became a permanent part of the political landscape by the end of the 1940s, aligning these theological liberals more closely with political liberalism. The World Order movement also created an ideological environment in which controversial ideas seemed more reasonable because they were presented in a global context. This global outlook pushed some ecumenical Protestant activists further to the left. Nolde moved in a more secular direction and committed to a broad understanding of human rights, and Stevens criticized racism and called for economic reform. Dulles, on the other hand, moved toward anti-communism. This divergence presaged some of the fault lines along which ecumenical Protestantism would fracture during the Cold War. And the Cold War would soon take its toll on the United Nations and human rights. But the institutionalization of the World Order movement assured that the one-world idealism of the wartime years would be no fleeting moment. It would reverberate through religious groups and through American politics for years. Its most immediate impact would be on Jim Crow.

CHAPTER 4

"A Non-Segregated Church and a Non-Segregated Society"

In the spring of 1946, at the tail end of the World Order movement, the Federal Council of Churches condemned segregation for the first time in its history. "The Federal Council of Churches of Christ in America hereby renounces the pattern of segregation" as "a violation of the Gospel of love and human brotherhood," the largest Protestant body in the United States announced. The organization pledged to "work for a non-segregated Church and a non-segregated society."[1] This new attitude spread quickly to other ecumenical Protestant groups, who had previously criticized "race prejudice" but until 1946 had said little about Jim Crow in the South or segregation in the North. Nor had they said very much about racism within Protestant churches, which were among the most thoroughly segregated institutions in the United States. In 1946 ecumenical Protestants moved from criticizing race prejudice, which had focused attention on changing the hearts and minds of individuals, to attacking segregation, which called for social action, structural thinking, and political solutions.

The ecumenical Protestant turn against segregation was brought on by changes during World War II, when Japanese Americans were dispossessed of their homes and businesses, and forced into makeshift concentration camps in barren landscapes, from the deserts of California to the prairies of Texas.[2] In these same years, Black migrants from southern states moved to cities in the North and along the West Coast in search of freedom and work. As they arrived, they were forced into segregated slums and barred from well-paying jobs.[3] At first, American ecumenical Protestants responded haphazardly to these developments and scrambled to come to terms with the changes World War II produced. But by 1946 they were clear: Segregation was incompatible with Christianity.

The sea change in attitude toward segregation among ecumenical Protestants was a product of the World Order movement, which linked domestic racism to global events. Just as African Americans launched the Double V Campaign against fascism abroad and racism at home, so too did ecumenical Protestants connect the creation of a postwar peace with a desegregated United States. An interracial coalition of activists, empowered by the World Order movement, engineered the ecumenical renunciation of segregation. The short-lived Commission on Church and Minority Peoples, composed of some of the most important anti-racist activists of the generation before the civil rights movement, drew on Protestant globalism and the new language of human rights as they convinced ecumenical Protestant groups to denounce segregation. The attack on Jim Crow became the first, and perhaps the most vital, way in which Protestant globalism transformed the United States.

Mobilizing Against Japanese American Internment

In the 1940s, ecumenical Protestant leaders closely connected to international organizations were some of the loudest critics of Japanese internment. Missionaries, in particular, played a vital part. In the 1920s and 1930s ecumenical Protestant missionaries in Japan had made connections between their evangelism, anti-racist activism, and a commitment to ending imperialism. They also loudly protested the 1924 Immigration Act, which banned immigration from Japan.[4] During the early 1940s these missionaries were deeply worried about the domestic impact of the impending war with Japan.[5] After years of embargoes, protests by the Roosevelt administration, and the first peacetime draft in the history of the United States, most Americans could see that war was on the horizon. Missionaries to Japan and China, many of whom had been recently expelled by the Japanese military and forced to return to the United States, worried about violence against Japanese Americans as tensions between Japan and the United States worsened in 1940 and 1941.[6] In California, former missionaries Galen Fisher, Ruth Kingman, and Harry Kingman organized around fair treatment of Japanese Americans through the Committee on Fair Play for Citizens and Aliens of Japanese Ancestry, which they founded in October 1941.[7]

Galen Fisher had begun working as a missionary in Japan in the late nineteenth century and headed the Japanese YMCA there until his return to the United States in 1919. He continued his interest in Japanese affairs upon his return and joined the Institute of Social and Religious Research and the Institute on Pacific Relations, two prominent think tanks on East Asian affairs.[8] Fisher was among the many American missionaries to Japan to speak out against the 1924 Immigration Act and to work in the 1920s and 1930s to diminish anti-Japanese racism.[9] He also worked as the East Asia expert on William Ernest Hocking's 1932 report, *Re-Thinking Missions*. By the 1940s he was also the chairman of the Pacific School of Religion.

Harry Kingman was born in Tianjin, China, the son of Congregationalist missionary parents. He spent his later childhood in California, excelling in sports and playing two seasons with the New York Yankees. In 1916 he accepted a job with the YMCA located next to the University of California, Berkeley, where he would remain until he retired in 1957. During this time, he periodically travelled to China and Japan as a missionary. Upon retiring he and his wife, Ruth, moved to Washington, DC, and worked as lobbyists for civil rights groups that were too small to hire their own.[10] Ruth met Harry during her time as a student at UC Berkeley. She was born in California in 1900, the daughter of an itinerant Methodist minister. Her parents were briefly missionaries in Hawaii. Not long after she graduated from college she joined Harry in China, where she worked as a music director. They were married in Shanghai.[11]

In 1941 Ruth Kingman, Harry Kingman, and Galen Fisher focused the activities of the Fair Play Committee on dispelling rumors and stereotypes about Japanese Americans. The idea of "fair play" drew on the long-standing belief promoted by the YMCAs and YWCAs that democracy, like sports, required playing by the rules.[12] When those rules were broken in local outbursts of anti-Japanese hysteria, they believed that the best way to handle these crises was to create civic unity organizations. Such groups usually included church leaders, government officials, and liberal corporate executives who could work with the local government to deal with racist incidents, property disputes, or even race riots.

Fisher wrote to the Reverend John M. Yamazaki, who was starting a branch of the Fair Play Committee in Southern California, to explain how to start a civic unity group. "Let some one or more well-known white Americans (not Japanese-Americans) take the initiative," Fisher advised. "Secure some prominent man to be chairman, preferably not one who is known simply

Figure 6. Former missionaries Ruth Kingman and Harry Kingman organized against Japanese internment during World War II. They are pictured here in Washington, DC, where they moved in 1957 and founded the "Citizens Lobby," which represented ordinary Americans in congressional debates about civil rights legislation. Courtesy of Springfield College Archives and Special Collections.

as a Japanophile, [and] ask Governor Olson to be Hon. Chairman." While businessmen and politicians provided cover, the real power and initiative should remain with the churches, Fisher stressed. He told Yamazaki to consult with the "County Committee on Church and Community, especially its special committee on Racial Unity. Possibly that committee would take the initiative in pushing the whole plan."[13] Many civic unity groups, which grew in popularity during World War II, were formed in this way.

The Japanese attack on Pearl Harbor in the early morning of December 7, 1941, came as a shock to the West Coast and changed the circumstances under which Fisher was working. He continued to speak out in defense Japanese Americans even as the Native Sons of the Golden West, racist politicians, and farmers and shop owners who jealously eyed Japanese property called for the expulsion of all Japanese Americans from the West Coast. The FBI had arrested thousands of Japanese and Japanese Americans immediately after the Pearl Harbor attack but, not finding any evidence of disloyalty, released most of them soon after. Still, fear and anger persisted, and, at the behest of West Coast politicians, President Franklin Roosevelt issued Executive Order 9066, which permitted the military to create an exclusion zone along the West Coast, where people of Japanese ancestry could not live during the war. Two days after Roosevelt's order, the House Select Committee Investigating National Defense Migration, known popularly as the Tolan Committee, began public hearings on moving the Japanese out of the West Coast.[14]

Carey McWilliams, a liberal activist who was then working for the Immigration and Housing Department in California, had invited Tolan to come to the West Coast. McWilliams hoped the committee would welcome testimony on behalf of Japanese Americans. In February and March of 1942, civic unity groups testified that Japanese Americans were loyal to the United States and that removing them from the West Coast would be a terrible mistake. Ecumenical Protestants, and especially Quakers, offered testimony in front of the committee. So too did socialists like Norman Thomas, and a handful of liberals like McWilliams. But McWilliams's hopes were dashed as nine out of every ten witnesses at the Tolan Committee spoke in favor of internment. By the end of the hearings it became clear that internment was inevitable. The army ordered all people who had at least one Japanese great-grandparent to report to relocation centers on March 31, 1942.[15]

When internment began in the spring of 1942, ecumenical Protestants faced a perennial dilemma. Should they make a public show of their opposition to internment or should they use their political connections to work with the government in a quieter but perhaps more effective way on behalf of Japanese Americans? Protestant pacifists viewed their options as a choice between complicity in a totalitarian attack on the citizenship rights of Japanese Americans or protest against it. Historic peace churches—Quakers, Brethren, and Mennonites, denominations more inclined toward pacifism— were the most critical of internment in its early days. Realists, on the other hand, viewed the choice as between responsibility or inefficacy. John Bennett, who was Reinhold Niebuhr's right-hand man, told colleagues in April 1942 that they should "assume evacuation" and that trying to prevent it was "not good policy."[16] Like Bennett, most of the groups—from the Fair Play Committee to the Federal Council of Churches—preferred behind-the-scenes lobbying to direct confrontation with the government.

But even private lobbying could be quite critical of government policy. For example, the president of the Federal Council and other prominent leaders wrote to Roosevelt in 1942 in favor of review boards for Japanese Americans, so that each individual could be processed and released from the camps. The letter to Roosevelt called internment an "abrogation of the rights of citizens" characterized by "race discrimination." It pointed out that internment "savours of totalitarianism and discrimination" and would be used by the enemies of the United States to "undermine America's prestige and influence" abroad.[17] It was quite a thing to tell a wartime president his policies were totalitarian.

The Federal Council's passionate protest against internment stood in contrast to the tepid response of many other ecumenical Protestant organizations. Ecumenical Protestants often donned the mantle of Christian service, charity, and goodwill when speaking publicly about internment. The Berkeley Council of Churches opened up their facilities to Japanese Americans awaiting relocation. As an act of goodwill it wanted to "make the burdens of this trying time easier for [Japanese-Americans]." Lacking any sense of complicity in the government's racist actions, it described the service of the churches, the service of American soldiers, and the "service" of the Japanese Americans in the same patriotic language that avoided serious discussion of the moral or legal implications of internment. "We rejoice to know that many of you are facing [internment] in the same spirit in which others are facing the possible loss of their sons, for much longer than the duration," the Berkeley Council of Churches wrote to Japanese Americans on their way to Manzanar and other concentration camps.[18]

Others spoke out against internment publicly. Reinhold Niebuhr's recently launched *Christianity and Crisis* issued a harsh editorial about Roosevelt's actions. Niebuhr was disconnected from the pacifist and missionary groups that first brought the treatment of Japanese Americans to national attention. But Henry Smith Leiper, a former missionary to China and a major architect of the international ecumenical movement, was more attentive to the plight of Japanese Americans. In April 1942, only a few months after American entry into war and amid anti-Japanese hysteria, Leiper wrote "A Blot on Our Record." This editorial denounced internment because it was so much like Germany's Nuremberg Laws, the Nazi statutes that deprived Jews of citizenship. (This comparison to the Nazis also appeared in other publications, like the *Christian Century*).[19] The cause of internment was clear to Leiper: racism and unscrupulous politicians standing to gain from the exploitation of some sixty thousand citizens were to blame.[20]

The readers' response to this editorial was swift, outraged, and came largely from ordinary churchgoers. *Christianity and Crisis*, a small magazine that rarely printed letters to the editor, dedicated nearly half of its pages in the following issue to angry responses to the Leiper article. Mrs. W. M. Mayes from Ojai, California, regretted the loss of civil rights of Japanese Americans but argued that internment prevented violence from breaking out. Mary Lillian Dodd of Millbrook, New York, was less generous. Leiper's article "may serve the Axis propaganda better than our cause," she wrote. Another letter—this one from a chaplain—accused the journal of succumbing to the idealism that its realist editors claimed to be fighting against. Leiper's editorial had "all the gossamer grandeur of the era of utopian perfectionism." Polley Dougherty from Santa Ana, California, went against the grain. She applauded Leiper for calling out the "injustice, unconstitutionality, and un-Americanism" of Japanese internment and she likewise feared "for the future of our country when it adopts such Hitlerian methods." But she was in the minority. Most of the letter writers agreed that rights do not need to be respected during wartime. Besides, wrote Mayes, it was unfair to compare American camps to Nazi ones because "no internment is pleasant, but the main camp, Manzanar, is located in a part of the state famous for its scenic beauty and health-giving air."[21]

Niebuhr personally responded to the torrent of criticism. He understood he was on thin ice with his constituency. He defended Leiper's article but in a cooler tone, without the Nazi comparison. What was left of the original critique in Niebuhr's hands was a firm commitment to due process of law without regard to race, which was no small commitment in 1942. In the wake of this outburst Niebuhr, Leiper, Bennett, and the other editors of *Christianity and Crisis* decided to avoid discussing internment. No further comments on Japanese internment appeared in the journal for the next several years. Niebuhr had more in common politically with pacifists, it must have seemed, than he did with his realist readers.

Other ecumenical Protestant groups sought to put Japanese internment front and center with an unrivaled intensity. The pacifist Fellowship of Reconciliation remained consistently critical of government policy. Among its most vocal members was Caleb Foote, a Quaker who was hired by the fellowship to open an office in Northern California in 1941. Foote repeatedly denounced Dillon Meyer, the head of the War Relocation Authority, who other ecumenical leaders saw as a cooperative liberal bureaucrat.[22] Foote even proposed using nonviolent resistance to protest internment, including picket lines and sit-down strikes at the entryway to the camps. Nevin Sayre, another fellowship official, entertained this idea, but he doubted that it would work and was certain that it would offend some of the nonpacifist Japanese prisoners in the camps.[23] In the end, nothing came of the proposal, but the fellowship kept protesting internment throughout the war.

Aside from public condemnation and private lobbying, ecumenical Protestant organizations mobilized their resources to combat anti-Japanese prejudice. But it took time, partly because of their large bureaucracies. The Congregationalists' Social Action Committee reported, "this work got really under way at and following the General Council meeting at Durham, June 1942" after money was allocated.[24] Soon after, they mobilized a lobbying campaign to implement review boards meant to quickly differentiate the "loyal" and "disloyal" Japanese Americans. In 1943 and 1944, these boards allowed Japanese Americans deemed loyal to resettle outside the exclusion zone if they could find sponsorship by an outside group.

The Federal Council of Churches, the Foreign Missions Conference, and some denominational bodies cooperated in finding homes and jobs for Japanese Americans away from the West Coast. The Congregationalist Social Action Committee worked closely with the historic peace churches in setting up hostels and employment centers in cities like Chicago and Philadelphia, and they raised funds to support Japanese and Japanese American college students in universities away from the West Coast.[25] The Midwest branch of the American Friends Service Committee reported in late 1944 that it had helped 3,500 Japanese Americans relocate to Chicago, providing them lodging in a hostel, helping them find jobs and permanent homes, providing medical services and even small loans.[26] By 1945, church groups had placed more than 4,000 students in colleges and universities away from the West Coast.[27] As the war wound down, on January 2, 1945, the army lifted the exclusion order, and Japanese Americans were allowed to return to their hometowns on the West Coast. Ecumenical Protestant relocation efforts were redirected to California, Oregon, and Washington, where most of the internees had lived.

Ecumenical Protestants also mobilized during the war against further expansion of anti-Japanese laws. Congregationalists, for example, successfully acted to stop an alien land law from being passed in Colorado, which would have kept Japanese Americans from owning land in the state. The political efforts continued after the war, as activists demanded reparations for the harm done to Japanese Americans. The Federal Council also sent its staff to congressional hearings to testify on behalf of establishing an organization that would help internees rebuild their lives as they returned to their West Coast communities.[28]

The same commitments that led ecumenical Protestants to rebuild Japanese American communities also drove them to reform the immigration system. Viewing immigration reform as primarily a racial justice issue, Walter Van Kirk worked closely with Congressman Walter Judd to end Chinese exclusion in 1943. Van Kirk had spoken out on behalf of China, a wartime ally, but he waited until 1946 to push for Japan to be placed on the immigration quota system. He testified in Congress and organized letter writing campaigns on behalf of a bill proposed by Judd to end Japanese exclusion. Despite the best efforts of Judd and Van Kirk, the bill failed to pass in 1949. By the time Japanese exclusion was finally ended with the McCarran-Walter Act of 1952, Van Kirk believed that the quota system itself was racist because it privileged Northern and Western Europeans. When Congress passed the act over Truman's veto, the Methodist student magazine *motive* condemned it as "a bipartisan bit of racial bigotry." Evangelicals, on the other hand, remained steadfast in their opposition to immigration reform and insisted that only groups capable of assimilating to the "American Christian Heritage" of the United States should be let in. Van Kirk and his allies regrouped for a long fight that ended with the Immigration Act of 1965, which did away with the quota system and eventually led to increased Asian immigration to the United States.[29]

During the World War II era, the ecumenical Protestant mobilization on behalf of Japanese Americans occurred within an integrationist framework. As Japanese internees began returning to the West Coast, ecumenical

Protestant leaders used the tragedy of internment to further integrate Japanese American Christians into white churches and white neighborhoods. Because the wartime hysteria had roots in ignorance and segregation, ecumenical Protestants reasoned that putting Japanese Americans in the company of white Protestants would lessen racism and make it less likely that this terrible history would repeat itself. Younger Japanese American pastors and religious workers rarely favored returning to the prewar pattern of separate Japanese churches and church associations.[30] A Japanese American churchgoer believed that "the war and the resultant evacuation has wiped away almost all vestiges of the segregated Japanese churches." He warned Japanese Americans and Protestant churches to "take this unusual opportunity to start on the road to integration."[31] Ecumenical leaders' desire for integration meant that Japanese Americans would be asked to blend in and risk losing their culture and language.

There were a few exceptions to this pattern. Whenever integration seemed unrealistic in the immediate future, ecumenical groups backed reconstituting Japanese American communities. Responding to reports that some Japanese Buddhists were unwilling to leave relocation camps because they feared being separated from their religious communities, the Congregationalists created a program that was "administered by Buddhists, subsidized by non-Buddhists." "The thought which has guided us in making this proposal was that such a Buddhist ministry would encourage persons in the camps to relocate. If they knew they could continue their religious affiliations, they would leave the camps more readily," the Congregationalists explained.[32] But this was the exception to the rule. By 1945, ecumenical Protestants involved in fighting the internment of Japanese and Japanese Americans had decided that integrated churches must be the norm in postwar America. And their integrationist ethos carried over into their work fighting the segregation of African Americans.

Toward Desegregation: The Commission on Church and Minority Peoples

As some ecumenical Protestants rallied in the early 1940s to protect Japanese Americans, others responded to the dramatic protests by African Americans. The March on Washington Movement was among the most important. It began in 1940, when A. Phillip Randolph and a delegation of civil rights leaders met with President Franklin Roosevelt, during America's arms buildup, to press him to give African Americans access to defense jobs. They had as much right as anyone else to help defend the United States from the fascist threat, Randolph told the president. The Oval Office meeting was cordial, and the Black leaders were optimistic that Roosevelt would come to their aid. But the president announced a few weeks later that he would take no action integrating defense work. Feeling betrayed, Randolph called for a nationwide protest to converge on Washington, DC, in 1941.

Roosevelt was worried about the march because it would show disunity as he was rallying Americans against Japan and Germany. To avert the public display of division, he made a deal with Randolph. Roosevelt issued Executive Order 8802 on June 25, 1941, which established the Fair Employment Practices Commission (FEPC) to review cases of discrimination in defense industries, albeit with no real enforcement powers. In response, Randolph called off the march.

Some ecumenical Protestants were early supporters of the March on Washington Movement. A. J. Muste, leader of the pacifist Fellowship of Reconciliation, sent his lieutenants, James Lawson and James Farmer, to work with Randolph. When the march was called off, Lawson and Farmer carried on by forming the Congress of Racial Equality in 1942. The new organization would be a pillar of anti-racist activism through the 1960s.[33]

On the whole, however, the initial Protestant response to the March on Washington Movement was muted. The issue of access to defense work for African Americans was brought up at a meeting of the Federal Council's Executive Committee in 1940, before Randolph met with Roosevelt. Dr. Wilbur T. Clemens, a white Methodist minister from New York, suggested that "the government in wording contracts . . . attach a rider to the effect that any contract which is found to be discriminatory in its labor policy shall suffer a financial penalty." But the Federal Council decided not to pursue the issue.[34] Like some of the Black press, even sympathetic ecumenical Protestant leaders initially worried about Randolph's ability to mobilize African Americans and the possibility of a backlash against the movement. For example, Buell Gallagher, a white ecumenical Protestant who was the president of Talladega College and an NAACP vice president, worried that the march would incite violence by white southerners.[35]

But once Randolph succeeded in pressing Roosevelt to create the FEPC, ecumenical Protestants eagerly joined in calls for the expansion of rights for African Americans. Black church leaders, including Federal Council Race

Relations secretary George E. Haynes, wrote to Roosevelt in February 1942 to proclaim their loyalty to the United States and to push the president to use his emergency powers to expand the FEPC and to desegregate the military. Haynes pleaded with Roosevelt to expand the rights of African Americans out of "respect for the dignity of their personality" and the need for unity in fighting fascism.[36]

Ecumenical Protestants justified their support for the FEPC by arguing it would make a big difference to both Christianity and the United States abroad. "The experience of our missionaries in dealing with people of India, China, Africa and other lands has shown conclusively that we need to achieve justice and fellowship among racial groups in our own land in order to show the sincerity of our belief in the Gospel," the Federal Council announced.[37] Time and again, foreigners would ask American missionaries to square their religious views with the racist violence taking place in their Christian homeland. In response, some missionaries pleaded for their fellow believers back home to do something about racism, especially lynchings. The lessons learned from the missionary movement were applicable to the war effort, the council reasoned. America "has united with other nations to fight and work for justice and democracy in the world." To continue do so, Americans needed to "set our own house in order."[38]

The ecumenical Protestant embrace of the FEPC legislation was widespread. Harry Kingman, who had fought against Japanese internment, became the West Coast head of the FEPC in 1943. Methodist bishop G. Bromley Oxnam lobbied Congress in 1944 for a permanent FEPC. And Walter Van Kirk, the head of the Federal Council's International Department and the secretary of the Dulles Commission, and whose "Religion in the News" broadcast reached millions of listeners weekly, noted in his book on Christianity and the postwar order that "the colored peoples of India, Africa and Asia are watching the churches," and he made a permanent FEPC the centerpiece of his domestic reform program.[39] In 1945, Haynes sent a letter to ten thousand ministers, asking their congregations to pray for the FEPC, and he urged them to send letters to their senators and representatives.[40] Support for the FEPC was broad among ecumenical Protestant leaders and caused quite a bit of excitement because it was one of the few anti-racist policies (in addition to anti-lynching legislation) that Protestant activists could rally around in the early 1940s.

The cause of the FEPC was not enough for some ecumenical Protestants who protested Japanese internment and African American economic segregation. Many of these activists were displeased with the churches' record and wanted a long-term approach that would shift ecumenical institutions from piecemeal, local work to a more organized and forward-looking effort against racism. After all, the churches were talking about reshaping the postwar world order, and few things mattered more to peace than the racism that had motivated the Nazis' treatment of the Jews, Japanese treatment of the Chinese, and the American treatment of its Black and Japanese citizens. Their efforts led to the Federal Council's pathbreaking renunciation of segregation in 1946.

The path toward renouncing segregation began inauspiciously, with a memorandum sent by Haynes. In June 1941, Haynes asked other Federal Council departments whether they would support a broad study of the areas of life "where interracial conflict needs to be lessened."[41] He had suggested that the proposed committee be composed of different racial groups. Samuel McCrea Cavert, the perennial Federal Council bureaucrat, told Haynes to stress expertise. "Have it done by people who look at it as social scientists rather than as advocates of some particular interest," Cavert argued, which would make it look more objective. Cameron Hall, of the Labor Division of the Federal Council, told Haynes and Cavert to fill the group with "church people" rather than social scientists. Churchgoers "will not take the work of non-church groups in the same 'at homeness' as if it comes from the churches."[42]

Others chimed in, arguing that the problem of racism must be studied in a global context. Missionary head Ralph Diffendorfer argued that a narrow focus on racism would ignore "the larger issues involved," and, instead, he "would like to see this problem set in the midst of a broad base that would really register in the total life of the Church." Channing Tobias, head of the YMCA's Colored Work Division, retorted that "we are not isolating this subject. It is the church itself that is isolating it." Speaking just before the 1942 Delaware conference, Tobias went on: "On the Dulles Commission they have not only dealt inadequately with it as a basic problem within our own nation but it has not been dealt with adequately from the national groups that come within the whole picture. Questions are raised by people of other countries as to our sincerity when we attack problems and overlook race."[43]

Cavert disagreed with Tobias. The Dulles Commission "can hardly deal with race adequately insofar as that is a domestic measure." Cavert did believe there was a need to study racism in the United States, but if it was taken up by the Race Relations Department it "would be regarded as a special group of pleaders." He had a solution: Tackle the race issue but make sure the study came from the Federal Council as a whole. Conditions had changed over the past twenty years, he said, and Protestants needed to think more deeply about the meaning of democracy. "The relationships between groups is all-important to what we mean by democracy," he said. Cavert wanted "something that would attract public attention." In the end it was decided that Haynes would be sent to the 1942 Delaware conference to see what the Dulles group was doing, but that this inquiry into democracy should be kept separate and should involve a broad membership of church people.[44]

The bureaucratic wrangling had ended, and what began as an outline for a study of "democracy" and its relationship to "minorities" was turned into a campaign that would transform ecumenical Protestantism's relationship to Jim Crow. The study commission continued a long-standing focus on "our ethical and religious concerns," but it also broadened its scope to include "our civic and social activities" outside the churches. Although the phrasing was ambiguous enough to escape the watchful eye of conservatives, it nevertheless brought the relationship of racism and the churches into the political arena. The study also sought to describe the connection between racism and "the international problems and the bases for a just and durable peace."[45] The anti-racist initiative would benefit from the publicity of the Dulles Commission as Haynes, Cavert, and Tobias popularized an argument that gained tremendous moral force during World War II: that racism at home mattered deeply to American and Christian interests abroad.

The idea that white people could remain objective, while others were merely lobbyists for their racial group's narrow interests, was widespread among ecumenical Protestants in the 1940s. So when the Federal Council approved the proposal for a twenty-five-person Commission on Church and Minority Peoples, it requested that a "large majority . . . be white persons, in order to guard against creating the impression that the study is merely 'special pleading.'"[46] The ever-present Tobias was on the commission, along with Haynes and Benjamin Mays. Haynes and Tobias were born in 1880 and 1882, respectively, and Mays was born a little more than a decade later in 1894. These three African Americans were born in the South and initially educated in the region at Black colleges with ties to Northern Protestant denominations. It was through their tremendous talents and these denominational networks—Baptist for Mays, Congregationalist for Haynes, and Methodist for Tobias—that they secured admission to research universities in the North, combining a religious education with graduate work in the social sciences. Haynes, for example, was the first African American to receive a PhD at Columbia University. These men were particularly adept at crossing the boundaries between Black and white institutions, and often moved between the North and the South. Each one was shaped by a religious upbringing in a Black congregation and a lifelong commitment to seeing African American churches thrive. But they were also critical of some aspects of Black churches, especially the role of uneducated ministers, the preponderance of women in the pews, and their otherworldly theology. "The Negro ministers will be challenged to assume more and more the role of a true prophet," Mays announced in an influential book on the "Black church" in 1933. The minister must become "the one who interprets the will of God to men—in personal, social, economic and religious life."[47]

Mays, Tobias, and Haynes took on important institutional roles that they used to combat racism. Mays would become the first African American to serve as vice president of the Federal Council. He was also president of Morehouse College in Atlanta, where he would mentor a young Martin Luther King Jr. Haynes coordinated the Federal Council's anti-racist initiatives for two and a half decades. And Tobias was a longtime YMCA leader who would serve as chairman of the NAACP in the 1950s. These giants of mid-century anti-racism were also adept at negotiating with white liberals. Although they would occasionally publicly embarrass their white colleagues for their prejudices, they tended to prefer negotiation, behind-the-scenes pressure, and bridge building over confrontation.[48]

The composition of the Commission on Church and Minority Peoples revealed the long-standing links between ecumenical Protestants and organizations supporting better treatment for African Americans. Eugene Barnett, the YMCA secretary, who was also a regular at Federal Council meetings, joined the group. The commission also contained a group of white southerners. The southern Methodist Dorothy Tilly joined the Federal Council's commission. (She would later serve on the 1946 Presidential Committee on Civil Rights, along with Tobias). Tilly was joined by white southerners Howard W. Odum and Will W. Alexander, both members of the Commission on Interracial Cooperation.[49] (Tobias had also served on the Commission on Interracial Cooperation from 1935 to 1942). Lastly, the group had a number of prominent officials who cooperated but had little immediate impact except to lend prestige (and money) to the organization, like Anson Phelps Stokes of the Phelps Stokes Fund, a philanthropic organization that supported

Figure 7. George E. Haynes led the Federal Council of Churches' efforts to combat racial prejudice from 1919 until his retirement in 1946. A trained sociologist, he was the first African American to receive a PhD at Columbia University. Courtesy of James Weldon Johnson Memorial Collection in the Yale Collection of American Literature, Beinecke Rare Book and Manuscript Library, Yale University.

African American groups. A prominent exception was the best-selling author Louis Adamic, who consistently showed up to meetings and contributed to discussions.[50]

Bradford Abernethy was transferred from the Dulles Commission to run the day-to-day operations of the group. In many ways he was a typical product of the culture the Protestant establishment had created. He was not a standout figure during the 1940s, yet he and countless others like him worked largely behind the scenes to make the socially engaged programs of the Protestant establishment possible. Abernethy was the son of William Abernethy, the senior pastor of the Cavalry Church in Washington, DC, during the 1920s and 1930s, who was a major figure among American Baptists. The younger Abernethy received his bachelor's of divinity at the premier Baptist seminary, Colgate-Rochester Divinity School, in 1933. While there, he married the school president's daughter. He went on to become a pastor in Columbia, Missouri, where he stirred controversy within his congregation by supporting the Missouri Supreme Court decision to admit an African American to the dentistry school in the 1930s. Growing frustrated by local church work and annoyed at the racial conservatism of his congregation, Abernethy gave more and more attention to ecumenical work, heading the Missouri Council of Churches immediately prior to being summoned to work for the Dulles Commission. As Walter Van Kirk noted, Abernethy had traveled extensively prior to his arrival in New York, including to Edinburgh and Oxford for study, as well as to Scandinavia, Continental Europe, the Middle East, and to Mexico for a year. By the time he transferred to the Commission on Church and Minority Peoples, Abernethy had all the qualities and experiences of ecumenical leaders: a high-quality education at a leading university and liberal seminary, involvement with idealistic youth groups, firsthand experience with Jim Crow, international expertise that included contact with non-Europeans, and a deep knowledge of bureaucratic procedures.[51] His formative experiences made him an ideal person to work with both local churches and Federal Council leaders.

As the Commission on Church and Minority Peoples began its work in 1942, it found that Protestantism was deeply segregated in the United States. There was "a tendency toward self-examination of the policies and practices of the churches' own institutions," like hospitals and schools. Moreover, denominational meetings tended to be carried out under nonsegregated conditions, and the denominations were looking more favorably at sending nonwhite missionaries abroad. But virtually all churches were segregated.

No denominations had a stated policy on the admission of nonwhites into white churches. Few nonwhite students were being admitted to Protestant schools, and college and seminary faculties had few, if any, nonwhite professors. Moreover, denominations had no stated policies about segregation at their hospitals, leading to widespread de facto segregation.[52] While the commission held out hope that denominations were becoming more self-critical, their assessment of the situation was bleak. As Frank Loescher, one of the commission's researchers, wrote in a widely circulated manuscript, "Protestantism, by its policies and practices, far from helping to integrate the Negro in American life, is actually contributing to the segregation of Negro Americans."[53]

Church segregation garnered attention partly because of the massive movement of peoples during World War II. In California, for example, the availability of jobs along with more hospitable attitudes toward African Americans attracted a large influx of Black women and men from the western edges of the South, where conditions for African Americans were much harsher. The Black populations of California cities like San Francisco and Berkeley, and especially Oakland and Richmond, skyrocketed. Many Black residents who lived in the region prior to the migration of the 1940s commented on the worsening race relations in the area. Informal segregation and a relatively liberal atmosphere gave way to animus against African Americans.[54]

Some liberal clergy tried to capitalize on these changes and create integrated churches. The first was the Community Church in Berkeley, California, led by the white Congregationalist minister Buell Gallagher, followed shortly by a church in San Francisco headed by African American theologian Howard Thurman. Gallagher's and Thurman's churches were two of several dozen experimental churches created in northern and western cities during World War II.[55] With roots in the interfaith and interracial activism of the 1930s, their proliferation during World War II was an attempt to create integrated neighborhoods, especially in places that appeared to be "transitioning" from a previously all-white to an all-Black neighborhood. These churches usually had both a Black and a white minister, along with integrated staffs, and tried to attract multi-racial congregations.

Ministers hoped that by creating integrated churches, they would freeze the transition from white to Black neighborhoods mid-way. But it did not work. The Community Church in Berkeley attracted African Americans from the neighborhood, but virtually all of the white members were supportive racial liberals from other areas, undermining the attempt to create integrated neighborhoods.[56] Despite their limits, Gallagher regarded these churches as a "prophecy" of an unsegregated nation and hoped these few integrated churches would be "the spiritual center of the integrated community."[57] By 1945, just about every metropolitan area in the United States, outside of the South, had a self-consciously integrated church.[58] But these churches were the exception in a religion that was largely segregated by race. Integrated churches did important work, like providing gathering spaces for anti-racist organizations. They also dramatized what most people already knew: that the vast majority of American churches were segregated.

The nearly total segregation of America's churches presented a roadblock to the Commission on Church and Minority Peoples. The commission tried to get local churches to go along with desegregation by meeting with minister after minister and asking for their input. During three weeks in March 1944, Bradford Abernethy and Will Alexander traveled to five cities in different regions to listen and discuss local views on race relations. Abernethy reported that local leaders appreciated being consulted, but he and Alexander were disappointed with the views they encountered. Abernethy reported, "Although churchmen have a troubled conscience on this issue, there was lacking a sense of prophetic zeal and earnestness about the church's relation to the problem of race and culture. Only rarely is a 'Thus saith the Lord' heard."[59]

In the North and the South there was "not enough difference in the pattern of segregation to warrant drawing any sharp distinction between attitudes," the commission found. In all the regions, hostility breaks out about the same issues: "housing, employment, transportation, blood bank, etc." There were a few hopeful signs, like some interracial churches and a "very definite mood . . . for clarifying the matter of 'social equality.'" And as activists knew, all conversations eventually involved a heated discussion of interracial marriage. This difficult subject, which most anti-racist activists avoided, needed to be faced head-on in the commission's study, Abernethy believed.[60]

The other great challenge the commission members faced was the lack of a statement by African American religious leaders unequivocally denouncing segregation. Many white Protestants were skeptical that African Americans themselves wanted an end to segregation. There was a grain of truth to this skepticism. The segregated religious bureaucracy gave many Black men and women experience in leadership positions and secured jobs for them in tough times.⁶¹ Integration of an organization often meant simply the integration of the membership, while the leadership positions of the new organization would go mostly to whites. This was the kind of integration African Americans did not want.

The mistrust between Black and white leaders made the statement produced by the African American members of the Commission on Church and Minority Peoples, and signed by 106 prominent Black religious leaders, all the more remarkable for its forthright denunciation of segregation in church life. The statement was organized by Benjamin Mays, who was elected vice president of the Federal Council in 1944, a first for an African American. He used his clout to press the Black clergy to denounce segregation. It received widespread coverage in the press as the first collective condemnation of segregation in American churches produced by Black religious leaders.

The statement was surprising to both the white and Black press, since both thought of Black church leaders as conservative, apolitical, and obliging on the issue of segregation. It was part of a long-standing critique of the Black church. "In the first half of the twentieth century, the dominant political narratives treated African American religion with despair and disdain" before the southern civil rights movement offered "a powerful and startling departure from that story," writes Barbara Savage. A long tradition of social scientific literature, including writings by Mays himself, had categorized the "Black church" as a problem to be solved.⁶²

The ministers' statement itself contradicted all of this, demonstrating that African American clergy had a long tradition of anti-racist activism. They called for an "open-door" church for people of all races. This open letter to white church leaders emphasized that segregated churches fell short of the Christian ideal of the fatherhood of God and the brotherhood of man. "Freedom of worship, if it means anything, means freedom to worship God across racial lines and freedom for a man or woman to join the church of his or her choice," Black church leaders insisted. There might still be Black and white churches after the religion desegregated, but they would be operating according to "the requirements of the Christian ideal." Sensing that the wind was at their backs, the Black leaders called for immediate action, both religious and political. After all, "the time is always ripe to correct a wrong." Now was the time to "equalize educational and work opportunities; to administer justice in the courts; to give the ballot equally to all citizens, irrespective of race; to provide opportunities for all to live in a healthy environment;

and to guarantee equal access to health and hospitalization."[63] The Commission on Church and Minority Peoples could now clearly say that Black clergy were against the segregation of religion. And they could do so with the confidence that both Black and white voices in the ecumenical leadership were speaking the same language.

Soon after the letter was published, in early 1945, the commission finalized their plans for a large conference on racism and the churches. To their dismay, they were unable to find a suitable location. Restrictions on wartime travel made it difficult to gather large numbers of people. The Dulles Commission, with its close ties to the State Department, was able to regularly circumvent these restrictions, but the Commission on Church and Minority Peoples was not able to meet as they had hoped. Instead of a 250-person conference somewhere in the Midwest, they settled for a 26 person, three-day conclave in Princeton, New Jersey, beginning May 8, 1945.

At Princeton, they charted a path forward. Liston Pope wrote the plan. Pope—an awkward name for a Protestant—was a young Yale professor of social ethics, who would later become editor of the influential *Social Action* magazine and dean of the Yale Divinity School. Like Will Alexander, Pope was a white southerner, a fact that privileged him at these kinds of meetings. But as organizers quickly found out, he viewed Jim Crow and Christian racism as great evils. His blistering condemnations were frequently edited by other commission members for the sake of diplomacy.[64]

Some of Pope's recommendations were reminiscent of older strategies, like breaking down stereotypes through face-to-face meetings. At the local level, he urged white churchgoers to socialize with non-whites, to establish interracial youth camps, to choose a co-pastor from a minority group, and, if "the church is willing to take this stand," to publicize that people of all races were welcome.[65]

In addition to these traditional "race relations" techniques, Pope urged activism and political agitation. He argued that congregations should start drives against restrictive covenants and lobby union locals to admit non-whites. In addition, local councils of churches should make sure that minorities were represented in local government. At the denominational level, leaders should critically analyze the policies of their institutions to make them more inclusive, especially hospitals and schools. This should apply not only to patients and students but also employees and executives. One of the ways to do this was to no longer inquire about race on job applications, Pope wrote. Denominations should also use "experience gained in missionary work for the illumination of interracial problems at home," he advised. Pope also anticipated future calls for socially responsible investing when he urged ecumenical Protestant institutions to "invest denominational funds in housing projects open to members of minority groups, and in other such projects which are remunerative socially as well as financially." But most especially, denominations should outlaw discrimination based on race within their group and abolish their segregated bureaucracies. At the highest levels of the ecumenical movement, leaders should press for an international bill of human rights and an end to colonialism.[66]

Pope's program was revolutionary because it went beyond changing individual hearts and minds and focused attention on political and structural issues. Racism was not only a matter of attitudes but also of laws, institutions, and economics. But these ideas still flew below the radar in 1945. Because of its small size, the Princeton meeting did not produce the kind of publicity generated by the Dulles Commission. Instead, Princeton became largely a strategy meeting, with commission members seeking to refine their arguments and create a clear plan for influencing the Federal Council.

Pope's plan for influencing the Federal Council began with theology, "so that initial debate, if any, would be on Christian Principles rather than Church Procedure."[67] The theological statement he submitted to the Federal Council began by recognizing the fatherhood of God and the brotherhood of all men, which was at the heart of building "the Kingdom of God on this earth." It chastised Christians for the sin of arrogance and pride in seeking the promotion of the interests of some over the interests of the whole. "Any discrimination within the Church because of race, negates the nature of the Church. Let the Church be the Church, cleanse its own life, and so live out its principles as to create new faith, new conscience, new hope in the world."[68]

Protestant personalism figured prominently in Pope's efforts. Personalism's emphasis on dignity and human personality played an influential role in both anti-racist efforts and in debates about human rights. The Commission on Church and Minority Peoples argued that learning from different peoples was part of "God's purpose" to see "the creation, development, and enrichment of human persons," who are invested with "infinite dignity and promise." The commission further stated, "Human progress is measured and human institutions are judged by the extent to which the sacredness of human personality is recognized, enriched and fulfilled, and the opportunity offered to all men to live in the dignity and freedom proper to those who are God's children."[69]

The theology of anti-racism simultaneously drew on multiculturalism—the celebration of difference—as well as color-blind liberalism, which emphasized instead the similarity of all people. On the one hand, ecumenical Protestant theologians argued that "the true principle of human society is unity in diversity." At other points in the same statement they played down diversity and emphasized the similarities of all people: "In God all men are brothers regardless of the accidents of antecedents, entitled to equal and un-segregated opportunity for self-development without distinction either in law or fact on account of race or nationality."[70] Thus ecumenists promoted color-blind liberalism while sowing the seeds of a multiculturalism that became popular in later decades. The Federal Council officially adopted this anti-racist theology in 1945.

All of the institutional wrangling that Haynes, Mays, and Pope were doing would eventually sway ecumenical Protestants to take a public stand against segregation. With the Federal Council's official approval of the theological statement decrying racism, the members of the Commission on Church and Minority Peoples pressed on. They saw an opportunity at the emergency meeting of the Federal Council in Columbus, Ohio, in the spring of 1946. The meeting was called by Federal Council president G. Bromley Oxnam, who decided that there was a need for ecumenical Protestants to speak quickly and decisively about the postwar world order as World War II came to an end.

Responding to Oxnam's call for an emergency meeting on international affairs, Haynes sent out two memos on November 19, 1945, urging Oxnam to tackle racism. Haynes recalled the violence after World War I, when he began working for the Federal Council, and he believed World War II would follow a similar pattern. He also noted attempts to defund the FEPC and the new self-confidence shown by returning Black and Japanese American veterans. Most of all, local churches needed guidance. "Local church leaders," he wrote, "are eager to do something and are anxious for guidance on what to do and how to gear their local church groups into methods of doing them. A program of action is the call of the hour."[71]

The Commission on Church and Minority Peoples, unable to bring attention to racism 1945, would have a second chance at Columbus. The Columbus meeting began on March 5, 1946, following the long-established pattern of several hundred Protestant leaders gathering with prominent intellectuals, politicians, businessmen, labor leaders, military officials, and State Department officials. Even President Harry Truman attended. But despite the staid bureaucratic procedure, it felt like a new day was dawning. The United Nations was a reality. There were "religious, social, economic, and political" tensions in the world, especially "in the case of the Soviet Union and the western democracies" but the United Nations would create "sympathetic understanding" and undertake "constructive tasks of common concern."[72] The sense of hope that a new world was coming in the spring of 1946 was also palpable for theologians. At the Columbus conference, a group of biblical scholars released the Revised Standard Version of the New Testament, a theologically liberal translation that threatened the dominance of the popular King James Version for the first time. This hopeful feeling was mixed with a sense of responsibility. According to the Federal Council, the church "must come to grips with and speak to the issues which imperil the very existence of humanity: imperialism, militarism, racism, nationalism, and class conflict."[73]

Despite the millenarian spirit of 1946, it was not entirely clear which way the Federal Council would go on segregation. And Mays's experience at Columbus shows why. On the second day of the 1946 Columbus conference, President Harry Truman arrived to give an address. Mays was originally scheduled to sit with other Federal Council dignitaries on stage behind the president, he recalled in his autobiography.[74] An unnamed conference organizer decided, however, that sitting a Black man behind the president would be inappropriate and moved Mays's seat to the front row, away from the gaze of cameras. Only a last-minute intervention by a New York delegate got Mays back behind the podium. Mays's case underscored the Federal Council's indecision about the place of African Americans in the United States.

Mays hoped to turn the tide against segregation, as well as the Federal Council's indecision, by appealing to Protestant globalism. The working group on "race relations" at Columbus, staffed largely by members of the Commission on Church and Minority Peoples, announced that "as a nation, our world leadership is imperiled by the existence of undemocratic patterns at home." Moreover, "Large numbers of Negro, Japanese, and Spanish veterans who fought in the United States Army against these theories of racial superiority are now denied free access to an opportunity to earn a living" and have "only restricted citizenship."[75]

Mays decided to use one of the latest examples of the harmful effects of segregation on the world stage that resonated with an ecumenical Protestant constituency enthralled by the United Nations. The location of the UN headquarters was still in doubt as of early 1946, but it seemed increasingly likely that it would be located in an East Coast American city, which brought worries about the treatment nonwhite dignitaries might experience. The Indian delegation complained loudly about their encounter with segregation in Washington, DC.[76] Indeed, large swaths of America were never seriously considered as a UN site because of segregation.[77] The Federal Council called it a "source of great embarrassment to our leaders" and "a discouraging factor" as the United States was beginning "to play our part in the new world unity upon which our future existence depends."[78]

Mays and Haynes had skillfully positioned racism at the center of the Federal Council's postwar plans, but it would be white activists who shepherded a clear-cut denunciation of segregation through the Columbus conference. Alexander had recovered from surgery for cancer in time to attend, but it was recently retired Union Theological Seminary president Henry Sloane Coffin whose role was decisive at Columbus. Coffin, an heir to the W. & J. Sloane fortune, chaired the working group on race at Columbus and used his clout to denounce segregation. It mattered to other Federal Council delegates that a white, wealthy, and well-positioned clergyman said it was time for Jim Crow to go. During a fiery speech by Coffin, "The southern members got up and left," recalled Alexander. "They knew what was coming and they quietly got out. They didn't bolt, or anything. They just got away so they could say when they got back home that they weren't there."[79]

But it was not only southerners who opposed integration. At least one Methodist bishop from the North understood the implications of the attack on Jim Crow for the segregated Methodist hierarchy. Realizing that what Coffin was proposing indirectly called for the Methodists to desegregate, the bishop "was pretty violent in saying they weren't going to do it." But with the southern exodus and the strong support for the resolution, Alexander reported, "The brethren handled him pretty roughly, and passed the thing overwhelmingly. It was a pretty sensational thing for a church body to do."[80]

In 1946, the Federal Council officially renounced segregation "as unnecessary and undesirable and a violation of the Gospel of love and human brotherhood" and pledged to prove its sincerity by working "for a non-segregated Church and a non-segregated society." It was a once-in-a-generation shift. The Federal Council had for years decried "race prejudice," but it had not attacked Jim Crow. The Federal Council continued to emphasize lessening prejudice through education and moral suasion among individuals, in order to "create new men with new motives." But now the Federal Council also attacked something that the churches had "neglected" to do:

"to deal adequately with the fundamental pattern of segregation in our society." Creating "a non-segregated society" would mean focusing on structural patterns and political solutions.[81]

The Federal Council's new attitude toward segregation went far beyond anything it or its predominantly white member denominations had said about Jim Crow. The report anticipated the 1954 *Brown v. Board* decision because of its insistence that segregation "has always meant inferior services" to minorities and that segregation is "always discriminatory." Segregation expressed the sense of superiority held by "vast numbers of Americans" and helped transmit that attitude "from one generation to another." Moreover, it denied jobs and an adequate standard of living to millions of Americans, hampered the effectiveness of the armed forces, disenfranchised citizens, encouraged demagoguery, and incited racial violence. Worst of all, segregation was given "moral sanction" by churches, which had "accepted the pattern of racial segregation in their own life and practice."[82]

For the Black press, the "Non-Segregated Church" statement was like a bolt of lightning coming from a clear blue sky. Calling the Columbus conference "history-making" and the Federal Council's actions "revolutionary," the front-page headline of the *Chicago Defender* announced that "Jim Crow and the church were divorced this week by the Federal Council of Churches of Christ in America."[83] Ecumenical journals likewise understood the importance of the statement calling for a non-segregated church. The *Christian Century* called the declaration on race relations "the most far-reaching denunciation of racial segregation ever to emerge" from a body of American Christians.[84]

Despite the pathbreaking renunciation of segregation, Haynes, Alexander, Pope, and Tobias did not get everything they had hoped for. Interracial marriage was the most challenging issue for church leaders and that was precisely why some commission members had pushed for a forthright statement on the matter. A draft of the Federal Council's "Non-Segregated Church" statement had emphasized the need to stop using miscegenation as an excuse for segregation. It was unlikely that much interracial marriage would occur, given previous experience with seminaries and schools that were integrated, Pope and others reasoned. Interracial marriage was treated by the Federal Council not as a moral right but as a legal one that should not be abridged, particularly because miscegenation laws had done nothing to stop elicit interracial relationships. The anti-racist activists stressed "that each race is rightfully grateful for its own heritage and desirous of preserving its own identity," reassuring church leaders that Black people did not really want to marry whites, and vice versa. This pluralist language is striking because it provided such a strong counterpoint to the color-blind attitude present in virtually everything else written about race by ecumenical Protestants during the 1940s.

Despite assurances that African Americans did not really want to marry whites, the section on interracial marriage was crossed out of the working draft of the "Non-Segregated Church" statement. Exactly who called for this section to be deleted is unclear. Perhaps it was the strongly pluralistic language or the difficulty of the issue that led to its removal. One of the drafters wrote "finally deleted" on the last revision of the statement, likely with a measure of relief.[85]

Federal Council officials were also weary of the political implications of the "Non-Segregated Church" statement. The Federal Council publicized some of the goals enumerated by Pope. But in an act of censorship, the Federal Council's Executive Committee refused to print many of them, fearing what churchgoers would think of their new anti-racist agenda and its social and political implications. The most widely distributed pamphlet communicating to everyday churchgoers what the Federal Council had decided on segregation at Columbus simply listed a number of self-interrogating questions ecumenical Protestants should ask themselves: Is your church racially segregated? Is racial segregation practiced in the administration of your church-affiliated school, college, seminary, hospital, or youth camp? Does your church hire minorities? Does it hire enough of them? In 1946 the Federal Council had empowered anti-racist activists to act politically against segregation, but it did so in hushed tones. Ecumenical leaders, aware of the gap between their critical stance on segregation and the widespread support for segregation among churchgoers, kept the implications of their views hidden from their congregations.[86]

Instead of political mobilization and structural thinking, churchgoers received a course on the "Clinical Approach" to "race relations." It was based on the thinking of Haynes, who was a human relations expert. He believed misinformation and stereotypes caused racial conflict. By the late 1940s, "human relations" emerged as an interdisciplinary field of study, funded by the Rockefeller Foundation, as well as the Ford and Carnegie philanthropic arms. Human relations explained racism as a problem of individual behavior and offered a solution to prejudice through adjustment of attitudes. If only people of different races could be brought together in a neutral atmosphere and confronted with the facts on race, they would have their prejudices broken down and, over time, they would change their beliefs and behaviors.[87]

Haynes had studied with sociologist William Graham Sumner, whose notion of "folkways" underpinned Haynes's approach. For Sumner, folkways resulted from community experience securing its basic human needs and were deeply ingrained in ethnic groups. For him, the tenacity of folkways was a reason why ethnic groups should be left alone and kept apart. But in Haynes's view, folkways could be undone under the right circumstances because he had a more expansive definition of basic human needs. For Sumner, basic needs were material, like working and eating. But for Haynes they included spiritual needs, which could be tapped to overcome the drive for economic and social dominance.[88] What exactly these religious and spiritual needs were, however, was never clearly spelled out. They reflected Haynes's optimism about the transformative power of religion.

What made Haynes different from many social scientists of the era was that he did not separate out the scientific inquiry into racism from reformist activism to diminish it. And despite its resemblance to earlier efforts, Haynes's "Clinical Approach" was far more ambitious than interracial Sundays, a yearly event that urged churches to cross the color line and worship together. Haynes's "clinics" not only encouraged people to overcome prejudices but to make plans of action for their communities. Haynes's goal was to get church people to cooperate with "the leaders of social, labor, business and civic agencies of the community" to diagnose and "deal with such questions as discrimination in employment, housing, education, health and leisure-time activities." With a strong emphasis on "factual analysis and through democratic agreement" these groups would "formulate a community-wide plan of action" to solve these problems. For Haynes, the goal was always "social action."[89]

By the end of World War II, ecumenical Protestants pushed a two-pronged approach to the problem of segregation. On the one hand, they revamped earlier "race relations" efforts under the banner of "human relations" and civic unity campaigns. For example, Fisher's Fair Play Committee merged with the California Federation for Civic Unity shortly after World War II.[90] This was the public face of ecumenical Protestants' efforts and the one they communicated to most churchgoers. On the other hand, the Federal Council and its allies took a stand against Jim Crow for the first time and empowered their intellectuals, activists, and policy makers to fight Jim Crow from city halls to the halls of Congress. This important departure had been engineered by activists who seized upon the enthusiasm for postwar peace planning and showed that it could not be done without ending segregation. After all, as they put it, a just and durable world peace and an effective United Nations required a democratic and desegregated America.

From Anti-Prejudice to Anti-Segregation

Soon after the Federal Council condemned segregation in 1946, a half dozen denominations, the YWCA, and YMCA followed its lead in opposing Jim Crow.[91] Between 1942 and 1946, American ecumenical Protestant leaders had taken a major leap from mild resolutions criticizing "race prejudice" to clearly denouncing segregation. While other white liberal groups continued to attack "prejudice," which emphasized changing white attitudes, the Federal Council and its allies began, however haltingly and ambivalently, to denounce Jim Crow and work for its abolition. The move from anti-prejudice to anti-segregation signaled a more political and structural critique of racism, and a growing determination to use legal and political tools to dismantle segregation. The willingness to name segregation as the problem signaled an important shift in the attitudes of ecumenical Protestants toward racism.

It took a war fought against fascism, and a moment when the global ramifications of racism were made crystal clear, to get ecumenical Protestants to commit to creating a non-segregated church and a non-segregated society. It also took an ad hoc emergency commission—the Commission on Church and Minority Peoples—to gather the clout to push through the "Non-Segregated Church" statement. Finally, the Federal Council's attack on Jim Crow required a special context—the World Order movement—when Protestant globalism dominated the minds of the Protestant establishment and desegregation seemed to fit neatly with the ecumenical vision of the postwar world.

The public call for desegregation marked an end of an era, and several figures took the opportunity to move on. Haynes, one of the architects of the turn against segregation, retired soon after the 1946 Columbus conference, where the call against segregation was first heard. After twenty-five years of work on "race relations" on behalf of the Federal Council, he had succeeded in getting ecumenical Protestant leaders to formally renounce segregation and to commit to a program of interracial clinics that he had designed. It was the culmination of his career. Soon after his retirement, Haynes felt the pull of global Protestant institutions. He was approached by the YMCA's world headquarters to study the organization's work on the African continent. In January 1947, he embarked on a tour of fifteen colonial territories in Africa, which resulted in a massive study called *Africa: Continent of the Future.*[92]

Tobias also retired soon after the conference. He had been senior secretary of the Colored Work Department of the YMCA, but the position itself disappeared when the organization desegregated its administration in 1946 in concert with the Federal Council's "Non-Segregated Church" statement. That same year he became the first Black director of the Phelps-Stokes fund and one of the members of the President's Commission on Civil Rights. Tobias stayed involved in the NAACP, becoming its chairman in 1953.

Other members of the Commission on Church and Minority Peoples moved on as well, including the young Bradford Abernethy, who accepted the position of University Chaplain at Rutgers University. Abernethy stayed connected to anti-racist activists, helping Quakers send students to the Global South and bringing figures like Benjamin Mays and Bayard Rustin to his campus. He later worked with New York's James Robinson to set up the Operation Crossroads Africa program, a predecessor of the Peace Corps.[93] In these ways, the anti-racist work done by ecumenical Protestants during World War II rippled through other institutions in the United States and beyond.

Protestant globalism had enabled the ecumenical turn against segregation. American ecumenical Protestant commitment to anti-racism and desegregation would, in turn, shape how the Universal Declaration of Human Rights was understood and would help make anti-racism a mainstay of human rights politics for much of the twentieth century.

CHAPTER 5

The Anti-racist Origins of Human Rights

At the end of World War II, American ecumenical Protestants had denounced segregation as a theological heresy and a political tragedy. In the course of the World Order movement, international events made it easier for the Federal Council of Churches to attack segregation. The flow of influence would soon reverse course, as the domestic criticism of segregation, in turn, began to shape discussions of international human rights. Ecumenical Protestants focused the international community's attention on the incompatibility between human rights and segregation.

That human rights came to be understood as an indictment of racism may seem like a natural development. After all, the universal nature of human rights implies that all human beings are equal. But in the 1940s the link between human rights and anti-racism was anything but obvious. Competing human rights declarations, including those produced by the Catholic Church and by lawyers' guilds, said little about racism. Indeed, the American Anthropological Association announced in 1947 that human rights were antithetical to decolonization. Ecumenical Protestants, however, argued that diminishing racism and ending colonialism went hand in hand with the spread of human rights. In doing so, they joined anti-colonial activists in the Global South and anti-racist activists in the United States in highlighting the anti-racist implications of human rights. Ecumenical Protestants used their public platform to broadcast these views widely.[1]

Ecumenical Protestant intellectuals were at the forefront of creating an anti-racist understanding of human rights. The work of missionary expert Edmund D. Soper and social ethicist Buell G. Gallagher, who are the subjects of this chapter, was especially important. Building on the anti-racist mobilization of the World Order movement, Soper and Gallagher developed comprehensive accounts of the link between anti-racism and international events. Soper penned the first systematic academic study of racism as a global phenomenon, while Gallagher produced one of the most forceful attacks on Jim Crow written by a white American prior to the 1960s. Both elevated anti-racist human rights above other priorities, like religious liberty and economic rights, which ecumenical Protestants were also drawn to. And their intellectual labor created the foundation of an understanding of human rights that went far beyond the specifically American and religious milieu. Soper and Gallagher promoted an anti-racist understanding of human rights that became popular across the world.[2]

Ecumenical Protestant intellectuals writing about racism in the 1940s moved increasingly toward structural criticism of racism, and they adopted a global framework. They also took steps away from color-blind liberalism and toward ensuring ethnic and racial pluralism. As this chapter shows, Soper and Gallagher criticized racism by drawing on social science and the missionary movement and by celebrating the racial cosmopolitanism of Brazil and the racial pluralism of the Soviet Union as two models for the United States to emulate. Their ideas, rooted in a global exploration of racism, made their way into the Federal Council of Churches' pathbreaking statement on human rights in 1948, which was popularly understood as a condemnation of segregation. Human rights would be the most important and enduring expression of these new commitments.

Racism as a Global Phenomenon

A new anxiety gripped American ecumenical Protestants during World War II. Some began to wonder if the world was dividing itself into racial blocs that would one day go to war with one another. Soper warned his fellow Protestants in 1943 that "world racial consciousness . . . binds the minority groups together in a growing solidarity." In the 1930s and 1940s ecumenical Protestants took seriously Japan's claim that it was building a pan-Asian sphere of influence. The intensity of the rhetoric of the "master race" coming from Germany, combined with the ruthlessness of what one historian has called a "race war" between the United States and Japan, made the organization of the world into racial blocs seem not only plausible but likely.[3] Some ecumenical Protestant intellectuals warned about looming race wars and worried that racism was the biggest danger to the postwar order they were working to create.

Decolonization was ascendant, but European powers showed little appetite for giving up their colonies. "I have not become the King's First Minister in order to preside over the liquidation of the British Empire," announced Winston Churchill in 1942.[4] Imperial and anti-colonial forces, some ecumenical Protestants feared, were on a collision course and had the potential to realign global politics around race. As Gallagher put it, "Peace built on white supremacy is the guarantee of tomorrow's global war on race lines."[5]

Anxiety about a potential anti-imperialist coalition of colonial and post-colonial nations was built on a long history of warnings from cheerleaders of the West's supremacy. Lothrop Stoddard warned white Americans in his 1920 book *The Rising Tide of Color Against the White World-Supremacy* that World War I had weakened global European domination and that "the colored world, long restive under white political domination, is being welded by the most fundamental of instincts, the instinct of self-preservation, into a common solidarity of feeling against the dominant white man."[6] Stoddard was especially concerned about immigration and called for America to stop the tide of foreigners from flooding the country. Turning Stoddard's argument on its head, Gallagher and Soper argued that the United States could only avert war with the nonwhite world by renouncing white supremacy, ending imperialism, and distributing the world's resources more equitably.

Ecumenical Protestant intellectuals were not the only Americans changing their minds about racism. As they began earnestly engaging with the complicated issues of race in the 1940s, they drew upon the social scientific research conducted in prior decades. Anthropologists, especially secular Jews and women in that profession, had done more than any other academic community to change the public dialogue on race by undermining the biological arguments that supported white supremacy. The first major challenge to biological racism came from the German Jewish émigré and Columbia University anthropologist Franz Boas, whose 1911 book, *The Mind of Primitive Man*, made the case for treating race and culture separately.[7] Boas pioneered cultural relativism as a methodology, and he insisted that the environment shapes human difference. Later, his students declared that race has nothing to do with culture. Ruth Benedict made this same point in her popular works, including *Race: Science and Politics* (1940) and *The Races of Mankind* (1943). The latter book was co-authored with Gene Weltfish, another of Boas's female students, who grew up in a German-speaking Jewish family. Ecumenical Protestant intellectuals cited these books frequently.

Jewish groups also mobilized against racism in the 1940s and focused on combatting antisemitic attacks emanating from Nazi Germany and from fascist sympathizers in the United States. Responding to antisemitism meant embracing both religious and racial tolerance through the framework of "human relations."[8] Catholics also experimented with new ways of combating racism. The most novel approach was the lawsuit launched in California with the help of the Catholic Interracial Council, which culminated in the 1948 court case *Perez v. Sharp*. The plaintiffs (a Mexican American woman, who was legally designated as white, and an African American man) were denied a marriage license because of a ban on interracial marriage. They argued that this was a violation of their religious freedom because their Catholic religion made no racial distinctions among the faithful. Although the court case eventually overturned California's miscegenation laws on the grounds of the 14th Amendment, and not on the grounds of religious liberty, it nonetheless demonstrated that some Catholics were finding new ways to challenge segregation with arguments grounded in their religious tradition.[9]

On the whole, however, Catholic churchgoers and Catholic priests resisted integration in the 1940s. A commitment to the territorial boundaries of the parish system, along with congregations organized around ethnicity and language, often translated into resistance against a growing African American population in urban centers.[10] Many Jews began to leave urban areas in the 1940s, moving to suburban areas from which African Americans were largely excluded.[11] Protestants also moved to newly built suburbs in large numbers. Like most other American religious groups, ecumenical Protestantism remained thoroughly segregated by race.[12]

American ecumenical Protestants, Catholics, religious and secular Jews, and women all made important contributions to the dialogue on race in the 1940s, but, in that decade, it would be a foreigner who penned the most influential treatise on race in America. The Swedish sociologist Gunner Myrdal's *An American Dilemma*, published in 1944, set the terms of the debate about segregation.[13] Myrdal's central thesis was that most Americans believed in a set of liberal principles, including "the essential dignity of man" and "the importance of protecting and cultivating his personality" against "the doctrines of caste, class, and slavery."[14] While Americans believed this "American Creed," Myrdal argued, they rarely put these values into practice. Myrdal's American Creed was more wishful thinking than a description of Americans' beliefs in 1944, historians now argue.[15] But Myrdal's thesis was a powerful rhetorical weapon, and it echoed what some Protestant activists had been saying for many years. Along those lines, ecumenical Protestant intellectuals argued that Christianity stood in opposition to racism and that most Protestants knew it. The solution ecumenical Protestant intellectuals like Soper and Gallagher proposed was for the faithful to begin acting more like Christ.

While ecumenical Protestants borrowed from anthropologists and sociologists, and built upon their own long-standing concerns about racism, they also viewed diminishing white supremacy as central to the implementation of their postwar vision. American ecumenical Protestants worried that their World Order movement would run aground on the rocks of white supremacy. The two intellectuals who offered the clearest course to ending colonialism and racism were Soper and Gallagher. A social ethics professor at the Pacific School of Religion in Berkeley, California, Gallagher was a lifelong anti-racist activist. He had spent the 1930s as president of the historically Black Talladega College and served as a vice president in the NAACP. He represented a wing of Protestantism long involved in the Black freedom struggle in America.

Soper was a professor of missions at Garrett Theological Seminary in Evanston, Illinois. For two decades he had written about the missionary movement and the encounter between different world religions.[16] He represented a wing of Protestantism rooted in the missionary project, which grew concerned about racism because of the obstacles it created for the spread of Christianity in the Global South.[17] Although their interests in combating racism emerged under different circumstances, Gallagher and Soper agreed that white supremacy was the chief challenge for the postwar world.

Soper's efforts on the issue of global white supremacy began in 1942, when he was asked to prepare a position paper on "race" for a Methodist meeting, which was attended by such leftist luminaries as Vice President Henry A. Wallace (who would run for president in 1946 on the Progressive Party ticket) and Methodist bishop Francis McConnell, the sponsor of the left-wing Methodist Federation for Social Action. Soper, the consummate professor, dove deeply into the history and practice of racism by organizing an ongoing seminar on race in 1942 and 1943 at Garrett Seminary, an endeavor that included biblical scholars and church historians, but consisting mostly of missionary experts.[18] Soper brought together the many ideas expressed by these professors into a single, authoritative statement on the Methodist views of race.

After hearing reports from fellow missionaries from around the world, Soper concluded that a "growing solidarity" between nonwhite peoples was emerging. Soper also warned that communism was spreading in places like China and among African Americans because it was convincing people that it was "the only movement which is taking seriously the task of brotherhood among men." As Soper argued, Americans were constrained by their history, making it hard for them to oppose racism. If Protestants would rise up to challenge white supremacy, they would have to overcome racism, which is, as he put it, "of long standing and is rooted in our colonial history, in the feeling of superiority toward the Indians, and that this same feeling was carried over into our dealings with other races in other lands as well as in our relations with the Negroes."[19]

Soper's solution was in line with broader ecumenical Protestant thinking on racism in the 1940s. He called for a "Pacific Charter," to be modeled on the Atlantic Charter, to grant self-determination and better economic conditions to the peoples of Asia. Moreover, eradicating racism at home, Soper concluded, would have global ramifications for the missionary movement. At home, he urged Christians to eliminate antisemitic references in their literature, and he pushed for Congress to eliminate the poll tax, extend the Fair Employment Practices Commission, and eliminate inequalities in education and social services among racial groups.[20]

Soper understood that he had to tread carefully. After all, the Methodist Church was segregated, and criticism of these arrangements would provoke church leaders more than discussions of poll taxes would. Without ever denouncing segregation, Soper called for a study on the segregated jurisdiction system of the Methodist Church ("to ascertain whether this plan involves anything else than separation for the largest mutual service," he wrote cryptically) and to open up church schools and hospitals to African Americans.[21] Ralph E. Diffendorfer, who served as executive secretary of the Board of Missions of the Methodist Church from 1939 to 1949, was so impressed with Soper's work that he came to believe racism and colonialism would be the central issues for the missionary movement after the war ended. Diffendorfer therefore provided funds and connections for Soper to carry on research into racism across the globe.

Soper was no activist, but he arrived at many of the same conclusions held by Benjamin Mays, Dorothy Tilly, Channing Tobias, Thelma Stevens, Will Alexander, and Liston Pope during the World Order movement. Soper had been unaware of their work for the Commission on Church and Minority

Peoples in 1942 and 1943, but by 1944 he had begun to collaborate with these figures, especially Stevens. He also began working closely with sociologist Robert Redfield and Howard University professor Rayford Logan, who lent social-scientific expertise to Soper's research. In the mid-1940s, Soper regularly spoke with virtually every major Protestant intellectual who had an interest in racism.[22] His efforts would result in the most systematic study of racism as a global phenomenon at the time.

The years of discussions and studies Soper headed in the 1940s culminated in the publication of his 1948 book, *Racism: A World Issue*. This text was the first systematic study of the past and present of racism across the world.[23] That such a pioneering study emerged in the ecumenical Protestant milieu demonstrates the importance of international affairs for this community, and the academic resources it wielded at mid-century. *Racism* took a historical perspective, with each chapter devoted to exploring how racism emerged in a different region of the world. Chapters began with a description of the genesis of ethnicities in a given country, followed by a chronology of the migrations of peoples in and out of the area. Soper then demonstrated that racism in each country was not a timeless phenomenon but that it had emerged at some moment in history for specific purposes. In the countries he surveyed, including India, China, Japan, Indonesia, and South Africa, Soper revealed the tenacity of racism by showing its links with economic, religious, and linguistic differences. Soper's book emphasized the variability of patterns in race relations, both historically and comparatively, and the complexity and uniqueness of racism in different regions of the world. A product of missionary thinking, *Racism: A World Issue* reflected a global frame of reference among ecumenical Protestants that was decades in the making.

Brazil and the Soviet Union as Model Societies

While Soper was deeply influenced by missionary activity, Buell Gallagher was shaped by his experiences within the United States. Gallagher had a long history of working closely with African Americans, which made him more sensitive to their mistreatment than were other Protestants. Gallagher was more critical of segregation, more open to working with secular organizations, and more willing to offer concrete political solutions to America's domestic and international problems. One of the more notable features of his 1946 book, *Color and Conscience*, was his familiarity with the contemporary writings on African American history and culture. Because Gallagher had spent a decade in the Jim Crow South, his outlook was strongly shaped by the Black-white binary. His understanding of world events was distinctly American.

Color and Conscience emerged at the same historical moment as Gunner Myrdal's more famous *An American Dilemma*, and both books emphasized the chasm between ideals and practices. As Gallagher put it, "Our difficulty is that, while we give theoretical assent to the idea [of racial equality], we postpone the day of ethical action until the irreversible course of history has carried us beyond the point where affirmative action is creative."[24] Gallagher's *Color and Conscience* was, in a way, a radical Christian's guide to *An American Dilemma*.[25]

The two books diverged in important ways. Historians sometimes chide Myrdal for turning segregation into a moral issue, rather than a political or economic one.[26] But Gallagher wove morality together with a structural understanding of racism. And he wrote with an urgency missing in Myrdal's book. "Our racial caste system has its historical roots in slavery but thrusts its contemporary tentacles into every crevice and cranny of the social structure throughout the nation," Gallagher told his readers. "Slavery as ownership of chattel is gone: as a caste system, it remains."[27]

Gallagher understood American racism in an international light with important consequences for America's role in the world. "The fanatical glee with which Radio Tokyo seized upon reports of racial difficulty in the United States and beamed them toward India and the Americans south of the Rio Grande is not accidental. [The race riots in] Los Angeles, Detroit, Houston, Beaumont, Sikenston, New York, Philadelphia, and other American cities have made headlines in the nonwhite world."[28] Gallagher made an argument that would later be mobilized by Cold War liberals against Jim Crow: that racism at home undermined America's fight against totalitarianism abroad.[29] The history of American imperialism and the news of white supremacy at home aided Japan, Gallagher told his readers. If the United States wanted to gain allies against fascism, it would have to jettison white supremacy more quickly than it was doing.[30]

Gallagher's goal was not only to condemn white supremacy but also to help Americans imagine an integrated future. When Protestant intellectuals imagined an America without racial segregation they looked abroad, especially to Brazil and the Soviet Union. The comparative perspective appealed to them because American history seemed to offer so little hope.

One could hardly find a "better" time for race relations that America could return to. It would not be until 1955 that C. Vann Woodward wrote the pioneering work *The Strange Career of Jim Crow* and popularized the idea of a usable past in race relations. Woodward argued that white and Black people lived together without strict segregation for a long period after the end of slavery in 1865 and before segregation was systematically implemented in the 1890s. If Jim Crow was constructed so late, and for political reasons, Woodward argued, it could also be undone.[31] But the 1940s were a period dominated by the historian U. B. Phillips, who depicted slavery in positive, uplifting terms, and the Dunning School's books on post–Civil War Reconstruction, which argued that Reconstruction was an irresponsible failure on the part of northern radicals. Gallagher, who was thoroughly conversant with the writings of W. E. B. Du Bois, Alain Locke, and Melville J. Herskovits, came closest to a historically rooted path to ending segregation in the United States. But, in general, ecumenical Protestant intellectuals believed comparisons with other nations were the best means of provincializing American racism and imagining other ways to organize their society.

Soper and Gallagher were taking part in a broader project among mid-century intellectuals to provincialize segregation. The work that bears most resemblance to their efforts was Frank Tannenbaum's 1946 book *Slave and Citizen.*[32] Tannenbaum, a German Jewish historian of Latin America at Columbia University, focused his book entirely on a single question: Why were descendants of enslaved people in the United States segregated, while in Latin America they experienced fewer barriers? Tannenbaum argued that the differences in postemancipation societies, especially the differences between the United States and Brazil, were shaped by different legal and religious traditions. The Iberians inherited the Roman system of slavery and viewed the enslaved person as a contractual partner, Tannenbaum argued, and therefore, "the element of human personality was not lost" when slavery was implemented in Spanish and Portuguese colonies in the Americas.[33] In British colonies, however, there was little legal precedent for slavery, and therefore few customs and legal barriers existed against the dehumanization of the enslaved person and their complete exploitation. In the United States, with its British inheritance, the slave was not subject to protection by the state nor targeted as often by Christians for conversion. In postemancipation societies, these differences in treatment carried over from slavery. "The nature of our problem is conditioned by the time it will take for the Negro to have acquired a moral personality equal to his legal one," Tannenbaum argued. "The 'solution' of the Negro problem is essentially a matter of establishing the Negro in the sight of the white community as a human being equal to its own members."[34]

Soper took up Tannenbaum's cause. He emphasized the centrality of human personality, the importance of religion, and an emphasis on just how unusual the United States was in its strict racial segregation. He also spoke with ease about racial boundary crossing, including "miscegenation" and "amalgamation." Soper shared Tannenbaum's exaggeration of differences between Brazil and the United States, ignoring what historians now note as enduring racial hierarchies in the Latin American nation.[35] Nevertheless, Brazil provided a model for the United States.

Soper noted that Brazil had slavery far later than the United States and only banned the practice in 1888, when the remaining 700,000 enslaved persons were freed by national decree. Before 1888, slavery was becoming incrementally less important to Brazilian society, and manumissions were frequent. The end of slavery in Brazil appeared easy to Soper in comparison with the United States, which fought a civil war over the issue. Although Brazilians shared with the United States a history of slavery, their Catholic faith and preservation of human personality of enslaved peoples created a nonsegregated postemancipation society, he argued.

The lax racial boundaries in Brazilian society were transmitted to the country by the Portuguese, Soper argued. Early in their history, the Portuguese brought enslaved Africans to Portugal, but they did not create strict racial separation. Over time, the enslaved Africans intermarried with the local population. "All the peoples of southern Europe are more liberal than those of northern Europe with respect to intermarriage with other races," Soper wrote. But "none of them mingle their blood, however, more freely than do the Portuguese. They seem to be 'color blind.' This characteristic they naturally carried with them into Brazil."[36]

In the 1940s, nothing embarrassed Protestants like an unfavorable comparison with Catholics. Readers of Soper's book understood that Portugal and Brazil were Catholic nations, whereas the northern Europeans he chastised were predominantly Protestant. To dramatize the point, Soper employed an idea developed by historian Arnold Toynbee that racism was more prevalent in Protestant societies. Toynbee was a popular historian who in the 1940s was half-way through his ten-volume history of the world. Toynbee's emphasis on religious ideas as central characteristics of civilizations made his work especially popular in the United States, which remained more religious than the United Kingdom, Toynbee's home country. One of his claims, which ecumenical Protestant intellectuals dubbed the "Toynbee thesis," attracted the most attention. Toynbee argued in his sixth volume that it was no accident that the nations with the strictest forms of racial segregation (including the United States, South Africa, Australia, and Canada) were predominantly Protestant ones. Protestants, argued Toynbee, interpreted differences between themselves and racial others as divinely ordained and they had a peculiar anxiety about their racial dominance because, as the Bible prophesized, "the last will be first and the first will be last." The fear of reversals of power and reprisals by nonwhites made white Protestants cling tenaciously to their feelings of superiority, Toynbee argued.[37]

Ecumenical Protestant intellectuals used the Toynbee thesis to criticize ministers and churchgoers, particularly those who held fundamentalist views and affirmed the biblical literalism that Toynbee seemed to blame for racism. Galen Fisher, the former missionary and activist against Japanese internment, was the strongest proponent of the thesis. It was at the heart of a position paper he delivered to the Commission on Church and Minority Peoples in April 1945.[38] Fisher thought that the contrast Toynbee made between Protestant and Catholic civilizations was too clearly cut, but he was equally insistent that "racism today is most acute where Whites of Protestant antecedents dominate." With the Boers of South Africa in particular, their explicit use of Old Testament metaphors to justify their oppression of native Africans and their rebellion against the British confirmed the thesis for Fisher. Aside from its explanatory power, the Toynbee thesis affirmed the theological liberalism of ecumenical Protestant intellectuals and bolstered their confidence about leading the more conservative laity and clergy away from their outdated beliefs.[39]

Soper was no radical, but by contrasting the United States with Brazil he occasionally celebrated ideas that in the 1940s were more often associated with the Communist Party than with Protestant ministers. For example, he praised the Catholic acceptance of interracial marriage. He argued that, in the Brazilian context, it was good for the "serious" Europeans to mix with the "gay" Africans. There was already a lot of intermixture by 1890, when the last census that included race as a category was taken in Brazil. Soper relativized the American conventions of racial classifications by attacking the "one-drop rule." In the United States, "'a drop of black blood' in a person makes him a Negro," he wrote, but "in Brazil a slight amount of white blood in a person makes him a white."[40] Political leaders of Brazil also applauded the creation of a distinctly Brazilian race, according to Soper, and celebrated each of the racial heritages of this new people. In contrasting the two societies, Soper exaggerated the racial inclusion of Brazil. He did not ignore the social differences between light- and dark-skinned people in Brazil, but he did minimize them. "The problem is clearly one of caste, or social and economic standing, and not of race, but it is just as evident that it has racial roots," wrote Soper.[41] He believed Brazil was in the process of overcoming the racial divide. Nonetheless, his point about the differences between the two countries was startling. In the 1940s it was quite a thing to be celebrating the racial mixing of Brazilians and promoting the country's racial practices as a model for Americans to follow.

Soper used Brazil's example to argue that the social conventions of the United States are not only provincial but also that they could be rapidly transformed. The racial fluidity in Brazil pointed to the malleability of human nature. "Brazilians are a part of our humanity, but with a different background, exposed to a different social attitude, and definitely educated to think of races as equal, not innately inferior or superior," Soper wrote. "These people have shown that human nature can react very differently to the fundamental problem of racial intermingling. Increasingly we must study the problem from their angle and learn the values which they find in practices far different from our own."[42] Soper was instructing his fellow Americans that alternatives to segregation existed. They only had to look beyond America's borders.

Gallagher and Soper looked to the Soviet Union, along with Brazil, for an example of state policy and social practices that offered an alternative to American segregation. They were buoyed by the American wartime alliance with the USSR and sought to promote Soviet nationality policy while muting their criticism of communism and holding out hope for incremental reform in the communist country. Gallagher and Soper did so at a perilous time following World War II, when politicians like Harry Truman and Winston Churchill were sounding the alarm about communist aggression. Yet Soper and Gallagher found much to like in Soviet practices, and they believed, however naively, that a shared respect for the rights of ethnic and racial minorities could become a basis for cooperation between the two nations.

The Soviet Union's rapidly transformed attitude toward Jews stood out to Gallagher and Soper. "At no point can the Russian change in attitude toward alien groups be studied more advantageously" than in the case of the Jews, wrote Soper.[43] In the early twentieth century, the Russian Empire sponsored violent pogroms against Jews. But only a few decades later, the USSR celebrated national differences and incorporated all peoples into the state and society, and welcomed Jews into public life, Soper believed. The scale of the migration from the Pale of Settlement to Moscow, Saint Petersburg, and other Soviet cities dwarfed the immigration of Jews to the United States and Palestine prior to World War II.[44] Like other observers, Soper missed the rising antisemitism in the postwar USSR. And he said little about the forced expulsion of Germans, Tatars, and other nationalities during the war, which were matters of public knowledge. Despite these omissions, he got a lot right about the socialist country. Soper lauded the Soviet policy of promoting indigenous languages, barring discrimination by law, promoting a respect of national cultures and traditions, and involving peripheral peoples in all aspects of social and political life.

It made sense for Soper to see the Soviet Union as a model society in the 1940s. He looked to a country that, according to Yuri Slezkine, "was the world's first state to institutionalize ethnoterritorial federalism, classify all citizens according to their biological nationalities and formally prescribe preferential treatment of certain ethnically defined populations."[45] While Karl Marx wrote about imperialism as a force that would thrust the backward peoples of Asia into the modern world, Vladimir Lenin, the Soviet Union's first leader, used anti-imperialism as a weapon in his revolutionary struggle. During World War I and the Russian civil war that followed, he renounced territorial concessions, called for national independence for colonial nations, and granted cultural autonomy to many nationalities in the former Russian Empire. According to Francine Hirsch, Soviet experts pursued a policy of "double assimilation" within the USSR, which encouraged people to become Soviet by becoming members of an ethnonationality.[46] Lenin created new republics, like the Belarussian and Uzbek Soviet Socialist Republics, which would have some linguistic and cultural autonomy, while remaining part of the Soviet Union's political community.[47]

The Soviet Union provided a model for how to deal with a plurality of racial minorities in one nation, according to Soper. The differences between the USSR and United States resulted from the differing legal regimes, he explained. The United States practiced the "melting pot theory," in which immigrants were expected to "merge, lose their former distinctive features, and become completely amalgamated," whereas the USSR had a policy of "local and racial autonomy," with a stated purpose of retaining "distinctiveness, language, traditions, and customs." The USSR also incorporated anti-racist language into its constitution. Soper tied together the problem of racial bias with enumerated rights, arguing that we are "beginning to realize that the racial problem is not a problem by itself but one which is a part of another, that of basic human rights."[48]

Gallagher also applauded the USSR, praising the country's legislation "against any expression, oral or written, of any kind of antipathy or prejudice between national and racial groups within the Soviet Union."[49] Gallagher was especially appreciative of the active recognition bestowed on minorities in the USSR: "The Soviets have made a thoroughgoing effort to recognize the values of each minority and its culture, however small in numbers. It is not merely that the negative job has been done in making sure that 'race' constitutes no disadvantage to any person within the Union. It is much more than that. The positive values of each distinctive culture—in language, customs, costumes, dietary habits and tastes, art, literature, drama, education, religion, and the like—are openly encouraged and carefully nurtured."[50] It was not enough to get rid of racism, Gallagher argued. The United States needed to do more to actively include racial minorities in the cultural, social, and political life of the country. Gallagher and Soper both praised ethnic pluralism and celebrated the USSR as a model multicultural society.

In 1947, Soper's celebration of Soviet policy was surprising and unusual. The Cold War had begun, and ministers across the country were warning about the dangers of Soviet atheism. Just a few years later, evangelist Billy Graham would be catapulted to fame, in part, for attacking the USSR. Despite this hostility, or perhaps because of it, Soper continued to insist that there was plenty to praise in the communist country. He was hoping to bridge the Cold War divide by finding common goals for the two countries to work on. Soper argued that the Soviet Union's casting away of barriers to fundamental freedoms was "one of the greatest steps forward in human progress," which placed "man, the common man, equal and free . . . in the center of the entire program."[51] According to Soper, this was the misleading part about the USSR: Stalin might seem like "virtually a dictator," but at the bottom of society, at the level of the soviet, "there is real democracy."[52] And he argued that this ought to give Americans hope for the future of the USSR and for Soviet-American relations.

Soper defined democracy in ethnoracial terms, arguing that true democracy is constituted by people working together to run their society while celebrating their ethnic differences. Again, Soper returned to language, saying that the Soviet policy was a good one, requiring everyone to learn a single language while also cultivating regional ones. There was much to be done in the USSR, particularly in improving the treatment of religious minorities, he wrote. However, "With all this the Soviet Union stands before the world as the only land, with the exception of Brazil, where racism is completely repudiated; where no assumption of inherent superiority of any group over any other is allowed; where the minority groups are possessed of a new self-respect; where youth can allow their ambitions to soar, knowing that there is no extraneous, arbitrary barrier to fulfillment, except the limits of their own abilities and perseverance."[53] Resisting the emerging logic of the Cold War, Soper insisted that the Soviet Union was a model of racial pluralism and urged Americans to take it seriously.

While discussing race and ethnicity in the Soviet Union, Soper challenged the conventions of the United States and of Protestant Christianity. He argued that when Soviet policy is "reviewed against the background of the Russian past it fills one with hope" for countries like the United States. It should remind us that "no fundamental change can be expected . . . without some powerful motivation" like communism.[54] It went without saying that Soper believed Christianity would be that "powerful motivation" in the United States.

In order to shame American Christians, Gallagher turned to the work communists in the United States had been doing to help African Americans. Calling Christian activities on behalf of minorities "meager, halting, and largely ineffective," he chastised "the Christian Church, which includes well over half the adult population of these United States," for not producing "an ethical attack on color caste which approaches the vigor and virility of the attack launched by the American Communists."[55] Gallagher was no fan of communism, but he also recognized the shortcomings of American Protestants in light of the energy the Communist Party devoted to fighting racism.[56]

Both Gallagher and Soper called for a Christian crusade against racism, which would aid America's domestic minorities and the country's foreign relations. The Cold War was just beginning, and, Gallagher pointed out in 1946, the Soviet Union would not cooperate with the United States so long as segregation continued. And the nonwhite peoples of the world would not come to America's aid if tensions with the USSR worsened. Whether American Protestants wanted friendly relations with the USSR or saw communism as Christianity's main competitor, they needed to jettison racism quickly. Gallagher and Soper were providing models for their country to do just that.

What gave these authors such confidence in Christianity's ability to overcome racism? For Gallagher the sources of his hope were in the historical precedents of abolitionism and the wave of missionaries to the American South in the wake of Reconstruction. He was also encouraged by the World Order movement. Others, like Galen Fisher, saw hope in the work of missionaries around the world. Fisher credited ecumenical Protestant missionaries working in India, China, and other nations for stoking a racial and national self-respect among colonial peoples. He took pride in the overrepresentation of Christians in the Korean independence movement and in the professional classes of China. He also noted the contribution of the YMCA to Indian autonomy. The organization appointed an Indian to run its national bureaucracy, and he became the first Indian to head a nationwide organization in the colony. Fisher believed that Christianity abroad was promoting modernization and decolonization.[57]

The faith that Gallagher, Soper, and Fisher placed in the missionary movement is hard to square with the long history of Christian imperialism.[58] Yet their generous assessment was shared by many others in the 1940s, including the elder statesman of Pan-Africanism, W. E. B. Du Bois. In his 1945 book, *Color and Democracy: Colonies and Peace*, Du Bois began a chapter on "Missions and Mandates" with a call for the creation of "a new mandates commission implemented by that unselfish devotion to the well-being of mankind which has often, if not always, inspired the missionary crusade."[59] Like Gallagher, Du Bois drew inspiration "especially in the Christian missions of the eighteenth and nineteenth centuries; in the suppression of slavery and the slave trade; and in the various attempts to alleviate, if not abolish, poverty and to do away with ignorance."[60]

Du Bois, who was Gallagher's longtime acquaintance, also noted Christianity's history of imperialism and chauvinism, but quickly moved past it. According to Du Bois, "It is all too clear today that if we are to have a sufficient motive for the uplift of backward peoples, for the redemption and progress of colonials, such a motive can be found only in the faith and ideals of organized religion."[61] As it happened, Du Bois and the NAACP were cooperating with the Reverend Michael Scott, a white missionary in South West Africa. At the United Nations, Scott publicized the devastating effects of South Africa's policies in the trusteeship of South West Africa and successfully prevented South Africa from annexing this former German colony.[62] Du Bois disavowed personal faith, but he believed in the ability of the Christian missionary project to undermine colonialism.

The belief that the ecumenical Protestant churches would rise up against segregation was a faith that the Protestant establishment maintained through the 1940s and well after. But for those who investigated the history of American churches, the real tenuousness of this faith became clear. As the Commission on Church and Minority Peoples had already shown, segregation ran deep in the country's churches. It was not surprising that Gallagher had to reach back one hundred years to the abolition movement or that Soper had to reach beyond America's shores to find models for fighting racism.

Two observations haunted Gallagher and Soper. The first was that the officially atheistic USSR and Catholic Brazil, along with the Communist Party in the United States, were taking the lead in fighting racial segregation and white supremacy. The second shock was the widespread acceptance of segregation among white Protestants in the United States. Soper and Gallagher hoped that the World Order movement would change the hearts and minds of American Christians. Since little in Protestantism's recent history had been effective in overcoming segregation, a departure was needed from the recent past. Like advocates of the social gospel, who reached back to a distant past to justify their theological departures, so too did white anti-racist intellectuals reach back to earlier traditions like abolitionism and outward to the missionary movement to justify their attack on racism and segregation. They also linked their worldwide explorations of racism to the new language of human rights.

Soper and Gallagher encouraged ecumenical Protestants to see human rights as a condemnation of structural racism and a call for political solutions. Like the Commission on Church and Minority Peoples before them, Soper and Gallagher viewed racism as a structural problem. The first step Soper and Gallagher took toward a structural view of racism was in separating out prejudice and segregation. Soper pointed out that "ill will" toward African Americans was often not present in segregated churches. Segregation maintains itself not in fear or hatred of other races, but through "racism, the assumption of inherent superiority of white over black." Racism can be expressed in "benevolent pity" or charity, but it always presumes a racial hierarchy, Soper wrote.[63] This solidification of racial attitudes into social conventions occurred all over the world, with India's caste system standing as a prominent example. In India, Soper argued, early feelings of racial superiority had created the caste system, but the early motivations had faded away. He felt that in the United States, as in India, racism could not be overcome without dismantling segregation.[64]

As an expression of this structural understanding of racism, Gallagher enumerated a series of rights that the Federal Council had been promoting in the 1940s. These included color-blind hiring and the right to join a union; the "opportunity and encouragement to register, vote, run for office, and serve when elected"; and access to housing and public facilities, including "restaurants, hotels, trains, and buses."[65] These social and economic rights had been explored by the wartime Committee on Church and Minority Peoples, affirmed by the Federal Council in 1946, and prefigured the social and economic human rights expressed by the Federal Council and the UN's Universal Declaration of Human Rights in 1948.

Following through on this understanding of racism, Gallagher went further than Soper in seeking a political solution to Jim Crow. He ran for Congress in 1948 on a platform that emphasized "strengthening the United Nations and correcting the immoralities of racism, narrow nationalism, and kindred evils which endanger permanent world peace."[66] He had been recruited by unions in Berkeley and Oakland to run for office, and, although he ran as a Democrat, Gallagher aligned his platform with Henry Wallace's Progressive Party, the left-wing alternative to Harry Truman's Democrats.[67] Although Gallagher found broad support in the Bay Area, he could not overcome the Red-baiting attacks waged against him by his anti-communist opponent. He lost by a very narrow margin of 49 to 51 percent.[68]

Few ecumenical Protestant intellectuals became so directly involved in electoral politics as Gallagher had. But the ideas that drove him to run for Congress were becoming more widespread among ecumenical Protestant clergy. The global frame of reference promoted by the World Order movement and the politically oriented anti-racism developed by the Commission on Church and Minority Peoples merged together in the postwar writings of Gallagher and Soper. The global understanding of racism they promoted fit neatly with the universal character of 1940s-era human rights talk. Although neither Gallagher nor Soper were directly involved in the Federal Council's deliberations about human rights, their work influenced the organization's pathbreaking declaration of human rights in 1948.

Human Rights and the Attack on Global Racism

The leaders of the Federal Council of Churches believed that a distinctly Protestant statement on human rights was needed in 1948, just as the United

Nations was completing its work on the Universal Declaration of Human Rights. Unlike the vast majority of human rights declarations that came out in the late 1940s, the Federal Council was virtually alone among predominantly white American groups in focusing attention on racism. And, as it turned out, the Federal Council's 1948 human rights statement would announce the organization's stand against segregation to American churchgoers, to the US public, and to the world.

The Federal Council had already gone on record in 1946 in opposition to segregation but did its best to keep its political implications from everyday churchgoers and from the American public. The human rights statement, on the other hand, could not be kept under wraps. For one thing, Harry Truman's President's Commission on Civil Rights had delivered in 1947 its report, *To Secure These Rights*, which asked Congress and the president to implement reforms that would diminish segregation in the United States. Congress demurred, but Truman acted to slowly desegregate the military and the federal workforce on his own authority. He also incorporated many of the commission's recommendations into his reelection planks in 1948 as he faced Republican nominee Thomas Dewey, the Progressive Henry Wallace, and the segregationist candidate, Strom Thurmond. In this tense political atmosphere, any statement on segregation by the Federal Council was bound to attract attention. Human rights became the means through which ecumenical Protestants publicly announced their attack on segregation.

The Federal Council's human rights statement came out of their regular biennial meeting, which took place at the end of 1948 in Cincinnati, Ohio, yet another city from a state whose convention industry proved so hospitable to interracial assemblies.[69] The sixteen-member commission drafting the human rights declaration was composed largely of veterans of the Federal Council, representing four of its departments, and many were old hands of the Commission on Church and Minority Peoples and the Department of Race Relations, including Channing Tobias, Will W. Alexander, Liston Pope, and Dorothy Height. The group drafting the human rights statement also included University of Texas president Homer P. Rainey and Methodist minister Nelson Cruikshank, who was then working for the American Federation of Labor and would later write the 1956 Social Security Act. They were joined by Frederick Nolde, the head of a church commission that had been working on human rights and religious liberty for several years.[70]

The drafting committee began its work on November 6, 1948, which left its members less than a month to outline a human rights statement. The quick pace meant that the authors had to rely on precedent. The document's global viewpoint, its emphasis on social, economic, and political rights, and its singling out of racism as the biggest threat to world order all pointed to the influence of the works produced by ecumenical Protestant intellectuals in the 1940s. Whereas the World Council of Churches, dominated in large part by European theologians, made a statement in 1948 that emphasized the human right of religious liberty, the Federal Council's emphasis on desegregation was unmistakable.

The Federal Council's 1948 statement on human rights began by observing that human beings "are God's creatures and have infinite worth in His sight." People had a responsibility to obey God's moral law, but they also had God-given rights, which are meant "for the state to embody . . . in its own legal system and to ensure their observance in practice." The first rights listed were "Personal Rights," including freedom of religion and conscience; freedom of speech, press, and inquiry; freedom of association and assembly; and freedom from arbitrary arrest, police brutality, and mob violence. The Federal Council argued that the rights "have been for long generally recognized in our society" but were "in jeopardy at present." The ecumenical Protestant leaders added an anti-racist emphasis that had been previously missing in discussions of personal freedoms. The Federal Council announced that these rights "cannot be obtained under a system of racial segregation," and it reaffirmed its earlier "renunciation of the pattern of segregation as . . . a violation of the gospel of love and human brotherhood. As proof of their sincerity, the churches must work for a non-segregated church and a non-segregated society."[71]

Economic and social rights were newer to Americans. Among the economic human rights the council enumerated were an adequate standard of living and a family wage, the right to employment with fair compensation, and the right to join a labor union. And all Americans were entitled to the social right to adequate living space, the right to education and professional training, the right to recreational facilities, to use communal social services, to adequate health services, to transportation on the basis of equality, and "to receive equal service from businesses and persons serving the public, such as stores, theaters, hotels and restaurants." The political rights included the right to vote secretly for alternative choices, equality before the law, the right to run for public office, the right to participate fully in all branches of government, including the military, and the right to organize peaceful political activity.[72] As with personal rights, the ecumenical leaders stressed that the social, economic, and political rights were incompatible with Jim Crow. The Federal Council's list of human rights encompassed virtually every demand of the African American political struggle of the era.

Americans took notice of ecumenical Protestants' denunciation of segregation. Front-page headlines across the country pronounced, "End of Racial Segregation Asked by Churches' Council," according to the *New York Times*, and "Protestant Council Indorses Complete End of Segregation," according to the *Washington Post*. The *Chicago Defender* noted that a Federal Council delegation brought the human rights statement to a White House meeting with President Truman. An array of religious institutions—radio programs, the religious press, schools, and local churches—spread this message from coast to coast. The Federal Council took a public stance in 1948 that racism within the United States was a human rights issue.[73]

While the press spread the Federal Council's message that racial equality was a human right, others resisted it. Defenders of segregation understood that human rights were a challenge to Jim Crow. John M. Alexander of the Southern Presbyterians was on the drafting committee for this document. The Southern Presbyterian denomination had joined the Federal Council in 1944 and proved to be the organization's most devoted supporter of segregation. It was typical for commissions like the human rights working group to include one or two conservative white southerners in order to represent what was often called the "Southern viewpoint," and Alexander served his role by delivering a sharp criticism of the human rights document. Clashing with the new perspective of ecumenical Protestants swayed by the ideas of Gallagher and Soper, Alexander chastised his fellow Protestants for failing to recognize that "social attitudes change slowly." Contrary to Soper's belief that the law could change attitudes, as it had in the USSR, Alexander argued that when laws move ahead of public opinion they do more harm than good. Instead of social engineering through the law, it is better to cultivate "patience and good will," he argued. Furthermore, "constitutions should not be ignored" when discussing laws, Alexander said. It was a gesture to the states' rights argument that so many white Southern Protestants found persuasive.[74]

Alexander reminded the human rights drafting committee in 1948 that the South had a lot of peculiarities—slavery, war, reconstruction, and "conquered territory attitudes"—that would make change slower in that region than others. Referring to northern hypocrisy on the issue of segregation, he urged the Federal Council to take up the fight "in regions that do not have our inherent complexes." Changes in the North or West "would speak louder than statements and pronouncements." As for mob violence, Alexander argued to his colleagues, the South had done quite a bit of good on its own, without federal interference. He ended his comments with statistics that he believed showed that whites were rarely violent toward African Americans.[75]

Alexander's comments were received respectfully, but he was outvoted. At Cincinnati in 1948, the human rights statement was approved without dissent but with numerous abstentions. Even in defeat, Alexander did not want to air his grievances and create discord with his fellow Protestants despite the high stakes of the human rights document. But others did. J. McDowell Richards, also a Southern Presbyterian representative to the Federal Council, spoke out against the human rights statement and abstained from voting because, he said, "We are trying to achieve in a moment what will take many years to achieve," and that he believed a "measure of voluntary segregation is expedient." Then a Methodist bishop from Pennsylvania tried to bury the human rights statement by having it referred to the Executive Committee of the Federal Council so that it could be revised and perhaps gotten rid of.[76]

But they were both met with opposition. The last speaker on the issue, the Reverend L. K. Jackson, an African American minister from Gary, Indiana, gave a moving address. "Most of you do not know the horror of having money in your pocket and not being able to buy food or being sleepy and not being able to find a place to sleep," he told his mostly white colleagues. Jackson's speech was "roundly cheered."[77] The motion to refer the document to the Federal Council's Executive Committee was withdrawn, and the human rights statement became the official position of the Federal Council of Churches.

The fight was not over. Alexander waited until after the 1948 conference to publicly air his misgivings about the document. Reiterating the go-slow argument, he donned the mantle of Niebuhrian realism, arguing that "the realistic approach" was to "start where we are, that is to say, within the framework of social segregation" and to use the formula of "equal but separate" to ensure "progress for the Negro in the South." Quoting a "prominent theologian"— probably Niebuhr himself—Alexander warned against the dangers of the "perfectionists" whose utopian goals cannot be reached right away.[78]

It is not surprising that the Southern Presbyterians dissented from the human rights statement, given the then recent developments in their denomination. In 1946, in the midst of a coordinated renunciation of segregation by a number of Christian organizations, the Southern Presbyterians formed a study commission to consider whether Black Presbyterian churches should be expelled from the denomination and placed into a new segregated denomination. Even though they did not follow through, the Southern Presbyterians were the only denomination affiliated with the Federal Council to become more supportive of segregation in the mid-1940s. Even the Southern Baptists, who were not members of the Federal Council, passed several resolutions calling for better race relations and improved conditions for African Americans during this period.[79]

Southern Presbyterians like Alexander and Richards, and others from different denominations and regions who shared their views, were segregationists of a particular kind. They were what Martin Luther King Jr. would describe in "Letter from a Birmingham Jail" as white moderates who were "more devoted to 'order' than to justice" and "paternalistically" believed they could "set the timetable for another man's freedom."[80] To the right of these white moderates, in the 1940s (and in the 1960s) were theological racists. Theological racists argued that God ordained the races to live apart from one another and cited stories like the curse of Ham in the book of Genesis to support their cause. Theological racism was especially widespread among the grassroots of southern denominations.[81]

White moderates abetted the political goals of theological racists, but they refused to do so on the grounds of biblical curses and God's commandments. By the end of 1948 very few ecumenical Protestant leaders were willing to publicly support white supremacy, and fewer still were willing to root it in Christian teachings. Even Alexander and Richards acknowledged desegregation as an ultimate goal. Sensing the ground shifting beneath their feet, Alexander and Richards were merely proclaiming what had been common sense among white ecumenical Protestant leaders a few years earlier. They spoke about race in the same way that ecumenical leaders had in the 1930s: that Christianity was committed to better race relations but improvement would be slow, would occur largely through education, and changes would only happen in some indefinite future. Many ecumenical Protestants, now committed to human rights, were leaving Alexander and Richards behind.

The Federal Council's 1948 commitment to human rights showed that ecumenical Protestants leaped beyond their past moderation on civil rights. They did so in contrast to white moderates like Alexander and Richards, as well as organizations like the National Council of Christians and Jews, which was committed to combatting "prejudice" while remaining politically neutral toward legal discrimination and segregation.[82] That human rights were widely seen in opposition to segregation demonstrates that ecumenical Protestants believed, along with Soper and Gallagher, that racism was a serious threat to world order. Moreover, it is clear from both the Federal Council's support and from the strong reaction of Alexander and Richards that calls for human rights were reshaping America's religious politics.[83]

Whereas the 1946 "Non-Segregated Church" statement provoked only a few minor quarrels, two years later the Federal Council's statement on human rights led to a public fight between anti-racist activists and white moderate Protestants. The 1948 human rights statement caused open controversy, exposing a widening fault line between a faction of ecumenical Protestants moving quickly to the left on the issue of segregation and white moderates who defended the status quo on Jim Crow. Human rights marked the culmination of the international and structural thinking on race by ecumenical Protestants like Gallagher and Soper. Human rights also signaled decades of bitter battles to come between anti-racist activists and defenders of segregation that would leave American Protestants deeply divided.

From One World to Two

Ecumenical Protestant intellectuals' concerns about Jim Crow at home led them beyond America's shores in search of an unsegregated future for the United States. They found it in the racial cosmopolitanism of Brazil and in the nationalities policy of the Soviet Union. When ecumenical Protestant intellectuals thought about human rights, they were imagining a future for the United States in which the country's racial conventions would be overcome and the examples of foreign models would be followed.

As human rights became the vehicle through which the new structural and global understanding of racism was delivered to the American public, race became one of the first fault lines to emerge among ecumenical Protestants in the postwar era. As some ecumenical Protestant leaders moved from a personal to a structural and global understanding of racism, which they codified in the form of human rights in 1948, others resisted. Alexander and Richards defended the racial status quo and publicly sparred with their fellow Protestants. In the process, both the criticism of segregation by Soper and Gallagher, as well as the defense of Jim Crow by Alexander and Richards, contributed to the polarization of their religious community.

The belief that racism ought to be seen in a global context, linking together domestic and foreign concerns, would be reframed easily enough as the Cold War took hold of American politics. Ecumenical Protestants would join other liberals in arguing that segregation in the United States undermined America's role in the world and its Cold War against the Soviet Union.[84] But the Cold War would pose a broader challenge for ecumenical Protestants, threatening to undermine the very foundation of the universalism they had so carefully crafted during the war years. As their "one world" outlook was confronted with the bipolar framework of the Cold War, Protestantism itself would become increasingly divided into two worlds.

PART II

Two Worlds

CHAPTER 6

Beyond the Cold War

On March 5, 1946, the former British prime minister Winston Churchill stood before a crowd of dignitaries gathered at Westminster College and announced that the Cold War had begun. Churchill's "Sinews of Peace" speech was delivered in the small college town of Fulton, Missouri, but its message was heard across the world. "From Stettin in the Baltic to Trieste in the Adriatic," Churchill roared, "an iron curtain has descended across the Continent."[1] Delivered with Harry Truman's blessing and with the president in attendance, Churchill's speech was a first draft of what would become Cold War orthodoxy only a few years later.

"Sinews of Peace" was a call to arms. "The Communist parties or fifth columns constitute a growing challenge and peril to Christian civilization," Churchill warned. He was "convinced that there is nothing [the Soviets] admire so much as strength, and there is nothing for which they have less respect than for weakness, especially military weakness."[2] In a brief forty-six minutes and twenty-four seconds, Churchill had called upon US president Harry Truman to join forces with the British Empire, to strengthen Western military alliances at the expense of the United Nations, to defend "Christian" nations against communist infiltration, and to oppose the Soviet Union with force.

Soon after Churchill finished his speech, he and Truman boarded a train that barreled toward Columbus, Ohio, arriving the following day. An emergency meeting of the Federal Council of Churches had just begun in Columbus, and Truman was due to deliver the keynote address. Welcomed by a crowd of 35,000 onlookers, Churchill made a brief public appearance in his pajamas. But the seventy-two-year-old statesman was too tired to attend the Federal Council's conference and opted for a nap on the train instead. Had he joined Truman at the Deshler-Wallick Hotel, where five hundred

ecumenical Protestant leaders gathered with another three hundred prominent intellectuals, politicians, business and labor leaders, military officers,
and State Department officials, Churchill would have encountered a vision
of the postwar world starkly different from his own.[3]

G. Bromley Oxnam, the Federal Council president, had called the emergency meeting in May 1946 precisely to oppose Churchill's outlook and to
push for the human rights vision ecumenical Protestants had articulated
during the war. Oxnam differed from Churchill in his hope to reduce armies
and end conscription, to move colonies toward autonomy, and to limit national sovereignty for the sake of the United Nations, while expanding the
rights of racial minorities and lessening poverty.

This ecumenical Protestant vision for the postwar world had emerged
out of the debates and struggles of the wartime years, but it was difficult to
square with the emerging Cold War. In the decade that followed, American
ecumenical Protestants would find it hard to reconcile their one-world universalism with the bipolar world that Churchill had announced in Fulton
and that Truman would soon make real. From 1946 to 1958, ecumenical
Protestant leaders struggled to maintain their commitment to a UN-centered
world order, all while grappling with a new and increasingly urgent sense
that communism was a danger that needed to be opposed.

At first, American ecumenical Protestants responded to Churchill's challenge by trying to make peace with the Cold War. Their interests dovetailed
with Truman's political initiatives at times, but they never entirely overlapped.
Because of the important differences between Churchill and Truman's Cold
War and the globalism of ecumenical Protestants, Oxnam was never willing
to fully accept the new international framework that came to dominate the
postwar world. Although ecumenical Protestants took a winding path after
1946, one that led them to focus on Asia rather than Europe, by the mid-
1950s they openly rejected the Cold War framework. American ecumenical
Protestants subtly transformed their carefully crafted wartime doctrine in
ways that offered Americans a robust alternative to the Cold War.[4]

One World versus the Cold War

In 1946, Oxnam called an emergency session of the Federal Council of
Churches in order to weigh in on the postwar settlement. As president of the
organization, Oxnam hoped the meeting would be a defining moment that

would see the churches reaffirm the UN-centered vision they had so carefully elaborated during the war. But, just days before the conference began,
the Soviet Union failed to meet a deadline for withdrawing its troops from
Iran. The impasse and the subsequent war scare hovered over the conference, leading ministers and foreign policy experts to huddle in the hallways
and conference rooms in Columbus, asking one another whether a third
world war was on the horizon. The outlook seemed even more grim because
the United States had developed atomic weapons only a year earlier. This
terrible new weaponry promised to wreak havoc on cities and made imagin-
able for the first time in human history, as the Federal Council put it, "the
prospect of swift ruin for civilization and even the possibility of a speedy
end to man's life on earth."[5]

These circumstances were drastically different than just one year before,
when American ecumenical Protestants had proudly proclaimed that a new
international order had arrived. Many of the anti-communist dignitaries at
the Columbus conference referred to their present moment as a time of
choosing. Congressman Walter Judd, a Congregationalist layman, referred
to 1946 as "the year of decision" in his address at the Ash Wednesday service.[6] In his keynote address, President Harry Truman said that the world
stood "in the doorway to destruction or upon the threshold of the greatest
age in history." Reflecting on the paradox of 1946, John Foster Dulles spoke
of being "full of hope because the situation is so hopeless."[7] All three made
the case that a UN-centered world order was incompatible with the values
promoted by the Soviet Union. Whether Oxnam liked it or not, the Cold
War was already beginning to shape discussions among members of the
Federal Council.

There was good reason to be skeptical of the United Nations in 1946. The
UN charter's call to "reaffirm faith in fundamental human rights, in the
dignity and worth of the human person, in the equal rights of men and
women and of nations large and small" was undermined from the start by a
security council that gave outsized power to the five permanent members,
including the ability to shut down any talk of human rights in their home
countries.[8] As Mark Mazower notes, some of the United Nation's founders
treated the ideals of the organization's charter "as promissory notes" that
were "never intended to be cashed."[9] But this was not exactly what Dulles
and Judd were thinking. They were enamored with the aims of the United
Nations in 1946 and it was their passion for liberal internationalism that
drove their opposition to illiberal countries like the Soviet Union. There were

certainly ecumenical Protestant critics of the United Nations who treated the organization as a new form of imperialism.[10] But most ecumenical Protestants were neither fervent anti-imperialists nor committed anti-communists. They hoped that the United Nations would be effective.

The United Nations remained wildly popular among ecumenical Protestants, who hoped that the organization was just a beginning. In surveys conducted during 1951–52, Episcopalians were asked whether "it would be a good thing if U.N. were some day replaced by some kind of world gov't." The polls were taken at a flashpoint of the Cold War, when the Korean War was raging and when Ohio senator John W. Bricker first introduced legislation designed to limit what he called the United Nation's promotion of "human slavery." The Episcopalians were among the most politically restrained of ecumenical denominations, representing as they did some of the wealthiest Americans. And yet their bishops and priests said yes to world government overwhelmingly. Even parishioners, who were generally more conservative than the clergy and national leaders, said yes by a wide margin. As the Cold War reached a fever pitch, bishops nonetheless affirmed a world government by a margin of 60 percent "yes" to 15 percent "no", priests 60 percent "yes" to 22 percent "no", and churchgoers 47 percent "yes" to 33 percent "no." The hope ecumenical Protestants projected onto the United Nations in the 1940s and 1950s was not solely about what the organization was then but about what the organization could one day become.[11]

There was a utopian quality to ecumenical Protestant thought about the United Nations that dimmed in the late 1940s but never went away. In 1946 anti-communism was only beginning to emerge as the primary international posture of the United States. And it was only just becoming clear that the United States would soon take over many of the functions of the British and French empires in the world. The ideals and hopes that ecumenical Protestant leaders and churchgoers projected onto the United Nations did not prevent them from supporting some of the anti-communist policies of the Truman administration, but they did serve as an alternative to "containment" and the Truman Doctrine.

Most ecumenical leaders did not prioritize fighting communism in 1946. At the Columbus conference, they acknowledged a world of differing "religious, social, economic, and political patterns ... particularly true in the case of the Soviet Union and the western democracies."[12] Differences, however, were not to prevent "sympathetic understanding [and] every friendly negotiation," especially the undertaking of "constructive tasks of common concern" through the United Nations.[13] Echoing the Six Pillars of Peace produced by the Dulles Commission in 1943, they called for an international agreement negotiated through the United Nations to reduce armaments and end peacetime conscription worldwide. Oxnam and his allies also called for the strengthening of the UN mandate system, for the creation of a path to independence for colonial nations within definite time frames, and for a more equitable distribution of wealth among the world's nations.[14]

Most notably, American ecumenical Protestants were among the most forceful backers of the internationalization of atomic energy. A theological who's who—consisting of Robert Calhoun, Reinhold Niebuhr, H. Richard Niebuhr, Roland Bainton, John Bennett, and Henry Pitney Van Dusen—delivered a stern condemnation of the US use of nuclear weapons against Japan and called for the United Nations to safeguard the weapons.[15] They directly repudiated Churchill, who had insisted that "it would be criminal madness" to entrust atomic secrets to the United Nations and risk the possibility of it getting into communist hands.[16]

Ecumenical Protestants once again called on the United States to demonstrate that it too subscribed to the new international norms proclaimed by the UN charter. At the 1946 meeting at Columbus the Federal Council broke decisively with Jim Crow, pledging to create a "non-segregated church and a non-segregated society."[17] In addition, the Federal Council of Churches called for "full employment," because "the nature of man and the structure of modern industrial society have caused the right to an opportunity for employment at an equitable wage to become a basic right."[18] For the ecumenists gathered at Columbus, expanding rights at home went hand-in-hand with a rights-based internationalism centered on the United Nations.

In the spring of 1946, ecumenical Protestants reaffirmed their faith in the United Nations and mostly ignored Churchill's warnings about communism. Instead, they continued to push for the development of a moral and legal framework that applied to all nations and necessitated actions, like disarmament and internationalization of nuclear power, at odds with Truman's plans. But in the ensuing years they faced a test of loyalties between the United States and the United Nations. How ecumenical Protestants should react when the US government behaved in line with their values but did so unilaterally, thereby undermining the United Nations, became an urgent problem.

The dilemma first arose with the European Recovery Program, which was better known as the "Marshall Plan." It was announced by Truman's

secretary of state, George Marshall, during the Harvard commencement address he delivered in June 1947. The United States would help rebuild the
economies of European countries, as Marshall put it, to engineer the "return
of normal economic health in the world, without which there can be no political stability and no assured peace."[19] Between 1948 and 1953, approximately $13 billion in aid was sent to Europe. Britain, France, West Germany,
and Italy were the biggest beneficiaries, along with Belgium, the Netherlands, Greece, Turkey, and Norway.[20]

Ecumenical Protestants enthusiastically embraced the Marshall Plan as
"one of history's most momentous affirmations of faith in the curative power
of freedom and in the creative capacity of free men."[21] But they had a problem on their hands. Eastern Bloc countries and the Soviet Union did not
participate in the plan. Soviet leaders chaffed at the economic and political
requirements that came along with the aid, and they interpreted the plan as
a form of American imperialism.[22] So too did leftist critics in Western Europe. Ecumenical Protestants acknowledged Western Europeans' fears "that
the United States may seek to make Europe over in its political and economic image," and they disliked how the plan bypassed the United Nations
and therefore undermined the multilateralism that ecumenical Protestants
believed the new organization encouraged. In spite of these reservations,
however, the Marshall Plan fit so well with ecumenical Protestants' belief in
altruism that they called on the government to implement price controls to
fund the program. Focusing on the "moral and spiritual" motives and insisting it "should be above political partisanship," ecumenical Protestants
refused to recognize that the Marshall Plan was driving the United States
toward a standoff with the Soviet Union.[23]

Ecumenical Protestants paid little attention to the Marshall Plan's Cold
War consequences, but Truman's more militaristic policies could hardly be
ignored. In 1947, Truman announced to Congress that communist infiltra-
tors in Greece and Turkey would topple the nations' governments unless the
United States intervened with massive military aid. Americans were led to
believe—wrongly, it turned out—that the Soviet Union had stoked these
civil wars. This was the Truman Doctrine, which proclaimed that the United
States would defend countries against external communist threats anywhere
in the world. "The situation is an urgent one requiring immediate action
and the United Nations and its related organizations are not in a position to
extend help of the kind that is required," the president announced to Congress in 1947. But he assured Americans that "the United States will be giving

effect to the principles of the Charter of the United Nations" by "helping free and independent nations to maintain their freedom" against "coercion" and "subterfuges."[24]

Truman knew many Americans remained devoted to the United Nations in 1947, a popularity that ecumenical Protestants had promoted with a messianic fervor. The president cleverly split apart the "principles" of the United Nation from its institutional mechanisms. Forced to choose between the aims of the UN preamble, on behalf of which Truman claimed to speak, and the actual organization, which the president bypassed, ecumenists had only a muddled response. The Federal Council applauded Truman for opposing "the attempted subjugation of peoples by armed minorities and outside powers using coercion and infiltration." "If Soviet foreign policy is aggressive and expansionist in character, we have the obligation not only to discourage expansionist action but also to seek a comprehensive settlement," the Federal Council insisted. Not only did they temporarily put aside their opposition to America's large military budget but also their commitment to the United Nations, recognizing that it was "not yet equipped to deal with all the immediate problems" in Greece and Turkey.[25]

The Federal Council tried to have it both ways about the United Nations. The United States should "give the United Nations full information" about the aid to Greece and Turkey, and should "seek the counsel and cooperation" of the United Nations in how the funds were distributed, in addition to inviting UN inspectors to monitor the distribution of aid, the Federal Council pleaded.[26] Ecumenical Protestants did not praise the massive military aid to Greece and Turkey in the way they had done for the Marshall Plan, but they did lend their support, with important caveats, to the Truman Doctrine in 1947.

The Federal Council had only recently begun to grapple with Soviet-American tensions. The first major statement from the Federal Council on the subject had come in October 11, 1946.[27] This was the statement that philosopher George A. Coe would later say signaled the abandonment of the principles of the wartime World Order movement and marked the beginning of the Protestant drift toward complicity in the Cold War.[28] Written under John Foster Dulles's oversight, the report began with a sharp contrast between both Christian and democratic values and the ideals of the USSR. The only way the two sides could find peace, Dulles argued, was through worldwide acceptance of liberal values. "All men must renounce the effort to spread abroad their way of life by methods of intolerance," he wrote.

International peace "begins with recognition of the sacredness of the individual human personality." Freedom of conscience was paramount to global peace, with individuals "free to believe as their reason and conscience dictate." For Dulles in particular, religious freedom had become a weapon to use against the Soviet Union.[29]

Although the Federal Council was critical of the Soviet Union in late 1946, the organization was not endorsing the emerging Cold War. It made clear, in language that was difficult to imagine only several years later, that "the United States should set an example by renouncing the acquisition of new military bases so far distant from the continental United States and so close to the Soviet Union that the offensive threat is both disproportionate to the defensive value to the United States." While this principle applied to all nations, the authors argued, America should go first in good faith.[30] Moreover, the Federal Council avoided the rhetoric of Truman and Churchill that presented the United States and the USSR as polar opposites. "Neither state socialism nor free enterprise provides a perfect economic system; each can learn from the experience of the other," the organization pronounced. The American economy had yet to prove that it could "assure steady production and employment" or "continuously provide industrial workers with that sense of individual creativeness which gives greater satisfaction than mere material possession."[31] To show the world the value of democracy, the United States should first tackle "certain inadequacies of democracy" that could be fixed through "remedial action within their own borders." In a self-critical spirit, the Federal Council called on the United States to observe human rights at home. "There is need to bring about greater observance of human rights and freedoms for all without distinction as to race or religion," Federal Council leaders wrote. "Particularly must America do away with the widely prevalent double standard of personal relations and citizenship applied to Negro Americans."[32] While critical of the Soviet Union, American ecumenical Protestants took pains to demonstrate that human rights were not merely an anti-communist weapon.

The tension between anti-communism and support for Protestant globalism troubled G. Bromley Oxnam. He insisted in 1947 that the United States *must be strong* because Russians "respect strength." But the threat of communism was not solely or even primarily a military threat, Oxnam argued. It was the spread of communist ideas that needed to be fought most urgently. Instead of weapons, the best defense of political democracy was the eradication of poverty and the spread of economic democracy. "Communism makes no headway where plenty exists and justice abounds. Poverty is the open door through which [communism] enters," Oxnam wrote. To make the United States immune from communism, full employment needed to be guaranteed and democracy needed to be extended to industry "so that the worker may participate fully in determining the conditions under which he works, and share equitably in the wealth he produces."[33] He urged the United States to avoid military competition and focus instead on the welfare of its citizens.

Oxnam argued that civil society, not the military, should take the lead in Soviet-American relations. He proposed exchanges of "religious, educational, scientific, artistic and business leaders" between the two countries in order to establish personal ties, build trust, set a precedent of regular dialogue, and create an atmosphere more conducive to sorting out big problems. As Oxnam put it, "The only way to get rid of an iron curtain is to lift it."[34] But Oxnam recognized that exchanges between civil societies were long-term solutions at best. Tensions between the Soviet Union and the United States were mounting, and the ideological differences appeared too stark to overcome.

Reaffirming his faith in the United Nations, Oxnam suggested that the United States announce its "intent to work through the United Nations, with or without Russia, that we are ready to abolish the veto, and will stand consistently for the facing of these issues in terms of the democratic decision of the representatives of the peoples of the world."[35] By calling for the abolition of the veto, Oxnam was trying to save what he saw as the most important function of the United Nations: checking the autonomy of each nation, including the United States, by embedding it in a broader community of nations. This would ensure that any decisions the United States made in its foreign policy would be broadly multilateral. If war should ever come between the United States and the Soviet Union, "we will be doing it in terms of the judgment of humanity, rather than in the decision of a single nation," Oxnam explained.[36] He was speaking for a broad swath of ecumenical Protestants when he spoke of "humanity" in narrow terms.

While Oxnam struggled to find a way forward with the USSR, others, like Dulles and Reinhold Niebuhr, became more hawkish toward the Soviet Union. Earlier, Dulles had urged the United States to relinquish some of its national sovereignty for the sake of international cooperation, but he dropped this demand in 1945 at the UN negotiations in San Francisco. There were subtle shifts in his outlook over time that were partly motivated by his antipathy toward the Soviet Union. But Dulles's globalism was always easy to reconcile with US priorities, such as free trade and the proliferation of liberal values. Unlike most ecumenical Protestant leaders, he was rarely critical of the United States when he spoke about world order. His vision of the postwar world did not require Americans to significantly change their values or behavior.

Niebuhr, on the other hand, was more subtle in his anti-communism than was Dulles. He called on the United States to behave more responsibly in wielding its power and drew attention to the ironies and contradictions of US global supremacy. And yet, he repeatedly attacked the pacifist wing of ecumenical Protestantism, helping silence some of the most trenchant critics of American militarism. In the 1930s his calls for Americans to cast off their "innocence" sounded prophetic because of deep divisions about US foreign policy at the time. But repeating those calls in the late 1940s, and especially in the 1950s, when there was near unanimity among policy makers about the Cold War, sounded more like an endorsement of the status quo. In the early days of the Cold War, Niebuhr and Dulles often found themselves on the same side of key issues. Only later would their differences become magnified and lead to public fights over US foreign policy.

The emphasis Niebuhr placed on the necessity of US power came at the expense of his earlier advocacy of an American demonstration of goodwill through unilateral disarmament and through international control of atomic energy. Symbolic of this embrace of the Cold War by many realists, some of the same theologians who had earlier advocated handing over nuclear weapons to the United Nations now believed it would be immoral for their country to do so. "For the United States to abandon its atomic weapons, or to give the impression that they would not be used," Niebuhr and the other theologians reasoned in 1950, "would leave the non-Communist world with totally inadequate defense."[37] It was not only nuclear weapons that troubled ecumenical Protestants. In the late 1940s there was an abiding sense that conditions had changed drastically since 1946, when ecumenical Protestants confidently proclaimed their postwar plans. The editors of the *Christian Century* observed, "The problem of securing a just and lasting peace grows more baffling, more difficult with every passing week. The 'one world' hope which flamed high four years ago has all but vanished in the presence of a two-world reality."[38]

Sensing the uncertainty that the Cold War was producing, Dulles decided in 1949 to gather ecumenical Protestants at another mass meeting.

The first large-scale gathering organized by the Dulles Commission took place in 1942 in Delaware, Ohio, and had created the first outlines of a postwar international organization. At the second meeting in Cleveland, Ohio, in 1945, the Dulles Commission had detailed a plan for the United Nations. Dulles hoped that the third meeting, in March 1949, which would take place again in Cleveland, would produce the outlines of a united Protestant approach to the Cold War.

With Dulles at the helm, criticism of his close ties to the US government resurfaced. James A. Craine, the executive secretary of the Commission on World Order of the Disciples of Christ, complained that "the leadership of the churches since [1945], has been too closely affiliated with the policies of the State Department to make our witness effective." Craine urged the Federal Council to express Christian convictions in "positive terms" that are "unmodified by the precautions and expediencies which are necessary in political negotiation."[39] The desire to distance Christianity from US government policy was growing among a wing of ecumenical Protestants.

The growing divide among ecumenical Protestants over the Cold War came to a head during the debates over the North Atlantic Treaty Organization (NATO), which was being negotiated as Dulles gathered ecumenical Protestant leaders in 1949. Many ecumenical Protestants were suspicious of NATO. They were deeply attached to the United Nations, which was partly their creation, and feared that a regional military alliance would undermine the mission of the United Nations. The State Department was so concerned with ecumenical Protestant opinion that it sent one of its senior experts on the USSR, Charles E. Bohlen, to Cleveland for a one and a half hour off-the-record discussion. Bohlen apparently did not release any information about the NATO pact that was not publicly available. He was there to interpret the treaty and answer questions. Were the Scandinavian countries being forced into the treaty? Was NATO a violation of the UN charter? Would NATO take the power to declare war out of the hands of the US Senate? Did this treaty create the potential for minor conflicts between proxy nations to trigger a global war that no one could win? Bohlen tried to reassure ecumenical Protestants. For example, he told listeners that the treaty would not force the United States to go to war. An attack on an ally could be "considered" an attack on the United States, but the Senate would still have the prerogative on whether to declare war or handle the matter in some other way, he explained.[40]

Despite Bohlen's assurances, the NATO issue led to an intense debate. Dulles spoke more than anyone else during the NATO discussion, urging caution and humility in crafting a position about a treaty whose text was not yet available for public scrutiny. Others were not so cautious. Ernest Edwin Ryden, the editor of the *Lutheran Companion*, called NATO a "military scheme" that would destroy the United Nations.[41] If Dulles wanted explicit approval of NATO, his hopes now fell short because of organized opposition. Instead, Dulles urged that no action be taken until there was more information. In the end, the delegates could not come to an agreement on NATO in Cleveland.[42]

For Dulles, the outcome of the conference was less important than the platform the occasion provided him. Dulles took full advantage of the coverage *Time, Newsweek*, and the *New York Times* provided, deciding to use the occasion to criticize Secretary of State Dean Acheson. Dulles supported NATO, but he was critical of the idea of arming Scandinavian countries. At a news conference after the close of the first day of the Cleveland conference he declared that Norwegian sources had told him there would be no American bases placed in that country. He called for an explicit statement on the matter in order to publicize the defensive nature of the alliance. Journalist Walter Lippmann praised Dulles's comments as a responsible alternative to the views of the more aggressive members of the State and Defense Departments, who would "back the Russian into a corner."[43] But Acheson did not respond kindly to Dulles's criticism. A report noted that Acheson was "boiling mad" and "blew up" after reading Dulles's speech, complaining that "Dulles just can't get over the fact that Dewey lost the [1948] election and he isn't now Secretary of State."[44]

Dulles was acting like a shadow secretary of state and that placed the ecumenists in the uncomfortable position of having their views at the center of a political controversy. Not only was Dulles engaging in partisan politics, but he was widely perceived to be the steward of these ideas at a moment when his values diverged with those of many ecumenists. The 1949 Cleveland meeting was widely reported as a one-man act. *Time* depicted Dulles as a paternalistic figure giving aid to a clergy that were largely out of their depth.[45] Referring to him as an "expert and conscientious coach," the *Time* reporter explained that "from the moment U.N. Delegate John Foster Dulles ended his opening address, most of the delegates looked to him for guidance on the question for which he had done his best to prepare them: the North Atlantic Security Pact." The editors of the *Christian Century* complained

that every single position Dulles took at the Cleveland conference was ratified.[46]

The drift away from the United Nations and toward US unilateralism
in 1949 by a wing of ecumenical Protestants was captured by a document
called "Moral Responsibility and United States Power: A Message to the
Churches."[47] Niebuhr drafted the document. Niebuhr began by calling
American power providential. This did not mean that the United States at-
tained its power "as chiefly the fruit of virtue." Rather, that power was
granted to the United States so that it might be used wisely and responsibly.
The United States "has the confidence of many in other lands who believe
that our people have no lust for conquest and genuinely desire a just and
lasting peace in the free world," wrote Niebuhr. "Freedom-loving peoples
look to us for leadership, and without that leadership there would be demor-
alization in the world." Niebuhr worried about US inexperience at wielding
power and that it might use this power for its own advantage.[48]

Niebuhr was rehearsing many of the ideas that appeared in his 1953
book, *The Irony of American History*.[49] The book garnered him invitations to
meetings of the State Department and made him a favorite of Henry Luce's
publishing empire. Yet the same qualities that made him America's most
important Cold War theologian opened him up for criticism from his fellow
ecumenical Protestants. After all, Niebuhr never explained why he believed
the United States would exercise its power responsibly. In Niebuhr's formulation, irresponsible use of power was something that *could* and *might* happen, not something that was already occurring. Niebuhr's unwillingness to
criticize American power sounded to his critics like a capitulation to the
state at a moment when many others were calling for distance from the government.[50]

Paul Hutchinson, who had taken over as editor of the *Christian Century*
from Charles Clayton Morrison in 1947, took the lead in attacking Niebuhr
and Dulles. The *Christian Century* editorialized soon after the close of
the 1949 Cleveland conference that Niebuhr's writings were "cautious and
equivocal, secularist and confused. The conference itself was groping, baffled and herd-minded." Niebuhr and Dulles's "discussion of justice and
human rights consistently dealt with these in terms of expediency, as means
to curb Russia rather than to express Christian brotherhood," ecumenical
Protestantism's most important journal argued.[51] Hutchison went on to list
what he saw as the "amazing blind spots" of Niebuhr's analysis: "The use in
war of atomic and other weapons of mass destruction, the continuance of

peacetime conscription, the reduction of our colossal arms budget, the curb-
ing of our worldwide spy network, the threat of universal military training,
the reduction of the number of military bases around the world or the relax-
ation of military domination of education, industry, commerce and science."[52]
What the editors viewed as the heart of the matter—the confrontation between
Christian values and the naked power the US government was resorting
to—was dodged by the Dulles Commission. They charged Niebuhr with
placing "the stamp of church approval on the bipartisan foreign policy of
our government."[53]

   Time magazine, whose publisher, Henry Luce, had a very different agenda
for the postwar world than did the editors of the *Christian Century*, also
pronounced the conference a failure because it did not endorse Luce's vision
of the "American Century." The Federal Council's position on NATO "bore
none of the ringing affirmations that distinguished the conference's meetings of 1942, when it called for a postwar world organization, or of 1945,
when it called for the Christian concepts of justice, law and human rights in
the UN Charter. The delegates sidestepped the issue" of NATO.[54] To a wide
range of observers, the Federal Council offered little of value in the face of
the Cold War. And the old rivalry between pacifists and realists reemerged
in a new form, once again dividing ecumenical Protestants.

China and the Search for an Alternative to the Cold War

American ecumenical Protestants reached a stalemate on the Cold War in
Europe at the end of the 1940s. Split between rival factions, they did not present a united front on the most important policy debates, including NATO.
But by the end of the 1950s, ecumenical Protestants finally had an answer to
the challenge the Cold War presented. Focusing mostly on Asia, while the
gaze of Dulles and Niebuhr was fixed on Europe, ecumenical Protestant intellectuals found a new way of understanding world politics. Rather than
seeing the world in spatial terms by imagining the globe split into a first
world, second world, and third world, they came to conceive of international
affairs as governed by "revolutions" taking place both between nations and
within each country. The pioneers of this theology of revolution argued that
movements for justice, both abroad and at home, were part of a providential
plan, and they urged religious and political leaders to take them seriously. In
contrast to anti-communism, the theology of revolution emphasized the

need to accommodate demands for land reform, decolonization, economic redistribution, and desegregation—even if those demands came from socialist movements. It was an outlook that would become widespread among ecumenical Protestants by the 1960s and would lead them to more fully embrace the social movements of that era.

Why did Asia become the focus of attention by ecumenical Protestants in the 1950s? Ecumenical Protestants had long been concerned about the effects of imperialism, the spread of Western modernity, and the question of cultural and religious pluralism in Asia. The postwar debates about US economic power in Western Europe and the "Coca-colonization" of the Continent did not carry the same weight for ecumenical Protestants as the century-long criticism of imperialism in places like China and India.[55] And ecumenical Protestants with connections to Asia believed that the Truman and Eisenhower administrations did not appreciate just how much US policy in the region would have to depart from the imperialism of the past.[56] In Asia, the context and the salient issues were different from those in Europe. Intellectuals like Kenneth Scott Latourette, John Mackay, and Richard Shaull came to believe that the Cold War could be avoided in Asia. Understanding international affairs as a process of revolution and accommodation presented ecumenical Protestants with an alternative to the Cold War framework, belatedly offering a reply to Churchill's challenge.

In developing an alternative to the Cold War framework, two important things changed for ecumenical Protestants. First, partly through the crucible of McCarthyism, ecumenical Protestants could no longer take for granted that US interests closely aligned with Christian interests. Although they had paid lip service to this idea before, the oppositional posture toward US policy was something quite new for ecumenical Protestants in the 1950s. Second, rethinking the Cold War in Asia involved relocating the locus of humanity away from the United Nations and toward the revolutionary movements of the Global South and among movements for economic and racial justice mobilizing within every country. In this way, American ecumenical Protestants reinvented their 1940s-era universalism in light of two of the twentieth century's most important developments: the Cold War and decolonization.

With all eyes on Europe, Americans only belatedly recognized East Asia as an important region where world-historical events were unfolding. On October 1, 1949, Mao Zedong founded the People's Republic of China. The creation of a new country under the communist banner capped decades of fighting in the country between "Red" and "White" forces that began in the 1920s, was interrupted briefly by the Japanese invasion in 1937, and resumed in full force in 1945. By 1949, Chiang Kai-shek's White forces had fled to the island of Taiwan, ceding control of the mainland to Mao.

It is hard to overemphasize how troubled US ecumenical Protestants were by this development. For a century, China was imagined as a new frontier for the spread of Christianity, a land of backward peasants living in the depth of depravity, who hungered for charity, compassion, and conversion. More recently, the Chinese people had become long-suffering protagonists in the novels of Pearl Buck and heroes of the resistance against Japanese aggression. That the land that Protestants had devoted themselves to winning for Christianity was now in communist hands weighed on their minds. Ecumenical Protestants worried so much about losing ties with China that they elected Zhao Zichen, a strong supporter of Mao's communist government, as one of the World Council of Churches' co-presidents in 1948.

Ecumenists considered their options in a political climate that vilified liberals for "losing" China. Congressman Walter Judd, who had so eagerly participated in the World Order movement during World War II, was also Congress's most vocal supporter of Chiang Kai-shek, and he became the most outspoken critic of the State Department's experts on the country, who were widely known as "China hands."[57] In order to navigate this maze of changing circumstances, the Federal Council of Churches asked Kenneth Scott Latourette to take charge. Latourette headed the small but influential part of the Dulles Commission called the Committee on East Asian Affairs. Throughout the 1940s Latourette acted as the liaison between the Federal Council and the State Department on issues relating to East Asia. Now, in 1949, he was being asked to revise Protestant views in light of the communist consolidation of China.[58]

Latourette had been a missionary in China in the early 1910s and he continued working with missionary organizations in the decades that followed. He was also a professional historian who had written books on the country's past. In a vacuum of serious scholarship on China, Latourette became the dean of Chinese studies from his position as professor at Yale Divinity School. By 1945, he had completed his seven-volume *History of the Expansion of Christianity*, which detailed the long history of the missionary movement. Serving as president of the American Historical Association in honor of his large body of scholarship on China, he delivered the organization's presidential address in December 1948 on the Christian understanding of history.[59]

What made Asia different from Europe, to Latourette's mind, was the long history of Western imperialism and racism. Drawing on long-standing discourses on religious and racial pluralism, Latourette found a way of understanding events in Asia that resembled the wartime universalism of the World Order movement and allowed him to downplay the importance of the Cold War in Asia. As the historian looked at contemporary events in China, he predicted a long period of instability in the country resulting from a population explosion, economic devastation, and a cultural transition resulting from the decline of Confucianism and the intrusion of Western ideas. For these reasons, Latourette was confident that "Communism will probably not have a long life in China" because "it will be unable to solve China's basic problems." "The Chinese cannot be regimented in the thoroughgoing fashion that long pre-communist precedent had facilitated in Russia," he believed. Chinese nationalism was too strong for China to become a puppet state of the Soviet Union, and China's weak economy and frayed social structure would prove to be a liability rather than an asset for the USSR.[60]

The United States was powerless in the situation, Latourette cautioned. American military intervention would only provoke Chinese nationalism. Chinese Christian churches would face a tough time under communism, he acknowledged, but they would survive. The best policy was to focus on economic aid to China, no matter who was in charge, and to let events play out.[61] Latourette saw little reason to alter the main tenets of the World Order movement's policy toward East Asia, which included massive developmental aid, an end to colonialism, ending race-based immigration quotas, and a spirit of partnership and good-faith negotiation. Latourette insisted that communism's growth should not change this position.

Henry P. Van Dusen, president of Union Theological Seminary since 1945, disagreed with Latourette's assessment of the situation in China, and he argued that Chinese communism was dangerous precisely because it was different from Stalinism. Van Dusen believed that China's indigenization of communism meant that it was likely to spread throughout Asia and needed to be stopped by military force. To emphasize this early version of the domino theory, which held that the growth of communism in one Asian nation would quickly spread to neighboring countries, Van Dusen quoted from one of Latourette's historical monographs, reminding Latourette that in the middle ages "[only] armed force has . . . made it possible for the spirit of Jesus to survive."[62]

Van Dusen insisted that military force was the best means of controlling the spread of communism in East Asia but his pessimism about China's future was not shared by other members of the group charged with coordinating the Federal Council's Asia policy. Van Dusen suggested to Walter Van Kirk that his comments might be incorporated into the position paper on East Asia being written in advance of the 1949 Cleveland conference but only if "others share my misgivings about Ken's paper." If the "criticism is mine" alone, Van Dusen wrote, "by all means disregard the matter."[63] From the records of the committee, it appears that Van Dusen's objections were promptly disregarded. Latourette's view became the Federal Council's official stance.

By the end of 1949 ecumenical Protestants formalized their policies on East Asia. The Foreign Missions Council called on the United States and the United Nations to "labour incessantly for the observance of human rights and fundamental freedoms for the peoples of Asia."[64] The Federal Council urged the American government to fight poverty rather than communism in China.[65] Drawing on the ideas of Latourette, the Federal Council argued that communism takes advantage of poverty, and the best means of stopping communism was not through military aid but through the creation of economic prosperity and social stability. "Neither the creation of a Pacific military alliance, nor the granting of military assistance by the United States to the non-communist forces of the Far East, would alone suffice to establish in that area the conditions of a just and durable peace," the Federal Council warned. "The primary resources with which the West must promote peace in the Pacific are ideas, not atomic bombs; food, not guns; plowshares, not swords; tools of production, not implements of destruction."[66]

Ecumenical Protestant leaders were heading toward a call for the diplomatic recognition of "Red" China at the end of the 1940s. They staked out this position with little backing from churchgoers. One poll in November 1949 showed that 42 percent of Americans opposed recognition of mainland China, with only 12 percent supporting it. College graduates, who were more likely to be represented by ecumenical Protestant denominations, also stood in opposition. Fifty-two percent of US college graduates opposed diplomatic relations with mainland China, while 33 percent favored recognition.[67] The policies of the Federal Council of Churches were unpopular with their constituency, but they pursued them nonetheless.

After completing a tour of East and Southeast Asia in 1949, Princeton Theological Seminary president John Mackay announced in January 1950 his support for recognition of China in order to bring it into the community of nations. "Otherwise," Mackay wrote, "we will be alienating the Chinese people who by their attitude repudiated the other regime."[68] A few months later, a group of sixty-eight missionaries endorsed the diplomatic recognition of China, and Mackay elaborated some of the reasons for the endorsement. The arguments were grounded in both geopolitical and religious concerns, and they repeated many of Latourette's earlier points.[69] Mackay presciently emphasized that Chinese nationalism created a possibility for the United States to court China and lead it away from the Soviet Union. He also believed that diplomatic recognition would help protect the Christian minority in China. Proud of the missionary encouragement of self-rule and national development, Mackay believed that "Communists in China, despite their Marxism, have no natural quarrel with the Christian religion as Communists in Russia had good reason to have." Echoing Oxnam's observations of the USSR in the 1920s, Mackay believed Russia's Orthodox Church had been the handmaid of the oppressive monarchy prior to the Russian Revolution. But in China, Christianity was represented by missionaries who encouraged national development and progressive measures against poverty. Surely the communist government would recognize this history, Mackay believed.[70]

By the time he clarified his position in the *New York Times* it was two months after the Korean War had begun, and Mackay acknowledged "new complications" and admitted "it may indeed be advisable, and even necessary, to postpone such recognition."[71] Diplomatic recognition of China remained off the agenda for the duration of the Korean War, which began in 1950, and for several years after the armistice in 1953.

As the Korean War broke out, a new organization—the National Council of Churches, which succeeded the Federal Council in 1950—took the lead in formulating ecumenical Protestant policy. The National Council was created through a merger between the Federal Council of Churches with several other large national bureaucracies, including the Foreign Missions Conference of North America, the Home Missions Council, and the United Council of Church Women. By the end of the 1950s this yet larger bureaucracy moved from their midtown offices in Manhattan to the nineteen-story modernist Interchurch Center on the Upper West Side of New York City, directly across the street from Riverside Church. The new building, which occupied a whole city block and was affectionately nicknamed the "God Box" after its uninspired architecture, housed many of the same committees, councils, and commissions that had operated under the Federal Council.

Figure 8. Princeton Theological Seminary president John Mackay surveying the 38th parallel on the Korean Peninsula in 1949. Mackay would later become one of Senator Joseph McCarthy's fiercest critics. Image courtesy of the Presbyterian Historical Society and the Presbyterian Church (USA).

The National Council of Churches gave full support to the Korean War. The new organization saw the North's invasion of South Korea as a violation of the moral aims of the United Nations, and ecumenical leaders applauded the use of the United Nations as the coordinating body defending South Korea. If there must be war, ecumenical Protestants reasoned, it should be a war organized through the United Nations and fought in the name of humanity. In fact, the National Council believed that the credibility and efficacy of the United Nations were at stake in the war. "Because the fate of the United Nations is closely linked with the fate of Korea," the organization announced, "the armed attack on the Republic of Korea presents a grave menace to the whole effort to develop an effective international organization for peace." The National Council reminded Americans that the South Korean Republic was established through the United Nations, and the international organization continued to monitor elections. "And even as the United Nations Commission on the scene sought a peaceful solution to the problems of Korea, the attack from North Korea was launched," the National Council explained. "The aggression is a most direct challenge to the authority of the United Nations as an instrument for the maintenance of international peace and security."[72] Thus, in 1950, their solidarity with the United Nations led ecumenical Protestants to support the Korean War.

Protestant globalism could sometimes lead to criticism of US policy, as it had in the cases of Latourette and Mackay, or to support of it, as it had during the Korean War. The patriotic atmosphere during the Korean War muted earlier criticism. So too did McCarthyite attacks on the National Council. The climate of the early Cold War also emboldened evangelicals in their attacks against ecumenical Protestant leaders for being insufficiently patriotic. And American Catholic clergy, like Cardinal Francis Spellman, were among the loudest anti-communist voices in the country.[73] As a consequence, ecumenical Protestants were forced to turn their attention from shaping international affairs to protecting their right to simply speak out on them.

Ecumenical Protestant leaders became terribly worried when Senator Joseph McCarthy appointed J. B. Matthews to be his chief anti-communist investigator in 1953. Matthews was an unlikely choice for such a role because he was a product of ecumenical Protestantism. He grew up in a Methodist household and departed in 1915 for Java (today, part of Indonesia) for six years of missionary work. Matthews had been ordained as a Methodist minister when he returned to the United States, but his passion was for languages (he was proficient in Arabic, Aramaic, Hebrew, Malay, Persian, Sanskrit, and Sudanese). Having received degrees at Drew University, Union Theological Seminary, Columbia University, and the School of Oriental Languages at the University of Vienna, he went on to teach languages at Methodist-run schools. He later taught at the historically Black Fisk

University and Howard University as an expression of his commitment to anti-racism. As a proponent of the social gospel, Matthews worked on behalf of many left-wing causes in the 1920s and 1930s, including serving as a secretary for the Fellowship of Reconciliation and becoming a dues-paying member of the Socialist Party of America in 1929. In many ways, this was a typical profile for an ecumenical Protestant leader. But during the Great Depression he veered further left than most. In 1935, he had accused Protestant clergy of being "partners in plunder" with American capitalists.[74]

Like a handful of others, Matthews had been put off by the aggressive tactics of the Communist Party. By 1938 he had switched sides from the Far Left to the Far Right and began accusing Protestant churches of being run by communists and fellow travelers. Shortly after publicly breaking with the Left, he became a witness for the Dies Committee and served as the committee's research director until he left in 1945 to conduct investigations on communism for the newspapers of the anti-communist Hearst Corporation. In 1953, Senator McCarthy hired Matthews to lead the staff of the Senate Permanent Investigations Subcommittee.[75]

Matthews's appointment coincided with the publication of his article "Reds and Our Churches" in the *American Mercury*, a right-wing paper.[76] The article was provocative by design, insisting that "the largest single group supporting the Communist apparatus in the United States today is composed of Protestant Clergymen."[77] "Reds and Our Churches" was so inflammatory that both Republican and Democratic senators rallied against Matthews. After reading the article, John McClellan, a Democratic senator from Arkansas who generally supported McCarthy, "was so enraged by the article that he promptly assumed leadership of the group" attacking Matthews. Shortly after the story broke on the front pages of newspapers across the country, countless clergy called their senators in protest. After the episcopal bishop from Detroit put pressure on the Republican senator from Michigan, Charles E. Potter, Potter withdrew his support for McCarthy during this controversy and called for Matthews's resignation.[78]

Ecumenical Protestant leaders not only swayed senators to oppose Matthews but also had a direct line to the White House. Eisenhower's closest aides worked with ecumenical Protestant leaders and religious leaders from other faiths to engineer a protesting note to be sent out by Eisenhower. The president called the attack on Protestant clergy "unjustifiable and deplorable" and an attack on "the principles of freedom and decency." Eisenhower's statement was put out as response to a letter written by members of the

National Council of Christians and Jews. As the *New York Times* noted, "the President's reply was apparently immediate," which revealed coordination between the administration and religious leaders. The President's sharply worded rebuke led to Matthews's resignation the following day.[79]

Matthews was unrepentant and claimed he had proof that seven thousand clergymen were communists or fellow travelers. But both McCarthy and the House Un-American Activities Committee (HUAC) had refused to let him testify. A few years later, Matthews revived his career by cooperating with state-level Un-American Activities Committees in the South, helping white southern politicians discredit civil rights leaders with accusations of communism.[80] In Congress, however, Matthews's resignation was a major coup for McCarthy's opponents. According to Robert Griffith, this episode "proved that McCarthy could be beaten, that the 'myth of invincibility' was just that."[81]

Matthews had resigned on July 10, 1953. Eleven days later, on July 21, G. Bromley Oxnam testified before HUAC.[82] When members of HUAC began to raise accusatory questions about his association with several popular front groups during the 1930s, Oxnam initially hoped to stave off a public confrontation. After unsuccessfully pursuing a private settlement with the committee's chairman, Oxnam became disillusioned, and he instead prepared for a public fight. He now insisted on testifying before the committee in response to charges calling him a communist and a fellow traveler first made by fundamentalist Carl McIntire and later repeated by HUAC staff and witnesses. When Oxnam testified, most of the questions came from McIntire's list of accusations.[83]

Oxnam testified about his involvement with left-leaning organizations, clarified his views on communism, and explained his past associations with individuals suspected of being communists. His testimony also delved into some of his close associates and fellow Methodists, like Harry F. Ward and Jack McMichael, whom he publicly criticized in front of the House committee. For example, he refused to call his former teacher and mentor Harry Ward a friend. Oxnam spoke about an episode "in 1940 when the American Civil Liberties Union took action barring anyone who believes in totalitarianism from the organization. Professor Ward resigned in protest, which indicated, I think, his attitude upon several matters."[84]

Similarly, Oxnam made public his disagreements with Jack McMichael, the secretary of the embattled Methodist Federation for Social Action. "I did not know that he was a member of the Communist Party but I found myself

Figure 9. Methodist bishop G. Bromley Oxnam is sworn in for testimony at a meeting of the House Un-American Activities Committee (HUAC) in 1953. Photo by George Skadding / The LIFE Picture Collection via Getty Images

in such fundamental opposition to Jack McMichael that I had to face one of two decisions, either to stay in [the Methodist Federation for Social Action] and get him out or to get out myself," Oxnam announced. "And it seemed to me wiser to resign and sever all relations because I was a little fearful it would take a bit longer to get him out than I had time to give."[85] Oxnam then went on to assure HUAC that he already knew that McMichael was a Communist Party member and was willing to share his source of the information with the committee in private.

In the process of vindicating himself, Oxnam had thrown Ward and McMichael under the bus. Like countless others, Oxnam sought to protect his own authority by touting his anti-communist credentials and by disassociating himself with the Far Left of his own community. His tactics were cruel but successful. Richard M. Friend concludes that "after Oxnam's effective rebuttal, HUAC soon moved on" from attacking ecumenical Protestants. And Angela M. Lahr concluded that "media response overwhelmingly favored Bishop Oxnam." His testimony and disavowal of the Protestant Left

made it safer for ecumenical Protestants in positions of power and encouraged governmental anti-communist crusaders to move on from focusing on
religious groups.[86]

John Mackay's "Letter to Presbyterians" capitalized on the momentum
created by Matthews's resignation and Oxnam's vindication. It was written
in the fall of 1953 and distributed to Northern Presbyterians across the
country. Mackay's letter was the product of a newfound confidence that the
tide was turning against Red-baiters. Earlier that year, when Matthews had
publicly accused Protestantism of supporting communism, he singled out
Mackay. In his response on July 10, 1953, the day Matthews resigned, Mackay
previewed many of the arguments that would reappear in his "Letter to
Presbyterians." Mackay defended his right to join any cause he believed was
worthwhile, even if communists had joined the same cause. Calling McCarthyism a "New Inquisition," Mackay announced that "we have come to a moment when in certain circles in our country you can be anything you want, if
you are anti-Communist. You may be a liar, a rake, or a Fascist: everything is
condoned so long as you vociferate against communism." Calling out Mc-
Carthy in all but name, Mackay wrote that "the new inquisition already has
its 'Grand Inquisitor,' who, like his famous prototype, thinks in patterns
which have been made familiar to the world by totalitarian regimes."[87]

When Mackay wrote the "Letter to Presbyterians" later in the fall of
1953, he was more measured in his rhetoric but emphasized the same points.
He again referred to an inquisition that was confusing dissent with treason.
Referencing religious freedom, Mackay warned that "the shrine of conscience and private judgment, which God alone has a right to enter, is being
invaded" by congressional committees.[88] The political developments were
leading to a "fanatical negativism" and a "spiritual vacuum" that could "be
occupied with ease by a Fascist tyranny."[89] The problem of communism was
being solely dealt with as a police problem. Instead, Mackay suggested that
a providential reading of history—that the "revolutionary forces of our
time are in great part the judgment of God upon human selfishness and
complacency"—should lead us to "a sincere attempt to organize society in
accordance with the everlasting principles of God's moral government of
the world."[90] Mackay wanted Americans to "always be ready to meet around
a conference table with the rulers of Communist countries . . . whatever
their ignominious record, and regardless of the suffering they may have
caused."[91] Quoting a passage from Isaiah, "Come now, and let us reason together," Mackay insisted that dialogue was a Christian duty.[92]

The Northern Presbyterian denomination asked every one of their ministers to read and discuss Mackay's letter with their congregations. Mackay's letter grabbed nationwide headlines and became a model for other Protestant denominations.[93] By 1953, Mackay had returned to his earlier calls for direct dialogue with communist China, and through his battles with McCarthyism he developed a critical spirit toward US foreign policy.

Theology of Revolution

In his fight against McCarthyism, Mackay hinted at a new idea that would become Protestant orthodoxy by the 1960s. In his "Letter to Presbyterians" he suggested that "revolutionary forces" represent God's judgment on humanity.[94] The idea that "revolution" was happening worldwide and that it provided clues to God's work on earth, if only it were read in light of the Christian conception of time and history, did not receive much attention. But other ecumenists, most notably Presbyterian missionary educator in Brazil Richard Shaull, took up this idea of seeing world events as a series of providential revolutions. Shaull developed the theology of revolution as an alternative to the bipolar Cold War outlook. He argued that the world was not divided between capitalism and socialism or between democracy and communism. Instead of dividing the world spatially, he believed that all nations faced internal revolutions against injustice. The choice each country had to make was between accommodating revolutionary movements by transforming its society in the name of justice or risking the turmoil and violence that often result from revolutions. This theology of revolution led some ecumenical Protestants to see the struggles for economic justice, racial justice, and decolonization as providential and to more fully embrace these movements.

Ecumenical intellectuals writing about revolution in the mid-1950s pushed further than their predecessors in a few directions. First, the new dialogue made clearer that Christians should not view communism as the religion's enemy. Rather, they should recognize, and even embrace, some aspects of socialism. Second, ecumenical authors argued that their religion was political in nature and that their fellow believers should more fully embrace political activism, including protest movements. Third, ecumenical Protestants more clearly shifted their focus to the Global South, with greater attention to the destabilizing effects of US power in Asia, Africa, and Latin America. Finally, a new sense of urgency about the need to quickly transform the world replaced notions that Christianity was a "leaven" that changed society imperceptibly over long stretches of time. On the whole, the theology of revolution offered an alternative to the Cold War framework and it pushed some ecumenical Protestants to embrace the protest movements of the 1960s.

Ecumenical intellectuals developed a theology of revolution partly because they listened to their fellow Protestants abroad who were on the front lines of revolution. Zhao Zichen, a Chinese Protestant minister and a supporter of Mao who sat on the World Council of Churches' governing body, wrote to the *Christian Century* in 1949, announcing that China has a distinctive history and its adoption of communism should come as no surprise. He pointed to the long history of Euro-American imperialism in the country and praised Mao for liberating China from both the West and from the country's feudal past. In the new era that was dawning, religion would no longer be the handmaiden of imperialism, wrote Zhao. The task henceforth was for Christianity to "confess its sins and shortcomings in seeking to save its own life by occasionally siding with reactionary forces," he wrote. At a moment when ecumenists were uniting their coreligionists from many lands and translating their religious values into a purportedly universal system of human rights, Zhao insisted that China would go its own way and that Protestants should accept, and even celebrate, national differences.[95]

American ecumenical Protestants listened carefully to foreign critics like Zhao. They also listened to American missionaries, who were themselves on the front lines of revolutionary movements. M. Richard Shaull was one of these figures. His 1955 book, *Encounter with Revolution*, was an influential account of international affairs that abandoned the bipolar divisions of Cold War thinking.[96] The book reads like an open letter to Protestants from a missionary whose work abroad endowed him with a cosmopolitan knowledge Americans desperately needed. Shaull's goal was to explain to Americans why people abroad become communists, and how to combat the spread of the ideology. But he also wanted Americans to look beyond communism and to see God's hand in the revolutionary movements across the world. The book was a clear illustration of the shifting dialogue in the mid-1950s from the threat of communism to the causes of revolution. *Encounter with Revolution* was adopted as a study manual by the Student Volunteer Movement and was frequently cited by ecumenical Protestant activists in the 1960s who had joined the New Left.[97]

Warnings that the spread of Western modernity was destabilizing other parts of the world were not new. Ecumenical Protestant intellectuals had long warned about the destabilizing effects of capitalism in the Global South. William Ernest Hocking gave a full account of the harmful effects of modernity in Asia in his 1932 report on the missionary movement. "Modernization has arrived" in Asia, Hocking had announced, and brought with it "problems similar in character to those which accompanied such development in the West."[98] In 1937, theologians meeting in Oxford, England, echoed Hocking's conclusion that the "same forces which had produced material progress have often enhanced inequalities, created permanent insecurity, and subjected all members of modern society to the domination of the so-called independent economic 'laws.'" India and China witnessed modernization in other nations and observed firsthand "economic exploitation by capitalistic powers," prompting "a widespread demand for radical social change through which the benefits of industrialization might be secured and the evils from which the industrialized nations of the West are suffering might be avoided," ecumenical Protestants explained. "A consequence of this development of capitalism was the rise of socialism and communism," they argued in 1937.[99]

Shaull built on these earlier criticisms as he implicated the United States in the world's disorder and held it responsible for its consequences. The root of the problem was the spread of industrialization and technological modernity across the world promoted by the United States and Western Europe, Shaull wrote, along with promises of a better life, and the failure of the West to deliver what it promised. Peasants and workers across the world were demanding a rapid end to poverty. Shaull pointed out the irony that "Communism appeals to many of these people as the one power capable of *finishing* the revolution which the United States and Western Europe *started*."[100] This view contradicted the widely held notion that American capitalism was an inherently attractive alternative to communism because of the consumer goods it offered to the masses.[101] Instead, capitalism was creating instability that often led to communism, according to Shaull.

Shaull's diagnosis of revolutionary movements led him to conclude that US Protestants must undo the harm their country was causing. To do so, ecumenical Protestants had to support political movements that could rival the communist parties in appealing to the masses. A new movement was needed in the Global South, Shaull argued, and ecumenical Protestants should lead the way. Repeating a well-worn criticism of secularism that had become orthodoxy in some ecumenical circles, Shaull argued that liberals were not up to the job because their rationalism "makes them unaware of the irrational forces in men and society, and blinds their eyes to the depth of the revolution." China's Nationalist Party, the Guomindang, was a tragic example of this defunct liberal spirit, according to Shaull. The party's leadership was full of Protestants, including its leader Chiang Kai-shek, but this did not keep Shaull from blaming their flaws on liberalism. These Chinese leaders were Christian in name only, Shaull argued, and their politics had little to offer the Chinese masses, who yearned for land reform.[102] Despite Shaull's hazy assessment of liberalism, his call for a more politically engaged Christianity, one that veered leftward, was clear. Prophetic Christianity offered an alternative to both liberalism and communism, according to Shaull.

By proposing a third way between capitalism and communism, Shaull smuggled in socialist ideas into his book under the banner of Christianity, making it safer for Americans to discuss these taboo ideas. "We are living 'between the times,' in a moment in which many of the political and social structures of the past have collapsed and in which new ones, more adequate for the future, have not yet been born," he wrote. Events "may demand radical changes in our thinking and in our lives." Dealing with revolution may "require confiscation of land, government planning, and in some cases, a degree of socialism."[103] Shaull took ideas long circulating in ecumenical Protestant circles, made them systematic, and offered them explicitly as an alternative to the predominant Cold War framework. Subtly, he shifted the focus of ecumenical Protestants from the United Nations and the problem of the anarchy of nation-states to emancipating peoples from the dominating forces of imperialism and poverty. He urged readers to look past Cold War geographic divides and see poverty as the world's central problem. "The Communist 'liberation' of China, the Mau Mau revolt in Kenya, the unrest in Southeast Asia and South America—all these are but tongues of a revolutionary flame that smolders in the depths and threatens to burst out and engulf us all," he warned. "As we Americans peer into the mouth of the volcano, we see only the red fires of Communism and assume that it, and it alone, is the cause of all our trouble. Here is our first great mistake."[104] Accommodating revolutionary demands was the next great task for American Christians.

Recognizing "Red" China

By articulating an alternative to the Cold War framework, Shaull helped justify crossing its spatial divisions. And although he did not address the issue of China's isolation directly, his ideas created a context in which recognition of the People's Republic made sense. Shaull had little hope for the Soviet Union, but he believed other communist nations could reform themselves. He cited Yugoslavia as an example of a country that was critical of the USSR and open to dialogue with the West. Shaull believed "it is possible that similar movements may develop in other parts of the world. . . . If we refuse to enter into contact with them, we force them into Russia's arms. If we keep all doors of contact open to them, we offer them this possibility of development in encounter with the thought and movements of the Western world."[105]

Amid the receding sway of McCarthyism and the new understanding of world "revolution," Mackay called again for diplomatic recognition of mainland China in 1956.[106] He reemphasized the freedom of American and Chinese Christians to meet one another, a human right that the state could not take away. When exchanges between American and Chinese Protestants were endorsed by the National Council of Churches later that year, the *New York Times* reported that "some observers described it as the first major move to crack what has been called the Bamboo Curtain."[107] In fact, ecumenists had pursued the strategy of meeting with Christians in communist nations with success earlier that year, when a major meeting of the World Council of Churches executive committee took place in Budapest (a month before the Hungarian Crisis of 1956) and a National Council delegation visited Moscow shortly thereafter.[108]

The National Council took up the cause of recognizing mainland China and became the idea's most enthusiastic backer. The organization spotlighted the issue of diplomatic recognition at the Fifth World Order Conference in 1958. Dulles, who was now Dwight Eisenhower's secretary of state, reunited with many old friends at the conference. But the reunion was not a happy one. As evangelical critic Carl Henry observed, the ecumenists "virtually repudiated major facets of Free World strategy shaped by Secretary of State John Foster Dulles, one of the National Council of Churches' own elder statesmen."[109] Dulles spoke out against diplomatic recognition of China in an address at the conference and was publicly humiliated and personally insulted when ecumenical Protestants overwhelmingly passed a resolution that called for recognition.[110] John C. Bennett explained why excluding China from the international community was wrong. Isolating China "helps to preserve a false image of the United States and of other nations in the minds of Chinese people. It keeps people in ignorance of what is taking place in China. It hampers negotiations for disarmament. It limits the functioning

Figure 10. Secretary of State John Foster Dulles speaking in 1958. That year, the National Council of Churches became the first large US organization to call for the diplomatic recognition of mainland China and for its inclusion in the United Nations, which Dulles personally lobbied against. Image courtesy of the Library of Congress.

of international organizations. We have a strong hope that the resumption of relationships between the peoples of China and of the United States may make possible also a restoration of relationships between their churches and ours."[111] For these reasons, in 1958 the ecumenists called on the United States to diplomatically recognize the People's Republic of China and to allow it to join the United Nations.

Bennett understood the call for recognition would not translate into policy immediately. He described the repudiation of Dulles as "part of a larger consideration—the attempt to move beyond more rigid Cold War attitudes of recent years."[112] By this time even Van Dusen had come around to support the recognition of China, and defended the position to his good friend Henry Luce. Both Luce and Van Dusen agreed that China would eventually need to be recognized, but Van Dusen worried that the State Department was not giving any thought "as to how the American public is to be prepared for this inevitability."[113] The call for recognition was one piece of a broader effort to wind down the Cold War and offer an alternative worldview.

When ecumenical Protestants discussed China in the 1950s, they emphasized the long history of imperialism and racism, while minimizing concerns about communism. They saw the communist takeover of mainland China as a product of economic and ideological upheaval, and they believed that communism would have a short life there. They consistently refused to see communism as monolithic, and while they affirmed the need to oppose the Soviet Union militarily, ecumenical Protestant leaders saw the way forward with China through economic development. The debates over Chinese recognition were one of the ways they had come not only to oppose specific policies of the United States but also criticize the Cold War itself. In doing so, however, they invited attacks by their enemies.

The Evangelical Countermobilization and the Clergy-Laity Gap

The National Council of Churches' "Red China" resolution of 1958, which signaled a more confrontational stance toward the US government, occurred at the precise moment that evangelicals completed their nationwide consolidation. Evangelist Billy Graham reached the height of his powers, commanding enormous audiences and receiving regular access to President

Eisenhower. Evangelical intellectuals, like Carl F. H. Henry, also began building bridges with disaffected ecumenical leaders like John Foster Dulles, Walter Judd, and Daniel A. Poling. Henry, the editor of *Christianity Today*, which was the evangelical alternative to the ecumenical *Christian Century*, criticized the National Council's stance on China.[114] He also orchestrated an attack on the National Council designed to drive a wedge between the organization and its denominations, and between national leaders and their local constituencies.

The budding alliances between disillusioned ecumenists and neo-fundamentalists like Henry were central to the increasing salience of the term "evangelical," which distinguished this group from ecumenical Protestants, who were less and less interested in evangelization in the orthodox sense of the term. Only a decade before, during the World Order movement, Dulles, Judd, and Poling were active participants and supporters of the movement to create a just peace based on Protestant principles. In the late 1940s they began diverging from other ecumenical leaders because of the Cold War. But these divergences were tentative, and the three leaders kept their worries about the National Council private until the mid-1950s. Dulles and Judd continued to participate in events sponsored by the National Council, and Poling rarely went after ecumenical policy in his journal, the *Christian Herald*. But by the mid-1950s their reluctance to criticize their fellow ecumenical Protestants disappeared.

Their new willingness to attack ecumenists was aided by the National Council's quarrel with the Eisenhower administration. Calling the Red China statement "rank hypocrisy" and "a brutal betrayal of our Protestant brothers in China," Poling declared, "With every influence that I have, I repudiate it." Judd likewise condemned the statement as soon as it came out, arguing that it would hurt American morale.[115] Henry highlighted evangelicals' dissatisfaction in the pages of *Christianity Today*, and the newfound common political grievances against the ecumenists made Judd and Poling more willing to think of evangelicals as natural allies.

Dulles also repudiated ecumenical views on China. "I attach great weight to judgments taken by church people which relate primarily to the realm of moral principles and the like," he told journalists. "When it comes down to practical details such as whom you recognize and whom you don't, then I think the judgment does not carry the same weight."[116] Henry, aligning himself with Dulles, gave the secretary of state a respectful treatment in *Christianity Today*. Henry's own words about ecumenical Protestants were less judicious. "The modern Herods and Pilates crowded God out of central-ity in ecumenical deliberations" about China, he wrote.[117]

In an editorial published shortly after the National Council called for the recognition of mainland China, Henry's *Christianity Today* blasted the ecumenists for their "naïve confidence . . . that recognition and admission into the family of nations has a reformatory effect." This struck at the core of the ecumenical worldview, which held that all nations could be brought into greater accord through their participation in the United Nations and through their exposure to human rights norms.[118] Henry also chastised ecu-menists for being far too sympathetic to the atheistic Soviet Union and too critical of the United States. He wondered "whether the antithesis between Christianity and unbelief had now been diluted." Henry also criticized the direct political intervention by the National Council, lamenting that "the historic American principle of separation of church and state is clearly on the wane." Henry's attacks on ecumenical Protestant politics were disingen-uous. After all, many of the institutions he helped organize were designed to create greater political influence for evangelicals. Henry's more incisive crit-icism was aimed at the clergy-laity gap. "Direct pressure upon government policies by religious leaders of institutionalized Protestantism . . . is more and more approved, despite a lack of mandate at the grass-roots level," he observed, "and frequent conflict with convictions of lay constituencies" has been occurring. This was inevitable "when political influence and power is concentrated in any religious collectivity."[119] For Henry, the problem was that a small group of ecumenical Protestant elites was speaking on behalf of a constituency that did not agree with them.

Henry recognized the discord among ecumenical denominations and between the laity and the clergy—and he fanned the flames. *Christianity Today* surveyed its readers about recognition of "Red China."[120] Unsurpris-ingly, the 1,400 responses overwhelmingly disapproved of the positions taken by the National Council, a fact that *Christianity Today* used over and over to insinuate that the National Council had lost connection with every-day churchgoers and was increasingly acting like the Catholic Church.[121] The journal repeatedly called on the National Council's executive commit-tee to repudiate the "Red China" report, and it kept the coverage of the issue alive for many months after the conference.[122]

When it became clear the National Council was not backing down, Henry focused on the denominations. The editors applauded the Southern Baptists, who expressed their "shock" over the proposals on China, and supported the Southern Presbyterians, who "deplored the actions" of the National Council.[123] Based on "independent surveys," the call for recognition of China was "contrary to the convictions of the vast majority of their constituencies," *Christianity Today* insisted. "Yet NCC-affiliated denominational leaders maintained public silence or, at most, curiously emphasized that the conference did not speak for the NCC, while ignoring the question whether the delegates authentically represented their respective denominations."[124] This was not merely an evaluation but a threat. "In this climate of affairs, denominational silence will inevitably be taken for acceptance," Henry insisted.

Henry scored a victory when the Northern Baptists repudiated the Red China report by a close vote of 245 to 234. And under the leadership of O. K. Armstrong, a former congressman known for his hawkish views on communism, the Northern Baptists went on record against admitting mainland China into the United Nations until the country showed respect for human rights.[125]

The National Council did not appear especially shaken. While a few denominations repudiated the China recommendations, most did not. And support for the National Council remained strong. The Southern Presbyterians, for example, affirmed their "basic support" for the National Council while disapproving of their specific stance on China.[126] In general, ecumenical Protestants showed that they were willing to oppose government policy publicly and dramatically, and were willing to suffer the consequences of their actions.

From Protestant Globalism to a Theology of Revolution

By 1958, ecumenical Protestants had shown themselves willing to confront US foreign policy and to challenge Cold War orthodoxy with a new understanding of international relations. In the decade-long process of reconciling a UN-centered globalism with anti-communism, American ecumenical Protestants came to terms with a fact they had long had the luxury of ignoring: They could no longer take for granted that the interests of the US government and of Christianity were aligned. In the process, they had lost some of their allies and ceded some of their public stature to old and new rivals.

But ecumenical leaders were emboldened by the controversy they had created in their calls for the recognition of China. Mired in indecision about US foreign policy in Europe and split over NATO, ecumenical Protestants turned their sights on Asia in the 1950s. With Asia on their minds, intellectuals like Latourette, Mackay, and Shaull built on a strand of anti-colonial thought missing in the discussions of Europe to offer an alternative to the prevailing Cold War framework and focus attention instead on the theology of revolution. Most importantly, their deliberations on China paved the way for their influential opposition to the Vietnam War in the following decade.[127]

In the crucible of the Cold War, US ecumenical Protestants preserved their earlier emphases on universalism, anti-colonialism, and social-democratic and anti-racist reforms. Without ever giving up on the United Nations, which they continued to revere for both its moral aims and its institutional workings, they shifted their attention toward revolutionary forces. They had originally conceived of the United Nations and human rights as a means of solving the crisis of unlimited national sovereignty. From the 1930s to the 1950s, ecumenical Protestants debated whether Protestant globalism would free countries in the Global South from European and American domination or whether it would force newly emergent nations to behave in accordance with Christian and Western values. By the late 1950s, ecumenical Protestants moved decisively toward liberation. The new focus on revolution provided ecumenical Protestants with an escape from Cold War orthodoxy.

The ecumenists' new confidence in opposing government measures and in the need to engage politically on behalf of providential revolution had immediate effects. Ecumenical Protestants recognized that a "revolution" was taking place against segregation in the United States. Inspired by events abroad, ecumenical Protestants mobilized on behalf of revolutionary movements at home in the schools of Little Rock and in the streets of Selma.

CHAPTER 7

Segregation Is a Sin

In 1948, the Federal Council of Churches announced that segregation was incompatible with human rights. Soon after, prominent voices and influential institutions rededicated themselves to creating a "non-segregated church and a non-segregated society." By denouncing segregation in light of global moral standards, ecumenical Protestant leaders empowered activists to do more to fight racism.[1] If African Americans were endowed with universal rights, these Protestant activists argued, then the United States should reflect human rights norms in both custom and law. In other words, it was time for Jim Crow to go.

Among the activists empowered by the human rights movement were Dorothy Tilly, Benjamin Mays, J. Oscar Lee, and Eugene Carson Blake. These women and men made important contributions to the movement to end Jim Crow from the 1940s to the 1960s. Tilly's participation in Harry Truman's President's Commission on Civil Rights, for example, transformed theological commitments into a political platform. In such ways, ecumenical Protestants helped shape the very terms of the debate about racism. But it was not only a matter of ideas and platforms. Ecumenical Protestant activists knocked on doors to get signatures on petitions against restrictive housing covenants, filed briefs with the Supreme Court in cases that overturned discriminatory laws, and mobilized to pass the Civil Rights Act of 1964. Although historians have been slow to appreciate their contributions, especially during the 1940s and 1950s, ecumenical Protestants fought segregation in both word and deed.[2]

Among the important legacies of ecumenical Protestant activism against segregation was the polarization of their religious community. As some ecumenical Protestants sought to end Jim Crow, they encountered massive resistance among their own ranks. Some white ministers and churchgoers did not take kindly to the attacks on segregation, and they resisted in whatever ways they could. Ecumenical Protestants split along the fault lines of race and region, as well as along the clergy-laity gap. Segregationists affiliated with the Federal Council of Churches (after 1950, the National Council of Churches) subtly shifted their defense of Jim Crow over time. By the 1950s the days of evoking the curse of Ham and other biblical stories were largely gone. More and more, they turned to political arguments like states' rights and constitutional originalism in support of the racial status quo in the South. This subtle but important transformation acted as a bridge for some believers to the modern conservative movement.

The resistance to integration ecumenical Protestants encountered forced them to shift tactics in the mid-1950s. Despite their important political accomplishments, ecumenical activists made virtually no headway in integrating churches themselves. As 11:00 A.M. on Sunday morning remained the most segregated hour of the week, ecumenical Protestant activists turned their attention instead to universities and their students. Ecumenical Protestant college students were exposed to some of the more radical ideas about "revolution" circulating in international Protestant institutions. They emerged in 1960 on the front lines of the fight for racial justice in the United States. On the whole, the ecumenical Protestant mobilization against racism in the 1940s and 1950s made important contributions to desegregation and served as a tributary to the civil rights movement while also dividing America's religious communities.

From "Social Enlightenment" to "Social Reform"

Ecumenical Protestants' human rights talk caught the attention of poet and critic Alain Locke in 1946. He believed that "many churchmen are returning to [an antiracist Christianity] after years, almost generations, of temporizing and compromise." Pronouncements at that time gave Locke "renewed hope" that progress against segregation would be made. He cautioned that "one cannot, of course, expect social enlightenment automatically to convert itself into social reform, but one is a necessary preface to the other, and throughout history they have never been far apart."[3]

In fact, ecumenical Protestant activists were making a major push for social reform in the 1940s. The most important sign that Locke was onto something was the ecumenical Protestant participation in Harry Truman's

President's Committee on Civil Rights. The group's groundbreaking October 1947 report, *To Secure These Rights*, would set the civil rights agenda for the next two decades. The President's Committee was formed when the National Emergency Committee Against Mob Violence approached Truman in 1946. This umbrella group, which included the Federal Council of Churches, was concerned about a wave of lynchings across the country that targeted Black veterans returning home from the war. In December 1946 Truman issued Executive Order 9808, which created the President's Committee on Civil Rights. It was nicknamed the "Noah's Ark" for having pairs of representatives from major Democratic Party constituencies—two labor leaders, two businessmen, two southerners, and two African Americans.[4] The committee also reflected the Judeo-Christian trinity of a rabbi, an ecumenical Protestant minister, and a Catholic layman.

Despite this burgeoning pluralism, most of the committee members belonged to ecumenical Protestant denominations, reflecting the continued power of the religion. Three of the committee's members had close ties to ecumenical Protestant life. White southerner Dorothy Tilly and African American activist Channing Tobias had been on the Federal Council's wartime Committee on Church and Minority Peoples and had a long record of anti-racist activism.[5] Tilly had grown up in rural Georgia, the daughter of a Methodist minister. Throughout her life, she had been active in the Methodist Church, especially in its social action committees and women's organizations. Exposure to the poverty of African American children led Tilly to a long career of activism against lynching, unequal education, racism in the courtrooms, and ultimately against Jim Crow itself.[6] Joining Tilly and Tobias on the committee was Episcopal bishop Henry Knox Sherrill, who would later serve as the first president of the National Council of Churches.[7]

To Secure These Rights framed the issue of civil rights in global terms, it emphasized the role of the federal government in dismantling Jim Crow, and it outlined a step-by-step program for carrying out its agenda. The report borrowed the ideas and language of Gunner Myrdal's pathbreaking book, *An American Dilemma*, declaring that "the greatest hope for the future is the increasing awareness by more and more Americans of the gulf between our civil rights principles and our practices."[8] The American liberal tradition, the report argued, was best articulated in the United Nations' call for "international cooperation and action" on "human rights." With international attention focused on human rights, "It would indeed be ironical if in our own country the argument should prevail that safeguarding the rights of the individual is the exclusive, or even the primary concern of local government," the report's authors pointed out. Committee members also demonstrated their anti-communist credentials by arguing that lynchings undermined America's fight against the Soviet Union. Broadening civil rights was the right thing to do in light of America's commitment to human rights, the committee argued, but it would also aid the country's foreign policy aims.[9] Finally, like the Federal Council, *To Secure These Rights* announced that the segregationist formula of separate but equal "brands the Negro with the mark of inferiority and asserts that he is not fit to associate with white people."[10] Separate but equal, they declared, was never practiced and never could be. Nothing short of desegregating the country could fulfill America's liberal principles.

When it was issued, the report outlined specific policy proposals, many of which had already been endorsed by ecumenical Protestant groups. *To Secure These Rights* included support for a federal anti-lynching law, ending poll taxes, reparations for Japanese American families, removal of Asian exclusion laws, desegregation of the military, a permanent Fair Employment Practices Commission, legislation outlawing restrictive covenants, and integration of public services.[11]

There were important divisions within the commission. Tilly believed that the strategy of going after segregated schooling in the South was a mistake. When the issue of withholding federal aid to segregated schools came up, Tilly opposed it on the grounds that it would harm southern children, both Black and white, and would undermine progress in the region. "The South will stay ignorant before it will be forced to having non-segregated schools," Tilly warned. Although Sherill agreed with Tilly, they were outvoted by a majority that included Tobias, who urged the federal government not to fund segregated schools.[12]

Despite these disagreements, Bishop Sherrill's endorsement of *To Secure These Rights* was a bellwether of postwar ecumenical Protestantism. Sherrill possessed a conservative temperament, and his Episcopalian denomination tended to be circumspect about controversial topics like race.[13] And so he was cautious on the President's Committee: Little that he endorsed in the report had not already been endorsed by several ecumenical bodies. After *To Secure These Rights* was issued, the Federal Council strongly supported it. "We cannot hope to influence other peoples to accept the Christian way of life or other nations to accept the democratic principles we proclaim, unless we can demonstrate in our own community living that we take them seri-

Figure 11. J. Oscar Lee speaking about US segregation in Nuremberg, Germany, in the early 1950s. Lee headed the Federal Council of Churches' (after 1950, the National Council of Churches') Department of Race Relations. INTERFOTO / Alamy Stock Photo.

ously and are striving to translate them into effective practice."[14] By 1947 ecumenical Protestant activists fighting segregation no longer felt isolated. Powerful leaders like Sherrill supported their work.

To Secure These Rights provided a roadmap for ecumenical Protestants working to get rid of Jim Crow. Since George Haynes was now retired and Tobias had moved on from the YMCA, leadership of the Federal Council's efforts was passed on to the young activist J. Oscar Lee, who became the new head of the Federal Council's Department of Race Relations. He had grown up in Philadelphia and attended nearby Lincoln University, a historically Black college. He received degrees from Yale, Union Theological Seminary in New York, and Union Seminary in Virginia. Lee had spent World

War II organizing migrant workers in Connecticut. At the Federal Council, Lee was the only African American to hold an executive position.[15]

Limited by a modest budget, Lee focused on coordinating ecumenical Protestant groups in the late 1940s. He organized annual retreats with social action groups, which allowed him to take the pulse of Protestant anti-racist activism. Some of what Lee heard was not new. The Northern Presbyterians created an institute for local ministers to learn "the techniques of building an integrated church." They also created a program called "Adventures in Brotherhood," which encouraged "exchange visits" between Black and white children. Northern Presbyterians were working to integrate some of their youth councils, including several in the South. Galen Weaver, the head of the Congregationalist denomination's anti-racist activities, led roundtable discussions about race that had involved 2,200 Protestant leaders. Weaver also helped orchestrate the "Vermont Plan," which sent African American children from New York City to stay with white families.[16]

Lee noticed that these well-worn tactics were accompanied by a new emphasis on lawsuits. The Congregational Council for Social Action, for example, had filed two amicus curiae briefs in landmark civil rights cases. The first was the groundbreaking *Shelley v. Kraemer* (1948) case, which made racial housing covenants—contracts designed to prevent nonwhites from purchasing a house—unenforceable. The second was *Takahashi v. Fish and Game* (1948), which overturned bans on fishing licenses for Japanese immigrants.[17] The Detroit Council of Churches took on two civil rights cases. One was a police brutality case, stemming from the shooting in the back of fifteen-year-old Leon Mosley in 1948. The other was the "Harrison Street" housing case, pursued on behalf of an African American family trying to purchase a home in a predominantly white neighborhood.[18]

Getting more involved in party politics was also becoming the norm in the late 1940s. The Virginia Council of Churches worked with legislators in the Virginia General Assembly in 1947 to introduce a bill to end de jure segregation in the state. The YWCA representative Dorothy Height reported to Lee that she regularly appeared before congressional hearings. Like the Congregationalists, the YWCA filed amicus curiae briefs in several civil rights cases. Height was among a cohort of influential African American women, which included Anna Hedgeman and Pauli Murray, working to expand the political activism of the YWCA. Height had recently outlined a series of planks, based on *To Secure These Rights*, which she was planning on introducing at the 1948 Democratic and Republican Conventions.[19]

As ecumenical Protestants were becoming more involved in legislation and party politics in the late 1940s, housing and employment emerged as the two most important issues. The Los Angeles Council of Churches organized a drive against racially restrictive housing covenants and the San Francisco Council of Churches members passed out leaflets on housing covenants' harmful effects. San Francisco's council lobbied the federal government to create nonsegregated veterans housing in the city.[20] The Congregationalist denomination pushed the United Packinghouse Workers to desegregate their union.[21] All of these efforts were aided by the twenty new Protestant lobbying organizations set up in Washington, DC, during the World Order movement.[22] As Lee must have noticed, in the late 1940s ecumenical Protestants had created a sophisticated political advocacy infrastructure.

This political mobilization was occurring just as the Supreme Court heard two court cases on the separation of church and state, *Everson* and *McCollum*, in 1947 and 1948, respectively. With church-state relations in the news, the old question of the propriety of religious leaders getting involved in politics was raised once again. And the issue was only heightened by the charges of clericalism that ecumenical Protestants directed at the Catholic Church (and because evangelicals regularly accused the Federal Council of acting just like the Vatican). The Catholic Church emerged from World War II with an upwardly mobile laity and an increasing political confidence, partly rooted in a strong commitment to anti-communism. Catholic leaders began asking for greater aid to parochial schools, which became one of the most hotly debated public policy issues in the late 1940s. When the Supreme Court introduced the metaphor of a "wall of separation between church and state" in the 1947 court case *Emerson v. Board of Education*, Protestants chastised the Catholic Church for failing to meet this standard.[23] Ecumenical Protestant criticism of Catholics sharpened the debates about the proper boundaries of political action. The Supreme Court cases shaped the context in which debates about the ecumenical Protestant political mobilization to end segregation took place.

Lee wanted to find out how far he could push political advocacy without setting off alarm bells about church-state separation. Like other ecumenical Protestant leaders, he did this through trial and error. Lee asked the Federal Council to press Republicans and Democrats to adopt anti-racist planks in their party platforms. Advocacy of this sort had already been done by Height on behalf of the YWCA, a voluntary group. On behalf of another group, the United Council of Church Women, Georgiana Sibley asked both Republicans and Democrats in 1948 to include in their platforms support for the United Nations, lower trade barriers, the UN Covenant and Declaration of Human Rights, and to implement these statements "in the laws of our own country," to ensure civilian control over policy, and to eliminate "lynching and mob violence," the poll tax, and "discrimination in employment practices, housing, and education."[24] Could this advocacy also be done by an organization that officially represented America's Protestant churches? The strategy had some advantages: Party platforms were expressions of general principles rather than proposals for specific legislation.[25] Nevertheless, the Federal Council's leaders balked at Lee's proposal. They worried about such direct mixing of church and state, especially on issues that were clearly divisive. For similar reasons, the Federal Council rejected giving money to organizations that targeted specific congressional campaigns.[26] The council was reluctant to get involved in conventions and campaigns, while other groups, especially women's groups, were more comfortable with such direct intervention.

Ecumenical Protestants were getting more comfortable in national politics, but they largely avoided civil disobedience in the 1940s and 1950s. In those same years the Fellowship of Reconciliation, a pacifist Protestant group, was developing a less cautious approach. The Congress of Racial Equality (CORE), which arose from and remained connected to the fellowship, initiated sit-ins during World War II, and the Fellowship of Reconciliation organized "Journeys of Reconciliation" in 1947, which was a precursor to the Freedom Rides of the civil rights movement.[27]

George Houser, who worked for both the Fellowship of Reconciliation and CORE, wrote to Lee in June 1947. Houser proposed the Federal Council and the fellowship hold a joint conference "to face up to this whole question of segregation in the church."[28] With Lee absent, his assistant replied to Houser, believing that Houser must not have heard about the Columbus conference of the previous year or the work the Federal Council was now doing.[29] Houser, of course, knew about both developments but was unimpressed with the cautious programs and the glacial pace of change. He "had in mind something more complete than has been done to date. I was thinking of a conference which would deal exclusively with what churches can do and ways of implementing decisions made," giving a "good deal of attention" to the "interracial church."[30]

When Lee returned to the office he rejected Houser's proposal himself. Was it because the fellowship cooperated with sympathetic leftists during a wave of anti-communist agitation or because the ecumenical leadership's

sense of self-importance made Lee dismiss pacifists like Houser?[31] Both
reasons likely played a role, but an adherence to bureaucratic procedures
and the confidence in the "Non-Segregated Church" statement as a break-
through were equally important. Lee said that Houser's proposal "is an interesting one" but reminded him that the "Non-Segregated Church" statement
came about only because of "extensive study." "The big task," Lee wrote, was
"to implement the statement of policy adopted there." For Lee, progress
came about through exhaustive study of the facts and in placing incontro-
vertible proof of social problems to responsible Protestant leadership. Lee
was doing just that, and he believed progress was being made.[32] Now was no
time for more conferences.

Lee's rebuff was final. Houser was not invited in the coming years to
Lee's retreats, and Lee avoided working with the Fellowship of Reconciliation. Houser worked on the margins of Protestantism, finding more willing
allies on the secular left than among religious organizations, as he developed tactics of civil disobedience that would later be embraced by many ecumenical Protestants, especially young people, in the 1960s.[33] As Lee and his
allies struggled to figure out what human rights advocacy would look like in
the context of American politics in the late 1940s, their position-paper liberalism held them back.

Sweatt v. Painter, Brown v. Board, and the Protestant Divide over Segregation

As ecumenical Protestants pushed the boundaries of church and state with
their politically active anti-racist agenda, the issue would come to a head
when Lee and the Federal Council became involved in the court cases that
would lead to the groundbreaking Supreme Court decision, *Brown v. Board
of Education*. Although civil disobedience remained out of bounds for most
ecumenical Protestants, the political mobilization against segregation—
including legal action—was far more than anything they had done in the
past. By 1948 many ecumenical Protestant groups had successfully intervened in lawsuits designed to get rid of racist laws. When the Federal Council
would do the same in the *Sweatt v. Painter* case, it led to a major controversy
about the proper relationship of church and state.

In January 1949, Galen Weaver, the director of Congregationalism's
pioneering desegregation efforts, wrote to Lee to encourage the Federal

Council to get involved in a developing court case on segregated higher education. The "McLaurin, Sweatt and Sipuel cases," Weaver reported, had been
discussed at a meeting organized by NAACP lawyer Thurgood Marshall.
Weaver urged Lee to join other ecumenical Protestant organizations in filing a joint brief in support of the plaintiffs.[34] Lee agreed to get involved.

The plaintiff in the case, Heman Marion Sweatt, was denied admission
to the University of Texas Law School and was told to apply instead to the
law school the state set up specifically for African Americans. The question
before the courts was whether the separate law school was, or could ever
become, equal. The NAACP was especially eager to have an organization
"charged with the moral leadership of our nation" write an amicus curiae
brief, because the *McLaurin* and *Sweatt* cases would be judged on the "facts"
not on the "law." These cases, an NAACP assistant special council emphasized, "involve for the first time a direct attack on the separate but equal
doctrine," which the Federal Council had recently denounced.[35]

Such direct political involvement was new for the Federal Council, and
Lee proceeded cautiously. Working with executive secretary Samuel McCrea
Cavert, Lee developed a justification for intervening in the court case rooted
in the 1946 "Non-Segregated Church" statement, the Universal Declaration
of Human Rights, a 1948 statement on racism by the World Council of
Churches, and the Federal Council's 1948 human rights statement.[36] When
finished, the amicus brief reiterated the Federal Council's position that
"'Separate but equal facilities' in the matter of public education tends to
maintain a permanent pattern of imposed inferiority and subjection." Segregation "is a denial of the equal protection of the laws, of the dignity and
inherent rights of the individual human being and of the Christian concept
of universal brotherhood." The brief also repeated the argument, so important during the World Order movement, that segregation would hinder "a
durable peace throughout the world." "We do not believe that in the human
tempest which has been shaking the world for several decades, our form of
government and way of life can permanently endure on the basis of discrim-
inations and segregations," the Federal Council told the US Supreme Court.
Referencing Lincoln and emancipation, the organization wrote that "it is
still true that this country cannot exist half slave and half free."[37]

Despite Lee's careful preparation, the brief stalled in the Federal Council's bureaucracy because of opposition by Southern Presbyterians J. Mc-
Dowell Richards and John M. Alexander.[38] They disagreed on principle with
the Federal Council's commitment to human rights and urged the churches

not to get involved in such controversial political matters. They were backed by some moderates, who went to great lengths to placate the Southern Presbyterian denomination, which was the Federal Council's newest member.[39]

F. Ernest Johnson, the Federal Council's research director, was "distressed" that the organization was trying to bury the brief. Even worse, the Executive Committee was about to pass rules making it more difficult for Lee to testify before Congress.[40] Johnson was not alone in his anger. Lee demanded that the Executive Committee stop equivocating on segregation. He warned that "secularism as well as Catholicism and Communism are making increasing inroads" among African Americans, who are "losing faith in the willingness and the ability of Protestants to deal with the racial problems that deny them worth as persons." Protestants "do not have unlimited time to convince those with troubled consciences" to match their practices with Christian principles. Appeasing segregationists will not change their minds, Lee wrote, but neglecting racial justice will surely alienate racial minorities and sympathetic whites. The Executive Committee needs to choose whether it will perform a "prophetic" function of blazing "new trails"—as it had in "international relations, segregation, human rights, and economic life"—or whether it will withhold action until "unanimous agreement" is reached. Lee urged the Federal Council not to become hostage to "those groups in it which have the least social conscience."[41]

Lee won the battle. In the wake of Lee's challenge, the Federal Council's Executive Committee reintroduced the amicus brief with the condition that denominations disagreeing with the brief could have their dissent recorded.[42] The brief noted that the Federal Council supports human rights and is unalterably opposed to the "separate but equal" doctrine. A footnote in the amicus brief stated that "the Presbyterian Church in the U.S. Dissociates [sic] itself from this brief."[43] Approved initially in May of 1949, the legal document did not gather much publicity until the end of the year, when the brief was given final approval in December, after the Sweatt case made its way to the Supreme Court. Unusually, the Federal Council's Executive Committee was meeting in Atlanta, and the southern byline attracted more attention in press reports than Federal Council meetings usually received.[44]

White southern liberals had mixed reactions to the brief. One American Baptist minister from Washington, DC, noted that an influential layman in his church, who was of a "rather liberal view toward the Negro race . . . seems terribly upset" over the Federal Council's brief. The minister shared the layman's concern because, he believed, "legal procedures" undermine "Christian influence."[45] The more partisan ecumenical Protestant institutions become, the less seriously people will take their ideas, he argued.

Other southern liberals gave enthusiastic support. South Carolina US District Court judge J. Waties Waring expressed his faith that racial segregation would end "through the churches." He insisted that opponents of segregation possess the "weakest line of defense ... in the religious area. And there really is no semblance of an argument when the approach is made from that standpoint." Overestimating ecumenical leaders' authority over churches, Waring urged a trickle-down initiative, encouraging the Federal Council to share its resolutions with its denominations, which would share it all the way down to the pews. By "reaching millions of American citizens," the Federal Council would force the Senate to "begin to realize there is a great wave of religious backing to the abolition of segregation," and "they will stop playing petty politics and wipe out the bane of filibustering."[46]

Waring showed little knowledge of the Federal Council's publicity efforts amid widespread apathy, and some hostility, in the pews. However, he did identify a rhetorical advantage that ecumenists had over their segregationist opponents with regard to racism. Over the past several decades, theologians had confronted an alternative theology of race that recognized racial differences as God-given and white supremacy as part of the natural order. To those who cited Galatians 3:28 ("There is no longer Jew or Greek, there is no longer slave or free, there is no longer male and female; for all of you are one in Christ Jesus") theological racists retorted with Deuteronomy 32:8 ("When the Most High apportioned the nations, and when he divided humankind, he fixed the boundaries of the peoples") and Acts 17:26 ("From one ancestor he made all nations to inhabit the whole earth, and he allotted the times of their existence and the boundaries of the places where they would live"). Theological racists told biblical stories about God's curses and punishments of those who defied his orders to keep the races apart. According to Jane Dailey, "Narratives like these had two key pedagogical aims: to make the case for segregation as divine law, and to warn that transgression of this law would inevitably be followed by divine punishment."[47]

By 1946 ecumenists had won the battle against theological racism among the leadership of the Federal Council and its denominations. While theological racism persisted at the grassroots, especially in the South and among Southern Baptists, fundamentalists, and evangelicals, it was largely banished from the leadership of ecumenical institutions. That did not mean that every ecumenical Protestant leader supported integration—they did not. But decades of work to lessen prejudice had made it difficult for segregationists in the ecumenical denominations to appeal to racist theology in defense of Jim Crow.

Instead, defenders of segregation moved from theological racism to political arguments, appealing to states' rights, majoritarianism, and church-state separation. They rooted this politics in the ecclesiology of majoritarianism and individualism, and sometimes realism. Opponents of integration appealed to anti-hierarchical and individualistic forms of church organization, arguing that the Federal Council had no right to speak on behalf of those in the pews or on behalf of individual churches. But they also tacitly accepted some of the theological grounds of the anti-racists. As they moved from theological to political arguments, the fights about ecclesiology that had roiled ecumenical Protestantism in the 1930s merged with debates about church-state separation of the late 1940s.

When Southern Presbyterian representative J. McDowell Richards defended his opposition to the *Sweatt* brief in the *Presbyterian Outlook* in 1949, he made a constitutional argument, not a theological one. The role of the courts is to decide what the law is, he wrote, not what it ought to be. He also noted that most churchgoers in the Southern Presbyterian denomination approved of segregation and therefore his vote against the amicus brief represented the will of the majority. Cautioning against the "immediate abolition of segregation," he counseled his fellow Presbyterians that racial injustices should be undone by "education rather than by legislative fiat."[48]

When publicly pressed by critics, Richards elaborated his own views. To the question, "Is segregation Christian?" Richards responded, "My answer to that question must necessarily be an unequivocal 'No'." Segregation was unchristian, he admitted. But this did not lead him to support desegregation efforts, at least not through anything beyond education. He reiterated the constitutional argument and suggested that "voluntary" segregation is preferable to "enforced" segregation. Richards warned that forcing desegregation on the region might provoke "violence and strife," which were "far less Christian even than segregation."[49] Ceding theological ground, Richards took on more explicitly political arguments against the Federal Council's attack on Jim Crow.[50]

Amid these public disagreements among ecumenical Protestants, Texas attorney general Price Daniel challenged the Federal Council on its right to file a brief in the *Sweatt* case. The amicus brief needed the consent of both the plaintiffs and the defendants, and Daniel refused to approve the brief unless it clearly described the actual practices of the Protestant churches. He charged "that the religious denominations represented by the Federal Council maintain separate churches, separate church schools, separate denominational colleges, and separate congregations for white and Negro citizens in Texas and fourteen other Southern states."[51] What right did these hypocrites have to challenge the racial practices of others when they also practiced segregation? he seemed to be asking. The Federal Council had no reply to this embarrassing criticism and skirted around Daniel's objection by getting permission directly from the Supreme Court to file the brief. Despite the Federal Council's best efforts, its hypocrisy became national news.

The national controversy over the *Sweatt* case encouraged churches in the South to oppose the Federal Council's desegregation efforts. The Lynchburg, Virginia, *News* editorialized that "more and more it becomes evident that the Federal Council of Churches of Christ has outlived, or rather destroyed, its usefulness." The Federal Council's Virginia branch had recently become involved in a political campaign to end segregation in that state, the newspaper noted, and now the Federal Council itself was filing a brief in the *Sweatt* case. The *News* objected to the amicus brief on democratic and antipolitical grounds, calling for "withdrawal from the Council of Churches of Christ of all churches that hold to the doctrine that their members speak for themselves" and believing "that churches are concerned with things religious and not with things political."[52]

The Virginia *News* made two underlying assumptions about religion and politics. The first was based in ecclesiology, or the organization and structure of the Christian church. The authors held to the "congregational" model of church organization, which insisted that there was no higher authority than the individual congregation in theological matters and was deeply suspicious of church hierarchy. In this libertarian model of church life, groups like the Federal Council had no right to speak on behalf of church congregations, especially if the Federal Council's opinions were not shared by the churchgoers they represented. The second assumption of the Federal Council's opponents was a clear distinction between religion and politics, which ecumenical Protestant leaders refused to make. They argued that congregations should be concerned with religious life—by which they usually meant emphasizing individual piety—and leave politics to the private judgment of God-fearing Christians. In both their ecclesiology and their views of church-state relations, the views of these objectors had more in common with the views of evangelicals than with the beliefs of the leaders of their own ecumenical denominations.

Only one church followed through on the threat to secede from their denomination, in this case the United Methodist Church, because the denomination was a member of the Federal Council. A newspaper editor and a judge led the board of Stewards of the First Methodist Church in Talladega, Alabama, to repudiate the actions of the Federal Council and leave the Methodist denomination in late 1949.[53] In response, Samuel McCrea Cavert insisted that the filing of the brief had been carried out through a "democratic and representative process" and suggested that the issue "is one for the Methodists to handle through their own channels and in their own way."[54] Another Methodist Church in South Carolina condemned the Federal Council for "injecting the Church into what would otherwise be exclusively a matter of state" but stopped short of secession. The amicus brief undermined "good will" between the races and went against the wishes of "a large segment of Methodist Laymen," according to the church. In the future, the church leaders insisted, a poll of the Methodist laity should be taken before such actions are carried out.[55]

Two years later, another secession took place. This time, it was Adam Clayton Powell's Abyssinian Baptist Church in New York City, which served the African American population of Harlem. Powell, a Black minister who was also a member of Congress, had enough of ecumenical Protestants' equivocation on racism after the organization attempted to bury a proclamation critical of segregation. Adopting a position that religion and politics can never be separated, Powell wondered, "How can we expect the legislators of America to be more Christlike than their clergymen?" As white southerners rebelled against the Federal Council's politics, some African American groups criticized the Federal Council for not going far enough.[56] These protests by African Americans and by southern laymen signaled more trouble ahead for ecumenical Protestantism.

Soon after the Federal Council filed the amicus brief in the case of *Sweatt v. Painter*, the Supreme Court ruled unanimously in 1950 that Heman Sweatt must be admitted to the University of Texas Law School. The ruling noted that the separate Black and white law schools in Texas were grossly unequal. The justices also argued that the mere separation of Black and white students constituted a form of inequality. Four years later, in the 1954 *Brown v. Board* decision, the Supreme Court extended this line of reasoning to its logical conclusion. "In the field of public education, the doctrine of 'separate but equal' has no place," the unanimous ruling read: "Separate educational facilities are inherently unequal."[57]

Shortly after the *Sweatt* ruling in 1950, the Federal Council had merged with several other ecumenical Protestant organizations to create the National Council of Churches. The merger marked a backward step for women's organizations, which lost some of their independence from their male colleagues.[58] But the bureaucratic transition did not have a big impact on the ongoing anti-racist initiatives. Lee's Department of Race Relations was renamed the Department of Racial and Cultural Relations, but not much else changed. Rather, external circumstances drove an increasingly conservative approach to anti-racist initiatives in the first few years of the 1950s. The National Council's leaders feared repeating the drama of their earlier intervention in the *Sweatt* case. Amid the high tide of McCarthyism and the Korean War, the National Council largely kept quiet about racism. At least for this organization, the years immediately before *Brown* meant backsliding on the commitment to human rights made in the 1940s.

Yet when the 1954 *Brown v. Board* decision announced the beginning of the end of Jim Crow in the United States, ecumenists were ecstatic and saw the court case as a culmination of the responsible work they had been carrying on for a decade. The *Christian Century* called the case "historic" not only because it brought America's "democratic professions" in line with "actual social practices" but also because it restored America's "claim to world democratic leadership." "Any American missionary can testify—and hundreds have—that no handicap he has encountered has had more damaging effect than the belief, widespread in Asia and Africa, that our national practices on race matters have been immoral and hypocritical," the editors wrote. The National Council even proposed a national holiday dedicated to celebrating the decision.[59]

Brown v. Board expressed the kind of law ecumenists had been fighting for internationally and domestically—one underwritten by "broad human interests" rather than by "rigid conformity to past legal precedents," according to the *Christian Century*. *Brown* cited "psychological and sociological studies" rather than "law-case citations" in its decision, which demonstrated the "humanitarian construction of our law" as developed by "Brandeis, Holmes and Cardozo."[60] Whereas opponents of desegregation backed strict construction of the Constitution, ecumenists celebrated the liberal constructionism that matched their own theological liberalism.

The *Christian Century* noted that the Supreme Court did not order the immediate desegregation of the South, and it praised the delay in implementation as a "wise decision." Confident that history was on their side, the editors mistakenly believed the delay would "work against the race demagogues," giving the "responsible elements in the south time to reassure the frightened [and] to draw up constructive proposals." The journal assumed a reservoir of goodwill existed in the South, with a "silent public opinion" that believed segregation to be "doomed," and that racist demagogues were "growing less influential." Public opinion "will swing behind efforts to give it honest implementation," the editors wrote.[61] Theologian Reinhold Niebuhr agreed. The delay avoided "undue shock" and lessened "resistance by southern authorities," he counseled. "No law can be enforced if it is not generally accepted by the people."[62]

Adding to the ecumenists' confidence were widespread endorsements of the *Brown* ruling, even by those skeptical of federal intervention. John Bennett pointed out that the Southern Presbyterian denomination, which vigorously opposed the *Sweatt* brief, had endorsed the *Brown* verdict. It signaled that "there has developed in the south a considerable body of opinion which never took part in the struggle against segregation but which is now ready to support the law." Bennett argued that for many this was merely "acceptance of the law as law," but for others it was a sign that they were "ready to change their position" on segregation. Bennett hoped these newly emergent moderates would have time to work things out and that "the Negro leadership, especially in the north, will avoid the kind of pressure which will harden the lines as they are instead of encouraging this new middle group to change the lines which divide people in the south."[63] For Bennett, who was overconfident in the authority of denominational leaders, this *Brown* decision was yet more evidence that ecumenical strategy on segregation was on the right track.

Even the Southern Baptist Convention, which was not a member of the National Council, endorsed *Brown*. The *Christian Century* reported that while a few Southern Baptists spoke at the denomination's national convention about the biblical curse of Ham as justification for segregation, and others raised the specter of white women marrying Black men, the overwhelming majority (nine thousand to fifty, according to the journal) voted to comply with the *Brown* ruling. There was deep resistance to integration among Southern Baptist churchgoers, but the *Christian Century*, which subscribed to a highly hierarchical understanding of social change, thought that Southern Baptist leaders would convert their flocks to integration in due time. Since most of the seven million members of the denomination

lived in the South, the Southern Baptist move would make a "decisive difference," the journal argued.[64]

The ecumenical Protestant condemnation of segregation gained a global
dimension in the months following the *Brown* decision. Ecumenists from
across the world gathered for the second meeting of the World Council of
Churches in Evanston, Illinois, in 1954. The World Council brought together
1,674 delegates from 163 Protestant and Orthodox denominations in 48
countries to the campus of Northwestern University. The "saffron and white
robes of the Church of South India" and the "turbans" of the African Gold
Coast captured the attention of audiences that reached as many as 150,000
people.[65] The timing of the meeting and its location in the United States
meant that segregation would receive a lot of attention. Benjamin Mays,
who had been so involved in the anti-racist debates of the World War II
years, would not let the opportunity go to waste. He pushed the global body
to strongly condemn segregation.

Mays laid out his challenge to the World Council in 1954. In an article
that appeared shortly before the organization met in Evanston, Mays argued
that both science and Scripture give no basis for segregation. The logic of
segregation had been undermined in the last fifty years by biologists, who
showed there to be no physiological differences between people of different
races, and church historians, who showed that until modern times Christians paid little regard to racial differences, according to Mays. The task for
the World Council in 1954 was to move beyond the equality of races, which
scientists and theologians widely accepted, onto the concrete task of how to
"make new creatures of men and women in the area of race." Calling for a
new "Pentecost"—a miraculous event described in the Book of Acts, when
people from different nations could suddenly understand one another—
Mays demanded that the "American Church open its doors to all peoples,
irrespective of race."[66] Mays repeated these demands at the World Council
meeting. Standing before thousands gathered at Northwestern's McGaw
Memorial Hall, Mays received a standing ovation when he declared that
"segregation remains the great scandal in the church."[67]

Swayed by Mays, the World Council of Churches declared segregation to
be incompatible with Christianity. Christians "cannot approve of any law
which discriminates on grounds of race, which restricts the opportunity of
any person to acquire education to prepare himself for his vocation, to pro-
cure or to practice employment in his vocation, or in any other way curtails
his exercise of the full rights and responsibilities of citizenship."[68] Christians

Figure 12. Benjamin Mays in the audience of the World Council of Churches meeting in Evanston, Illinois, 1954. Photo by Larry Burrows / The LIFE Picture Collection via Getty Images.

should "renounce all forms of segregation or discrimination and . . . work for their abolition within their own life and within society," the World Council went onto say. "If Christian obedience leads to suffering, that is part of the price."[69] The World Council also announced it opposed laws banning interracial marriage. Ecumenical Protestants had not been willing to go this far at the 1946 Columbus conference. Now, a global body of Protestant and

Orthodox churches appeared unflinching in their call to dismantle Jim Crow, as well as apartheid, in all of its forms.[70]

The meeting also revealed divisions within the global body about segregation. The main defender of segregation was Ben J. Marias, a South African and a member of the Dutch Reformed Church, who urged Protestants to "take account of long established social patterns" without losing track of the ultimate goal of nonsegregation. "Different churches based on language or race may be useful and even preferable in some extreme cases," Marais cautioned. To "force integration," he advised, "would only lead to a rich harvest of chaos and disaster."[71] The disagreement between Mays and Marais mirrored some of the conflicts between Lee and the Southern Presbyterians over the amicus curiae brief a few years earlier, especially in the way that Marias tacitly accepted the theological anti-racism of the ecumenical movement while finding other ways to defend apartheid.

But Marias was no match for a well-organized group of African American leaders who demanded integration of the churches from top to bottom. Leaders of the all-Black denominations not only pushed for an open-door policy for local churches but also criticized white Protestant leaders for excluding African Americans from participation in the church bureaucracy. The Reverend J. Clinton Hoggard challenged his colleagues, asking them to "take a look at the leaders of the assembly. Do you see any Negroes among them? In fact, the only full-fledged Negro delegates here are from Negro denominations, not integrated denominations." The World Council leaders responded to the criticism by electing two African Americans to the governing body of the organization, a symbolic move that was hailed as a "forward step" by the *Chicago Defender*.[72] The World Council, like some of the national bodies of ecumenical Protestants, proved themselves to be responsive to pressure to change their segregationist practices. In 1954 the largest Protestant and Orthodox body in the world, swayed largely by American ecumenical Protestants, had condemned segregation.

The Civil Rights Movement

Because ecumenical Protestants publicly supported desegregation but called for slow-paced change and devoted few resources to the cause, it largely fell to African Americans to see through the promise of *Brown v. Board* in the South. Benjamin Mays's former student, the twenty-six-year-old Martin Lu-

ther King Jr., suddenly became a national leader of the Black freedom struggle as he led the boycott of the segregated bus system in Montgomery,
Alabama. King had grown up in the Black church, where he first heard the
anti-racist theology for which he would later become famous. At sixteen, he
enrolled in Morehouse College and became close with its president, Benjamin Mays, who was then publicly denouncing Jim Crow as a violation of
human rights. After graduating from Morehouse in 1948, King enrolled at
the predominantly white Crozier Theological Seminary in Pennsylvania.
The seminary was run by Edwin E. Aubrey, a member of the Dulles Commission and one of the organizers of the World Order movement. It was in
the ecumenical context at Crozier that King first encountered the works
of Mohandas Gandhi and his call for nonviolent civil disobedience. After
Crozier, King received his PhD from the Methodist-run Boston University,
where he worked under the supervision of theologian Edgar Brightman, a
philosopher committed to the personalist tradition that promoted the dignity and worth of human personality. King, already attuned to the Black
vernacular tradition of dignity, elaborated and systematized his thought
into a formal philosophical position. He brought these experiences with
him to Montgomery, where the boycott he led would end segregation on city
buses in 1956. He would soon help organize the Southern Christian Leadership Conference and attack Jim Crow under the banner of civil and human
rights.[73]

As King inaugurated the civil rights movement in the South, white su-
premacists tried to stop him. The Ku Klux Klan, steeped in a history of
Christian nationalism, revived and grew to a size not seen since the 1920s.[74]
While the Klan used terror to enforce the status quo, the more respectable
White Citizens Councils sprung up across the South, keeping pressure on
politicians not to relent to federal courts and Black activism. What became
known as "Massive Resistance" was later summarized by one southern governor's inaugural address: "Segregation now, segregation tomorrow, segregation forever!"[75]

Ecumenical Protestants believed that the *Brown* ruling proved their
strategy was the right path. But Massive Resistance was the first indication
that they were wrong in predicting a triumph of moderation in the South. In
March 1956, Brethren official Ralph Smeltzer urged the National Council to
recognize the "racial revolution" taking place and for ecumenical Protestants to organize a "bolder and broader program toward racial integration."[76]
The National Council did something far short of recognizing the racial

revolution. But it did depart from past practices by hiring a white southerner, Will Campbell, to travel through the southern states and organize the
white moderate and progressive pastors that the National Council believed
predominated in the South. The project was poorly funded and poorly
staffed but nonetheless represented a policy of more direct involvement by
the National Council in the civil rights movement.[77]

Campbell's first test was in Little Rock, Arkansas, where a clash over
segregated schools was taking place in 1957. The collegiate gothic facade of
Little Rock Central High School became a symbol of white intransigence
across the world. The governor of Arkansas, Orval Faubus, disobeyed federal
court orders to integrate the school and went so far as to mobilize the National Guard to prevent Black students from entering Central High. Because
of the international attention the crisis received, Secretary of State John Foster Dulles wrote urgently to Dwight Eisenhower in 1955 about the Little
Rock school desegregation crisis. "We are portrayed as a violator of the standard of conduct which the peoples of the world united to proclaim in the
Charter of the United Nations," Dulles wrote, "whereby the peoples reaffirmed 'faith in the fundamental human rights and the dignity and worth of
the human person.'"[78]

Eisenhower reluctantly intervened on the side of the federal courts. He
nationalized the Guard and sent in the Army's 101st Airborne division, allowing the first nine African American students—dubbed the "Little Rock
Nine"—to attend the school. In a televised address to the nation, written by
Dulles, Eisenhower told Americans that "at a time when we face grave situations abroad because of the hatred that Communism bears toward a system
of government based on human rights, it would be difficult to exaggerate the
harm that is being done to the prestige and influence, and indeed to the
safety, of our nation and the world."[79]

Faubus was unmoved. All public schools in Little Rock were closed for
the 1958–59 school year.[80] Worried about the events, the National Council
sent Campbell to investigate. Campbell organized a statewide committee of
ministers, leading a group to meet with the governor to press him to integrate schools. With Faubus steadfast in his support for segregation, Campbell organized a public condemnation of the governor by local ministers.[81]
At the end of 1959, the Supreme Court weighed in and ordered Faubus to
reopen the schools in 1960. Despite his efforts to organize moderate ministers, Campbell appeared to be a bystander as the larger drama of the civil
rights movement played out.

Other groups joined the National Council in becoming more active in the southern states. Congregationalists, who had few southern churches but ran many colleges in the region, took action. As early as 1952 their denomination began envisioning a post–Jim Crow South. They predicted that "considerable" repercussions would flow from the *Sweatt* and *Brown* cases unless "southern white leaders of prestige" would sway public opinion behind the Supreme Court. "We can do little," a Congregationalist race relations group declared, "except perhaps help discover a few key persons in the South" to take the lead in ushering in a nonsegregated society.[82]

Mrs. Albright, a representative of the Southeast convention of the Congregationalists, which encompassed Kentucky, Tennessee, Alabama, Georgia, South Carolina, and a part of northern Florida, reported that the "staff . . . definitely desire integration" but said "our churches are not ready." In the wake of the 1954 *Brown* decision, even fraternal activities, like inviting Black visitors to a convention, were now opposed by many white southern ministers. Albright reported that an integrated student meeting, which had previously aroused little suspicion, had only half of the previous number of participants at its latest gathering. Not sure what to do, Albright maintained that "if we of the staff move too fast, we will be defeated or replaced." "We would lose half of our white churches," she worried, if Congregationalists desegregated their bureaucracy. Trying to convey some of the hopelessness of the situation, Albright stated, "We do not even have freedom of discussion on this issue. Emotion aroused by the school decision has set us back."[83]

Church leaders were faced with unwavering opposition from the laity in the South. Robert G. Geoffroy, the manager of the Vicksburg, Mississippi, Chamber of Commerce, wrote to the Congregationalist leadership, "I violently oppose integrated schools in the South at the present time." Geoffroy recited many of the common arguments of the day against racial equality. "The Negro should first prove his responsibility . . . is consistent with our American heritage which has resulted in certain prerequisites being placed on the privilege of voting, of serving on juries, of holding office, etc." Geoffroy insisted he was no bigot, relaying a story of his time in Korea during the recent war. "I adopted and cared for a homeless Korean lad of 12. I loved him like a brother. I ministered to his needs. I respected his dignity. But I didn't for a minute think that with his combination of environment and heredity that he could participate in or compete in the same social structure as my daughter of the same age," he wrote. "To me it is only a matter of degree to substitute Southern Negro for Korean," Geoffroy concluded.[84]

It was not only churchgoers who objected to integration. Congregational churches were understood to be some of the more liberal ones in the South, and more supportive of ending Jim Crow than the Baptist and Methodist churches that predominated in the region. Yet a report detailing the views of southern pastors in the Congregational churches pointed out that they—not just their congregations—were extremely hostile to integration. White ministers in metropolitan areas tended to be the most accepting of integration, but those working in small towns and rural areas, who were the least likely to have a seminary education, responded to questions about desegregation "in violent terms." One pastor, asked about whether his church would send a delegation to an interracial meeting, replied "Yes, but to run the Negroes off; and I will be leading my delegates!"[85]

Large majorities of Congregationalist ministers in the South reported that, in their own opinion, their denominational conventions should remain segregated. In one survey, more than 60 percent of southern ministers reported that integrating the Congregationalist bureaucracy (not the churches themselves, which was never brought up) would "kill the church or drive it from the denomination."[86] The National Council's filing of the amicus curiae brief in 1950 had set off a couple of defections and a lot of derision. Now, in 1955, there was open rebellion. That year Congregationalists discovered just how widespread and deep-seated racism was among their own ranks. In the wake of *Brown*, any attempt to desegregate would seriously jeopardize the position of ecumenical Protestants in the South.

Worst of all, ministers who spoke out on behalf of integration found themselves under fire. The National Council offered help to ministers who were out of a job. They had identified eight individuals who were "under pressure due to their stand on desegregation" and aided four of them, while Church World Service funds were used to help three others.[87] Ecumenists working to dismantle segregation felt themselves besieged in the mid-1950s and did not know how to move forward with plans that suddenly seemed unworkable in the post-*Brown* world.

Denominational leaders were perplexed by the vitriol from southern churches and were unsure how to respond. The Congregationalists did briefly consider taking punitive action against constituencies that practiced racial segregation. The Council for Social Action inquired in 1955 whether representatives from segregated churches could be barred from its national meetings. The denomination's leadership replied that it was "theoretically conceivable" but "not practically likely because of the strong decentralizing tendency in Congregationalism." In part because of this laissez-faire ecclesiology, the "general tendency [is] to let this question die" because few people "wanted to apply punitive measures" against fellow Congregationalists.

As ecumenical Protestants debated what to do next, southern state governments exacerbated tensions between southern churches and the "outsider" religious leaders calling for desegregation. State legislatures targeted the United Methodist Church, passing laws designed to help churches break free from the denomination. The United Methodist Church was the legal owner of the buildings used by their churches. If congregations would break away, as they had been urged to do over the National Council's *Sweatt* brief a few years earlier, they would lose access to expensive property or, at the very least, suffer through protracted and costly legal battles. Southern states stepped in to encourage rebellion. Mississippi, for example, passed the Church Property Bill in 1960, which protected individual churches from lawsuits by the denomination. This was an attempt to "widen the breaches within our churches," complained Mississippi Methodist leader J. P. Stafford. Southern states entered the ecclesiological battles about religious structure and authority just as ecumenical Protestants were reevaluating their response to the civil rights movement.[88]

From Churches to Universities

When the Congregationalists (who were in the process of merging with the Evangelical and Reformed Church) finally outlined their post-*Brown* plan in 1955 and submitted it for financial backing from the Fund for the Republic, they chose universities and schools rather than churches as the institutional center of their program.[89] Placing their hope on students came after a long process of eliminating alternatives, especially the churches, which showed outright resistance to desegregation. The Congregationalists put together "The North Carolina-Virginia Project" and hoped it would "avoid fanfare" in this tense atmosphere of 1955 and 1956. The plan created an interracial team of two southern women, Pauline Puryear and Dorothy Hampton, who were appointed to be liaisons with Christian schools and get them to integrate their staffs and student bodies.[90] Their work with the churches was frustrating. "I would have to say that if I had known one year ago what the first nine months of this job would be I probably would not have accepted it," Hampton complained. But she saw promise in the students she worked with. "The youngsters will respond to me and perhaps add to my acceptance."[91]

With most Protestant churches resistant to interracial gatherings, much of the actual contact that took place between Black and white Protestants was among youths and college students. "The student Christian movement was biracial," writes Doug Rossinow. "In the 1950s, it facilitated an extraordinary degree of interaction between black and white youth."[92] Baby boomers in the ecumenical denominations became the first generation to regularly meet, face-to-face, across the color line. Although interracial contact harkened back to older strategies of dealing with "racial prejudice" rather than segregation, it now occurred in the tense, post-*Brown* atmosphere and with students being exposed to the searing anti-racist human rights rhetoric of ecumenical Protestantism. Simply meeting interracially became a controversial and politicized act in the South during the mid-1950s.

Increased interracial student contact occurred as the discourse of worldwide "revolution" was becoming popular among ecumenical Protestants. The November 1955 issue of *motive*, the official journal of the Methodist Student Movement, picked up on this new rhetoric. The student magazine ran a special issue on "Revolution and Reconciliation" that sought to dramatize the global dissatisfaction with Euro-American economic and racial imperialism. Coverage included a detailed report of the Bandung conference and decolonization movements across the world.[93] The Methodists, who were one of the few predominantly white ecumenical Protestant denominations with a large African American membership and a large white southern membership, began educating their students on the interconnection of Jim Crow, decolonization, and white supremacy.

M. Richard Shaull's *Encounter with Revolution* added to the deepening interest in decolonization, and the book made "revolution" a keyword in ecumenical students' understanding of world events.[94] Like *motive*, Shaull's book foregrounded global movements for social justice as the most important development of the era. Shaull was one of the authors who contributed to what Jeremi Suri calls "the language of dissent" of the youth movements of the 1960s.[95] Shaull warned that peoples across the world were rebelling against the spread of Western capitalism and modernization and demanded control over their lives. "The common man today wants to feel a new sense of dignity and responsibility that comes from the possession of power," Shaull instructed Americans. "He demands the privilege of helping to control the economic and political forces which dominate his life, and will give

his support to that political movement which offers to satisfy this ambition."[96]
Encounter with Revolution is an illustration of how earlier attacks on global white supremacy in the 1940s by critics like Edmund Soper and Buell Gallagher had become widespread by the 1950s.

Ecumenical youth seized on the diagnosis of world revolution offered by Shaull and pushed it in more self-critical directions. After all, they were living at a moment when books like C. Wright Mills's *White Collar* (1950), David Riesman's *The Lonely Crowd* (1951), and William H. Whyte's *The Organization Man* (1956) encouraged criticism of mind-numbing bureaucracy and the pettiness of middle-class life.[97] The same revolt against soulless technological modernity that was happening abroad was also happening at home, many students came to believe. Shaull's *Encounter with Revolution* had correctly diagnosed world events, a *motive* reviewer noted, but wrongly excluded America from the global revolution. The "grave error" Shaull made in his book was "presuming no Revolution in the United States [and] ignoring the Court decision on racial integration."[98]

The "Revolution and Reconciliation" issue of *motive* and Shaull's *Encounter with Revolution* both served as primers for Methodists students who were attending the Seventeenth Ecumenical Student Conference in Athens, Ohio, in 1955. The ecumenical student conferences were a traditional recruiting ground for young missionaries, and the revolutionary rhetoric among them signaled just how much the missionary movement had changed over the twentieth century. The location of the meeting was also significant. At a previous gathering in Lawrence, Kansas, in 1951, students had experienced Jim Crow firsthand when they left the University of Kansas campus and were denied accommodations at a local hotel and were refused service at a café. Bayard Rustin, one of the 1951 conference participants, organized a small group that included two visitors from India, a Canadian, and three Americans to press the conference leaders to do "all within our power to maintain human dignity and prevent further incidents of this nature from occurring." "As members of this international body of delegates," Rustin reminded the organizers, "we cannot continue to talk about the principles of Christian living and missionary service and at the same time allow such anti-Christian acts to go unnoticed."[99] Students at the conference discussed the event in small groups, and the organizers decried the incident. They decided to move the 1955 conference to the more hospitable location of Athens, Ohio.

At the 1955 Athens conference students came from more than eighty countries and included some Catholics, Hindus, and Muslims. The crowds were so large they quickly "overtaxed the facilities of Ohio University" and "many were accommodated in the gymnasium stadium cars and broom closets," the *New York Times* reported. Local residents "threw open the doors of their homes to white and colored alike."[100] Crowding into seminar rooms and lecture halls, students from across the world passionately discussed apartheid in South Africa and segregation in the United States. Speaking at the conference, Shaull warned that "violent revolt against our economic and political imperialism, as well as against our racial pride" is taking place across the world. "The great majority of the peoples of the world, who happen to be non-white, will not tolerate our attitude of racial superiority," and America will face "judgement."[101]

Southern students leaving Athens pledged to return home and continue meeting interracially. One white student from the University of Mississippi commented that the future meetings will "have to be at a Negro college—if we tried them at ours the state would come down on us like a ton of brick."[102] Students at the Athens conference, like students in ecumenical denominations more generally, came to see themselves as political actors in the mid-1950s and imagined themselves as one part of a global movement for social justice. For example, when a student delegation returned to Austin, Texas, from a meeting of the YMCA in 1959, they organized sit-ins across the city.[103]

The Eighteenth Ecumenical Student Conference, which took place over the winter break of the 1959–60 academic year, made an even bigger impression on the participating students. Billed as the West's answer to communist youth meetings, the 1959 conference in Athens, Ohio, had a decidedly political edge.[104] The nearly 3,600 students, half of whom were foreigners studying in the United States, heard yet again about the link between decolonization abroad and desegregation at home, and about the ongoing revolution across the globe. This time it was from Martin Luther King Jr., who told the students that "an old order is passing away, and a new order is coming into being." He added, "We have seen the old order in Asia and Africa, in the form of colonialism and imperialism" and "we have seen it in our own nation in the form of segregation and discrimination." He urged that we now replace the old order with a new one "in which all men respect the dignity and the worth of human persons."[105]

As students returned home from Athens, they continued meeting in "Study-Involvement" groups through the spring of 1960. They drew severe criticism in the segregated American South. White students at a Texas university who wanted to gather with African Americans were denied permission to meet on campus and were threatened with suspension when they decided to meet interracially off campus. They met despite the threats. Students from Atlanta and Memphis reported similar incidents, as did a group of students from Tuskegee, Stillman, and Alabama Tech.[106]

When four African American students in Greensboro, North Carolina, began sit-ins at a segregated Woolworth's lunch counter on February 1, 1960, launching a movement across the United States, attendees of the Athens conference were in the perfect position to participate. And they did so in disproportionate numbers. According to Ruth Harris, one of the conference organizers, "Between February 1 and June 1, 1960, more than two thousand students were arrested [at lunch counter protests], mostly African Americans. A study done later revealed that every lunch counter demonstration included at least one student who had attended the 1959 conference in Athens, Ohio."[107]

The National Council applauded the sit-ins, calling them "expressions of just and righteous indignation against laws, customs, and traditions which violate human personality."[108] The YWCA praised the protesters for seeking to eliminate "those practices which deny recognition of the common humanity of all as children of God."[109] The Episcopalians, Methodists, and Presbyterians followed suit.[110] Truman B. Douglass, the vice president of the Congregationalists' Board of Home Missions, addressed the graduation ceremony of the historically Black Dillard College in the spring of 1960, urging students to fight "white man's law imposed upon a multi-racial society."[111]

The National Student Christian Federation explained the students' new understanding of revolution. The student demonstrators were acting out of "our responsibility in a world of revolution" and the "particular burden and opportunity resting upon us as students in the USA in view of the world position of our nation." Breaking with the earlier attempts of religious leaders to maintain a plausible distance between church and state, the students now declared the "impossibility of neutrality as to political engagement." They insisted that "there is no true evangelism that is at the same time not a political event."[112] Ecumenical youths were casting off the debates about ecclesiology and church-state separation that had embroiled their elders, partly because they were working outside of denominational boundaries. More and more, they expressed their solidarity with nonwhite peoples across the world and viewed as their community the transnational student movement, not the segregated churches of their hometowns.

The affective identification between college students and third-world revolutionaries was remarkable. Needless to say, there were important differences between the activism of US college students, especially white college students, and the Marxist rebels in Mozambique and indigenous activists in Brazil with whom they identified. But looking abroad for solidarity was a common practice among many religious groups. According to Melani McAlister, American evangelicals began in the 1970s to identify closely with victims of anti-Christian persecution abroad and to view themselves as victims of oppression in the United States.[113] Evangelicals' "victim identification" had some parallels with ecumenical youths' solidarity with the victims of Western imperialism. But these two outlooks encouraged very different political behavior in the United States. The theology of revolution encouraged ecumenical students to work with nonreligious groups, to engage in civil disobedience, and to move politically to the left.

Ecumenical youths declared that God was speaking and acting in the world through revolutionary movements: "His actions are on the world scene in the struggle between powerful socio-economic and military blocs, in the far reaching movement of liberation of Asian and African peoples from imperialist and colonial status to independence with dignity, and in the United States in the student non-violent movement which is working for economic opportunity, racial freedom and dignity, and democratic equality and justice for all men."[114] This fiery rhetoric was new for many ecumenical leaders, but by the end of 1960 most ecumenical institutions and denominations were reorienting themselves to a more confrontational form of activism against segregation pioneered by young ecumenical Protestants. Even though they did not intend their youth to take part in sit-ins, ecumenical leaders nonetheless embraced the new activism and, in retrospect, saw it as a logical outgrowth of the ideas they had been espousing since the 1940s.[115] In doing so, they abandoned their search for a middle ground on Jim Crow and clashed with a laity that remained hostile to integration.

Emblematic of this new activist style was former National Council president and head of the United Presbyterian denomination, Eugene Carson Blake. A month and a half before the 1963 March on Washington, where he would deliver an address, Blake entered a segregated amusement park in Baltimore with a group organized by CORE. He was arrested soon after walking in. The event made headlines across the world because of his public stature. After a short stint in jail, Blake emerged as a hero to many antiracist activists.[116] Blake's arrest dramatized a major development in Ameri-

Figure 13. Eugene Carson Blake being led into a police van following his arrest
at a segregated amusement park near Baltimore, Maryland, in 1963. Because
he was the first white clergyperson of his stature to be arrested for civil
disobedience, the event garnered international headlines. Image courtesy of
the Presbyterian Historical Society.

can Protestantism. After rebuffing the Fellowship of Reconciliation in 1947,
the National Council began actively cooperating with its offshoot, CORE,
and other anti-racist groups by the 1960s. That Blake would willingly subject
himself to arrest shows how much ecumenical institutions had changed by
the 1960s.

Ecumenical youths helped bring about that change. Although Blake was
in his fifties, the *Chicago Defender* pointed out that the protesters at the Baltimore amusement park were "predominately white and of college age."[117]
Young ecumenical Protestants were the first generation to be exposed to an
officially integrationist philosophy and to interracial meetings while still
attending segregated churches and living in segregated neighborhoods.
Of course, it was not only youth who protested segregation. Ministers

throughout the country joined marches and freedom rides. As they took leave from their pulpits, they often encountered resistance from churchgoers, who could not understand why ministers of the gospel were getting involved with a political movement. The gap in values between laity and clergy had long been present in American Protestantism, but it widened and became more public during the civil rights movement.[118]

Ecumenical activism against Jim Crow contrasted with evangelical views on segregation. As ecumenical Protestants discarded their earlier moderation by embracing protest movements and anti-colonial rhetoric, some evangelical leaders were discarding their commitment to segregation and becoming racial liberals. Evangelicals started reading Franz Boas and Ruth Benedict in the 1950s and listening to their missionaries about the harmful effects of American racism on overseas evangelism.[119] Billy Graham began desegregating his crusades in the mid-1950s but shied away from structural criticism and treated racism as an individual problem best tackled through education and persuasion.[120] L. Nelson Bell, editor of *Christianity Today* and Graham's father-in-law, echoed the feeling among many of his fellow Southern Presbyterians in 1956, when he stated that although the Bible does not mandate segregation, "voluntary segregation" was preferable.[121] By the 1960s evangelicals' loud demand for law and order—a slogan that was racially coded in obvious ways—often drowned out their calls for racial equality.[122] As some evangelical leaders became moderates on civil rights, they were attacked from the right by figures like Bob Jones and Carl McIntire. Churchgoers in their congregations also resisted calls for racial equality. But because ecumenical Protestants had blazed the trail of racial liberalism decades earlier and had moved on to more expansive attacks on racism, evangelicals were able to occupy the middle ground vacated by their religious rivals and defend their newfound racial liberalism by contrasting it with the wrongheaded approach taken by Blake and ecumenical youths.[123]

The National Council and its allies became important players in the civil rights movement. Among the organization's biggest achievements was an enormous pressure campaign on midwestern senators and members of Congress to pass the Civil Rights Act in 1964. The effort was led by African American activist Anna Hedgeman, a longtime figure in Democratic Party politics. Hedgeman grew up in a Methodist household in a small town in Minnesota, where hers was the only African American family. She was the first Black graduate of Hamline University, a Methodist school in St. Paul. She settled in New York City, and, from the 1930s through the 1950s, she worked primarily in the realms of local, state, and national politics but was also a prominent member of the YWCA and Church Women United. She began working for the National Council in 1963, helping organize the March on Washington and mobilizing the vast majority of white attendees at the march. Hedgeman brought skill, experience, and political connections to the National Council, all of which were rooted in a long history of African American women's organizing against segregation.[124]

To promote the Civil Rights Act of 1964, Hedgeman organized letter-writing campaigns, spoke out publicly, and lobbied members of Congress and senators. According to James F. Findlay, ecumenical Protestants "exerted pressure on Congress not only in Washington and on Capitol Hill, but also from parishes a thousand miles westward in small places like Rochester, Indiana; Farley, Iowa; and Waseca, Minnesota."[125] About 40 percent of the letters received by Iowa senator James E. Bromwell, Illinois senator Everett Dirksen, and House minority leader Charles Halleck on the Civil Rights bill came from church groups.[126] Ecumenical Protestants became an important constituency lobbying for the passage of the pathbreaking Civil Rights Act.

The human rights advocacy of the 1940s shaped the anti-racist activism of the National Council and their allies into the 1960s, but also revealed its limits. Eugene Carson Blake lamented the failures of religious activism in front of hundreds of thousands at the 1963 March on Washington, announcing that "as of Aug. 28, 1963, we have achieved neither a nonsegregated church nor a nonsegregated society. And it is partially because the churches of America have failed to put their own houses in order."[127] The integrationist philosophy long held by ecumenical leaders was resisted in the pews but also increasingly challenged by the emerging Black power movement. The long-standing focus on white prejudice and reforming white men and women was increasingly overshadowed by calls to empower African Americans—including calls made by Hedgeman.[128] The goal of getting more African Americans employed at Protestant universities, hospitals, and seminaries finally received greater attention in the 1960s.

Most dramatically, African American activist James Foreman burst into Riverside Church—the cathedral of liberal Protestantism—during a service in 1969 and presented the "Black Manifesto," which demanded $500 million in reparations from white Christians. Soon, activists staged sit-ins at Union Theological Seminary and several sit-ins in the National Council's "God Box" in support of Foreman's manifesto. Similar protests had struck meetings of the World Council, including one chaired by George McGovern.[129] The Black and white students who made up the majority of these activists were mobilizing the ideology of "revolution" and the tactics they had learned in ecumenical Protestant institutions. They now used them against the National Council and World Council.

In response to these protests, there was "broad agreement" among ecumenical leaders that more had to be done about racism and colonialism, writes Findlay, but they were "fearful of constituent reaction back home." Churchgoers across the country were aghast at the events in New York City and wrote to National Council leaders pleading not to give into Foreman's demands. "The acceptance of this manifesto in any form will constitute an endorsement of its spirit, its methods, its forms of deciding culprits, and is totally foreign to the Christian Church," one churchgoer wrote. Other letter writers were openly racist. If African Americans were seeking reparations, why shouldn't whites "seek the same type of consideration for all of the senseless killing and riots promulgated by the black race?" A May 1969 Gallup poll showed that 92 percent of churchgoers opposed reparations, while only 2 percent approved of them. A slight majority of African Americans also opposed reparations but a much larger number, 21 percent, approved. Despite the deep unpopularity of reparations among their constituency, several ecumenical Protestant denominations agreed to some of Foreman's demands and raised about a million dollars for the Interreligious Foundation for Community Organization by 1970.[130] Needless to say, most white churchgoers did not take kindly to the demands of Black power activists and grew increasingly frustrated with ecumenical Protestant leaders for working with these radicals. The clergy-laity gap widened dramatically during the civil rights and Black power movements of the 1960s.

* * *

The activism of some ecumenical Protestants against segregation that began in the 1940s and reached new heights in the 1960s helped polarize this religious community along political lines. The differences between the clergy, especially those who served in leadership positions, and the laity became remarkably wide. The divide between Protestants in the South and the rest of the country only sharpened differences. The anti-racist activism of ecumenical leaders and youths encouraged members of this religious community to adopt political identities, whether they were on the side of the civil rights movement or stood against it. The political mobilization against segregation partly accounted for the divergence between "conservative" and "liberal" religious groups and the increased salience of these two identities.[131]

Those more sympathetic to segregation challenged the right of ecumenical institutions to do more than change hearts and minds. Supporters of segregation relied increasingly on the political ideas of the conservative movement, including restrictions on the reach of the government and a strict constructionist view of the Constitution. Unable to deploy theologically racist arguments, ecumenical Protestant defenders of segregation turned to political and ecclesiological arguments instead. At the same time, evangelicals mobilized politically on behalf of the grievance politics becoming popular among white Americans in the wake of the civil rights movement.[132] Groups like the Southern Presbyterians found themselves on a trajectory toward ideas more common among evangelicals and the newly emergent conservative movement than with the leadership of the National Council.

More and more, America's Protestants were split over racism, especially structural racism. Segregation, however, was not the only reason for the emergence of fault lines among Protestants. Divisions also emerged through fights over economic policy.

CHAPTER 8

The Responsible Society

In the wake of World War II, ecumenical Protestants hoped to build upon the successes of the New Deal and ensure the American economy took care of the country's citizens. Like their mobilization against segregation, the new economic campaign was inspired by the World Order movement and empowered by their commitment to human rights. They evoked the rights-bearing human person as they came together around a third way between capitalism and communism. In their view, a Christian economy was one that balanced freedom and order and was organized around a mixed economy that borrowed elements of both socialism and free enterprise. They called it the "Responsible Society." As the World Council of Churches explained in 1948, "A responsible society is one where freedom is the freedom of men who acknowledge responsibility to justice and public order, and where those who hold political authority or economic power are responsible for its exercise to God and the people whose welfare is affected by it."[1] With this pithy slogan, ecumenical Protestants defended a mixed economy from corporate and libertarian detractors.

The Responsible Society was forged in a context of competing constituencies, turbulent geopolitics, a hostile mass media, and occasionally disagreements among family members. Church leaders convened grand conferences in Pittsburgh in 1947, in Amsterdam in 1948, and Detroit in 1950. As they gathered an illustrious cast of business moguls and union organizers with leading theologians, ecumenical Protestants hoped to get around thorny church-state separation issues by getting the laity to translate Christian theology into a concrete economic reform agenda. What they encountered, instead, was the clergy-laity gap in values and the realities of a religion segregated by social class. The quest for a Responsible Society also ran headlong into the Cold War framework, which intertwined discussions of the economy with debates about geopolitics. In the crucible of the early Cold War, ecumenical Protestants subtly refashioned their economic views, even as they remained stalwart backers of the mixed economy.

As this chapter shows, ecumenical Protestants desired to preserve and expand upon the New Deal, and their efforts were both attention grabbing and influential. Contrary to still-too-common depictions of postwar "mainline" Protestants as virulent anti-communists and defenders of free enterprise, many ecumenical Protestants were reformers who were part of a growing international interest in the welfare state.[2] Ever focused on consensus and order, they built bridges between labor and capital, Republicans and Democrats. Although their efforts fell short of creating the consensus they so desperately desired, they bolstered unions, governmental regulation, and economic equality by connecting these issues to Christian theology and by mobilizing Americans on behalf of these religious ideas. Ecumenical Protestants made connections between their religious beliefs and the liberal political initiatives of the era, blessing them as Christian before a devout nation.

Toward a Middle Way

Things were looking up for ecumenical Protestant churches during the early years of the Cold War, but the clergy was in no celebratory mood. By most measures we have of religious devotion, ecumenical Protestantism was growing and expanding its influence. Church attendance and membership were rising, Americans read the Bible more often and prayed more frequently, and the number of their churches grew, especially in the suburbs. But despite the financial health of ecumenical Protestant denominations, many of their leaders worried that something was deeply wrong with American culture. And they blamed the economy, or at least Americans' veneration of it. "American civilization is secular at heart," remarked African American theologian George D. Kelsey to a group of Protestant students in 1951. The country is driven by "a practical materialism with no explicit philosophy." Kelsey, who worked for the National Council of Churches and as a professor at Morehouse College, where he mentored a young Martin Luther King Jr., saw religion being overtaken by capitalism. "In our cities the towering skyscrapers of business enterprise dwarf the few churches which have not yet retreated to the suburbs," he lamented. Kelsey held the philosophy of

Adam Smith "primarily responsible" for this development.[3] In a similar vein, Presbyterian minister George Docherty felt compelled to remind Americans that their country was more than "the material total of baseball games, hot dogs, Coca-Cola, television, deep freezers, and other gadgets."[4] Ecumenical Protestants were anxious about the new economic climate, despite their growing churches, swelling budgets, and the enormous public attention they continued to receive.

Ecumenical Protestants also contended with the Christian libertarianism of their co-religionists. As had been evident for at least a decade, broad swaths of churchgoers—especially those in positions of power in individual churches—were sympathetic to the laissez-faire economic policies championed by the Republican Party for much of the 1930s and 1940s. They also contended with the economic libertarianism of evangelicals. While evangelicals focused their criticism of "materialism" on the Soviet Union, communists, and "godless" union leaders, ecumenical Protestants' anti-materialism focused broadly on American culture and the country's economy. Eschewing the Cold War dichotomy between capitalism and communism, ecumenical Protestants searched for a middle path between the two.

Church leaders worried about the power of America's corporate elite and the effects consumer capitalism was having on everyday Americans. Ecumenical Protestants wanted to tame capitalism's harmful effects, but they also recognized that they had limited options in pressing for reform. Their churches were disproportionately middle class and much of the white working class was Catholic. And as churches relocated to the suburbs, it only worsened ecumenical Protestantism's disconnect from industrial life. Ecumenical Protestants' paths toward economic reform were circumscribed by these structural limitations. Their class-bound churches precluded mobilizing workers. Their anxiety about their own laity led them to work not through their economically segregated churches but around them.

Ecumenical Protestants focused their attention on the manufacturing belt along the Great Lakes, encompassing cities like Chicago, Detroit, Pittsburgh, and Buffalo. After all, the region's industrial output had just helped the United States win World War II by becoming an "arsenal of democracy," and much of the country's economic activity remained concentrated there. But on the horizon was the growth of the Sunbelt, stretching from Florida to Southern California. Because of cheap labor, government investment, and a political climate friendly to corporate interests, economic activity slowly pivoted toward that region. Not coincidentally, the Sunbelt was dominated by evangelicals.[5]

As ecumenical Protestants became involved in the postwar economic debates, they positioned themselves as mediators between labor leaders and corporate executives, casting themselves as a neutral party. Before the Federal Council of Churches brought the two sides together, the organization's chief researcher, F. Ernest Johnson, urged ecumenical Protestants to elaborate their values, so they could present a united front. In the new postwar economy and amid broad demographic changes, what economic values did American ecumenical Protestants hold? Johnson was the perfect person to lead the investigation. After all, he had run the Federal Council's research bureau since the strikes of 1919 and was an influential supporter of the New Deal. Johnson was born in a small town in Ontario, Canada, and grew up in central Michigan. He attended Union Theological Seminary in New York and was ordained in the Methodist Church before leaving the ministry in 1916 and becoming involved with the Federal Council in 1918. He stayed with the organization until his retirement in 1952. He had also taken an academic position at Columbia's Teachers College in 1931. Johnson was a devoted social gospeler throughout his life. As a Methodist and labor activist, he was drawn to personalism. Along with other Methodists, Johnson took the lead in translating the philosophical language of personalism into a language of the "rights" and "dignity" of labor.[6] By intervening at a decisive moment, Johnson hoped to do for the American economy what the Dulles Commission had done for the United Nations and the postwar settlement.

Johnson believed that the basic questions of Protestant values were already answered. Instead, his economic inquiry would focus on the major policy questions in the postwar United States.[7] Johnson's study ran from early 1946 through the end of 1950. His research assistants raised twelve questions about the economy and invited comments by theologians, academics, corporate executives, and labor leaders. Their studies, too technical for most churchgoers, outlined what Johnson presented as his religious community's consensus on the economy and paved the way for ecumenical Protestant leaders to bring labor and capital together.

The study hoped to find what social ethicist John Bennett referred to as "middle axioms." Expanding upon the idea first developed by British theologian J. H. Oldham, Bennett defined middle axioms as ideas that have a "substantial consensus" but which related broad theological postulates to "concrete reality." They are propositions that give guidance only at a particular time, rather than being true for all time, and help define the direction in which Christians should be moving. Bennett gave the example of the Six Pillars of Peace developed by the Dulles Commission as ideal middle axioms. They were specific enough to apply only to the World War II era and would have made little sense only a decade or two earlier. But they were also general enough to give guidance without offering the kinds of details that were best left to the experts. This, thought Bennett, was the best way to apply Christian ethics in the field of economics while leaving room for honest disagreement about technical matters.[8]

Bennett acknowledged that it was more difficult to find consensus around middle axioms in economic policy than in international affairs because Americans were so divided over the government's role in the economy. And economic matters were extremely complex, often leaving religious leaders at a loss in addressing them. Developing middle axioms was not a perfect solution, but it was the best way forward. And Bennett proposed two middle axioms of his own. The first was that the government ought to ensure full employment. The second was that private centers of power should not exceed government power, because the state was more responsive to the will of the people than were corporations.[9]

Inspired by Bennett's framework, Johnson began his study by identifying several problems that seemed most troubling in 1946. The first was the tension between freedom and social control.[10] The issue of social control had long been raised by critics of the New Deal, but it gained a new currency in the late 1930s when big business, reeling from loss after loss against the Roosevelt administration, reached out to ecumenical Protestant ministers like James Fifield for help. "Christian libertarianism," as Kevin Kruse calls it, grew in the late 1930s and flourished during the early Cold War. Christian libertarianism was the idea that Christianity was a radically individualistic tradition and that "the sacredness of individual personality" was threatened by the New Deal.[11] Christianity had promoted "thrift, initiative, industriousness and resourcefulness which have been among our best assets since the Pilgrim days," Fifield argued, but it was now being destroyed in the political realm by Roosevelt and in the spiritual realm by social gospelers like Bennett and Johnson. Echoing economist Friedrich von Hayek, Fifield condemned "America's movement toward dictatorship," which "has already eliminated the checks and balances in its concentration of powers in our chief executive."[12] Fifield, a Congregationalist and the minister to some of the wealthiest residents in Los Angeles, succeeded in promoting Christian libertarianism because, unlike fundamentalists, he shared the corporate elite's liberal theology, their denominational affiliation, and because he steered clear of bigoted and conspiratorial rhetoric fundamentalists often employed.

Johnson confronted Christian libertarianism by indicting classical liberalism and the "profit motive"—a target of criticism since at least the 1930s. Economic self-interest ran counter to the sense of selflessness that the Christian faith was supposed to instill. Many people eschew a search for profit in favor of some higher calling, Johnson argued, including administrators of cooperatives, public servants, inventors, and scientists. Likewise, workers value security, a good quality of life, and the "satisfaction from a job well done." Johnson argued the service motive would wither away if it was not expressed in all aspects of people's lives. "Service motives must find large expression in industry if they are to prevail in other sectors of our common life."[13]

Johnson was certain that ecumenical Protestants would lead America toward the "middle way" in economics. The "Christian religion," he assured readers, will provide Americans with a level of disinterestedness from economic gain because Christians sit "somewhat loose to earthly circumstances, to property, position and power." He was expressing the misleading but common view among ecumenical Protestants that they spoke on behalf of universal principles while others—Catholics, Jews, African Americans, Japanese Americans, women—merely pleaded on behalf of the special interests of their group. "The ingredients for the economy of a great age are here," he wrote assuredly, and ecumenical Protestants would help bring it about.[14]

Confident that ecumenical Protestants represented universal truths, Johnson delved into the issues that were "uppermost in the minds of most of our readers" in 1946. The most pressing, he argued, were tensions between labor and management. In January of that year, 750,000 steelworkers walked off their jobs in protest of low wages and high prices. Meatpackers, coalminers, and railroad workers soon followed suit. A general strike in Oakland, California, brought the city to a standstill. When Johnson printed his position paper defending the role of unions, he was taking a position that was unpopular with many middle-class churchgoers. Johnson reminded readers that labor unions arose out of a desire to uphold human rights. Although "work is a commodity," which could be freely contracted out by laborers, "the worker is not." Unions protect the humanity of the workers, Johnson argued, by ensuring living wages, creating equal bargaining power with employers, educating workers, training them, and pushing for regulatory legislation. Johnson placed some qualifications on his support for collective bargaining: It needed to be done in good faith, involve continuous communication, and respect the "reciprocal functions" of management and labor. In the long run, Johnson hoped unions would become more transparent, more professional, and rely more on voluntary participation. But the problems unions were created to address would not disappear anytime soon. He supported the "union shop"—meaning all workers at a factory must join the union, whether they want to or not—because labor unions arose and continue to exist "in a social situation that is full of injustices."[15]

The problems inherent in both labor and management, Johnson believed, meant that a third force, representing the common good, needed to step in between the two warring sides. "A combination of administrative and judicial authority vested in a permanent board or special court may, we believe without infringing any democratic principle, make decisions regarding the proper interpretation of existing contracts," Johnson wrote. This was especially necessary in industries like utilities, where the public interest would be greatly harmed by strikes. That mediating force would be the state, bolstered by the moral authority of Christianity, Johnson argued.[16]

In these ways, Johnson's studies articulated a Christian defense of the mixed economy and justified key middle axioms: the centrality of the service motive, support of the union shop, and an active state that mediated between labor and capital. The next big challenge was to place the studies in the hands of laypersons and have them put the new middle axioms into practice.

Mobilizing the Laity

The first great attempt to put Johnson's middle way into practice came at the National Study Conference on the Church and Economic Life, which was held in Pittsburgh in 1947. Two-thirds of the participants were laypersons, representing labor, agriculture, business, and cooperatives.[17] They arrived having pored over Johnson's economic studies and were ready to debate questions outlined by Yale Divinity School social ethicist Liston Pope. "What are the issues in economic life about which the Christian Church should be most concerned?" asked Pope. "What is the responsibility, function and contribution of the Protestant churches toward the resolving of these issues on Christian principles?" Most importantly, "What should be the program of the churches in discharging their responsibility?"[18]

Figure 14. The liberal Republican political leader Charles P. Taft, pictured here at a Senate hearing on unemployment in 1938, was a prominent layman and a proponent of ecumenical Protestant economic reform efforts throughout the 1940s and 1950s. Image courtesy of the Library of Congress.

The National Study Conference on Church and Economic Life was modeled on the gatherings put on by the Dulles Commission, which was held up as a model for Protestant consensus building and political mobilization.[19] And, like the Dulles Commission, the economic discussions were led by a well-connected layman, Charles P. Taft. He was the son of the former president William Howard Taft and brother of the influential senator Robert A. Taft. Like his father and brother, Charles was also involved in politics, devoting himself to the civic reform movements in Cincinnati, Ohio, as a longtime councilmember and briefly as the city's mayor in the 1950s. He also held federal administrative posts during World War II, including as an advisor to the State Department's delegation at the San Francisco UN conference. But unlike much of his family, Charles stood firmly in the liberal wing of the Republican Party and often feuded with his conservative brother. Charles was a lawyer by training, but his true passion was for religion. This devout Episcopalian had been the youngest head of the YMCA and in 1947 became the Federal Council's first layman co-president in the organization's history.[20] Charles Taft was as well positioned as anyone to bring labor and capital to a middle ground.

Taft joined the elites of America's corporations and unions at Pittsburgh. On the program committee alone were Eric A. Johnston, the president of the Motion Picture Association of America; William Green, president of the American Federation of Labor (AFL); Walter P. Reuther, president of the United Auto Workers (UAW); Charles E. Wilson, president of General Electric; James G. Patton, president of the National Farmers Union; Frank P. Graham, president of the University of North Carolina; and Frances Perkins, the former secretary of labor.[21] In addition, Fifield, the godfather of Christian libertarianism, joined numerous businessmen, labor leaders, civil servants, and several members of Congress. The Federal Council of Churches was flexing its muscles by gathering together this illustrious group, but finding a consensus on economic policy appeared unlikely.[22]

Proceedings were dull until a working group voted down Adam Smith and the profit motive. Smith's dictum that "the individual in pursuit of his selfish gain will be led by an invisible hand to work the common good" was an "unsatisfactory answer" to contemporary economic problems. The working group looked to the World Council of Churches for justification, citing the organization's statement that "Christians believe that property represents a trusteeship under God, and that it should be held subject to the needs of the community." They added that the profit motive was "irreconcilable [sic] with the emphasis of Jesus upon service as the basic motivation of life."[23]

The issue of the "union" or "closed" shop was among the most hotly contested subjects among ecumenical Protestants in 1947. Indeed, the topic was being passionately debated as the Taft-Hartley Act made its way through Congress (it passed a few months after the Pittsburgh meeting). Taft-Hartley prohibited the closed shop, which required that managers hire only union members. The legislation also allowed states to ban the union shop, which meant that individual workers in those states could refuse to join the labor union, even if the company they worked for was unionized. In these and other ways, the act would erode the power of unions.

With the law being debated in Congress, Representative Howard Buffett, Republican of Nebraska and active Presbyterian layman, wanted "some idea of the Christian viewpoint on the closed shop." After all, he would have to vote on the issue in a few weeks. Opinions in the room were sharply divided. W. L. Goldston, a Texas oil executive, urged his coreligionists to declare the closed shop "unchristian" because it impinged on individual choice. The Reverend Armand Guerrero of the leftist Methodist Federation for Social Action countered that "ministers have a closed shop of their own," and could therefore not go on record in opposition without being hypocrites. Sensing that the issue was divisive, Boris Shishkin, the AFL's director of research and the chairman of the group, moved to table the issue. The conference "skittered around the closed shop issue like an infielder dodging a hot grounder," the *Chicago Tribune* sarcastically put it.[24]

The controversy did not end there. "A section on wages provoked the sharpest discussion," according to an observer. After the group agreed that wages should provide a decent standard of living and be judged in terms of a company's income, the conversation got bogged down over Keynes's purchasing power parity theory. Proponents of Keynes's views argued that "wages ought to be set in terms of the purchasing power necessary for a prosperous and stable economy" and that "the Christian conscience can approve the goal." Charles P. Taft arrived in the room as Keynes was being discussed. He tried to dissuade the group from taking a position because the theory was "controversial."[25] Taft got his way. But the phrase reappeared in altered form when the committee charged with writing the official conference statement inserted it noncommittedly: "lack of sufficient purchasing power ... has been cited among the restrictions that may interfere with" a well-functioning economy.[26]

Labor, capital, and the ministry agreed that Christianity had a big role to play in the economy. But some dissenting voices thought churches had no business discussing the economy at all. This was a position more prevalent among southern laymen, who tended to eschew the social gospel and instead preferred one that focused on individual salvation. Ervin Jackson, a realtor from Birmingham, Alabama, urged the churches to stay out of economics: "Its job," a witness paraphrased him saying, "must be to promote a spirit of Christian love and respect for the individual man." Victor Reuther of the United Auto Workers could not have disagreed more. "The Church will gain authority only when it evolves a program in the field of economics and social relationships which will gain public respect."[27] He thought ecumenical Protestants had not done this yet.

In the tradition of such conferences, the organizers put out an official statement summarizing the conclusions they had reached. It conveyed little

of the controversy that had raged. Admitting the "sharp differences of opinion" aired at the conference, they nonetheless emphasized their "substantial
agreement." But the agreements were largely on questions, not answers. These
questions included how to balance "economic stability" and "progress" with
the "essential liberties of man," how full employment and equitable distribution of income ought to be achieved, what the effects of the "concentration
of ownership" on the economy have been, what role the government ought
to play in economic life, and how industrial relations could be "made more
harmonious." Answers would be found later.[28]

Organizers did offer a few tenuous conclusions, ones that were rooted in
the ethical deliberations of the clergy but not widely accepted by the ecumenical Protestant laity. They reasserted the primacy of the human person
"in religion and in human relations, including economics." The person "is
not primarily an economic self-seeker" and must be provided with "social
conditions, under which it will be less difficult to express in daily living the
spirit of redemptive love that is enshrined in the New Testament." Certain
"social institutions, such as the state, may serve to restrain man's egoism"
when moral instruction fails and that person is motivated more by profit
than by Christian teachings. Furthermore, where ownership by individuals
is "difficult to regulate for the common welfare, encouragement should be
given to further experimentation in the forms of private, cooperative, and
public ownership." And the American economy ought to provide an "adequate annual income for every family." The ultimate goal, ecumenical Protestants announced in 1947, was to work for "the abolition of preventable
poverty."[29]

Some business leaders expressed frustration about their inability to
make headway against the economic views of the ecumenical Protestant
leadership. And they recognized just how important religion was to the
postwar economy. In the wake of the Pittsburgh conference, they caught
on to the religious anxiety about the profit motive and to the explosion of
public religiosity in the postwar United States. The National Association
of Manufacturers (NAM), for example, renamed their journal *Trends in
Education-Industry Cooperation* in 1949 to *Trends in Church, Education and
Industry Cooperation*. The rebranded magazine extolled the piety of business leaders through biographical profiles and showed that businessmen
were promoting Christianity at work. NAM also held meetings between
management and religious leaders (leaving labor out, unlike at Pittsburgh)
that sought to reconcile the profit system with religious teachings. But they

struggled to get traction as economic regulation and labor unions remained popular during the postwar period, thanks in part to the work of ecumenical Protestants.[30]

As ecumenical leaders shrugged off the obvious attempt by NAM to co-opt Christianity on behalf of free enterprise, they nonetheless worried that their own efforts were too closely linked to corporate elites. They showed awareness that ecumenical Protestant denominations represented middle-class churches and that they had lost contact with the working class. Pittsburgh meeting organizers chastised the local churches for their history of excluding workers from membership and urged them to "avoid the stultification of a class Church." Protestant churches, the official Pittsburgh report said, have "tended to move out of an area as it became industrial," leaving working-class folks behind.[31] It was a trend that was accelerating with postwar suburbanization.

Statistics bore out these observations. According to polls taken in 1945–46, 23.9 percent of churchgoers belonging to the Congregational Christian denomination were in the upper class, 42.6 percent in the middle, and 33.5 percent in the lower class. Presbyterians (Northern, Southern, and others) collectively registered as 21.9 percent upper class, 40 percent middle class, and 38.1 percent lower class. Methodists were one of the few traditions to register a majority (51.7%) lower-class membership, thanks partly to their large southern and African American constituency. Protestants of all traditions were less likely to belong to a union than were Jews, and especially Catholics. If voting behavior is any indication of economic preference, polls noted that more Methodists, Presbyterians, Lutherans, Episcopalians, and Congregationalists voted for Republican presidential candidate Thomas E. Dewey in 1944 than for Franklin Roosevelt.[32]

Although these polls showed most ecumenical Protestant denominations, especially ones with few southern or African American members, were more affluent, educated, and individualistic in outlook than Americans as a whole, it is important to point out that they were divided on key issues. A plurality of Episcopalians, 34.7 percent, believed that working people should have more power, while a minority of 21.8 percent believed they should have less power. Methodists were even more supportive: 45.1 percent to 16.6 percent. Other surveys indicated that ecumenical Protestant churchgoers generally sided with individualistic economic ideas but also that there were substantial disagreements among the faithful. Asked whether the government's job is to "make certain that there are good opportunities for each

person to get ahead on his own" or "to guarantee every person a decent
and steady job and standard of living," the individualistic choice won out
in most ecumenical denominations. Presbyterians chose "on his own" at a
rate of 65.3 percent, Episcopalians at 64.9 percent, Congregationalists at
71.6 percent, and Methodists at 57.6 percent. But in each tradition a substantial portion of churchgoers preferred the "guaranteed economic security"
option: 31.1, 33.1, 25.8, and 37.9 percent, respectively.[33]

Although churchgoers in ecumenical denominations preferred economic individualism more strongly than Americans as a whole, the structure of ecumenical Protestant institutions made the situation even more
lopsided. Churchgoers with the most money were more likely to take leadership roles in local churches, which meant that they were more likely to
be sent as representatives to conferences like the 1947 Pittsburgh gathering. This only reinforced ecumenical leaders' feeling that they were disconnected from the working class. While the ecclesiastical structure of
ecumenical denominations produced a "laity" composed of wealthy members and conservative activists, ecumenical leaders had to go outside the
churches to represent their working-class members. At Pittsburgh, they
brought in union leaders who were not organically connected to church institutions to represent those Protestants who supported more economic
regulation.

Despite the disconnect with everyday churchgoers, most ecumenical
leaders thought the Pittsburgh meeting had been important because it empowered the clergy to get more involved in economic matters. Few went as
far as Taft, who thought the event "has succeeded beyond our hopes."[34] John
Bennett observed that the 1947 Pittsburgh conference "report is actually
more conservative than the Social Creed of the Churches of 1932." The major accomplishment, as Bennett saw it, was that the meeting "magnified the
function of the church" in economic matters. The Reverend Paul Silas Heath
thought that the conference gave local ministers a green light to get involved
in economic debates, which those in "the cloistered sanctuaries of the Seminaries" had been doing for years. Although the conference said little new
theologically, observed Heath, the propositions it endorsed "have never
been said before by the people who said them at Pittsburgh." In other words,
Protestant clergy were being encouraged to get involved in economic reform. Bennett agreed that although the conference was unimpressive "as an
episode in the history of Christian Ethics," it was successful as "a strategic
event in contemporary American Christianity."[35]

The postmortem of the Pittsburgh meeting raised old questions about the role of the laity, ecclesiology, and democracy in Protestant life. Fears of the "laity," a politicized term synonymous with conservative corporate executives and anti-clergy activists, were echoed in the wake of the Pittsburgh meeting. The unprecedented experiment with the laity was a step in the right direction, argued Walter George Muelder. But their ideas should be taken with a grain of salt. "The church, even in her accommodated social reality, bears a conscience and a Word quite other than the words of an agreement which a cross-section of the church membership might assent to," he wrote. In other words, what Christianity has to say about the economy was not up for referendum. According to Muelder, the point was not to convince everyone of the left-leaning ideas held by much of the clergy but instead to gain consent from the laity for the Federal Council to carry on its work. "Now that a large number of laymen have collectively agreed that the church has a responsibility in economic life," Muelder noted, "it will be easier to carry forward ethico-economic education in the churches."[36]

The National Study Conference on the Church and Economic Life in Pittsburgh in 1947 was a strategic victory for the Federal Council. It answered the critique that the laity did not have enough control over Protestantism while simultaneously ensuring that ecumenical institutions would continue to provide guidance on economic issues. The conference also expressed the ecumenists' confidence in the power of Christianity to discipline business and labor leaders. But the debates about who gets to speak on behalf of Protestantism and what the proper relationship was between church and state would not go away.

Taft emphasized that the Pittsburgh gathering was only a starting point and many hoped it would be the "Delaware" of Christian economics—a reference to the landmark conference organized by Dulles in 1942. Several participants suggested that a version of the Dulles Commission be convened for economic affairs and be charged with solving economic problems.[37] The idea of an independent commission that had free rein was a nonstarter in 1947. The Dulles Commission had been an unusually independent venture during the war, but in 1947 its independence had been curbed as it was reincorporated into the Department of International Justice and Goodwill. An independent commission on economics like the Dulles group, run by Taft, was therefore ruled out quickly for bureaucratic reasons.

But something new was needed. Taft was among those pushing for a broader approach to Protestant involvement in economic policy. Having

Taft on board was a major coup for the Federal Council. Not only did Taft lend prestige and facilitate political access for ecumenists, as had Dulles, but Taft's liberal Republican politics helped shield ecumenical Protestants from accusations of socialist sympathies. He believed a focus on the entire economy—not just industry and labor—would move ecumenical Protestantism away from what he considered an overly sympathetic view of unions. Federal Council secretary Samuel McCrea Cavert reported that Taft "apparently feels strongly that we need to do something in our organizational structure which will stand as a symbol of the fact that Pittsburgh marks a fresh method of approach." Cavert agreed with Taft that it would give the Federal Council "a psychological advantage" and ensure their ability to "lay hold continuously of the kind of personnel which we had at Pittsburgh."[38] At Taft's urging, the Federal Council reorganized the Industrial Division into the Department of Church and Economic Life.[39] The board of the newly organized department included many of the most prominent attendees of the Pittsburgh conference, including Walter Reuther (UAW), Boris Shishkin (AFL), Nelson Cruikshank (AFL), Paul Hoffman (Studebaker Corp), and James G. Patton (National Farmers' Union).[40] The representation of businessmen in the Federal Council was not new; the presence of labor leaders in the ecumenical bureaucracy, however, was a major development.[41]

The newly formed Department of Church and Economic Life was headed by Cameron Hall. He was a Presbyterian minister who had led the Northern Presbyterians' social action group. Hall, like the social gospel minister Walter Rauschenbusch before him, held a pastorate in the Hell's Kitchen neighborhood of New York City. Hall had only recently taken charge of the Federal Council's economic efforts, following the retirement of longtime activist James Myers (who joined the Socialist Party immediately after his departure).[42]

Hall's first task was to convene thirty follow-up conferences he called "little Pittsburghs."[43] They were weekend conferences sponsored by local and regional councils of churches, with participation ranging from one to two hundred people. Hall proceeded to organize conferences in cities mostly along the manufacturing belt "because of the importance of the area or community to the economic life of the country."[44] In places like Buffalo, Baltimore, Wilkes-Barre (PA), Chicago, Flint, and Kansas City, Hall was bringing the ideas and values of national Federal Council leaders to local churches.[45]

This regional approach strengthened ecumenical involvement in the industrial affairs of the country. Ecumenical Protestants became more involved in industrial disputes across the region and helped bring about a period of relatively stable relations between unions and corporations. But the regional focus also reinforced the territorial divide in political economy between ecumenical and evangelical Protestants. By focusing on the manufacturing belt, ecumenical Protestants ceded the Sunbelt to evangelicals. The Sunbelt's economy and evangelicals' economic views reinforced one another and, over the decades, the fortunes of evangelicalism rose with the growing wealth of the region. In the here-and-now of the late 1940s, however, the manufacturing belt predominated, and ecumenical Protestants made sure they were closely involved in the region's economic debates.[46]

The "Responsible Society" as a Middle Way Between Capitalism and Communism

Just as the Federal Council of Churches was promoting its economic views publicly, the World Council of Churches spearheaded a new economic doctrine that became known as the "Responsible Society." It became a rallying cry for ecumenical Protestant leaders in the postwar decades. The World Council was created in 1948 to give Protestants a single voice in world affairs, but it came into being in the early days of the Cold War, when the world was being split in two. The relationship between Christianity and the economy, which had been so contentiously debated in the United States, took on a global and geopolitical dimension at the World Council's inaugural meeting in Amsterdam. Given the immense press coverage of the event, American ecumenists traveling to Amsterdam knew they would be asked to take sides in the new bipolar world.

The Americans sailing to Europe in the summer of 1948 were torn between two rival impulses. The first was to criticize the Soviet Union and Marxism and to clearly distinguish their views from the materialist philosophy and the brutality of the USSR. This was especially important to the politicized laity at home, who were seeking to rein in the activism of the clergy. The other impulse was to create a truly global communion, one that would transcend the political divisions of the Cold War. Abroad, American ecumenists had to deal with foreign clergy who enthusiastically backed the welfare state and were sometimes sympathetic to communist regimes. Although the Russian Orthodox Church had not yet joined the World Council, many Eastern European and Chinese churches that lived under communist governments were represented at Amsterdam. Chinese theologian Zhao Zichen, for example, railed against Western economic imperialism and defended Mao's revolution.[47] He was elected co-president of the World Council at the Amsterdam assembly. And theologians like Zhao had important European allies, including the Swiss theologian Karl Barth, who had long sympathized with socialism. For these reasons, at Amsterdam the American ecumenists were hesitant about taking sides in the Cold War.

John Foster Dulles, however, was less hesitant. Transformed by the Cold War, Dulles was veering away by the late 1940s from an idealistic internationalism toward the stauncher nationalism that would characterize his career as secretary of state in the 1950s.[48] In his address at Amsterdam in 1948, Dulles focused on the evils of Soviet communism. His own views of the economy provided a striking contrast to the opinions of most ecumenical leaders. "I believe in the free enterprise system very strongly," he wrote to a friend in 1947. "I have that economic belief just as I have my own personal religious belief."[49] At Amsterdam, he told an audience of nearly 1,500 Protestant and Orthodox leaders from forty countries that Christianity provided two ideas central to world peace. The first was the idea that moral law undergirds international relations. The second idea was that "every human individual, as such, has dignity and worth that no man-made law, no human power, can rightly desecrate." His words echoed the human rights talk widely shared by his fellow believers, but their purpose was closer to the Christian libertarianism of James Fifield than to the social gospel tradition. For Dulles, the purpose of human rights was to protect individuals from the power of the state—especially the Soviet state—rather than to make industry more humane and democratic, as the Federal Council advocated. Dulles scored the USSR for being "atheistic and materialistic" and for constantly resorting to violence and coercion. In the face of this great evil, Christians ought to "more vigorously translate their faith into works" and provide "an example that others will follow."[50]

Theologian Josef L. Hromadka took exception to Dulles's words. Hromadka had spent the war years at Princeton Theological Seminary and had recently returned to Czechoslovakia, where he cooperated with the country's communist government. Hromadka's historical account of Soviet-American tensions stood in contrast to Dulles's. The theologian emphasized the destruction of the West's monopoly on power and the rise of "the underdogs of society." "I am not speaking about the fall or decline of the West," Hromadka told the same audience that Dulles had just finished addressing.

"What I have in mind is simply the fact the Western nations have ceased to be the exclusive masters and architects of the world." He argued that communism, although atheistic, represents "much of the social impetus of the living church from the apostolic age down through the days of monastic orders to the reformation and liberal humanism." Hromadka also insisted the ecumenical movement must transcend Cold War politics. "No kind of curtain, be it gold or silken or iron, must separate us one from another," he emphasized. "All national and class obsessions must be removed."[51]

Dulles soon left Amsterdam, disappointed that his words of caution against the USSR did not find a more receptive audience there. The creation of the World Council of Churches marked a dramatic breaking point between Dulles and many of his ecumenical allies. Despite long-standing concerns about his leadership, Dulles was used to getting his way at US gatherings. But he was marginalized and publicly criticized at this international meeting. Noting the alliances they were building abroad, Dulles soured on American ecumenical Protestants. A few years later, he would accuse in private the Federal Council of being filled with people of "Left Wing and Socialist tendencies."[52]

Dulles and Hromadka aired their conflict in public, but the World Council worked out the merits of capitalism and communism away from the prying eyes of journalists. "Church Council Closes Its Doors for Discussion of Communism," a *Washington Post* headline announced.[53] With Dulles absent, the group charged with economic policy went to work on this sensitive matter. It was chaired by C. L. Patijn, a member of the UN Social and Economic Council, which was then drafting the Universal Declaration of Human Rights. The group also included realists and former socialists, like Reinhold Niebuhr and John Bennett. Henry P. Van Dusen and Charles P. Taft, who were no fans of communism, were also on the committee.

Theologian Karl Barth hoped the World Council would issue a Christian manifesto that would rival the influence of the Communist Manifesto.[54] Although the World Council's call for a "Responsible Society" fell short of Marx's work, it nonetheless was an influential endorsement of the welfare state as a middle ground between laissez-faire capitalism and communism. "A responsible society is one where freedom is the freedom of men who acknowledge responsibility to justice and public order, and where those who hold political authority or economic power are responsible for its exercise to God and the people whose welfare is affected by it," the World Council announced. This dense sentence tried to capture the complexity of the many rights and responsibilities modern industrial societies needed to hold in tension with one another. "The basic problem of finding the right balance between planning and freedom, between centralization and the emphasis upon the initiative of many different units in society, individuals, small communities, voluntary associations, etc." can never be solved outright, the ecumenists argued.[55] Like other intellectuals, the World Council's theologians proclaimed the end of ideology in the postwar era.[56] What the world needed was the "experimental method," which borrows from a variety of systems in seeking to work out concrete problems. In this sense, "the Responsible Society is not another system," they explained. "It points to a society which accepts the fact of a deep tension between justice and freedom, a tension that will always force men to break through the stereotypes which are formed by history, and to seek new and fresh solutions."[57]

The ecumenists had no trouble pointing to concrete examples of the Responsible Society at work. It was evident in the "democratic socialism" being employed across Europe, where governments were building welfare states that carefully balanced freedom and social control, avoiding the pitfalls of both "doctrinaire Socialism and doctrinaire Capitalism." To the ecumenists, even the United States appeared to be heading in the same direction thanks to the New Deal and World War II–era regulations. "In the one remaining large center of Capitalism, the United States, in this respect the situation is less different from that in the partly-socialistic countries than is usually believed."[58]

The World Council was joining mid-century American liberals in promoting pluralism and pragmatism in economic policy.[59] Ecumenists agreed with Arthur Schlesinger Jr., who argued in his 1949 manifesto, *The Vital Center*, that "science and technology have ushered man into a new cycle of civilization, and the consequences have been a terrifying problem." The new system replaced personal communal bonds with impersonal corporations, which "had neither a body to be kicked nor a soul to be damned."[60] The new global economy turned business owners into ruthless profiteers and condemned workers to a life of servitude, where they would be treated more like machines than human persons.

What separated the World Council from liberal groups like Schlesinger's Americans for Democratic Action was the ecumenists' insistence that secularism was the cause of economic problems and that religion would be their solution. They argued, "Secularists assume that democracy itself is a sufficient object of faith, but to make a specific type of society its own absolute end is to destroy it." They repeated a well-worn argument that the only assurance that social order will not disintegrate into anarchy or devolve into totalitarianism is to worship something above the nation-state. Only through worship of a God who sits above all nation-states, the ecumenists explained, would the welfare state endure. The "responsible society will last only when responsibility is being learned in the practice of true religious faith."[61] But this criticism of "secularism" rarely prevented cooperation between ecumenical Protestants and liberals in the United States, who at that time appeared to be working toward the same goal. Just as European countries began building welfare states that would take care of their citizens from cradle to grave, and as the Truman administration pushed to expand the New Deal, the largest Protestant and Orthodox body in the world appeared to be endorsing both of these efforts.

The American ecumenists hoped to create a postideological world, but when they returned home from Amsterdam they found many of their fellow citizens were still deeply committed to the capitalist system. In their attempt to separate Christianity from all prevailing economic systems they had equated capitalism with communism, the Los Angeles Times charged. The theologians' ideas revealed "an all too prevalent bewilderment and a possibly dangerous misconception." Just look at how the two systems differ in practice, the editors exclaimed. Capitalism has not solved all the world's problems but "where there is free enterprise, the world is improving." The article claimed that by equating communism with capitalism, the theologians at Amsterdam were acting both foolishly and dangerously.[62]

The American ecumenists at the World Council tried to head off this criticism. Charles P. Taft convinced his colleagues to insert the modifier "laissez-faire" when talking about capitalism. After revision, the conference report read: "The Christian churches should reject the ideologies of both communism and laissez-faire capitalism." The new phrase placed emphasis on the theories of both systems, rather than their practices, and left open the possibility that some other forms of capitalism might be superior to communism. Upon his return from Amsterdam, Ralph Sockman commented that "the Americans were in a minority group because most of the delegates live under some kind of socialized government. . . . They don't know what our American capitalism really is." Sockman thought his country's economy was becoming more humane, and he was happy to criticize both capitalism and communism without necessarily equating the two. But according to the Los Angeles Times, the insertion of "laissez-faire" simply "evades the issue." "Genuine laissez-faire capitalism never has existed anywhere; there have been always some restrictions," they insisted, and added that the ecumenists' critique "either applies to existing capitalism or is meaningless."[63]

Some of the attacks were more personal. John Bennett was criticized by his uncle, who accused Bennett of having "harmed, rather than aided, the advance of spiritual leadership." Bennett's uncle admired Dulles's speech but felt that Bennett's committee did not measure up to that high standard. By equating capitalism and communism, the uncle wrote accusingly, Bennett was expressing his desire for "the Protestant Church to stand for revolution rather than evolution." Communists "can hardly fail to find comfort and gratification in the co-defendant named in your indictment."[64]

Bennett was nonplussed. "Dear Uncle Eversley," Bennett wrote back, "I am rather baffled that you should condemn [the Responsible Society] so strongly." He pointed out that it was the ideologies of capitalism and communism that the Amsterdam assembly condemned and not the actual operations of both systems. Bennett also believed that the criticism of communism was more "fundamental" than that of capitalism. Regardless, he ended his letter by urging his uncle to "take seriously the reasons why many people become Communists."[65]

The success of the World Council assembly at Amsterdam and its endorsement of a Responsible Society gave Bennett reasons to celebrate, despite both public and personal attacks. Ecumenism was a goal onto itself and the coming together of Protestant and Orthodox communions from across the world was a feat that he had spent his entire life pursuing. That many of the economic policies he had long advocated were reflected in the idea of the Responsible Society gave him further evidence of his world-historical role in transforming the economy. The meaning of a Christian economy would not be worked out by the laity or by the local church or, for that matter, by a referendum of workers and owners. It was not up for a vote, Bennett believed. It was for Americans to accept their responsibility to God and to the welfare of the human person, which obligated them to build a Responsible Society.

Back home, the American ecumenists were now empowered by a definitive theological statement on the economy, and they urged Americans to embrace its principles. In February 1950, they brought together laypersons at a conference in Detroit as a follow up to the dialogue begun at Pittsburgh three years earlier. They now had a more precise theological agenda to push.

But they also had to contend with increasing right-wing attacks and conservative suspicion of their work. "Many businessmen had not liked what they knew about the Pittsburgh conference and even less what came out of the Amsterdam Assembly," Cameron Hall reported. Another observer explained that Stanley High, author of "Methodism's Pink Fringe," and John T. Flynn, author of *The Road Ahead: America's Creeping Revolution*, were referenced "in muffled conversation" and "their writings, with rebuttals in both pamphlets and news reprints, formed at least a portion of the backdrop" for the Detroit conference. Opponents of the Federal Council "had filled the delegates' mail with pre-conference pamphlets and letters which implied, if they did not clearly state, that we had better watch out for communists, socialists and other unfortunate and misled characters," another participant reported.[66]

While businessmen were skeptical, labor leaders came with enthusiasm and a strategy for pressing their agenda among a group of ministers and theologians who they knew to be sympathetic to their cause. UAW leader Walter Reuther was not a layman, but his union values had been shaped by Protestant Christianity. During the strike wave in 1919, when Reuther was twelve years old, the minister at his Lutheran church in Wheeling, West Virginia, denounced unions in a sermon. Reuther's father, a committed Christian socialist, stood up from his pew, denounced the minister, and marched the family out of the church. Although Reuther's mother insisted that the kids continue to attend the church, Reuther and his siblings would be interrogated over lunch later in the afternoon about what they had heard in Sunday school and how it squared with their father's understanding of theology.[67] Reuther had developed a moralizing streak because of this upbringing.

When he arrived at Detroit in 1950, having recently survived an assassination attempt, he radiated a martyr's aura. Reuther delivered a "rousing" and "well staged piece of oratory," a businessman reluctantly admitted.[68] In his speech Reuther stressed the gap between the impressive technological efficiency of the modern economy and the poverty of the human and social sciences, which had yet to find ways to fairly distribute the benefits the modern world had to offer. Echoing the World Council's criticism of industrial modernity, Reuther lamented that "we know how to split the atom, but we don't know how to feed hungry people when there is too much to eat in the world."[69] Reuther knew his dramatization of human need amid industrial plenty would play well with the clergy that made up a third of the conference participants.

Reuther's words signaled a subtle but important shift in these ecumenical deliberations. More and more, ecumenical Protestants would emphasize poverty in an otherwise thriving economy. The New Deal had reformed capitalism and transformed the laissez-faire approach into a mixed economy. For this reason, ecumenical Protestants began focusing on the needs of the most vulnerable members of society. Earlier ideas, like government takeover of key industries, would fade away as poverty prevention took center stage. And new initiatives came to the fore, like using taxation to create greater economic equality. This transition began by 1950 among ecumenical Protestants. They would soon be joined by organizations like the Americans for Democratic Action and liberal intellectuals later in the decade.[70]

The new emphasis on alleviating poverty and inequality did not stave off controversy at Detroit in 1950. During a small-group discussion headed by Victor Reuther (Walter Reuther's brother) on the theme of "Freedom of Enterprise and Social Controls," the participants voted that using taxation to redistribute wealth was a Christian thing to do. "Extensive use of taxation to reduce inequalities" was desirable from a Christian standpoint as long as it did not severely disrupt the economy, the group concluded.[71] George S. Benson, the president of Harding College in Arkansas, which was affiliated with the conservative Church of Christ, shot back that redistributive taxation is "socialism regardless of who it is who holds the position." The "policy of taxing for the sake of erasing inequalities is socialistic and is totally contrary to the purposes of taxation in our past history."[72] Benson had just launched his own "Freedom Forums" that brought leading politicians, businessmen, and religious figures to Searcy, Arkansas, to rally for free enterprise. Harding College would become a leading center of evangelical economic thought and a counterpoint to the ecumenical gatherings.[73]

Many businessmen agreed with Benson, but they did not blame ecumenical leaders. Despite the bad things the businessmen had heard about the Federal Council prior to the Detroit conference, Hall reported that most had walked away with a feeling that "the churches are open to the participation and contribution of businessmen," even though they were repeatedly outvoted at the conference. While these managers and owners were annoyed with the Reuther brothers, they nonetheless "indicated a strong opposition to the extreme and 'intemperate' opponents of the Federal Council and the interest of the churches represented by the Conference." In other words, the 1950 Detroit conference convinced businessmen to defend ecumenical Protestants against attacks by the likes of Fifield and Flynn. Hall felt Detroit had carried Christian work on economics "beyond Pittsburgh" because businessmen were "ready and eager to work with the churches."[74] Reinhold Niebuhr agreed: "This is the most significant meeting of this kind in which I have taken part. It surpasses the Amsterdam conference in that it is more representative of all sections of life in a modern industrial economy."[75]

The labor delegation felt they had come out victorious. One labor delegate was delighted by the strong Congress of Industrial Organizations and AFL showing. Although he was hoping for "a Malvern Conference"—referring to the 1941 British gathering that endorsed the creation of a welfare state and had served as the inspiration for Dulles's Delaware conference—the union leader nonetheless came away with a good impression of the meeting. "The labor people found (I think somewhat to their surprise) a tremendous support for liberal ideas among the young clergy and the active leaders in the national Protestant organizations." In all, he reported, "the progressive view held" at Detroit.[76] Except for a few cranks, it seemed that everyone was happy with the Federal Council's leadership.

One delegate reported that the remarkable thing about the conference was that "nobody hit anybody else on the jaw, and nobody walked out!" But much more had been accomplished than simply getting capital and labor to behave. Hall pointed out that the statement on taxes "breaks new ground" because Protestantism had given so little consideration to taxes in the past. The conference affirmed the "Responsible Society" statement in all but name, urging a "middle way" between communism and capitalism. The ecumenists attacked communism and "practical atheism" but also argued that atheism "is present in contemporary capitalism" as well. The libertarian paper *Faith and Freedom* ungenerously dubbed this "The Extreme Middle," which captured the center-left character of ecumenical Protestant thought on the economy in 1950.[77]

Ecumenical Protestants had chimed in on practical matters as well. Amid partisan debates in Congress, the Detroit declaration urged federal aid for public education; "positive action" to assure "full access to adequate modern medical, surgical and other health services"; setting up "industrial councils" to mediate disputes between labor and management; and the use of the union label on church press materials.[78] These were some positions akin to Bennett's middle axioms. Ecumenical leaders were more forthright in their support for labor unions and for the government having a role in regulating the economy than they had been just three years earlier at Pittsburgh. At the end of the 1940s, a decade that had seen depression and world war, ecumenical Protestants succeeded in translating their support for economic and social human rights into a workable program. Whether in the theology of the Responsible Society or in their more concrete middle axioms, they pursued their theological and political agenda with great vigor.

The Revolt Against the New Deal That Wasn't

In the United States and in the international arena, ecumenical Protestants defended a middle way between capitalism and communism that they called the "Responsible Society." What they meant by the middle way differed in national and international contexts. The members of the World Council of Churches were more likely to defend the emerging welfare state, which had been articulated by the British bureaucrat William Beveridge in his famous wartime report and which was being put into place across Western and Central Europe (and served as inspiration to many nations across the world).[79] In the United States, most American ecumenical Protestants rejected the welfare state as a model for their country and instead defended the "mixed economy" created by Roosevelt and expanded by Truman. While many ecumenical Protestants hoped to create a political economy that would take care of people "from cradle to grave," as the welfare state aimed to do, they nonetheless tempered expectations by publicly insisting that American reforms would not need to go as far as the European ones. The desire to bring the laity along with them forced ecumenical leaders to compromise. As they made alliances, they moderated their sentiments and placed qualifiers in their speeches and writings. In the heated atmosphere of the early Cold War, they were repeatedly forced to reassure their domestic constituencies that the Responsible Society would not lead America on the road toward socialism.

By 1950 American ecumenical Protestants grew more articulate in their defense of liberal economics ("liberal" in the sense that Roosevelt and Truman used the term) in the face of libertarian detractors. They also worked successfully to bolster their authority to speak on these issues. They made great efforts to bring labor and capital together after World War II and, although they had little luck getting the two sides to agree on common principles, the clergy succeeded in getting assent from key constituencies in their community to carry on their work on behalf of a Responsible Society. And, by promoting the fiction that Christians could serve as impartial mediators by standing aloof from worldly events, they managed to defend more effectively the legacy of the New Deal—and to promote Harry Truman's Fair Deal, which promised to expand access to health care, education, and other critical services to more Americans. Under the guise of a "middle way," ecumenical Protestants smuggled center-left economic ideas into public discussions and defended a mixed economy by connecting it to Protestant Christianity. Their defense came at a critical moment, when these principles were under siege, and it proved crucial to the survival of the New Deal.

Promotion of the Responsible Society helped create the liberal economic consensus of the era. In 1946, the Republican Party regained control of Congress. They had run under the election slogan "Had Enough?"—a slogan that asked Americans whether they had had enough of the New Deal and wartime regulation.[80] Churchgoers in the ecumenical denominations should have been especially receptive to this call to bring the New Deal to an end. They voted Republican overwhelmingly in 1946, as they had in most elections. And their most active laypersons were often hostile to government intervention in the economy. With organizations like the National Association of Manufacturers turning their attention to religious organizations in the 1940s, with wealthy donors funding anti-statist Christian journals and universities, and with the threat of the USSR—an atheist state with a socialist economy—the ecumenical Protestant churches were primed to turn toward the Right in the wake of World War II. That did not happen. It is a testimony to the effectiveness of the maneuvering of ecumenical Protestants and the strong defense of the mixed economy they provided that the New Deal was not disassembled.

Indeed, partly through the efforts of Charles P. Taft, the liberal Republican faction cheered on president-elect Dwight Eisenhower as he accepted many of the changes brought about by the New Deal (much to the chagrin of Taft's brother, the conservative Senator Robert A. Taft). While Charles Taft celebrated the triumph of moderation in his party, Bennett, Hall, and Niebuhr lamented the limits of Eisenhower's plans. Hoping for a broad expansion of government programs to assure the welfare of all Americans, their efforts in the 1940s only managed to help preserve the status quo in the 1950s.

After 1950, however, the Federal Council—and its successor organization, the National Council of Churches—faced a challenge from a new alliance between corporate executives and evangelicals. In the 1950s ecumenical Protestants had to fend off new threats to their authority. Although initially successful, their efforts would pave the way for divisions within their own religious community and in American politics.

CHAPTER 9

Christian Economics and the Clergy-Laity Gap

Just as ecumenical Protestants called on the United States to become a "Responsible Society" in the late 1940s—one that respects the human rights of workers and gives them control over their working lives—their views came under attack from the wealthiest congregants of ecumenical churches. These business moguls, who mobilized under the banner of the laity, challenged the authority of the clergy and tried to wrest control of the cultural capital of Christianity from the ministers' hands. Although the fights largely took place over position papers and pronouncements, the corporate leaders understood that the stakes were in fact much higher. The conflicts between the laity and clergy were about who would get to decide what constitutes a "Christian" economy. And that answer mattered in a country as devout as the United States.

The most important tool that corporate executives wielded in their fight against the clergy was control over the National Council of Churches' purse strings. Much of the money that ecumenical Protestants relied on to build a just postwar world free from racism and poverty came from their wealthiest members, many of whom threatened to withhold donations unless the clergy stopped backing labor unions, supporting Harry Truman's universal health-care initiative, and championing redistributive taxation. But the corporate leaders also had allies in their fight against ecumenical clergy over economic policy, like the Catholic journalist John T. Flynn, the fundamentalist firebrand Carl McIntire, and the anti-communist congressman Walter Judd. These new alliances, formed in the 1940s and 1950s around a common enemy rather than a united outlook, foreshadowed the rise of the religious Right later in the twentieth century.[1]

The widening clergy-laity gap in the late 1940s and 1950s troubled the consciences of church leaders. The fights between clergy and laity were about economic policy but also about matters fundamental to Protestant theology and American democracy. In the tug-of-war between the laity, whose authority rested on their claim to speak on behalf of all churchgoers, and clergy, who claimed expertise over religious interpretation, important questions arose. If the Protestant tradition denied the special status of clergy, on what grounds did the clergy accumulate so much authority over economic affairs? If Protestantism was at the root of American democracy, as was widely believed at the time, did that mean the religious tradition itself needed to become more democratic? And what did this troubled relationship between clergy and laity mean for church-state relations, especially at a time when ecumenical Protestants attacked the Catholic Church for its alleged clericalism and authoritarianism? Ecumenical leaders like G. Bromley Oxnam, Douglas Horton, and John Bennett wrestled with these grave and pressing questions but never definitively answered them.[2]

The laity's war on the clergy raged from the late 1940s to the mid-1950s. This chapter focuses on three episodes of this conflict. The first is journalist John T. Flynn's attack on ecumenical Protestants in his best-selling 1949 book, *The Road Ahead*.[3] Building on decades of fundamentalists' investigations of their fellow Protestants, Flynn aired their Red-baiting accusations to a nationwide audience. Inspired by the attention Flynn's book garnered, Congregationalist and Methodist laymen, including Congressman Walter Judd, attempted to purge the "social action" groups of their denominations, which were responsible for political activity and were long a refuge for leftist politics. Finally, the oil magnate J. Howard Pew went after the National Council of Churches itself, attempting to use his generous pocketbook to censor its economic pronouncements. These efforts amounted to one of the most serious challenges ecumenical Protestants faced to their authority in the mid-twentieth century.

Despite the best efforts of Flynn, Judd, and Pew, the laity's war on the clergy failed to wrest control of Christian economics from the clergy. But the anticlericalism of the laity had three important effects. First, it devastated some parts of the Protestant Left. Secondly, it facilitated new alliances between evangelicals, corporate leaders, and politicians. Finally, the laity affected a subtle but important change in the economic ideology ecumenical Protestants promoted. By the end of the 1950s, ecumenical Protestants complained that an abundant economy, which created so much plenty for so many Americans, was leaving the poorest folks behind. Ecumenical Protestants were among those refocusing the attention of liberal politicians on the problem of poverty. The benefits of the postwar mixed economy, ecumenical Protestants argued by the end of the decade, needed to be expanded to all Americans.[4]

Mobilizing the Laity

The relationship between laity and clergy had long been a problem for American Christianity, but the issue took on a greater urgency during World War II, when ecumenical Protestants had mobilized politically in unprecedented ways. Methodist bishop G. Bromley Oxnam and Congregationalist leader Douglas Horton differed politically and theologically but they expressed remarkably similar concerns during the wartime years about the "clergy-laity gap." Both Oxnam and Horton wanted to encourage churchgoers to participate more fully in public life, they wanted to create more substantial ties to the labor movement, and they hoped to move away from the local church as the center of ecumenical Protestant life in the country.

Horton, the longtime executive secretary of the Congregationalist-Christian Churches, headed a denomination that was radically decentralized. Their bureaucracy was small. The denomination had virtually no power over individual churches, which imbued Congregationalism with both an ecclesiastic and political libertarianism.[5] The Congregationalists were also one of the wealthiest denominations in the United States. Oxnam's United Methodists, on the other hand, were less affluent (although, still wealthier than the population as a whole), more hierarchical, and more thoroughly bureaucratized. Many of the controversies about hierarchy that arose among Congregationalists carried little weight for Methodists. Oxnam had long been a social gospel advocate, unlike Horton, and had since the 1920s advocated on labor's behalf.

Oxnam and Horton lamented that their denominations' churchgoers were much wealthier than the average American, and they knew that the people in charge of most local churches—the deacons, the fundraisers, the accountants—were most likely to be the wealthiest members of the congregation. The problem only got worse the higher you went in the ecumenical Protestant bureaucracy. Horton observed that at his denomination's national meeting in 1944 only pastors and a few wealthy laypersons had the free time to attend and help shape policy. For Horton, this was symptomatic of a much bigger problem: "The Church does not maintain its contact with the other classes."[6] Oxnam, the social gospeler, agreed that Protestant churches needed to reestablish contact with workers because of labor's role in the coming transition toward economic democracy. "Dare we envision," Oxnam asked rhetorically, "the labor movement itself as a means through which the Christian ideal may indeed become real?"[7]

Worst of all, when ministers spoke to workers they exhibited "an old-fashioned missionary attitude," Horton complained. He may have been thinking of evangelicals, who, in the words of Billy Graham, also believed that "organized labor unions are one of the greatest mission fields in America today." Graham meant that ministers should proselytize to workers and "lead the laboring man in America in repentance and faith in Jesus Christ."[8] This kind of attitude, thought Horton, expressed an outdated belief, that "I have everything and you have nothing."[9] Oxnam called the labor movement "one of the greatest missionary opportunities of [Protestantism's] history," but he meant something quite different from Graham. Unions would transform Christianity as much as Christianity would transform labor unions, and the two would go on to transform the economy along social gospel principles. But this would only come to pass if Protestants put aside their paternalism and recognized labor's new dignity. Oxnam was still finding inspiration from abroad in 1944. "Anyone who has seen the workers of Russia," as he first did in 1927, "beholds this new spirit."[10]

Oxnam and Horton had been at the center of the economic controversies in the 1930s, when conservatives mobilized under the banner of the "laity" to demand more power for the wealthiest congregants of their denominations. They also navigated tricky church-state issues. In fact, Oxnam was one of the leading voices of Protestants and Other Americans United for the Separation of Church and State, an organization bent on keeping Catholic clergy out of politics. He therefore saw lay participation as a means of avoiding the very same accusations of clericalism he was directing at Catholics.[11] That was exactly what layman John Foster Dulles had done for Protestantism in international affairs and that was what others could do for the economy. Preachers and ministers would articulate general principles of Protestantism, but only the laity could put them into practice. "The social gospel is the layman's gospel," Horton emphasized, "for the layman is on the social front line as the minister cannot possibly be."[12]

Although there were many benefits to more lay involvement, the drawback was that those who claimed the mantle of the "laity" were the richest and most conservative members of Protestant denominations.[13] When the *Christian Century* declared 1946 the year of the "layman," they invited guest writers to submit articles on the subject. The editors hoped to attract new subscribers and raise more money, but what they got instead was fierce criticism of clerics. Stanley High wrote an article that accused Protestantism of being "preacher-ridden" and prone to "sonorous obscurities." (High, the son of a Methodist minister and a one-time candidate for the ministry, would soon author a Red-baiting article attacking "Methodism's Pink Fringe.") Henry R. Luce, the millionaire media mogul who offered up "the American Century" in contrast to Protestant globalism, likewise wrote in the pages of the *Christian Century* that Protestants were promoting "the most fantastically fuzzy ideas . . . about politics and economics, about war and peace."[14] Calls for more power for the laity usually came from the wealthiest segments of Protestantism and were intertwined with conservative political agendas. It became clear to the editors of the *Christian Century* that if the class structure of the church remained intact, Protestantism's laity would tilt toward conservative economic policies.

The outspoken conservatism of the Protestant laity meant that the church-worker relationship needed to be reestablished. And both Horton and Oxnam thought that this was unlikely to happen at the level of the individual church. Horton warned that "to date almost all of our thinking has been done at the level of the local church—and this is one problem which the average local church is too small to handle."[15] Oxnam likewise urged Protestants to refocus their efforts away from bringing labor into the churches and toward Christianizing the lives of people outside the church. "I am less interested in movements whose primary end is the Church," he wrote in 1944, "than in those endeavors whose primary purpose is to enthrone the Christian ideal in the practices of the common life and to create Christian spirit in the relations of that life."[16]

Oxnam focused on empowering working people, but Horton wanted to establish a role for churchgoers of all professions in order to balance political views and aim at what he viewed as a sensible middle ground. Horton proposed ad hoc groups of various professions gathering in cities across the country in order to discuss ways to mobilize churchgoers and Christianize their professions. To encourage the melding of Christianity and professional life, Horton urged churches to develop new sacraments focused on work. After all, so many sacraments emphasized family life—births, deaths, marriages—and none acknowledged work. From these informal groups, Horton hoped a laypersons' movement would emerge into something like a "Senate-House of Representatives relationship" between the clergy and the laity in his denomination, diminishing the distance between the two groups.

Moreover, Horton hoped "Christian guilds" would emerge in the professions, so that those professions "could be brought more effectively into a
Christian economy."[17] By the 1940s the local church appeared to stand in the
way as ecumenical leaders endorsed a bigger-is-better organization of Protestantism, and one that emphasized Christian practices outside the traditional
confines of Sunday-morning services.

Oxnam and Horton hoped that establishing a closer relationship between working life and Christianity would empower their activism and political advocacy. But the problem of disunity and division remained. As
Oxnam saw it, Protestant churches "speak [in] one voice when we deal with
values; but the moment the question of mechanics is raised, church groups
talk in many tongues, and the discussions are a modern reenactment of
Babel." The more specific Protestant proposals became, the greater the disagreement. Oxnam proposed a simple solution. To get around divisions, the
technical expertise of the laity was needed. Labor and capital would come
together and create a framework of cooperation, while theologians and experts on political economy, like Harold Ickes and David Lilienthal (who
"writes like the prophets of old") would be brought in to mediate between
the two groups. "The moment is at hand," Oxnam prophesized, "when the
engineering and organizing genius of the world must master the mechanics
essential to the realization of valid ethical ideals, create an adequate machine, and put the machine to work."[18] To Oxnam's mind, technical expertise and social ethics would easily find common cause.

For all of Oxnam and Horton's desire to get the laity more involved in
Protestant life and to reestablish connections with workers, their enthusiasm
for the laity in the 1940s would have ironic consequences. More laypersons did
participate, but they were overwhelmingly the wealthiest and most conservative members of ecumenical denominations, a development that undermined
Oxnam and Horton's hopes that a broad spectrum of churchgoers would take
part in ecumenical activities. In spite of Oxnam and Horton's best efforts, in
the postwar United States the very term "laymen" continued to be synonymous with a conservative revolt against liberal and leftist clergy.[19]

The Ambiguity of the Clergy-Laity Relationship

Corporate executives, operating under the banner of the laymen's movement, did not begin the war over Christian economics. Attacks on the eco-

nomic views of ecumenical Protestants had begun back in the days of the social gospel and had been ongoing for most of the twentieth century.[20] By the 1930s, a loose web of fundamentalists and their supporters had banded together to counter the Federal Council of Churches' support for the New Deal and organized an ill-fated anti-Roosevelt coalition. And during the 1940s, corporate executives, in concert with some Protestant clergy, promoted Christian libertarianism, though only with limited success. The ecumenical Protestant leadership largely shrugged off these mobilizations as misguided.

But it was hard to ignore the blow delivered in 1949 by journalist John T. Flynn. His book, *The Road Ahead: America's Creeping Revolution*—an unmistakable reference to Friedrich von Hayek's *The Road to Serfdom*—was wildly popular, peaking at number two on the *New York Times* best-seller list. The publication of *The Road Ahead* in 1949—at a moment when anti-communist hysteria was reaching a fever pitch in the United States and when the Federal Council was also engaged in controversies about segregation and America's relations with China—meant that Flynn garnered more attention than the Federal Council's earlier critics. *The Road Ahead* brought years of simmering controversy out into the open, especially in Flynn's tenth chapter, which targeted the Federal Council directly.

Flynn was no fundamentalist, but his book built on the work fundamentalists had done in the 1930s. In that decade, dozens of new groups formed to keep tabs on the Federal Council and its ecumenical allies. The most important was the Church League of America, founded in 1937 by Chicago-area businessmen and religious leaders. The Church League had appealed to the FBI to keep track of the Reds in America's churches. But J. Edgar Hoover rejected these appeals, viewing the Red-baiting accusations as an intramural fight among religious denominations that the government would do best to avoid. So the Church League organized itself as a religious version of the FBI, keeping detailed records of subversive clergy. Like other private intelligence-gathering organizations, including Verne Kaub's Council of Christian Laymen and Myers G. Lowman's Circuit Riders Inc., the Church League self-identified as a "laymen's movement" and took part in the budding fundamentalist-corporate alliance of the era. Headquartered in Wheaton, Illinois, the Church League accumulated three million index cards of information about thousands of religious individuals they suspected of communist activities. The organization publicized its findings in their *National Layman's Digest*. The Church League regularly shared information with fundamentalists like Carl McIntire, who wrote scathing books about radical clergy and warned of the communist connections in the Federal Council in his nationally syndicated radio program. When Flynn wrote *The Road Ahead* in the late 1940s, he did not have to dig deep for information on the Federal Council. He relied on the legwork done by the ecumenists' theological and corporate opponents.[21]

Flynn was born in 1882 outside of Washington, DC, to "a good Catholic home." His Irish-Catholic father, a lawyer, eventually moved the family to New York City, where Flynn continued his parochial school education and attended a small Catholic college, followed by law school at Georgetown University, a Catholic institution. He did not write much about religion before the 1940s, but he did gravitate to the religious socialism of Norman Thomas, who became a good friend. A precocious writer since his teens, Flynn contributed a regular column on economics, called "Other People's Money," to the *New Republic* in the 1930s, in which he regularly lambasted the rich.[22] What seems to have turned him rightward were international affairs.[23] Flynn became a member of New York's America First Committee and had spent the wartime years writing screeds against Roosevelt's foreign policy blunders, from Pearl Harbor to Yalta. After the war he emerged as a full-throated conservative, warning about creeping socialism and the loss of America's freedom. By the end of his life, according to his biographer, Flynn embraced "an agenda that was virtually identical to that of the John Birch Society."[24]

Flynn considered his attack on the Federal Council in *The Road Ahead* to be just one part of a bigger story of America's march toward socialism. "My purpose in writing this book," Flynn explained, "is to attempt to describe the road along which this country is traveling to its destruction." That road was paved by a creeping socialism promoted by a group of people "more dangerous" than communists, he argued, "because they are more numerous and more respectable and they are not tainted with the odium of treachery." Flynn called out these socialists, who occupied "positions of power" and who "have in their hands immense sections of our political machinery," in the hope that it was not too late to change the country's course.[25]

Chapter 10 of *The Road Ahead* focused on the clergy who occupied positions of power in the Federal Council of Churches. Flynn argued that since the 1932 "Social Ideals of the Churches," the Federal Council had supported socialism. The organization had repeatedly praised cooperatives, applauded federal interference in the economy, criticized capitalism, and argued on behalf of collectivism. And he showed that leading ecumenical thinkers approved of many parts of the Soviet economy and that they believed the United States had much to learn from the USSR. These accusations had a grain of truth to them, even if Flynn exaggerated their implications.

Flynn singled out G. Bromley Oxnam and John C. Bennett, who had long been targets of fundamentalist critics. Flynn accused Oxnam of mingling with "strange companions" at the Massachusetts Council for American-Soviet Friendship and in the Committee to Aid Spanish Democracy. Flynn was more fair-minded about what the evidence gathered against Oxnam revealed than other critics had been. "There is no point in calling him a Communist," Flynn counseled his readers. "He is a Socialist."[26] But to Flynn, this made Oxnam even more dangerous.

With his best-selling book of 1949, Flynn joined a wide chorus of critics attacking the clergy in the name of the laity. Flynn astutely identified the gap between the leaders of the Federal Council and the majority of churchgoers. Flynn quoted what he called John Bennett's "profound confession" in Bennett's 1948 book, *Christianity and Communism*: "The rank and file of Christians, still in considerable measure represent the conventional assumptions of their nation or class but what has happened is that the *change in thought and commitment on the part of those who exercise leadership* has been so marked that the churches are moving in a new direction."[27] "Here is an admission," Flynn exclaimed, "that these leaders are running away with the machinery of the churches of Christ without the knowledge or approval of the faithful."[28] Flynn went on to praise the efforts of the ecumenists' least favorite person—Carl McIntire—for his role in creating the American Council of Churches and the International Council of Churches, both of which Flynn claimed were resisting the Federal Council's tyranny.[29] Flynn's praise for McIntire, along with his use of information gathered by McIntire and other fundamentalists, signaled one part of the alliance he was forming.

The other part of the alliance was with the corporate elite, who welcomed Flynn as an ally against Truman's economic policies. Flynn's book was used as a weapon during the political debates over Truman's universal health-care initiative. Truman had first proposed universal health care in 1945, delivering on a promise in his "Economic Bill of Rights" to make real the "right to adequate protection from economic fears of . . . sickness." Among the changes Truman proposed was for all Americans to join a single insurance pool. "This is not socialized medicine," the president insisted in a speech that hardly satisfied critics.[30]

Corporate opponents of Truman's health-care plan were eager to ally themselves with Flynn. For example, the anti–New Deal "Committee for Constitutional Government, Inc." distributed Flynn's book at a discount to "all physicians, dentists, nurses, all in teaching professions, [and] clergymen." The American Medical Association sent a copy of the book to every member of Congress. One congressman from western New York even sent the book as a Christmas gift to some of his supporters. By the end of 1949, *The Road Ahead* had sold a total of two million copies, and an additional four million copies were read the following year when an abridged version was published by *Reader's Digest*, where Stanley High, another vocal critic of the Federal Council, worked as an editor.[31] Flynn acted as a bridge between the fundamentalist mobilization against the theological and political liberalism of the Federal Council and the corporate mobilization against the New Deal.

The Federal Council had previously responded to attacks by discrediting its opponents. In 1944, for example, it published a pamphlet defending itself from attacks by fundamentalists like McIntire by pointing out how many of their opponents "have been associated either with anti-Semitic or pro-Fascist groups, or both." The organization urged Americans to disregard the wartime attacks because "the unity of the nation is involved."[32]

Responding to Flynn required more subtlety. Bennett was one of the accused in Flynn's book, and he wrote a memorandum to Federal Council leaders defending himself and the organization. Bennett was defiant in the face of Flynn's criticism: "I am not sorry to have Mr. Flynn as an opponent and I do not regret the company in which he has placed me." Bennett insisted that Flynn misrepresented his positions and was either "careless beyond excuse" or "deliberately unfair." After showing where his words had been abridged or distorted, Bennett challenged Flynn's assertion that Bennett's emphasis had been entirely on the virtues of socialism. Bennett showed that his books included praise for aspects of capitalism that he believed "should find a place in any future economic system." These included the seriousness given to the problem of incentives, the encouragement of "many different centers of economic initiative," and the need to have part of the economy "left to automatic forms of regulation." But Bennett knew this would not satisfy Flynn, who viewed socialism and capitalism as polar opposites. Bennett continued to insist "that we should move toward an economy which might, from one point of view, seem to be a revised Capitalism, and from another point of view, a revised Socialism."[33]

The Federal Council's response to Flynn's attacks was one of the few times that the organization had to defend itself so publicly and so directly. Unlike Bennett, the Federal Council stayed away from the specifics of economic policy and instead presented itself as a moderate organization that promoted reasonable ideas. In a pamphlet titled *The Truth About the Federal Council of Churches*, its leaders insisted that it was an institution focused on education and evangelism, not on politics.[34] But it was clear that ecumenical leaders felt vulnerable and this had to do with the uncomfortable truth about the clergy-laity gap in values that Flynn had made public. "I recognize that Mr. Flynn does point to a real problem in Protestantism," Bennett admitted.[35] Catholicism does not share this problem, Bennett suggested, because clergy face few restrictions in espousing religious positions on controversial issues. For Protestants it was not that simple. Ministers and preachers had no special privilege in the interpretation of religious teachings, and yet their beliefs differed so much from those of churchgoers. Bennett believed simultaneously in the seriousness of theological understanding, which took years of training and study, and in the necessity of lay leadership and participation, which had been increasing in recent years. And because Bennett did not believe in biblical literalism, he could not cite lines from scripture as a straightforward guide to Christian economics in the way that evangelicals sometimes did. There was no clear way out of the dilemma for Bennett, except to continue the ambiguity of the clergy-laity relationship.

Bennett's answer to Flynn's criticism instead highlighted the reasons why Bennett thought the ideas of the laity should not be taken as gospel. Bennett had long been accustomed to staking out positions that were deeply unpopular with churchgoers, whether defending Japanese Americans during wartime incarceration or promoting left-of-center economic views. "It is too easy for Protestant Churches to reflect the prevailing opinion in the community rather than the convictions that have a distinctively Christian basis," Bennett warned. Controversial issues cannot be resolved by "majority vote," he insisted, and in that sense the "Protestant Churches are not democratic." Instead, "leaders in theology and in ethical thinking" should continue to push the churches to change, as long as their "guidance" is "distinctively Christian" and "comes from the revelation of God in Christ and in the historic teaching of the Church." While publicly espousing the democratic and inclusive nature of Protestant institutions, ecumenical leaders like Bennett defended their authority by stressing their unique ability to distinguish between "secular" and "Christian" beliefs.[36]

The significance of Flynn's attacks was not in the ideas his book presented but in the publicity those ideas received and in the bridges Flynn built between fundamentalists and corporate executives. The theological disagreements of the fundamentalist and ecumenical traditions stretched back decades and by 1949 had taken on an economic character. Flynn publicized these intramural fights to the public at large. *The Road Ahead* became one of the vehicles in which decades of fundamentalist criticisms were delivered to the American public. That Flynn's book was published at a moment when the Federal Council was already under siege from segregationists, communist hunters, and conservative business leaders made the impact of the work even greater. Economics became one of many fault lines in an American Protestantism that mixed theological and political concerns, and which weakened some alliances and strengthened others. While Flynn's book did little to dissuade Bennett and others from their economic views, it did raise difficult questions about the clergy-laity gap and foreshadowed the new alignment of the political Right.

The Laymen's War on the Protestant Left

The Federal Council managed to weather Flynn's attack by being more cautious about their economic pronouncements and by accelerating their earlier project of getting more of the laity involved in the organization's activities. As the Federal Council transformed into the National Council of Churches in late 1950, it continued to tout prominent laypersons, like John Foster Dulles and Charles P. Taft, as proof of the organization's moderation. In the early 1950s the National Council of Churches' activism was inhibited as warring factions of laity and clergy battled for control of the new organization. But the National Council survived. Nobody on its staff was purged or publicly repudiated. The same leaders carried on under the changed circumstances of the early Cold War.

Other ecumenical Protestant activists were less fortunate. During the late 1940s social action groups—long a haven for leftist activists—came under attack by committees of "laymen" for their alleged promotion of socialism. These attacks culminated in attempted purges in the early 1950s. The fates of the Congregational Council for Social Action (which survived the attacks) and the Methodist Federation for Social Action (which did not) show that a rightward turn in American ecumenical Protestantism occurred in the early 1950s but that the growing conservatism was only part of the story.

The Council for Social Action had to defend itself from the moment of its formation in 1934, when the Congregationalist denomination mobilized to fight the injustices brought on by the Great Depression. The council was created to be the brain trust of Congregationalism as well as its political arm. At the 1934 meeting where Congregationalist leaders voted to form the council, they also voted to denounce the "profit motive," which set off conservative wrath, especially by an organized laymen's group from Minneapolis.[37] These laymen believed that the council had been created to fight the profit motive, but their protests fell on deaf ears during the Great Depression. The Council for Social Action, under the leadership of John C. Bennett and Liston Pope, went to work and emerged during World War II as a sophisticated political lobbying group and a major force within its denomination.[38]

The Minneapolis laymen nevertheless continued their attacks on the Council for Social Action, and by the early 1950s they had incorporated themselves as the nationwide "Committee Opposing Congregational Political Action." Minneapolis had long been a home for fundamentalists, and after World War II it became a refuge for evangelicals. The founder of the World's Christian Fundamentals Association, William B. Riley, was the pastor of the First Baptist Church in Minneapolis and the president of nearby Northwestern College. Billy Graham, the scion of evangelicalism, took over Northwestern College in 1948, and, two years later, he located the headquarters of the Billy Graham Evangelistic Association in Minneapolis.

The Committee Opposing Congregational Political Action purported to oppose any kind of politics by official Congregational bodies, and it gained the most support when it played upon the ecclesiastically and politically libertarian inclinations in Congregational life. The conservative group's most famous member, the Republican congressman from Minneapolis Walter Judd, explained, "I am *for* both social and political action by Congregational-Christians. I am *against* political action by the Congregational-Christian church or its official agencies."[39] But the group's conservative political leanings were transparent. A pamphlet circulating in the early 1950s said that the Council for Social Action "thought our system of government was outmoded; they disliked the American way of doing business, freely, as individuals. Particularly, they did not like people to make profits." The pamphlet warned its Congregationalist readers that the council "has suggested to Congress that: you are for socialized medicine (compulsory health insurance) . . .

for national regimentation of the economy (full employment bill, peacetime price control and rationing)," and it went on to accuse the group of promoting socialism and associating with communists.[40]

The Council for Social Action worried about its critics, and it tried to stave off a confrontation by carrying out an internal audit. Its leaders heard testimony from opposing sides of the debate about the role of the state in the economy. Russell J. Clinchy represented the libertarian strand of the Congregationalist tradition, and his testimony was made more compelling by his role in helping found the council. He supported anti-poverty programs when they were done on a voluntary basis but balked at the statism of the New Deal.[41] "I believe that a great mistake has been made during the past 15 years in allowing the responsibility of persons and of private agencies in the fields of social welfare to be taken over into the functions of the secular state," he argued. It was quite clear to him that Protestantism taught individual responsibility through and through, and that transferring responsibility to the state was undermining this religious insight. The kind of collectivism the Council for Social Action advocated was not what Clinchy had signed up for.[42]

Another member of the Council for Social Action, Buell G. Gallagher, argued instead that "condemnation of the activities of the so-called 'secular' agencies which are 'invading the province of the Church' might legitimately be directed toward the institutions of religion." The state took over, he explained, because churches were not doing enough. Gallagher argued that Protestants should embrace all projects that are "of the essence of religious values," even if they are pursued by secular organizations. After all, "Who shall say that the Spirit has not been at work" in government efforts against poverty?[43]

The most forceful backer of Congregational political action was longtime council member Bennett. His retort to Clinchy was short. Acknowledging the risk of state tyranny, he nonetheless focused on corporate tyranny. Christian freedom was not the same thing as "the freedom of the strong to control the community in their own interests." In other words, while Clinchy worried about the rise of state power, Bennett saw both state and corporate power as twin threats to the human person, both capable of wreaking havoc on the lives of Americans and both in need of restraint. If anything, he argued, corporate power is a greater threat than the power of government because government is at least nominally controlled by the will of the people.[44]

Despite Bennett's defense, conservatives convinced enough Congregationalists that the Council for Social Action was acting too politically, and
by 1952 there was sufficient pressure to force an investigation of the council.
A nine-person committee—three from the council, three from the Committee Opposing Congregational Political Action (from Minneapolis and
from a Los Angeles auxiliary led by James Fifield), and three "neutral"
members—heard testimony and reviewed the actions of the Council for Social Action. Gallagher was among the supporters of the group, while Congressman Judd joined the critics. The neutral party included the president of
the Rockefeller Foundation, the president of the Standard Oil Company of
New Jersey, and the head of the YMCA.[45]

The investigators wrestled with the same questions about democracy,
representation, and the clergy-laity relationship that had plagued the Federal and National Councils. The big question was whether the Council for
Social Action ought to speak on behalf of its denomination at congressional
hearings or in the courts when churchgoers were divided on an issue. The
investigators gave a muddled answer. The Congregational Council for Social
Action should continue to be an effective witness for its denomination's social and political interests, the investigators concluded, but the organization
needed to be careful about how it did so. Sometimes the council should
speak out on behalf of "ends" but be careful about supporting specific
"means" to those ends. It "should be extremely cautious in linking the denomination to any particular program." Similarly, "when it lobbies it should
do so with a complete sense of its responsibility to the churches and should
not take a partisan position on matters on which the churches are not substantially united."[46] The investigation raised important questions about religious
politics but largely avoided answering them with any clarity. And despite
words of caution, the investigators found no reason to change the organization's mandate or its personnel.

The report was signed unanimously, but it was clear that Congressman
Judd was incensed. Judd urged the denomination to revoke the council's
mandate of "cultivation of public opinion" and the group's ability to "on occasion intercede directly in specific situations." The council, Judd believed,
should focus on talking to the churches, not the general public, and should
be expressly forbidden from advocating any political positions. He added
that the Washington office of the group, which regularly lobbied Congress,
should be closed. The staff should be fired and replaced ("engage new personnel," he advised), and the group should be defunded and forced to rely

Figure 15. Congressman Walter Judd, right, meeting with Chiang Kai-shek and
Soong Mei-ling, in Taiwan in 1953. Judd was among Chiang's most fervent
supporters. Image courtesy of Hoover Institution Library and Archives.

on voluntary contributions.[47] In other words, Judd wanted the council to do
nothing beyond presenting information to the local churches, and he wanted
it to pay its own way. He was not opposed to Christian action per se but insisted that those who engaged in it should first disassociate themselves from
church titles, like he did when he ran for Congress.

Unable to sway his own denomination to muzzle its progressive wing,
Judd sought out allies among evangelicals. In 1950, he reached out to evangelist Billy Graham, a fellow Minneapolis resident. Judd was good friends
with Graham's father-in-law, L. Nelson Bell, who, like Judd, had been a
medical missionary in China. Graham wanted a meeting with Truman, and
he asked for Judd's help. Graham was seeking greater visibility for evangelicals, and he wanted more influence in national politics for his growing religious movement. Judd wrote a letter of introduction to the president on
Graham's behalf, facilitating what would be the evangelist's first of decades
of visits to the White House. Graham obliged Judd, his patron, by reporting
back that he had spoken to Truman about the fate of China—the issue clos-

est to Judd's heart. "I brought up the Far Eastern situation," Graham assured Judd. Meeting with Truman just weeks after the start of the Korean War, Graham reported that "I urged [Truman] to total mobilization, pointing out that the Bible often implies that we should be prepared for war at any time."[48] It appeared that evangelicals were much more cooperative political partners than members of Judd's own denomination.

The same commitments that led Judd to oppose the Council for Social Action and to work with evangelicals also led him to oppose a denominational merger the Congregationalists were planning. Since the late 1940s, the Congregationalists had been in talks to merge with the Evangelical and Reformed denomination, a German American denomination that had over time lost much of its ethnic character. The eventual merger of these two denominations, one from the Congregational tradition and one from the Reformed tradition, was widely seen as an expression of ecumenism and a herald of a postdenominational Christian future. Despite Judd's opposition, the "organic union" was consummated in 1957, after years of setbacks and lawsuits, when the two groups merged and created the United Church of Christ.[49]

Judd's Committee Opposing Congregational Political Action reemerged as the League to Uphold Congregational Principles in the battle against the merger. Judd worried that the union would lead to greater centralization in the new denomination and more political action. For Judd, the Congregationalists were loosely affiliated individual churches that came together regularly to make joint decisions, like funding missionary endeavors. But in the Congregational tradition, individual churches were the ultimate judges of doctrine and politics. For Judd, there was hardly a "Congregationalism" to speak of. This was "the principle of decentralization," a principle that "is the foundation of our American form of government," Judd claimed. He did not see the necessity of organic union, by which he meant the merger of the two denominations into one. There were other means of cooperating that would leave the radical decentralization of Congregationalism intact, he insisted.[50]

Just before the creation of the United Church of Christ, a group of about 100,000 Congregationalists broke away and formed their own denomination, which they called the National Association of Congregational Christian Churches. Judd threw his support to this new denomination, which remained officially apolitical in the ensuing years and focused instead on missionary work and conversion.[51] Theological considerations had propelled Judd to oppose the political mobilization of Congregationalists and, by the late 1950s, the political battles in his denomination led him to vigorously oppose ecumenism. For nearly a decade, Judd had tried to stop the political activism of Congregationalists. Although he did not succeed, he managed to create a major rift within the denomination, causing it to lose 100,000 members. In the process, he created new alliances with the evangelical movement.

The Laymen's War on "Methodism's Pink Fringe"

The Congregational Council for Social Action survived the turmoil of the 1950s, but the Methodist Federation for Social Action, a left-leaning group that underwent a similar attack, did not fare as well. It was an ironic outcome, given the decentralized ecclesiology of Congregationalists and the greater tolerance for hierarchy and authority among Methodists. The Methodist Federation for Social Action was much older than its Congregationalist cousin, having been founded in 1908, when the Methodist Church and the Federal Council had adopted the "Social Creed of the Churches." This social gospel group was a voluntary one, officially unaffiliated with the denomination, freeing it to pursue more radical activism. But the federation enjoyed privileges from the denomination, including the use of office space in the denomination's New York City headquarters. And its membership included many leading Methodists.[52]

Having been closely tied to Harry F. Ward's pro-Soviet policies during the 1930s, the organization transformed during World War II, refocusing on the problem of racism while maintaining a leftist approach to economic policy. Local affiliates had accused the Methodist Federation of not doing enough to fight segregation. "It is said that the Communists and Labor Unions succeed better than Christians in divesting their thoughts and actions of all traces of race prejudice," one local group charged. In response, the Methodist Federation desegregated its locals across the country in 1945. By the end of that year the group even organized an unsegregated local in Alabama, which quickly mobilized against the poll tax in the state.[53]

Despite a long history of activism, it was not until a meeting in Kansas City in 1947, which was documented in a series of exposé-style articles in the *New York World-Telegram* by communist hunter and Pulitzer Prize winner Frederick Woltman, that serious trouble began. The meeting was addressed by Harry Ward and Jerome Davis, both of whom had faced accusations of

communist sympathy. At that meeting, the federation made history by electing Bishop Robert Nathaniel Brooks as president, the first African American to hold the position.[54] But the exposé focused instead on the allegedly
communistic ideas and affiliations of the participants. Chinese general Feng
Yuxiang, known popularly as the "Christian general" for his zealous efforts
to promote the religion among his troops, denounced Chiang Kai-shek at
the Methodist meeting, referring to the embattled Chinese president as
"cruel and unscrupulous."[55] The Methodist organization responded by calling on the United States to withdraw all military aid and all missionaries
from China, and for both the United States and the USSR to withdraw
troops from the Korean peninsula and hold elections there. They also attacked the emerging Judeo-Christian Cold War coalition, urging the United
States to "decline the call of the 'holy war' being preached by the Vatican,"
and arguing that "freedom of religion has been eliminated in Spain and
many other fascist or Catholic countries, while there is freedom of religion
in Russia."[56]

The ensuing controversy played out within the Methodist Church along
the fault lines already emerging, with those who supported anti-communism,
laissez-faire capitalism, and segregation emerging as the federation's biggest
critics. White southerners were especially incensed. A Houston, Texas, pastor's conference unanimously condemned the Methodist Federation and
called the federation's ideas "atheistic communism."[57] The drama played out
as far away as California, where the state's Joint Legislative Fact-Finding
Committee on Un-American Activities (a state-level HUAC) condemned
the federation as one of the "conspicuous fronts for Communist activity."[58]

The federation's leaders defended their actions, as did several prominent
Methodist bishops, who spoke out against the Red-baiting attacks. Some
blamed the Catholic Church for inflaming tensions. Black Methodist leaders, who recognized the importance of the federation's anti-racist activism,
blasted the "false and immoral report of the *New York World Telegram* and
other Scripps-Howard newspapers."[59]

Opponents of the Methodist Federation tried to censure the organization in 1948 at the national Methodist gathering, and again in 1950, but
with little luck.[60] In 1950, however, the charges of communism were revived
by Stanley High, who published an article in *Reader's Digest* called "Methodism's Pink Fringe." High revived many of the familiar charges, bolstered
by information he received from J. B. Matthews, who had worked for the

Dies Committee and would soon become Joseph McCarthy's right-hand man.[61] Now millions of Americans were reading about the alleged communist sympathies of the Methodist Federation.

A wealthy attorney for a Texas oil company named Clarence Lohman, who was also a prominent layman in Houston, used the sensation created by *Reader's Digest* to translate outrage into a purge of Reds in the Methodist churches. That was his hope for the new organization he founded in late 1950, which he called "The Committee for the Preservation of Methodism." This group wanted "to cleanse the churches as McCarthy is cleansing the government," he explained.[62] Frustrated by the clergy's unwillingness to disavow the leftist federation, in 1951 Lohman organized a conference of laymen in Chicago, and out of this meeting came the "Circuit Riders, Inc.," a name that recalled American Methodism's beginnings of itinerant preachers spreading the gospel across the country on horseback. The organization was headquartered in Cincinnati, Ohio, and headed by Myers G. Lowman, who styled the group after the Church League of America and other imitators of the FBI. The new Circuit Riders were spreading the gospel of anticommunism in Methodist churches from coast to coast.

Lowman finally brought down the Methodist Federation by getting the government involved. He lobbied the State of Georgia's House Un-American Activities Committee to investigate the Methodist Federation. Georgia's HUAC produced an eighty-eight-page report called *Review of the Methodist Federation for Social Action*, which the Circuit Riders distributed in support of their accusations.[63] In 1952 the Circuit Riders finally succeeded in censuring the federation, something others had tried to do for decades. The federation was asked to stop using the name "Methodist" and to leave its office space in the Methodist building in midtown Manhattan. The move also put pressure on clergy to disaffiliate from the organization and to abandon its leaders. Crushed organizationally, the group carried on with a skeleton staff, not recovering until 1960, when it returned to New York.[64] It was a crushing blow for the Methodist Left.

That was not the end of the story, however. The same clergy that censured the Methodist Federation also created an official denominational social action group to take over many of the functions of the federation. Its official status and denominational funding ensured that the new group would not go too far afield in its politics. And yet, it also meant that, like most other ecumenical Protestant denominations, the politics of the Methodist clergy had a political outlet and that the denomination would stake out political positions in an official capacity. The "laymen" were able to make a public showing of their opposition to leftist ideas, but their anti-ecumenical and Christian libertarian impulses failed to produce the results they hoped for. If anything, the trial of the Methodist Federation for Social Action only led to the expansion of the denomination's clerical bureaucracy. The Methodist Left was clearly wounded, but Methodist liberalism continued to thrive and the political mobilization of ecumenical Protestantism carried on even during the trying years of the early Cold War.

The Failed Laymen's Takeover of the National Council and the Drift Toward Evangelicalism

The mixed results that laymen achieved in their fight against the clergy's views on the economy, segregation, and foreign relations came at a moment when the National Council was advocating the "Responsible Society" as a middle way between capitalism and communism. In the wake of the 1950 Detroit conference, where the new ideology made its US debut, conservatives reevaluated their strategy of opposition to the newly created National Council. Oil magnate J. Howard Pew, the self-described "fundamentalist," had been bankrolling James Fifield's anti-statist organization, Spiritual Mobilization, and had recently helped finance the conservative Christian Freedom Foundation, which sent its journal, *Christian Economics,* for free to 175,000 ministers. Like other conservatives, Pew had failed to stop ecumenical Protestant economic reform efforts at Detroit. He now decided he would try to stop them by attempting to gain control of the National Council of Churches.[65]

The National Council had its own reasons for wanting to work with Pew. It continued to desire the legitimacy that arose from working with the laity, and it wanted to shield itself from Red-baiting by parading its conservative members. The National Council also felt confident in its ability to work with businessmen following the successful Detroit conference. It also wanted to enhance its prestige and access to power—both elements that Pew could provide. Finally, the National Council needed money. After all, it was the biggest Protestant organization of the time, with dozens of institutions to fund and countless new ventures to launch. Pew was happy to provide money to the organization, but he made clear that his connections and his pocketbook came with strings attached.[66]

Pew agreed to chair the National Council's new National Lay Committee, which was designed to fulfill the hopes of Oxnam and Horton for greater participation of the laity in ecumenical affairs. The new committee would help to guide the National Council and to fundraise for the organization. While the National Council's Department of Church and Economic Life was balanced between representatives from labor unions and corporations, "laity" in this case meant the participation of Protestantism's wealthiest churchgoers. Pew insisted, and the National Council agreed, that he appoint all of the nearly two hundred members of the lay committee, which he filled mostly with very conservative businessmen and a few moderate members of the American Federation of Labor.

Pew's most audacious demand was that the National Lay Committee have absolute autonomy and the ability to censor National Council statements, something National Council leaders never agreed to. At the first meeting of his new committee, Pew unilaterally announced to the group that its members would have the power to review all National Council proclamations before they went to the General Council (the successor to the Federal Council's Executive Committee and the organization's highest authority, consisting of representatives from member denominations). Appalled by this threat of censorship, Oxnam urged his fellow church leaders to "dare not set a precedent which in any way gives to a group of men not in the organization and not chosen by the churches the right to review, directly or indirectly, the pronouncements of a great church."[67] After a several-month inquiry, a compromise was reached, whereby ten Lay Committee members would join the National Council's General Council without voting privileges. In the ensuing years, the relationship between the Lay Committee and the National Council developed: Corporate donations rose by 60 percent, and Lay Committee members gained prominent positions within the sprawling National Council bureaucracy.[68]

Pew's push to silence the National Council's economic pronouncements coincided with attacks on social action groups, with McCarthyism, the Korean War, and a rapidly growing economy, all of which inclined the organization to moderate its proclamations. Lacking formal power, Pew repeatedly threatened to withdraw his sizable personal contributions and to shut off the stream of donations he had facilitated. The National Council's leadership tried placating him by agreeing to limit the number of their proclamations, by creating a "screening committee" to watch over the Department of Church and Economic Life's statements, and by occasionally censuring department head Cameron Hall over his close relationship with unions. As Elizabeth Fones-Wolf observes, "business leaders played an important role in helping to silence an important segment of the religious community and to prod the institutions of the church in more moderate directions."[69] However, even by this point, many economic ideas that had been controversial in the 1930s and 1940s had already become orthodoxy. In 1953 the ecumenists began pushing back against Pew's committee, either by issuing proclamations as individuals or by simply ignoring Pew. The following year, he was no longer able to stop National Council calls for more government intervention in the economy, for federal aid to education, and for more public housing. Pew, unwilling to accept overtures of compromise from moderates, allowed the Lay Committee to die in 1955.[70]

Following the collapse of the Lay Committee, Pew redoubled his efforts on behalf of evangelicals. He had already invested money into the evangelical Fuller Theological Seminary, but now he financed the 1956 launch of *Christianity Today*, which served as the main platform for evangelical views, and he helped Billy Graham become the new face of US Protestantism by financially backing the broadcasts of his New York City revivals in 1957.[71] From the very beginning, *Christianity Today* took a conservative attitude toward the power of unions and the reach of the government. Evangelicals did not yet see themselves as part of a broader conservative movement in the 1950s, but the emerging network of donors they cultivated and the alliances they created in opposition to their ecumenical counterparts moved them in conservative directions. According to Molly Worthen, "Despite Carl Henry's 1947 manifesto decrying fundamentalists' neglect of social justice, he and the other editors toed the conservative line on every significant political and theological issue from foreign policy and civil rights to evolution and the ecumenical movement" in the 1950s.[72]

In one of the first issues of *Christianity Today*, the magazine's editors attacked the power of labor unions. They also decidedly stood against "the plea for more foreign economic aid and for expanded welfare programs at home" because of the "coercive element" involved in taxation. Signaling that there was now a new voice in American Protestantism, the magazine declared, "even if influential Protestant clergymen during the past generation tried to make collectivism out to be Christian, and Capitalism satanic, they were false prophets. By their proclamations they revealed that they misunderstood Christianity, and that their devotion to the writings of Marx ran deeper than their fidelity to the Hebrew-Christian Scriptures." The editors proclaimed, "Capitalism is biblical."[73] The rise of evangelicalism, signaled by the ascendancy of Graham and *Christianity Today*, benefited from the growing rift between clergy and laity in ecumenical churches. Focused in their opposition to the ecumenical "false prophets," evangelicals cultivated alliances with corporate leaders, helping pave the way for the rise of the religious Right later in the twentieth century.[74]

Toward the Great Society

Just as evangelicals were finding their voice on economic matters, ecumenical Protestants proceeded down two separate tracks. Oxnam, Bennett, and other clergy began to once again call for an end to poverty and to proclaim their support for the Responsible Society. Their efforts would come to fruition in the 1960s in the Johnson administration's War on Poverty. Charles P. Taft, by contrast, influenced laymen to support a moderate program that led to the modest reforms of the Eisenhower years.

With Pew gone, Taft promoted the laity as a bastion of moderation standing between the radicalism of some clergy and the reactionary politics of the National Association of Manufacturers. Speaking in 1956, Taft, the National Council's best-known layman, recounted the brief history of Christian laypersons' economic thought. The liberal Republican began with the 1937 Oxford conference, where he, "a very green and ignorant young lawyer," had first joined the ecumenical movement. In 1947, the Federal Council had held a laity-dominated study conference at Pittsburgh and soon after created the new Department of Church and Economic Life, which Taft headed. He skipped over the 1948 meeting of the World Council of Churches, which introduced the Responsible Society (the meeting was dominated by clergy, after all), and instead went on to discuss the 1950 gathering in Detroit and a laypersons' meeting in Buffalo in 1952. Thanks to these "gatherings of laymen with their professional advisers," Taft said, "the churches have a reservoir of know-how and a far greater concern for what keeps laymen awake at nights." After the tug-of-war between clergy and laity for much of the 1940s and early 1950s, Taft concluded in 1956 that Christian economics were in the safe hands of those responsible men who, unlike clergy, had a realistic sense of how the economy works.[75]

Taft overstated the victory of the laity over the clergy, which still held tremendous sway over economic ideas in the United States. With the departure of Pew from the National Council, the organization's leaders once again issued broad pronouncements on economic policy that made nationwide headlines. And clergy could still hold forth on economic matters from tens of thousands of pulpits across the country. As important, Taft's maneuvering was a triumph for a certain kind of Christian economics, one that had little use for the Christian libertarianism of Pew, Judd, Flynn, and High. Taft supported the economic moderation of President Eisenhower, who refused to deliver on the Republican Party's promise, first made in 1936, to dismantle the New Deal. It had been so controversial for so long, but its acceptance by Eisenhower and Taft signaled that it had achieved mainstream status among some of the laity as well as the clergy.

During the second half of the 1950s, conflict ensued between Taft and the clergy. Taft would not entertain Christian libertarianism, but he also rejected the more ambitious reform efforts to tame corporate power and implement economic democracy. Meanwhile, Bennett and Oxnam continued to push to limit economic inequality and to give workers a greater say in the operation of industry. But these disagreements never reached the fever pitch of the 1930s debates about the New Deal or the fights over the Responsible Society in the early 1950s. The thriving economy had a lot to do with the level of civility. High tax rates on the rich and widespread unionization meant that income inequality was at a historic low and worker representation was at an all-time high in the mid-1950s. The stakes appeared to be lower than they had been previously. In this atmosphere, both sides began focusing on raising the conditions of the poorest Americans.

National Council leaders joined other liberal intellectuals in focusing attention on the problems of poverty. The popular economist John Kenneth Galbraith used his 1958 book, *The Affluent Society*, to direct Americans' attention away from "the obsolete and contrived preoccupations . . . rooted in the poverty, inequality and economic peril of the past" and toward the problems which arise from an affluent economy.[76] The Catholic socialist writer Michael Harrington complained that all this talk of affluence masked the persistent poverty of Americans being left behind in a thriving economy. "While this discussion was carried on, there existed another America," he wrote in his best-selling book. "In it dwelt somewhere between 40,000,000 and 50,000,000 citizens of this land. They were poor. They still are."[77]

National Council leaders likewise emphasized in the mid-1950s the persistence of poverty in an affluent society, a theme proposed by union leader Walter Reuther at the 1950 Detroit conference. In 1956, the National Council held a follow-up conference in Detroit on the theme of "The Christian Conscience and an Economy of Abundance."[78] The conference's focus helped sway the national dialogue toward the elimination of poverty in the language of human rights. "From the Christian standpoint, a minimum goal for the distribution of abundance is the right of all persons to a reasonable level of living, including food, shelter, clothing, health care, and access to cultural interests," announced the National Council.[79] The United States was leaving "past ages of economic scarcity" and was "entering a new age" in which "enough can be produced to meet the basic needs of man."[80] Many were better off, thanks to the "mixed economy" of the United States, but more needed to be done to "recognize the dignity of each person and each group." "One-fourth of all families in the United States," the National Council lamented, "do not share in the general abundance" and earn too little to "sustain a life of health and hope."[81]

According to the National Council, the more equal "distribution of income in our country" was profoundly encouraging, and the role of "the labor union" in bringing "some control over the worker's economic life back into his own hands" was praised. These things remained a source of friction between clergy and laity. "Our group is not agreed upon the extent to which the individual is free to effectively control his own role in the economy and community life," National Council leaders wrote in 1956. But they agreed on raising the poor up to the standard that Christian human rights and human dignity demanded. Providing a floor for the poor without necessarily providing a ceiling for the rich, an idea Samuel Moyn calls "sufficient provision," created common ground in the debates over Christian economics.[82]

*   *   *

This new human rights advocacy closed certain avenues but opened up new ones. The "poverty amid plenty" idea was broad and generative, at least in the United States. To take one example, four years after the 1956 Detroit meeting, a report on East Coast migrant workers conducted by the National Council made its way into a documentary called *Harvest of Shame*.[83] The program was narrated by Edward R. Murrow and was broadcast nationwide the day after Thanksgiving, 1960, on CBS. It was especially poignant because it dramatized conditions laborers had to endure to bring the middle-class viewers the meals they were enjoying. As Americans gathered around the television and ate their Turkey leftovers, they were exposed to the depths of poverty that millions of their fellow citizens continued to endure.

Harvest of Shame was one of the ways that ecumenical Protestant reforms gained traction in the 1960s. By drawing attention to the dissonance between poverty and prosperity, the National Council helped pave the way for the Great Society programs of the Lyndon B. Johnson administration. When Johnson called on University of Michigan graduates to help build the Great Society in 1964, he repeated many of the ideas expressed by ecumenical Protestants in the previous decade. It would be "a society where the demands of morality, the needs of the spirit, can be realized in the life of the Nation," according to Johnson. The Great Society "rests on abundance and liberty for all."[84] Protestant economic debates took a winding path in the 1950s in response to pressure from laypersons and evangelical critics, but the new understanding of Christian human rights still served as a tributary to the liberal economic policies of the Johnson administration in the 1960s.

The clergy-laity gap had several important consequences for the postwar United States. In the short term, it encouraged the National Council to create a platform for Charles Taft, whose efforts helped sustain the so-called consensus politics of the 1950s. But over the long term, the clergy-laity gap widened and transformed into something more than a division within a single religious community. The clergy-laity gap led to the realignment of coalitions and the formation of new partnerships, on the left as well as on the right, which became influential in the ensuing decades. The political mobilization by ecumenical Protestants against poverty reached its apogee in the liberal reforms of the 1960s while also fomenting a conservative, religious backlash that would challenge these initiatives in later years.

Global Gospel, American Fault Lines

A generation of ecumenical Protestant leaders came of age and traveled abroad in the 1920s, rose to power in the 1930s, mobilized during World War II, came under attack during the early Cold War, and shaped the movements of the 1960s. These men and women wielded tremendous influence in their religious community and in liberal politics. Inspired by Protestant globalism, ecumenical Protestants brought their religiously rooted concerns about race, poverty, and foreign relations into the corridors of power and deeply influenced national political debates around these issues. Caged in by a devotion to procedure and consensus, and by many blind spots, their activism shaped both the accomplishments and limits of American liberalism in the middle decades of the twentieth century.

Beginning in the 1960s this generation of leaders passed from the scene. Channing Tobias died in 1961, and G. Bromley Oxnam in 1963. Reinhold Niebuhr passed away in 1971 after years of declining health. Other members of the mid-century ecumenical Protestant elite retired in the 1960s and 1970s but lived into old age. Thelma Stevens retired from service to the United Methodists in 1968 and lived until the age of eighty-eight. Benjamin Mays retired in 1971 from Morehouse College and lived to the age of eighty-nine. John C. Bennett retired in 1970 and lived until the age of ninety-two. Most dramatically, Henry Pitney Van Dusen suffered a stroke in 1970, and, after five years of declining health, he and his wife, Elizabeth Van Dusen, jointly committed suicide by taking an overdose of sleeping pills. She passed away immediately, while Henry died of related medical complications two weeks later.[1] As this generation retired and passed, they relinquished their hold on American ecumenical Protestantism to a younger generation during the 1960s.

The change that this generational turnover brought was unmistakable. Harvard theologian Harvey Cox, for one, identified a "New Breed" of ministers who rejected the position-paper liberalism of their predecessors and embraced the tactics of the protest movements so popular in the 1960s. "In Buffalo, Philadelphia, Kansas City, Chicago, Oakland and dozens of other cities, the New Breed can be found organizing welfare unions, tenants' councils, rent strikes, and school boycotts," Cox wrote in 1967. "The Christian churches are now taking the leadership in social change," observed community organizer Saul Alinsky. There is a "pure flame of passion for justice you find in these young ministers today."[2]

Among the best-known members of this new generation was Eugene Carson Blake. He was in his fifties but nonetheless embodied the revolutionary spirit of the age. Already famous for getting arrested while integrating a Baltimore amusement park and for delivering an address at the 1963 March on Washington, Blake soon took his activism to the international arena. As the head of the World Council of Churches, Blake launched the Program to Combat Racism in 1969. This massive human rights mobilization sent $4 million of aid to independence movements and anti-apartheid groups. At a time when Amnesty International refused to sponsor Nelson Mandela as a prisoner of conscience because his organization engaged in violence, Blake's program unflinchingly sent aid to Marxist rebels, including Mandela's African National Congress.[3] The Program to Combat Racism was a response to the worldwide "revolution" ecumenical Protestants had diagnosed and an attempt at overcoming the Cold War divide. It was just one measure of how radical some members of this community had become by the 1960s.

The earlier developments in the ecumenical Protestant milieu chronicled in this book shaped the 1960s-era movements against racism, poverty, and colonialism. Ecumenical Protestants also helped popularize human rights in the postwar world, among both civil society groups and governments. In the 1960s, countries in the Global South adopted the language of human rights in debates at the United Nations. The countries' diplomats understood human rights as interweaving race and religion, much like American ecumenical Protestants.[4] Indeed, in the 1960s most Americans experienced human rights rhetoric as a condemnation of Jim Crow from people living abroad, which helped sway the federal government to back desegregation.[5] The language of human rights also permeated the church-based civil rights movement in the United States.[6] Beginning in the 1960s, veterans of the civil rights movement and activists in ecumenical Protestant organizations, especially missionaries and members of the Christian peace movements, began to take governmental positions and to staff secular NGOs that advocated for human rights. Ecumenical Protestants helped create new human rights organizations like the Washington Office on Latin America and the Committee for Human Rights in Korea. Ecumenical Protestants also swelled the ranks of these organizations.[7] Moreover, the promotion of human rights by ecumenical leaders to their Protestant communities in the 1950s, when such ideas otherwise dropped out of the national conversation, helped make human rights "an everyday vernacular" language by the 1960s and 1970s.[8] In both organization and popularization, ecumenical Protestantism was a critical part of the ascendancy of human rights by the time the Carter administration incorporated them into US foreign policy in the late 1970s.

Human rights serve as an example of how ecumenical Protestant activism, from the 1920s to the 1960s, transformed American liberalism—but it is only one of many. American ecumenical Protestant institutions served as gateways to a variety of progressive causes, including those that fought racism and poverty, and criticized American foreign policy. Historians have underplayed the contributions of ecumenical Protestants to these movements partly because religious actors sometimes worked outside the boundaries of church-based organizations. Increasingly, Americans who grew up in the ecumenical Protestant milieu found ways of expressing their political commitments outside the confines of their religious communities. And religiously motivated people, who continued to affiliate with ecumenical denominations, became more comfortable working with, or for, secular political organizations in the 1960s. From the 1920s to the 1960s, American ecumenical Protestants transformed American politics as Protestants working through Protestant institutions. But even after the 1960s many "post-Protestants"—those shaped by a Protestant upbringing but who no longer associated with religious organizations—ensured that ecumenical Protestant values endured into the late twentieth century and into our own day.[9]

Although ecumenical Protestants had addressed racial, economic, and international problems from the 1920s to the 1960s, critics from the left argued that it was not enough. Younger ecumenical Protestants, in particular, criticized organizations like the National Council of Churches and the World Council of Churches for not following through on their many proclamations. A torrent of criticism of the "middle way" and "middle axioms" emerged from grassroots activists. And Protestant leaders from the Global

South criticized the ideology of "globalism," which had underwritten ecumenical Protestant activism from the 1930s into the 1960s.[10] Globalism min-
imized the controversial issues of decolonization and the rise of American
power, and sometimes presented the United Nations as a panacea. But foreign and domestic critics urged American ecumenical Protestant leaders to
wholeheartedly back anti-colonial movements, to welcome marginalized
voices into positions of power, and to abandon their working relationship
with the US state. To be relevant in the modern world, religion must "speak
truth to power" instead of working with it, wrote a group of activists that
included Bayard Rustin and A. J. Muste.[11] Others criticized the decades-long
quest to find a middle ground between liberal activists and conservative
churchgoers. Critics argued that ecumenical Protestant leaders ought to
choose justice over consensus.

Although many of these newly empowered activists were indebted to the
ecumenical tradition, they nonetheless criticized the National Council of
Churches as a moribund bureaucracy too embedded in the structures of
American power to witness effectively on behalf of social justice. Students
at Union Theological Seminary, located on New York's Upper West Side,
staged sit-ins at the school in May 1969. Soon the sit-ins spread one block
west to Riverside Church, the cathedral of ecumenical Protestantism. Just
one block south, a months-long occupation began in the Interchurch Center. Students demonstrated in the offices of the United Presbyterians, the
United Methodists, the United Church of Christ, and the National Council
of Churches itself.[12] A year earlier, student delegates at the meeting of the
World Council of Churches had staged a sit-in, demanding the organization
do more to combat poverty and racial injustice.[13]

Many of these critics voiced the theology of revolution, a tradition that
emerged within the ecumenical Protestant milieu. In this way, the passionate criticism by ecumenical Protestant youths of the National Council of
Churches and the World Council of Churches built upon the work and
activism of their elders. The YMCAs and YWCAs, the Student Christian
Movement, the National Council of Churches, and the World Council of
Churches—along with university campuses, neighborhood organizations,
and civil rights groups—became places where radical politics could find expression, encouragement, and sometimes wield tremendous influence. Institutionally and ideologically, the mid-century ecumenical leadership and
the more activist generation of the 1960s were more entangled than either
group was willing to admit. Each one, in their own ways, would bring about

important changes to the Left-liberal tradition in the United States and to
American politics.

The Lasting Legacy of Religious Fault Lines

The new spirit of activism intensified divisions among American Protestants in the 1960s and 1970s along the fault lines that emerged in earlier
decades. While protests and sit-ins worsened generational divides and intensified the rift between liberals and the Left, still more criticism came
from the Right. Political conservatives, evangelicals, the laity, and many
southerners grew increasingly alarmed as the National Council of Churches
encouraged protests against the Vietnam War, segregation, and poverty
with unprecedented vigor. Meanwhile, the World Council of Churches
turned sharply against colonialism. The gap in values between ecumenical
leaders and ordinary churchgoers became extraordinarily wide. One mid-
1960s poll, which was gleefully promoted by evangelicals, reported that "on
civil rights, 67 percent of [National Council of Churches general] assembly
delegates thought change was proceeding too slowly, whereas 70 percent of
average Americans thought it was going too fast." The gap was as wide for
the Vietnam War. Fifty-two percent of National Council of Churches delegates wanted US troops withdrawn from Vietnam, but only 18 percent of
Americans did. In fact, 55 percent of Americans advocated increased bomb-
ings in Vietnam, according to the poll. Most devastatingly, it appeared that
Protestants who attended church regularly were more conservative on these
issues than Americans who rarely went to religious services.[14]

By the 1970s and 1980s, gender and sexuality became a more pressing
issue and drove a wedge between ecumenical Protestants, the laity, and
evangelicals. Ecumenical leaders had never championed women's rights
with the same intensity as they had the United Nations or desegregation.
But they had lent support for birth control, sex education, and sometimes
even spoke up in support of interracial marriage. After the rise of feminism
in the 1960s, and especially the legalization of abortion following the 1973
Supreme Court decision *Roe v. Wade*, gender became an intensely debated
topic among ecumenical Protestants. The role of women in church and
family life, abortion, the AIDS epidemic, and homosexuality became some
of the most pressing and divisive issues for ecumenical Protestant leaders.
Like the political controversies at mid-century, the fault lines were similar,

with ecumenical leaders largely accommodating the demands of feminists and LGBTQ groups, while evangelicals made the patriarchal heterosexual family and opposition to abortion the hallmarks of their political identity. The big difference at the end of the twentieth century, compared to earlier decades, was that many Protestants in the Global South supported a conservative line on gender and stood against the liberal leadership of ecumenical Protestant denominations. The more recent debates about gay clergy led to the split of the United Methodist Church, a further blow to the ecumenical movement. New York Methodist bishop Thomas Bickerton woefully observed in 2020 that "the line in the sand" over homosexuality "had turned into a canyon."[15]

For ecumenical Protestant leaders, political and theological divisions were exacerbated by demographic changes in their churches. Among the most significant of these changes was the exodus of youths from ecumenical churches and the aging of their congregations. Some Protestant youths, who turned further to the left than their elders, remained faithful members of their denominations.[16] But, beginning in the 1960s, and accelerating in the following decades, many ecumenical Protestant youths left their denominations altogether. They were shaped by the values promoted by national Protestant leaders but did not find those values expressed in their home churches. Many young activists sought out secular groups, like the Student Nonviolent Coordinating Committee or Amnesty International, which better expressed their religiously motivated ethical commitments to human rights than did Methodist, Congregationalist, or Presbyterian churches. Others, encouraged by the religious pluralism promoted by ecumenical institutions, explored other outlets for their faith or simply stopped believing. Although they were shaped by the values and politics of ecumenical Protestantism, some of these young people left the churches in which they grew up and never returned.[17]

Evangelicals held on to their young members, at least for a time, and Catholic churches were replenished by immigrants, while ecumenical Protestant denominations began shrinking in the late 1960s. The term "mainline Protestant" came into use in the 1960s and quickly became synonymous with "decline."[18] To the present day, these congregations are growing smaller and older with each passing year. According to the Pew Research Center, in 2014 ecumenical Protestants (which Pew calls "mainline" Protestants) constituted only 14.7 percent of the population, down from 18.1 percent in 2007 and nearly 30 percent of the population in the early 1970s.[19] As churches shrank, the average churchgoer aged. The number of Methodists, Lutherans, and Episcopalians over the age of fifty rose by 10 percent between 1957 and 1983.[20] As younger and more progressive members of ecumenical Protestant churches left, congregations sometimes became more conservative. Today, slightly more ecumenical Protestant churchgoers identify as Republicans than as Democrats.[21] As churches became more conservative, they began withholding funds from activist organizations like the National Council of Churches, which now struggles with financial shortfalls.[22]

As telling as these statistics are, what ecumenical Protestants have lost cannot be measured by numbers alone. Most crucially, ecumenical Protestants lost control of the cultural capital of Christianity to the Christian Right. From the 1920s to the 1960s, ecumenical Protestants had commanded the attention of the press, the sympathy of America's political elites, and a popular understanding that their specific religious tradition was at the heart of American democracy and represented the best hope for a more just and peaceful world. While historians have rightly celebrated the decline of Protestant hegemony and the burgeoning religious pluralism that followed, they have not fully accounted for the ways in which ecumenical Protestants used their privilege at mid-century and the effects that had on the United States and beyond. Ecumenical Protestants wielded their power in surprising ways, by choosing to fight racial injustice, poverty, and imperialism. These very initiatives were partly responsible for their sudden loss of status in American public life, which would be ceded to evangelicals and conservative Catholics.

Evangelical Protestants, in particular, positioned themselves as Christianity's defenders against the hostile forces of political and theological liberalism, which they viewed as a slippery slope to secularism. The modern evangelical movement was born in 1942, with the founding of the National Association of Evangelicals in the same year that ecumenical Protestants launched the World Order movement. Since that moment, it has been a Janus-faced movement, with Billy Graham representing the polite, purportedly apolitical wing, and Carl McIntire leading the dissenting, anti-ecumenical wing. At first, the evangelical movement was modeled on the ecumenical movement: the National Association of Evangelicals was inspired by the Federal Council of Churches, and the evangelical *Christianity Today* was modeled on the ecumenical *Christian Century*. But evangelicals were also innovators who sought out new ways to gain the public's attention. Soon, new models of worship, like megachurches and TV ministries, helped propel evangelicals to new heights and gave platforms to their more radical activists.[23] The fundamentalist wing—led by Jerry Falwell in the 1970s—emerged as the public face of evangelicalism as this religious group became a major player in Republican politics. Internationally, evangelicals expanded their missionary outreach in the 1970s, while ecumenical Protestants had pulled back because of concerns about cultural imperialism.

The evangelical movement in the 1970s was the mirror image of ecumenical Protestantism: It policed racial boundaries, attacked welfare programs, and voiced support for the Vietnam War and for South Africa's apartheid government on anti-communist grounds.[24] None of this was new. The political orientation and alliances of evangelicalism had been shaped, in part, in the 1940s in reaction to what ecumenical Protestants were doing, placing evangelicals on a path that led from opposition to the United Nations and human rights to support for Ronald Reagan and Donald Trump.[25] Despite the best efforts of their leaders, however, evangelicals could not replicate the cultural and political authority that the Protestant establishment had wielded at mid-century. Evangelicalism is politically effective but its power is derived partly from its partisanship. So long as religious pluralism remains an accepted norm in the United States, it is hard to imagine evangelicalism becoming more than it is now: one group among many competing for public influence.

It was no coincidence that American conservatism and American evangelicalism rose together, just as it was not coincidental that American liberalism and American ecumenism had risen together at mid-century. Ecumenical Protestants supported economic reform from Roosevelt's New Deal to Johnson's Great Society. They took part in anti-racist activism beginning during World War II and proved to be reliable allies for the NAACP and for the Southern Christian Leadership Conference. Less successfully but still significantly, ecumenical Protestants worked to diminish anti-communism, transcend the Cold War, and reduce the arms buildup in the United States.

Ecumenical Protestantism was at the heart of mid-century liberalism's rise and fall. This was the case because ecumenical Protestants were important players in liberal politics. It was also the case because they had tied their political initiatives so closely with their theology, thereby entangling religious and political battles in new ways. Ecumenical Protestants avoided partisanship, and it was partly their ties to the liberal wings of the Democratic and Republican parties that made mid-century liberalism as durable as it was. They worked alongside a group that historians call the "New Deal coalition"—an unstable alliance between Jews, African Americans, working-class European ethnics, and southern whites backing the Democratic Party. They also worked with liberal Republicans to press their agenda. The New Deal coalition came apart in the 1970s along many of the racial, regional, and economic fault lines that ecumenical Protestant human rights activism had widened. Moreover, many of the organizations that had supported mid-century liberalism began to collapse. Just as ecumenical Protestants faced declining numbers and rebellion among their ranks, so too did some labor unions and civil rights organizations. To take one example, in the same way as the laity rebelled against the political initiatives of ecumenical leaders, so too did workers in the 1970s rebel against the actions of union leaders.[26]

The ecumenical Protestant leadership's move away from consensus politics, and the unpopularity of their views with churchgoers, helped make it possible for evangelicals to capture the Republican Party and move it rightward. Divisions in the United States greatly sharpened in the 1960s and 1970s over segregation, affirmative action, and the Vietnam War—but also, as this book has shown, over religion. These divisions realigned American politics and created an opening for the rise of modern conservatism. Ecumenical Protestantism contributed to the rise of liberalism at mid-century, and the religion's decline accelerated the decline of political liberalism in the 1970s.

But the story of "mainline" decline is misleading partly because it misses the political work ecumenical Protestants have done—and continue to do—that shapes our world today. The most obvious example is that the National Council of Churches and the World Council of Churches, along with dozens of denominations and thousands of religious groups, continue to pursue a progressive political agenda. Leading voices calling for racial justice continue to come from ecumenical denominations—figures like Disciples of Christ minister William Barber and United Church of Christ minister Traci Blackmon. Liberal politicians, like Hillary Clinton and Barack Obama, continue to be shaped by an ecumenical Protestant heritage.[27] They are joined by the many people whose values were shaped by their Protestant upbringing but who are no longer churchgoers. Although they get less attention than evangelicals, ecumenical Protestants and post-Protestants continue their political work in towns and cities across the nation, in the nation's capital, and at the United Nations.[28]

Inspired by ecumenism and the political doctrine of globalism, ecumenical Protestants sought to reshape the world at mid-century. By bringing international ideas to bear on domestic politics, ecumenical Protestants assured that their global gospel would have its most dramatic impact on the United States. Their human rights activism would politicize and transform religious life in America. But their mobilization also had repercussions well beyond their churches. It reshaped American liberalism and polarized US politics in ways that reverberate into the present day.

NOTES

Introduction

1. "Text of Council Statement," *New York Times*, December 4, 1948, 11.

2. Ibid.

3. I use the term "ecumenical Protestantism" to emphasize a shared commitment among this group of Protestants to unite Christians (especially Protestants, but also Orthodox Christians and, after the 1960s, Catholics) across denominational, national, racial, and economic boundaries. "Ecumenical" gatherings—whether among a group of churches in a small town, at a meeting of the Federal Council of Churches, or at multinational gatherings across the world—brought together Christian realists and pacifists, whites and African Americans, clergy and laity, and Americans and colonial subjects. The globally minded outlook and the boundary crossing that ecumenism promoted are at the heart of the political and theological developments described in this book. The term "ecumenical" is coming into increasing use by historians who are dissatisfied with the three major alternative classifications: "mainline" Protestants, the "Protestant establishment," and "liberal" Protestants. As Elesha Coffman shows, the term "mainline" Protestants came into widespread usage only in the 1960s and quickly became synonymous with "decline." See Elesha J. Coffman, *The Christian Century and the Rise of the Protestant Mainline* (New York: Oxford University Press, 2013), 8. The "Protestant establishment" is a helpful term because it emphasizes the embeddedness of Protestants in the domestic power structures of the United States, and this book occasionally uses the term when discussing the cultural and political authority of this group. But as Heather A. Warren points out, "religious establishment" came into use in the early 1960s and "became synonymous with 'mainline' Protestantism." Like "mainline," the term "Protestant establishment" does not capture the international dimension of this community or the proliferation of its political and cultural values long after it had lost its "establishmentness" in the 1960s. See Heather A. Warren, *Theologians of a New World Order: Reinhold Niebuhr and the Christian Realists, 1920–1948* (New York: Oxford University Press, 1997), 4. On the Protestant establishment, see William R. Hutchison, ed., *Between the Times: The Travail of the Protestant Establishment in America, 1900–1960* (New York: Cambridge University Press, 1989). "Liberal" Protestantism—referring to a critical and historical understanding of the Bible and an openness to Enlightenment values, such as a respect for scientific inquiry and cosmopolitanism—has a much longer and more distinguished history. But, for the purposes of this book, it blurs the boundary between theological liberalism and political liberalism. On theological liberalism, see Gary Dorrien, *The Making of American Liberal Theology*, vol. 2, *Idealism, Realism, and Modernity, 1900–1950* (Louisville, KY: Westminster John Knox Press, 2003). See also

Matthew Hedstrom, *The Rise of Liberal Religion: Book Culture and American Spirituality in the Twentieth Century* (New York: Oxford University Press, 2012).

4. Gary J. Dorrien, *The Making of American Liberal Theology*, vol. 1, *Imagining Progressive Religion, 1805–1900* (Louisville, KY: Westminster John Knox Press, 2001); Dorrien, *The Making of American Liberal Theology*, vol. 2; William R. Hutchison, *The Modernist Impulse in American Protestantism* (Oxford: Oxford University Press, 1982).

5. The views of both ecumenical and evangelical Protestants changed over time, which means that definitions of either group must be historically specific. This book defines both groups in relation to their characteristics at mid–twentieth century and emphasizes the relational development of their identities. One of the more influential definitions of evangelicalism, which focuses solely on theology, is detailed in David W. Bebbington, *Evangelicalism in Modern Britain: A History from the 1730s to the 1930s* (London: Unwin Hyman, 1989). On postwar US evangelicalism, see Molly Worthen, *Apostles of Reason: The Crisis of Authority in American Evangelicalism* (New York: Oxford University Press, 2014).

6. Ecumenical Protestants were divided in their attitudes toward nonbelievers and whether the state should remain neutral toward nonbelief. See K. Healan Gaston, *Imagining Judeo-Christian America: Religion, Secularism, and the Redefinition of Democracy* (Chicago: University of Chicago Press, 2019).

7. C. Howard Hopkins, *John R. Mott, 1865–1955: A Biography* (Grand Rapids, MI: William B. Eerdmans, 1979), 665.

8. On the moral establishment, see David Sehat, *The Myth of American Religious Freedom* (New York: Oxford University Press, 2016). See also William R. Hutchison, *Religious Pluralism in America: The Contentious History of a Founding Ideal* (New Haven, CT: Yale University Press, 2003).

9. C. Wright Mills, *The Power Elite* (New York: Oxford University Press, 1956).

10. On the advent of mid-century globalism, see Or Rosenboim, *The Emergence of Globalism: Visions of World Order in Britain and the United States, 1939–1950* (Princeton, NJ: Princeton University Press, 2017); Susan Schulten, *The Geographical Imagination in America, 1880–1950* (Chicago: University of Chicago Press, 2001); Samuel Zipp, *The Idealist: Wendell Willkie's Wartime Quest to Build One World* (Cambridge, MA: Belknap Press of Harvard University Press, 2020).

11. On Christian nationalism, see Sam Haselby, *Origins of American Religious Nationalism* (New York: Oxford University Press, 2014); Matthew McCullough, *The Cross of War: Christian Nationalism and U.S. Expansion in the Spanish-American War* (Madison: University of Wisconsin Press, 2014); John Fea, *Believe Me: The Evangelical Road to Donald Trump* (Grand Rapids, MI: Wm. B. Eerdmans, 2018). See also Andrew L. Whitehead and Samuel L. Perry, *Taking America Back for God: Christian Nationalism in the United States* (New York: Oxford University Press, 2020).

12. John Foster Dulles, "The Problem of Peace in a Dynamic World," in Marquess of Lothian et al., *The Universal Church and the World of Nations* (London: Wilett, Clark, 1938), 152–53.

13. On ecumenical Protestant mobilization in support of the Cold War, see Jonathan P. Herzog, *The Spiritual-Industrial Complex: America's Religious Battle Against Communism in the Early Cold War* (New York: Oxford University Press, 2011); Stephen J. Whitfield, *The Culture of the Cold War*, 2nd ed. (Baltimore, MD: Johns Hopkins University Press, 1996). On ecumenical Protestant resistance to American militarism, see Andrew Preston, "Peripheral

Visions: American Mainline Protestants and the Global Cold War," *Cold War History* 13, no. 1 (2013): 109–30; Michael G. Thompson, *For God and Globe: Christian Internationalism in the United States between the Great War and the Cold War* (Ithaca, NY: Cornell University Press, 2015).

14. See, for example, Carol Anderson, *Bourgeois Radicals: The NAACP and the Struggle for Colonial Liberation, 1941–1960* (New York: Cambridge University Press, 2015); Carol Anderson, *Eyes off the Prize: The United Nations and the African American Struggle for Human Rights, 1944–1955* (New York: Cambridge University Press, 2003). On the personalist influence on the American understanding of human rights, see Rufus Burrow Jr., *God and Human Dignity: The Personalism, Theology, and Ethics of Martin Luther King, Jr.* (Notre Dame, IN: University of Notre Dame Press, 1992); Gene Zubovich, "American Protestants and the Era of Anti-Racist Human Rights," *Journal of the History of Ideas* 79, no. 3 (2018): 427–43; Samuel Moyn, *Christian Human Rights* (Philadelphia: University of Pennsylvania Press, 2015).

15. On the history of religion and human rights, see Marco Duranti, *The Conservative Human Rights Revolution: European Identity, Transnational Politics, and the Origins of the European Convention* (New York: Oxford University Press, 2017); Steven L. B. Jensen, *The Making of International Human Rights: The 1960s, Decolonization, and the Reconstruction of Global Values* (New York: Cambridge University Press, 2017); James Loeffler, *Rooted Cosmopolitans: Jews and Human Rights in the Twentieth Century* (New Haven, CT: Yale University Press, 2018); Moyn, *Christian Human Rights*; Sarah B. Snyder, *From Selma to Moscow: How Human Rights Activists Transformed U.S. Foreign Policy* (New York: Columbia University Press, 2018). On histories of human rights that spend little time on religion, see Elizabeth Borgwardt, *A New Deal for the World: America's Vision for Human Rights* (Cambridge, MA: Belknap Press of Harvard University Press, 2005); Mark Philip Bradley, *The World Reimagined: Americans and Human Rights in the Twentieth Century* (New York: Cambridge University Press, 2016); Stefan-Ludwig Hoffmann, "Human Rights and History," *Past and Present* 232 (2016): 279–310; Barbara J. Keys, *Reclaiming American Virtue: The Human Rights Revolution of the 1970s* (Cambridge, MA: Harvard University Press, 2014); Samuel Moyn, *Not Enough: Human Rights in an Unequal World* (Cambridge, MA: Belknap Press of Harvard University Press, 2018); Sarah B. Snyder, *Human Rights Activism and the End of the Cold War: A Transnational History of the Helsinki Network* (Cambridge: Cambridge University Press, 2011).

16. See, for example, Bradley, *The World Reimagined*.

17. "Resolution on the Report of the President's Committee on Civil Rights," November 18, 1947, Folder 16, Box 57, RG 18, Federal Council of Churches Papers, Presbyterian Historical Society, Philadelphia, PA (hereafter, FCC Papers).

18. Gary Dorrien, *Social Ethics in the Making: Interpreting an American Tradition* (Oxford: Wiley-Blackwell, 2009), 111–12.

19. "Text of Report on 'The Church and Disorder of Society,'" *New York Times*, September 3, 1948, 11.

20. "Statement of Guiding Principles," *Post War*, January 1943, 5, Folder 8, Box 29, FCC Papers.

21. Lillian Calles Barger, "'Pray to God, She Will Hear Us': Women Reimagining Religion and Politics in the 1970s," in *The Religious Left in Modern America: Doorkeepers of a Radical Faith*, ed. Doug Rossinow, Leilah Danielson, and Marian Miller (New York: Palgrave Macmillan, 2008), 211–31; Margaret Bendroth, "Women, Politics, and Religion," in *Religion and*

American Politics, ed. Mark Noll, 2nd ed. (New York: Oxford University Press, 2007); Ann Braude, ed., *Transforming the Faiths of Our Fathers: Women Who Changed American Religion* (New York: Palgrave Macmillan, 2004); Ann Braude, "A Religious Feminist—Who Can Find Her? Historiographical Challenges from the National Organization for Women," *Journal of Religion* 84, no. 4 (2004): 555–72; Virginia Lieson Brereton, "United and Slighted: Women as Subordinated Insiders," in *Between the Times: The Travail of the Protestant Establishment in America 1900–1960*, ed. William R. Hutchison (New York: Cambridge University Press, 1989), 143–67; Bettye Collier-Thomas, *Jesus, Jobs, and Justice: African American Women and Religion* (Philadelphia: Temple University Press, 2014); Susan Hartmann, "Expanding Feminism's Field and Focus: Activism in the National Council of Churches in the 1960s and Beyond," in *Women and Twentieth-Century Protestantism*, ed. Margaret Bendroth and Virginia Brereton (Champaign-Urbana: University of Illinois Press, 2005), 49–69; Melinda M. Johnson, "Building Bridges: Church Women United and Social Reform Work Across the Mid-Twentieth Century" (PhD diss., University of Kentucky, 2015); Natalie Maxson, *Journey for Justice: The Story of Women in the World Council of Churches* (Geneva: WCC Publications, 2013); Nancy Marie Robertson, *Christian Sisterhood, Race Relations, and the YWCA, 1906–46* (Champaign-Urbana: University of Illinois Press, 2007); Judith Weisenfeld, *African American Women and Christian Activism: New York's Black YWCA, 1905–1945* (Cambridge, MA: Harvard University Press, 1997); Martha Lee Wiggins, "United Church Women: 'A Constant Drip of Water Will Wear a Hole in Iron': The Ecumenical Struggle of Church Women to Unite Across Race and Shape the Civil Rights Century" (PhD diss., Union Theological Seminary, 2006).

22. For an influential account of the mid-century liberal political order, see Steve Fraser and Gary Gerstle, *The Rise and Fall of the New Deal Order, 1930–1980* (Princeton, NJ: Princeton University Press, 2001). See also Jefferson Cowie, *The Great Exception: The New Deal and the Limits of American Politics* (Princeton, NJ: Princeton University Press, 2017).

23. Compounding the trouble for liberal politicians in the 1970s was the simultaneous collapse of support from the labor movement. See Jefferson Cowie, *Stayin' Alive: The 1970s and the Last Days of the Working Class* (New York: New Press, 2012).

24. On religious polarization, see Robert D. Putnam and David E. Campbell, *American Grace: How Religion Divides and Unites Us* (New York: Simon & Schuster, 2010); Robert Wuthnow, *The Restructuring of American Religion: Society and Faith Since World War II* (Princeton, NJ: Princeton University Press, 1988).

25. Richard Hofstadter, *The Age of Reform: From Bryan to F.D.R.* (New York: Knopf, 1955).

26. On the absence of religion in post–Civil War US historiography, see Jon Butler, "Jack-in-the-Box Faith: The Religion Problem in Modern American History," *Journal of American History* 90, no. 4 (2004): 1357–78. On the recent growth of scholarship on US religion, see John McGreevy, "American Religion," in *American History Now*, ed. Eric Foner and Lisa McGirr (Philadelphia: Temple University Press, 2011), 242–260. The literature on evangelicalism is too voluminous to list here. One important account that emphasizes the anti-ecumenical politics of the Christian Right and the limits of its political reach from the 1980s to the present day is Neil J. Young, *We Gather Together: The Religious Right and the Problem of Interfaith Politics* (New York: Oxford University Press, 2016).

27. Sydney E. Ahlstrom, *A Religious History of the American People*, 2nd ed. (New Haven, CT: Yale University Press, 2004); Hutchison, *Religious Pluralism in America*; Martin E. Marty, *Modern American Religion*, vol. 3 (Chicago: University of Chicago Press, 1999).

28. Coffman, *The Christian Century.*

29. This book builds on an argument first put forward by sociologist N. J. Demerath, who argues that ecumenical Protestants continued to shape American culture in the late twentieth century despite their diminishing numbers, and it applies his argument to the political arena. N. J. Demerath, "Cultural Victory and Organizational Defeat in the Paradoxical Decline of Liberal Protestantism," *Journal for the Scientific Study of Religion* 34, no. 4 (1995): 458–69. Demerath's observation is further developed in David A. Hollinger, *After Cloven Tongues of Fire: Protestant Liberalism in Modern American History* (Princeton, NJ: Princeton University Press, 2013); Hedstrom, *The Rise of Liberal Religion.*

30. For an important variation on this theme, one that ties it to the rise of Christian nationalism, see Kevin M. Kruse, *One Nation Under God: How Corporate America Invented Christian America* (New York: Basic Books, 2015).

31. William Inboden, *Religion and American Foreign Policy, 1945–1960: The Soul of Containment* (New York: Cambridge University Press, 2008); Thompson, *For God and Globe*; Andrew Preston, *Sword of the Spirit, Shield of Faith: Religion in American War and Diplomacy* (New York: Alfred A. Knopf, 2012); Preston, "Peripheral Visions."

32. In the discussions of ecumenical Protestants and American power, Reinhold Niebuhr frequently emerges as a focal point. This book situates him in the religious community to which he dedicated most of his time and energy, including his writing, speaking, and political maneuvering. In doing so, it shows his contributions to the UN, the World Council of Churches, and the Cold War while also highlighting his blind spots on racism, human rights, and events in East Asia. This book argues that it was not any single person or group, but the debates and disagreements among a diverse group of people and perspectives—coming together under the banner of ecumenism and globalism—that shaped the religious politics of ecumenical Protestants. On books that focus on Reinhold Niebuhr and his allies, see David L. Chappell, *A Stone of Hope: Prophetic Religion and the Death of Jim Crow* (Chapel Hill: University of North Carolina Press, 2004); Mark Thomas Edwards, *The Right of the Protestant Left: God's Totalitarianism* (New York: Palgrave Macmillan, 2012); Mark Hulsether, *Building a Protestant Left: "Christianity and Crisis" Magazine, 1941–1993* (Knoxville: University of Tennessee Press, 1999); Donald B. Meyer, *The Protestant Search for Political Realism, 1919–1941*, 2nd ed. (Middletown, CT: Wesleyan University Press, 1988); Warren, *Theologians of a New World Order.*

33. Campbell Craig and Fredrik Logevall, *America's Cold War: The Politics of Insecurity* (Cambridge, MA: Harvard University Press, 2009), 10.

34. The important exception, albeit much smaller demographically, was the Communist Party. More generally, the interracial Left of the 1930s was critical of segregation long before liberal organizations like the Federal Council of Churches was. See Kevin Boyle, "Labour, the Left and the Long Civil Rights Movement," *Social History* 30 (August 2005): 366–67; Glenda Elizabeth Gilmore, *Defying Dixie: The Radical Roots of Civil Rights, 1919–1950* (New York: W. W. Norton, 2008); Jacquelyn Dowd Hall, "The Long Civil Rights Movement and the Political Uses of the Past," *Journal of American History* 91 (March 2005): 1233–63; Robert Korstad and Nelson Lichtenstein, "Opportunities Found and Lost: Labor, Radicals, and the Early Civil Rights Movement," *Journal of American History* 75 (December 1988): 786–811.

Chapter 1

1. Ira Katznelson, *Fear Itself: The New Deal and the Origins of Our Time* (New York: Liveright, 2014).

2. Franklin D. Roosevelt, Inaugural Address, March 4, 1933, *The American Presidency Project*, https://www.presidency.ucsb.edu/documents/inaugural-address-8.

3. Quoted in David A. Hollinger, *After Cloven Tongues of Fire: Protestant Liberalism in Modern American History* (Princeton, NJ: Princeton University Press, 2013), x.

4. Richard Hofstadter, *The Age of Reform: From Bryan to F. D. R.* (New York: Knopf, 1955). For an overview of the political coalition Roosevelt's New Deal inaugurated, see Steve Fraser and Gary Gerstle, eds., *The Rise and Fall of the New Deal Order, 1930–1980* (Princeton, NJ: Princeton University Press, 1989).

5. Charles DeBenedetti, *Origins of the Modern American Peace Movement, 1915–1929* (Millwood, NY: KTO Press, 1978); Richard W. Fanning, *Peace and Disarmament: Naval Rivalry & Arms Control, 1922–1933* (Lexington: University Press of Kentucky, 1995); Robert David Johnson, *The Peace Progressives and American Foreign Relations* (Cambridge, MA: Harvard University Press, 1995).

6. Bruce Barton, *The Man Nobody Knows: A Discovery of the Real Jesus* (Indianapolis, IN: Bobbs-Merrill, 1925).

7. Donald B. Meyer, *The Protestant Search for Political Realism, 1919–1941* (Berkeley: University of California Press, 1960), 8.

8. William R. Hutchison, *The Modernist Impulse in American Protestantism* (Cambridge, MA: Harvard University Press, 1976).

9. On fundamentalism, see Joel A. Carpenter, *Revive Us Again: The Reawakening of American Fundamentalism* (New York: Oxford University Press, 1997); Sara Diamond, *Spiritual Warfare: The Politics of the Christian Right* (Boston, MA: South End Press, 1989); Darren Dochuk, *Anointed with Oil: How Christianity and Crude Made Modern America* (New York: Basic Books, 2019); Darren Dochuk, *From Bible Belt to Sunbelt: Plain-Folk Religion, Grassroots Politics, and the Rise of Evangelical Conservatism* (New York: W. W. Norton, 2012); Robert Booth Fowler, *A New Engagement: Evangelical Political Thought, 1966–1976* (Grand Rapids, MI: Eerdmans, 1982); William R. Glass, *Strangers in Zion: Fundamentalists in the South, 1900–1950* (Macon, GA: Mercer University Press, 2001); R. Marie Griffith, *God's Daughters: Evangelical Women and the Power of Submission* (Berkeley: University of California Press, 1997); Barry Hankins, *Uneasy in Babylon: Southern Baptist Conservatives and American Culture* (Tuscaloosa: University of Alabama Press, 2002); Susan Friend Harding, *The Book of Jerry Falwell: Fundamentalist Language and Politics* (Princeton, NJ: Princeton University Press, 2000); D. G. Hart, *That Old-Time Religion in Modern America: Evangelical Protestantism in the Twentieth Century* (Chicago: Ivan R. Dee, 2002); Randall J. Stephens and Karl Giberson, *The Anointed: Evangelical Truth in a Secular Age* (Cambridge, MA: Belknap Press of Harvard University Press, 2011); Matthew Avery Sutton, *American Apocalypse: A History of Modern Evangelicalism* (Cambridge, MA: Harvard University Press, 2017); Daniel K. Williams, *God's Own Party: The Making of the Christian Right* (Oxford: Oxford University Press, 2010); Molly Worthen, *Apostles of Reason: The Crisis of Authority in American Evangelicalism* (New York: Oxford University Press, 2014).

10. Edward J. Larson, *Summer for the Gods: The Scopes Trial and America's Continuing Debate Over Science and Religion* (New York: Basic Books, 1997).

11. Harry Emerson Fosdick, "Shall the Fundamentalists Win?," *Christian Work*, June 10, 1922, 716–722.

12. Quoted in Robert Moats Miller, *Harry Emerson Fosdick: Preacher, Pastor, Prophet* (New York: Oxford University Press, 1985), 130.

13. Ibid., 117–43.

14. Heath W. Carter, *Union Made: Working People and the Rise of Social Christianity in Chicago* (New York: Oxford University Press, 2015); Susan Curtis, *A Consuming Faith: The Social Gospel and Modern American Culture* (Columbia: University of Missouri Press, 2001); Martin E. Marty, *Modern American Religion*, vol. 1, *The Irony of It All, 1893–1919* (Chicago: University of Chicago Press, 1986), 286–97; Paul A. Carter, *The Decline and Revival of the Social Gospel* (Ithaca, NY: Cornell University Press, 1956); Gary Dorrien, *Social Ethics in the Making: Interpreting an American Tradition* (Oxford: Wiley-Blackwell, 2009); Henry F. May, *Protestant Churches and Industrial America* (New York: Harper and Brothers, 1949).

15. Robert Moats Miller, *Bishop G. Bromley Oxnam: Paladin of Liberal Protestantism* (Nashville, TN: Abingdon Press, 1990), 74. In addition to urban reform, social gospel advocates were also active in rural areas. See Kathryn S. Olmsted, "The 1930s Origins of California's Farmworker-Church Alliance," *Pacific Historical Review* 88, no. 2 (May 2019): 240–61.

16. Carter, *Decline and Revival*.

17. Oxnam recorded his travels in diaries, some of which were later published. For the full collection, see "Diaries and Journals, 1903–1963," Boxes 1–32, G. Bromley Oxnam Papers, MSS35329, Manuscript Division, Library of Congress, Washington, DC (hereafter, Oxnam Papers).

18. Quoted in Miller, *Bishop G. Bromley Oxnam*, 96.

19. E. Stanley Jones, *Christ of the Mount: A Working Philosophy of Life* (New York: Abingdon Press, 1931), 11.

20. Quoted in Dana L. Robert, *Christian Mission: How Christianity Became a World Religion* (Oxford: Wiley-Blackwell, 2009), 90.

21. E. Stanley Jones, *The Christ of the Indian Road* (New York: Abingdon Press, 1925).

22. Miller, *Bishop G. Bromley Oxnam*, 93–97.

23. David A. Hollinger, *Protestants Abroad: How Missionaries Tried to Change the World but Changed America* (Princeton, NJ: Princeton University Press, 2017); Andrew Preston, "The Religious Turn in Diplomatic History," in *Explaining the History of American Foreign Relations*, ed. Frank Costigliola and Michael J. Hogan (New York: Cambridge University Press, 2016), 284–303.

24. The group included Henry Pitney Van Dusen, Alva W. Taylor, Arthur E. Holt, Kirby Page, Paul Blanshard, Jerome Davis, and Cameron Hall—all of whom would take on influential roles in Protestant institutions in later years.

25. G. Bromley Oxnam, "European Notes, Summer 1921," Box 4, Oxnam Papers.

26. On the post–World War I Red Scare, see Beverly Gage, *The Day Wall Street Exploded: a Story of America in Its First Age of Terror* (New York: Oxford University Press, 2009).

27. Sidney Webb et al., *Labor and the New Social Order: A Report on Reconstruction* (London: Labour Party, 1918).

28. Daniel T. Rodgers, *Atlantic Crossings: Social Politics in a Progressive Age* (Cambridge, MA: Harvard University Press, 1998).

29. "Hits Reds, Points at Mr. Oxnam," *Los Angeles Times*, April 26, 1923, 12. See also "Shall Radical Head Schools? Facts About G. Bromley Oxnam and Associates," *Los Angeles Times*, April 26, 1923, part II, 1.

30. G. Bromley Oxnam, *Russian Impressions* (Los Angeles: n.p., 1927), quote at 7. A copy is stored in the Oxnam Papers.

31. Ibid., 53.

32. Ibid., 54–55.

33. Miller, *Bishop G. Bromley Oxnam*, 77. On McPherson, see Matthew Avery Sutton, *Aimee Semple McPherson and the Resurrection of Christian America* (Cambridge, MA: Harvard University Press, 2009).

34. Oxnam, *Russian Impressions*, 55.

35. Ibid., 61.

36. Little has been written about the exportation abroad of the modernist-fundamentalist controversies. On the importance of travel in the development of fundamentalist thought, see Darren Dochuk, "Fighting for the Fundamentals: Lyman Stewart and the Protestant Politics of Oil," in *Faithful Republic: Religion and Politics in Modern America*, ed. Andrew Preston, Bruce J. Schulman, and Julian E. Zelizer (Philadelphia: University of Pennsylvania Press, 2015), 41–55. See also Dochuk, *Anointed with Oil*; Markku Ruotsila, *The Origins of Christian Anti-Internationalism: Conservative Evangelicals and the League of Nations* (Washington, DC: Georgetown University Press, 2008).

37. Oxnam, *Russian Impressions*, 67–70, 74–75.

38. William Ernest Hocking, *Re-Thinking Missions: A Laymen's Inquiry after One Hundred Years* (New York: Harper, 1937). On Hocking's report, see William R. Hutchison, *Errand to the World: American Protestant Thought and Foreign Missions* (Chicago: University of Chicago Press, 1987), 158–177.

39. Carter, *Decline and Revival*, 147.

40. Michael G. Thompson, *For God and Globe: Christian Internationalism in the United States Between the Great War and the Cold War* (Ithaca, NY: Cornell University Press, 2015), 50.

41. Curtis, *A Consuming Faith*, 167.

42. Quoted in Carter, *Decline and Revival*, 146.

43. Quoted in ibid., 151–52.

44. Graham Taylor, "The Church Keeps Up with Social Trends," *The Survey*, February 1933, 65.

45. *Federal Council Bulletin* 16 (1933): 9.

46. "Text of Gov. Roosevelt's Address at Detroit on Social Problems," *New York Times*, October 3, 1932, 2.

47. K. Healan Gaston, *Imagining Judeo-Christian America: Religion, Secularism, and the Redefinition of Democracy* (Chicago: University of Chicago Press, 2019); Kevin Michael Schultz, *Tri-Faith America: How Catholics and Jews Held Postwar America to Its Protestant Promise* (Oxford: Oxford University Press, 2011). For a pre-history of the Judeo-Christian idea, see David Mislin, *Saving Faith: Making Religious Pluralism an American Value at the Dawn of the Secular Age* (Ithaca, NY: Cornell University Press, 2015).

48. Quoted in Burton Wheeler, "Memo on conference at the White House with the President," August 4, 1939, http://www.lib.montana.edu/digital/objects/coll2207/2207-B11-F03 .pdf; Richard Breitman and Allan J. Lichtman, *FDR and the Jews* (Cambridge, MA: Belknap Press of Harvard University Press, 2013), 64–66; Gaston, *Imagining Judeo-Christian America*, 60–62.

49. David J. O'Brien, *American Catholics and Social Reform: The New Deal Years* (New York: Oxford University Press, 1968); Kenneth J. Heineman, *A Catholic New Deal: Religion and Reform in Depression Pittsburgh* (University Park: Pennsylvania State University Press, 1999).

50. Quoted in Michael Janson, "A Christian Century: Liberal Protestantism, The New Deal, and the Origins of Post-War American Politics" (PhD diss., University of Pennsylvania, 2007), 126–27.

51. Quoted in ibid., 134.

52. "Charles Clayton Morrison, Religious Leader, Dies," *New York Times*, March 4, 1966, 33.

53. James MacGregor Burns, *Roosevelt: The Lion and the Fox* (New York: Harcourt Brace Jovanovich, 1956); James MacGregor Burns, *Roosevelt: The Soldier of Freedom* (New York: Harcourt Brace Jovanovich, 1970); Kenneth S. Davis, *FDR*, 4 vols., (New York: Putnam, 1972–1993); Frank Freidel, *Franklin D. Roosevelt* (Boston: Little, Brown, 1952); Geoffrey C. Ward, *Before the Trumpet: Young Franklin Roosevelt, 1882–1905* (New York: Harper & Row, 1985); Geoffrey C. Ward, *A First-Class Temperament: The Emergence of Franklin Roosevelt* (New York: Harper & Row, 1989).

54. "Al Smith Vetoes Roosevelt," editorial, *Christian Century*, February 17, 1932, 213.

55. Carl Knudsen, "And What Shall This Man Do?," *Christian Century*, February 10, 1932, 188–90.

56. The full text of the speech was printed as "Text of Gov. Roosevelt's Address at Detroit on Social Problems," *New York Times*, October 3, 1932, 2.

57. Richard Wrightman Fox, *Reinhold Niebuhr: A Biography* (San Francisco: Harper & Row, 1987), 135–36.

58. Reinhold Niebuhr, *Moral Man and Immoral Society: A Study in Ethics and Politics* (1932; Louisville, KY: Westminster John Knox Press, 2001), 8–9.

59. Quoted in Fox, *Reinhold Niebuhr*, 123.

60. Ibid., 123–24, 129–30.

61. Niebuhr, *Moral Man*, 222.

62. Ibid., 91, 93.

63. Quoted in Elesha J. Coffman, *The Christian Century and the Rise of the Protestant Mainline* (New York: Oxford University Press, 2013), 117–18.

64. Ibid., 119.

65. Mark Thomas Edwards, *The Right of the Protestant Left: God's Totalitarianism* (New York, Palgrave Macmillan, 2012); Fox, *Reinhold Niebuhr*; Heather A. Warren, *Theologians of a New World Order: Reinhold Niebuhr and the Christian Realists, 1920–1948* (New York: Oxford University Press, 1997).

66. "Mr. Roosevelt's Dream for the Tennessee Valley," editorial, *Christian Century*, February 15, 1933, 211–12.

67. Frank Davis Ashburn, *Peabody of Groton, a Portrait* (Cambridge, MA: Riverside Press, 1967); Louis Auchincloss, *The Different Grotons* (Groton, MA: Trustees of Groton School, 1960); William Amory Gardner, *Groton Myths and Memories* (Groton, MA, 1928); James McLachlan, *American Boarding Schools: A Historical Study* (New York: Charles Scribner, 1970); James McLachlan, *Views from the Circle: Seventy-Five Years of Groton School* (Groton, MA: Trustees of Groton School, 1960).

68. "The Inaugural Address," editorial, *Christian Century*, March 15, 1933, 351–52. Italics in original.

69. Untitled editorial, *Christian Century*, March 15, 1933, 383.

70. Ibid.

71. Elizabeth Fones-Wolf and Ken Fones-Wolf, "Lending a Hand to Labor: James Myers and the Federal Council of Churches, 1926–1947," *Church History* 68, no. 1 (March 1999): 64–65.

72. James Myers to Cameron Hall, "Memorandum," May 26, 1947, Folder 21, Box 63, RG 18, Federal Council of Churches Papers, Presbyterian Historical Society, Philadelphia, PA (hereafter, FCC Papers).

73. James Myers to Berton Eugene Kline, December 24, 1924, Folder 20, Box 51, FCC Papers.

74. Fones-Wolf and Fones-Wolf, "Lending a Hand to Labor," 72, 77.

75. Jerold S. Auerbach, *Labor and Liberty: The La Follette Committee and the New Deal* (Indianapolis, IN: Bobbs-Merrill Company, 1966), 32.

76. "Three Faiths Back Wagner Labor Bill," *New York Times*, March 26, 1935, 12; Janson, "A Christian Century," 144–49.

77. "Two Groups Press for Wagner Bill," *New York Times*, March 22, 1935, 9.

78. On the demographic composition of Congregationalists of the era, see Bendroth, *The Last Puritans: Mainline Protestants and the Power of the Past* (Chapel Hill: University of North Carolina Press, 2015), 137.

79. "Traditionally, women evaluate . . ." [Untitled] [Signed Olive H. Carpenter?], and Unsigned, "Social Creed," in Folder 4 ("Laymen"), Box 25, General Council Records 1861–1961, Congregational Library, Boston, MA (hereafter, GCR).

80. R. Marie Griffith, *Moral Combat: How Sex Divided American Christians and Fractured American Politics* (New York: Basic Books, 2017), 44.

81. Olive H. Carpenter, "Traditionally, women evaluate," Folder 4 ("Laymen"), Box 25, GCR.

82. Ibid.

83. "Credo" ["HLT S" on top-left of page], Folder 4 ("Laymen"), Box 25, GCR.

84. Ibid.

85. Irene Jean Crandall, "Some Social Ideals," Folder 4 ("Laymen"), Box 25, GCR.

86. Ibid.

87. "History of Legislative Department—Council for Social Action," LC-4, Council for Social Action Papers, Congregational Library, Boston, MA (hereafter, CSA Papers).

88. Cyrus Ransom Pangborn, "Free Churches and Social Change: A Critical Study of The Council for Social Action of the Congregational Christian Churches of the United States" (PhD diss., Columbia University, 1951), 50–51.

89. Quoted in Bendroth, *Last Puritans*, 140–41.

90. For example, in an aggregate of surveys from 1945 and 1946, 71.6 percent of Congregationalists agreed that "the most important job of the government is to make certain that there are good opportunities for each person to get ahead on his own." Only 65.3 percent of Northern Presbyterians and 64.9 percent of Episcopalians agreed. See "Christianity and the Economic Order, Study No. 10," *Information Service*, May 15, 1948, 7.

91. Quoted in Bendroth, *Last Puritans*, 144.

92. Letter from Russell J. Clinchy "To the Members of the Council for Social Action," p. 3, 1938, Series 21, State Conferences, SC-3: Local Reports, 1937–38, CSA Papers.

93. Bendroth, *Last Puritans*, 143.

94. E. P. Thompson, *The Making of the English Working Class* (London: Gollancz, 1965). On the conservative politics of the laity, see Coffman, *Christian Century*, 164–71.

95. Pangborn, "Free Churches and Social Change," 53.

96. On the reemergence of the laymen's groups during the Cold War, see Chapter 9 in this volume.

97. Matthew Avery Sutton, "Was FDR the Antichrist? The Birth of Fundamentalist Anti-liberalism in a Global Age," *Journal of American History* 98, no. 4 (May 2012): 1061.

98. John Evans, "Red Influences Seen Pressing into Churches: Report New Dealers Heed Radicals' Pleas," *Chicago Daily Tribune*, August 14, 1936, 11.

99. Sutton, "Was FDR the Antichrist?," 1052.

100. "Capitalism Finds a Friend," editorial, *Christian Century*, August 26, 1936, 1125–26.

101. Rev. John Evans, "Keynoter at Church Rally Dares Radicals to 'Come Out,'" *Chicago Tribune*, August 13, 1936, 6.

102. "Attack Told by Minister," *Los Angeles Times*, August 16, 1936, 5; "Police Accuse Angeleno Pastor of Attack Hoax," *Los Angeles Times*, August 17, 1936, 3.

103. "Capitalism Finds a Friend."

104. Sarah E. Igo, *The Averaged American: Surveys, Citizens, and the Making of a Mass Public* (Cambridge, MA: Harvard University Press, 2007), 104.

105. John Von Rohr, *The Shaping of American Congregationalism, 1620–1957* (Cleveland, OH: Pilgrim Press, 1992), 388; "Faith & Followers," *Time*, June 7, 1948, 76.

106. "Christianity and the Economic Order, Study No. 10," *Information Service*, May 15, 1948, 2.

107. "The President Accepts Nomination," editorial, *Christian Century*, July 8, 1936, 955–56.

108. "Thursday, July 12th, 1934," Diary, Europe 1934, Box 6, Oxnam Papers.

109. "Radio Address on Brotherhood Day, February 23, 1936," in *Public Papers and Addresses of Franklin D. Roosevelt*, 13 vols. (New York: Random House, 1938–50), 5:85.

110. Alan Brinkley, *End of Reform: New Deal Liberalism in Recession and War* (New York: Vintage, 1996).

Chapter 2

1. Andrew Preston, *Sword of the Spirit, Shield of Faith: Religion in American War and Diplomacy* (New York: Alfred A. Knopf, 2012), 321–26.

2. Franklin D. Roosevelt, Annual Message to Congress, January 4, 1939, https://www.presidency.ucsb.edu/documents/annual-message-congress.

3. "American Malvern," *Time*, March 16, 1942, 44, 46–48, quote at 48.

4. Or Rosenboim, *The Emergence of Globalism: Visions of World Order in Britain and the United States, 1939–1950* (Princeton, NJ: Princeton University Press, 2017), 6–10; Samuel Zipp, *The Idealist: Wendell Willkie's Wartime Quest to Build One World* (Cambridge, MA: Belknap Press of Harvard University Press, 2020).

5. Henry P. Van Dusen, *For the Healing of the Nations: Impressions of Christianity Around the World* (New York: Charles Scribner's Sons, 1940), xix.

6. Henry Sloane Coffin, "Let the Church Be the Church," *Religion in Life* 7, no. 1 (Winter 1938): 54.

7. Graeme Smith, *Oxford 1937: The Universal Christian Council for Life and Work Conference* (New York: Peter Lang, 2004), 56.

8. Ernest Fremont Tittle, "The Voice of the Church at Oxford," *Religion in Life* 7, no. 1 (Winter 1938): 21.

9. For an overview of the Anglo-American discussions prior to and during the Oxford conference, see Smith, *Oxford 1937*.

10. "Report on Church and Community," in *The Churches Survey Their Task: The Report of the Conference at Oxford, July, 1937, on Church, Community, and State*, vol. 8, ed. J. H. Oldham (London: G. Allen & Unwin, 1937), 68.

11. William Adams Brown, *What the Oxford Conference of 1937 May Mean for the Life of the Church* (New York: Universal Christian Council for Life and Work, 1937), 13.

12. Udi Greenberg concludes that European Protestants hoped for unity in order to "unleash an uncompromising anti-secular crusade at home," but "American ecumenism had a different intellectual agenda and operated in a different political context than its European counterpart." See Udi Greenberg, "Protestants, Decolonization, and European Integration, 1885–1961," *Journal of Modern History* 89, no. 2 (June 2017): 314–54, quote at 315–16.

13. On European secularization, see David Blackbourn, *Marpingen: Apparitions of the Virgin Mary in Bismarckian Germany* (Oxford: Oxford University Press, 1993); Owen Chadwick, *The Secularization of the European Mind in the Nineteenth Century* (New York: Cambridge University Press, 1975); Ruth Harris, *Lourdes: Body and Spirit in the Secular Age* (London: Penguin Press, 1999); Jennifer Michael Hecht, *The End of the Soul: Scientific Modernity, Atheism, and Anthropology in France* (New York: Columbia University Press, 2003); John McManners, *Church and State in France, 1870–1914* (New York: Harper Torchbooks, 1972); Eugen Weber, *Peasants into Frenchmen: The Modernization of Rural France, 1870–1914* (Stanford, CA: Stanford University Press, 1976).

14. *Draft Report on The Universal Church and the World of Nations* (Geneva: Universal Christian Council for Life and Work, n.d.), 5, 6.

15. Marquess of Lothian et al., *The Universal Church and the World of Nations* (Wilett, Clarck, 1938), 17–18, 21.

16. John Foster Dulles, "The Problem of Peace in a Dynamic World," in ibid., 145–46.

17. John Foster Dulles, "As Seen By a Layman," *Religion in Life* 7, no. 1 (Winter 1938): 40, 43.

18. Dulles, "The Problem of Peace in a Dynamic World," 149, 154–57, 170. For background on Dulles's views, see Bevan Sewell, "Pragmatism, Religion, and John Foster Dulles's Embrace of Christian Internationalism in the 1930s," *Diplomatic History* 41, no. 4 (September 2017): 799–823.

19. Dulles, "The Problem of Peace in a Dynamic World," 157.

20. Dean Keith Thompson, "Henry Pitney Van Dusen: Ecumenical Statesman" (PhD diss., Union Theological Seminary, Richmond, VA, 1974 [University Microfilms International, 1978]).

21. George Dugan, "Dr. Henry Van Dusen, 77, Of Union Seminary, Dies," *New York Times*, February 14, 1975, 40; Marjorie Hyer, "Dr. Henry P. Van Dusen Dies at 77," February 15, 1975, B6; Mark Thomas Edwards, *The Right of the Protestant Left: God's Totalitarianism* (New York: Palgrave Macmillan, 2012), chaps. 1 and 2; Thompson, "Henry Pitney Van Dusen."

22. Heather A. Warren, *Theologians of a New World Order: Reinhold Niebuhr and the Christian Realists, 1920–1948* (New York: Oxford University Press, 1997), chap. 2.

23. For Van Dusen's correspondence during the trip, see Folder 11, Box 19, Series 5, Henry Pitney Van Dusen Papers, Burke Library, Union Theological Seminary, New York, NY (hereafter, HPVD Papers).

24. Willem Adolph Visser 't Hooft, *Memoirs* (London: SCM Press, 1973), 59.

25. William Ernest Hocking, *Re-Thinking Missions: A Laymen's Inquiry After One Hundred Years by the Commission of Appraisal* (New York: Harper & Brothers, 1932). On Hocking, see Chapter 1.

26. See Van Dusen, *For the Healing of the Nations*, part 1; Thompson, "Henry Pitney Van Dusen," 180–94.

27. Quoted in Van Dusen, *For the Healing of the Nations*, 127. See also Thompson, "Henry Pitney Van Dusen," 203.

28. Thompson, "Henry Pitney Van Dusen," 212.

29. Philip M. Coupland, *Britannia, Europa and Christendom: British Christians and European Integration* (New York: Palgrave Macmillan, 2006), 48.

30. Ibid., 49–50.

31. Mark Lincoln Chadwin, *The Hawks of World War II* (Chapel Hill: University of North Carolina Press, 1968), 139.

32. Alfred O. Hero Jr., *American Religious Groups View Foreign Policy: Trends in Rank-and-File Opinion, 1937–1969* (Durham, NC: Duke University Press, 1973), 283.

33. See Edwards, *The Right of the Protestant Left.* The beginning of Miller's activities and the organization of the Century Group coincided with a change of public opinion revealed by Roosevelt's internal pollsters, which began to shift in favor of greater aid to Britain beginning in the summer of 1940. See James T. Sparrow, *Warfare State: World War II Americans and the Age of Big Government* (New York: Oxford University Press, 2011), 43.

34. Francis Pickens Miller, *Man from the Valley: Memoirs of a 20th-Century Virginian* (Chapel Hill: University of North Carolina Press, 1971), 88–103. For a detailed account of the Roosevelt administration in the summer and fall of 1940 and its decision to back the Bases for Destroyers deal, see Ian Kershaw, *Fateful Choices: Ten Decisions That Changed the World, 1940–1941* (New York: Penguin Press, 2007), 184–242.

35. Coupland, *Britannia, Europa and Christendom*, 56.

36. On the negotiations over the Atlantic Charter and the ambiguity of its meaning, see Elizabeth Borgwardt, *A New Deal for the World: America's Vision for Human Rights* (Cambridge, MA: Belknap Press of Harvard University Press, 2005), 1–4, 14–45.

37. Preston, *Sword of the Spirit*, 392.

38. Henry P. Van Dusen, "Dear Friends," October 10, 1941, page 2, Folder 5, Box 19, Series 5, HPVD Papers.

39. Ibid.

40. On Wilson's foreign policy and religion, see Cara Lea Burnidge, *A Peaceful Conquest: Woodrow Wilson, Religion, and the New World Order* (Chicago: University of Chicago Press, 2016).

41. Eddy, quoted in Michael G. Thompson, "Sherwood Eddy, the Missionary Enterprise, and the Rise of Christian Internationalism in 1920s America," *Modern Intellectual History* 12, no. 1 (April 2015): 23. One example of the greater separation between Christianity and US culture took place in 1930s China, where the numbers of ordained ministers being sent to China as missionaries began to decline in that decade and the number of Chinese ministers began to rise.

42. Ernest Hemmingway, *A Farewell to Arms* (New York: Charles Scribner's Sons, 1929); Erich Maria Remarque, *All Quiet on the Western Front*, trans. A. W. Wheen (New York: Little, Brown and Co., 1929); *Report of the Special Committee on Investigation of the Munitions Industry* [the Nye Committee Report], US Congress, Senate, 74th Congress, 2nd session, February 24, 1936, 3–13.

43. Ray H. Abrams, *Preachers Present Arms: A Study of the War-Time Attitudes and Activities of the Churches and the Clergy in the United States, 1914–1918* (Philadelphia: University of Pennsylvania Press, 1933), xvi, 245.

44. For a list of supporters Wyland had enlisted by March 1941, see "Facts and Purposes of the National Committee on Food For the Small Democracies," Folder 11, Box 27, National Committee on Food for the Small Democracies Papers, Hoover Institution Archives, Stanford University (hereafter, NCFSD Papers). Among the most prominent backers of the Hoover plan were Albert Buckner Coe, Ralph E. Diffendorfer, Harry Emerson Fosdick, Georgia Harkness, John Haynes Holmes, Walter Horton, E. Stanley Jones, Rufus M. Jones, Charles Clayton Morrison, John R. Mott, Albert W. Palmer, Daniel A. Poling, Ralph W. Sockman, and Ernest F. Tittle.

45. Robert Moats Miller, *How Shall They Hear Without a Preacher? The Life of Ernest Fremont Tittle* (Chapel Hill: University of North Carolina Press, 1971), 438.

46. Chadwin, *Hawks of World War II*, 135–36; "Churchmen Assail Hoover Food Plan," *New York Times*, December 2, 1940, 16. Oxnam also publicly opposed Hoover's Plan.

47. Quoted in Chadwin, *Hawks of World War II*, 135–38.

48. For a sampling of *Christian Century* editorials, see "Europe's Specter of Starvation," August 21, 1940, 1020–21; "Churchmen Support a Needless Starvation," October 16, 1940, 1267–68; "In Humanity's Name," November 13, 1940, 1406–8; "Food for the Hungry In Europe," November 27, 1940, 1467; "The Incomparable Atrocity," December 11, 1940, 1543–45; "Britain Bars Food to Occupied Nations," December 25, 1940, 1603.

49. In addition to Woolley and Catt, the signatories included Union Theological Seminary president Henry Sloane Coffin, head of the Episcopal Church and future Federal Council president Henry St. George Tucker, and longtime YMCA and missionary leader Robert E. Speer. See "Churchmen Support a Needless Starvation," 1268.

50. Ibid.; "In Humanity's Name," *Christian Century*, November 13, 1940, 1406.

51. Gary J. Dorrien, *Soul in Society: The Making and Renewal of Social Christianity* (Minneapolis, MN: Fortress Press, 1995), 116.

52. Wyland memorandum, Folder 9, Box 115, NCFSD Papers.

53. Mark Hulsether, *Building a Protestant Left: "Christianity and Crisis" Magazine, 1941–1993* (Knoxville: University of Tennessee Press, 1999).

54. Richard Fox, *Reinhold Niebuhr: A Biography* (New York: Harper & Row, 1987), 152–53.

55. John Haynes Holmes to Rev. Henry P. Van Dusen, January 21, 1941, Folder 6, Box 139, NCFSD Papers.

56. Niebuhr quoted in Martin E. Marty, *Modern American Religion*, vol. 3, *Under God, Indivisible, 1941–1960* (Chicago: University of Chicago Press, 1996), 30–31.

57. "Churchmen Assail Hoover Food Plan," 16.

58. "Conflicts of Outlook," *The Advance*, February 1, 1941, 63.

59. "Churches Ask U.S. to Seek Peace Now," *New York Times*, March 1, 1940, 2.

60. Charles Daniel Brodhead, "Confer on U.S. Wartime Policy," *Christian Century*, March 13, 1940, 366.

61. "The Churches and the International Situation," *Federal Council Bulletin*, April 1940, 8.

62. *A Message from the National Study Conference on the Churches and the International Situation: Philadelphia, PA., February 27–29, 1940* (New York: Federal Council of Churches, 1940), 11.

63. Miller, *How Shall They Hear*, 435.

64. *Message from the National Study Conference*, 11–12.

65. Brooke L. Blower, "From Isolationism to Neutrality: A New Framework for Understanding American Political Culture, 1919–1941," *Diplomatic History* 38, no. 2 (April 2014): 345–76.

66. "The Churches and the International Situation," 8.

67. Walter W. Van Kirk, "Developing a Positive Peace Policy," *Federal Council Bulletin*, May 1940, 11–12.

68. Gene Zubovich, "William Ernest Hocking and the Liberal Protestant Origins of Human Rights," in *Christianity and Human Rights Reconsidered*, ed. Sarah Shortall and Daniel Steinmetz-Jenkins (Cambridge: Cambridge University Press, 2020), 139–57.

69. See, for example, Edwards, *The Right of the Protestant Left*; Warren, *Theologians of a New World Order*. On the important role of pacifists, see David A. Hollinger, "The Realist-Pacifist Summit Meeting of March 1942 and the Political Reorientation of Ecumenical Protestantism in the United States," *Church History* 76, no. 3 (September 2010): 654–77. See also Joseph Kip Kosek, *Acts of Conscience: Christian Nonviolence and Modern American Democracy* (New York: Columbia University Press, 2009).

70. Miller, *How Shall They Hear*, 421.

71. The commission was originally called the Commission for the Study of the Bases for a Just and Durable Peace.

72. Quoted in Robert Moats Miller, *Bishop G. Bromley Oxnam: Paladin of Liberal Protestantism* (Nashville, TN: Abingdon Press, 1990), 261. The speeches were printed in *When Hostilities Cease: Addresses and Findings of the Exploratory Conference on the Bases of a Just and Enduring Peace, Chicago Temple, May 27–30, 1941* (Chicago: Commission on World Peace of the Methodist Church, 1941).

73. *When Hostilities Cease*, 5.

74. Miller, *Bishop G. Bromley Oxnam*, 261.

75. Miller, *How Shall They Hear*, 444.

76. "After the Bomber Comes the Builder," *Methodist Woman*, July 1941, 3–4, quote at 3.

77. *When Hostilities Cease*, 111.

78. "After the Bomber Comes the Builder," 4.

79. *When Hostilities Cease*, 107.

80. Ibid., 107–8.

81. "Minutes," page 76, Folder 11, Box 1, RG 18, Federal Council of Churches Papers, Presbyterian Historical Society, Philadelphia, PA (hereafter, FCC Papers). The initial members were John Foster Dulles (chairman), Henry A. Atkinson, Edwin E. Aubrey, Roswell P. Barnes, Albert W. Beaven, John Bennett, James H. Franklin, Georgia Harkness, Harold A. Hatch, William E. Hocking, John Bassett Moore, Justin Wroe Nixon, G. Bromley Oxnam, Albert W. Palmer, Luman J. Shafer, Channing H. Tobias, Walter W. Van Kirk, Henry P. Van Dusen, and Mary E. Woolley. The following organizations were invited to send two representatives each: International Council of Religious Education, Foreign Missions Conference of North America, Home Missions Councils, National Council of Church Women, United Stewardship Council, Church Peace Union, World Alliance for International Friendship through the Churches.

82. Minutes, Committee of Direction of the Commission to Study the Bases of a Just and Durable Peace, New York, March 21, 1941, Folder 6, Box 29, FCC Papers.

83. "The Church's Thirteen Points: Statement of Guiding Principles Adopted by the National Study Conference on the Bases of a Just and Durable Peace," *Christian Century*, March 18, 1942, 349–50.

84. Ibid.

85. Coupland, *Britannia, Europa and Christendom*, 52; "American Malvern," 44, 46–48.

86. "The Churches and a Just and Durable Peace: Reports Adopted at the National Study Conference at Delaware, Ohio, March 3–5, 1942," *Christian Century*, March 25, 1942, 394–95. This leftward shift in economic thinking is all the more surprising because the conference lacked virtually any representatives of labor. Business owners, on the other hand, had a strong showing. Harvey S. Firestone Jr., of the Firestone Tire Company, and John Holmes, of Swift & Company, were among the representatives from major corporations. Yale social ethicist Liston Pope complained that "labor was not represented more adequately at the conference." Pope pointed out that during the discussion only a single person had been a member of a union, and he happened to be a member of a teacher's union at a university. See Liston Pope to James Myers, March 14, 1942, Folder 17, Box 11, Series 1, Group 49, Liston Pope Papers, Special Collections, Yale Divinity School Library (hereafter, Pope Papers). James Myers, who was in charge of organizing the economics section of the Delaware conference, agreed that the lack of labor representation was "a sad reflection on Protestantism and [reflective of] the actual fact of <u>relative</u> [*sic*] fewer labor people in our churches." See James Myers to Liston Pope, June 2, 1942, Folder 17, Box 11, Series 1, Pope Papers. Underline in original. On ecumenical Protestantism's relationship with labor, see Chapters 8 and 9 in this volume.

87. On Muste, see Leilah Danielson, *American Gandhi: A. J. Muste and the History of Radicalism in the Twentieth Century* (Philadelphia: University of Pennsylvania Press, 2014).

88. A. J. Muste, "Social Bases for a Just and Durable Peace," January 30, 1942, Folder 9, Box 28, FCC Papers; David A. Hollinger, *After Cloven Tongues of Fire: Protestant Liberalism in Modern American History* (Princeton, NJ: Princeton University Press, 2013), 65–66.

89. Nurser, *For All Peoples and All Nations: The Ecumenical Church and Human Rights* (Washington, DC: Georgetown University Press, 2005), 187.

90. Gene Zubovich, "American Protestants and the Era of Anti-racist Human Rights," *Journal of the History of Ideas* 79, no. 3 (2018): 427–43.

91. "Set Fair Play As Goal of a Future Peace," *Chicago Defender*, March 21, 1942, 4.

92. HPVD [Henry P. Van Dusen], "The Churches Speak," *Christianity and Crisis*, April 6, 1942, 1–2; "The Churches and the Peace," *Christian Century*, March 18, 1942, 342–43.

93. "The Churches and the Peace," 342.

94. "The Church Is Not at War!," *Christian Century*, March 25, 1942, 375–77; HPVD [Henry P. Van Dusen], "Is The Church at War?," *Christianity and Crisis*, April 6, 1942, 2–3. See also Herman Will Jr., "The Churches and the Post-War World: A Report of the National Study Conference at Delaware, Ohio," *motive*, April 1942, 47–49.

95. Hollinger, *After Cloven Tongues of Fire*; Matthew Hedstrom, *The Rise of Liberal Religion: Book Culture and American Spirituality in the Twentieth Century* (New York: Oxford University Press, 2012).

Chapter 3

1. On the World Order movement's impact on US foreign relations, see Robert A. Divine, *Second Chance: The Triumph of Internationalism in America During World War II* (New York: Atheneum, 1967), esp. 160–62; Andrew Preston, *Sword of the Spirit, Shield of Faith: Religion in American War and Diplomacy* (New York: Alfred A. Knopf, 2012), 384–410.

2. On divisions among ecumenical Protestants about international affairs after 1945, see William Inboden, *Religion and American Foreign Policy, 1945–1960: The Soul of Containment* (New York: Cambridge University Press, 2008), 29–62.

3. On the links between international planning and domestic reforms, see David A. Hollinger, *After Cloven Tongues of Fire: Protestant Liberalism in Modern American History* (Princeton, NJ: Princeton University Press, 2013), 56–81; Andrew Preston, "Peripheral Visions: American Mainline Protestants and the Global Cold War," *Cold War History* 13, no. 1 (2013): 109–30; Michael G. Thompson, *For God and Globe: Christian Internationalism in the United States Between the Great War and the Cold War* (Ithaca, NY: Cornell University Press, 2015).

4. By locating the emergence of one strand of the American human rights discourse in the ecumenical Protestant milieu, including the emphasis on economic concerns, race, and religion, this chapters builds on the new scholarship on the history of human rights. The influence of US domestic concerns on international human rights, albeit without reference to religious organizations, has been most fully explored by Elizabeth Borgwardt, *A New Deal for the World: America's Vision for Human Rights* (Cambridge, MA: Belknap Press of Harvard University Press, 2005). Carol Anderson has spotlighted the role of race in the human rights debates of the 1940s, especially among African Americans. See Carol Anderson, *Eyes off the Prize: The United Nations and the African American Struggle for Human Rights, 1944–1955* (New York: Cambridge University Press, 2003). On the use of human rights by racialized minorities in the 1940s United States, including Asian Americans and Native Americans, see Mark Bradley, *The World Reimagined: Americans and Human Rights in the Twentieth Century* (Chicago: University of Chicago Press, 2016), 92–121. The importance of religion and race for human rights in the 1960s has been chronicled by Steven L. B. Jensen, *The Making of International Human Rights: The 1960s, Decolonization, and the Reconstruction of Global Values* (New York: Cambridge University Press, 2017). This chapter also builds on Samuel Moyn's work, which has demonstrated the importance of religious groups in articulating human rights in the 1940s. But this book shows that ecumenical Protestant evocations of human rights are best understood in a liberal, not conservative, context. See Samuel Moyn, *Christian Human Rights* (Philadelphia: University of Pennsylvania Press, 2015). The role of ecumenical Protestant organizations in the modern human rights movement is often mentioned but has not yet been fully explored. On the role of ecumenical Protestants in the human rights movements of the 1960s and 1970s, see William Patrick Kelly, *Sovereign Emergencies: Latin America and the Making of Global Human Rights* (New York: Cambridge University Press, 2018), 67–77; Sarah B. Snyder, *From Selma to Moscow: How Human Rights Activists Transformed U.S. Foreign Policy* (New York: Columbia University Press, 2018).

5. Philip M. Coupland, *Britannia, Europa and Christendom: British Christians and European Integration* (New York: Palgrave Macmillan, 2006), 55–56.

6. Present on the American side were the members of the Dulles Commission, along with the president of Hunter College, the head of Princeton's Institute for Advanced Studies, and an executive on the Council on Foreign Relations.

7. Coupland, *Britannia, Europa and Christendom*, 60–61.

8. "Notes of Meeting on 'Peace Aims'" [marked "Highly Confidential"], Balliol College, Oxford, July 15–16, 1942, Group No. 3, Series IA, Box No. 163, Folder 22, Kenneth Scott Latourette Papers, Yale Divinity Library, New Haven, CT (hereafter, KSL Papers).

9. On Toynbee's ideas about international relations, see Andrea Bosco and Cornelia Navari, eds., *Chatham House and British Foreign Policy, 1919–1945: The Royal Institute of International Affairs During the Inter-War Period* (London: Lothian Foundation Press, 1994); Christopher Brewin, "Arnold Toynbee, Chatham House, and Research in a Global Context," in *Thinkers of the Twenty Years' Crisis: Inter-War Idealism Reassessed*, ed. David Long and Peter Wilson (Oxford: Clarendon, 1995), 277–301; Maurice Cowling, *Religion and the Public Doctrine in Modern England* (Cambridge: Cambridge University Press, 1980), 1:19–45; Ian Hall, "'Times of Troubles': Arnold J. Toynbee's Twentieth Century," *International Affairs* 90, no. 1 (2014): 23–36; Ian Hall, "'The Toynbee Convector': The Rise and Fall of Arnold J. Toynbee's Anti-Imperial Mission to the West," *The European Legacy* 17, no. 4 (2012): 455–69; Kenneth Thompson, *Toynbee's Philosophy of World History and Politics* (Baton Rouge: Louisiana State University Press, 1985).

10. Coupland, *Britannia, Europa and Christendom*, 63.

11. John Nurser, *For All Peoples and All Nations: The Ecumenical Church and Human Rights* (Washington, DC: Georgetown University Press, 2005), 57–58.

12. Coupland, *Britannia, Europa and Christendom*, 60–61.

13. "Notes of Meeting on 'Peace Aims.'"

14. Ibid.

15. Ibid.

16. "Churchmen Detail 'Pillars of Peace,'" *New York Times*, March 19, 1943, 1.

17. Ibid.

18. Arthur Hays Sulzberger, "Six Pillars of Peace," Folder 14, Box 29, RG 18, Federal Council of Churches Papers, Presbyterian Historical Society, Philadelphia, PA (hereafter, FCC Papers).

19. "Churchmen Detail 'Pillars of Peace.'"

20. Charles F. Boss to Walter W. Van Kirk, June 24, 1943, Folder 14, Box 29, FCC Papers.

21. Bishop Wilbur E. Hammaker to Rev. Charles F. Boss, June 21, 1943, Folder 14, Box 29, FCC Papers.

22. Preston, *Sword of the Spirit*, 394–96.

23. Ibid.

24. Coupland, *Britannia, Europa and Christendom*, 66.

25. Ibid.

26. The Federal Council of Churches cooperated with the Foreign Missions Conference, the Home Missions Council, the International Council of Religious Education, the Missionary Education Movement, and the United Council of Church Women.

27. Preston, *Sword of the Spirit*, 399; Walter W. Van Kirk, "Christian Mission Prepares Ground for Church Action," *Post War World*, December 15, 1943, 1; "Drive for World Order of Nations Opened by Christian Church Group," *New York Times*, October 29, 1943, 1.

28. Quoted in Van Kirk, "Christian Mission Prepares Ground for Church Action."

29. "Johnstown Churches Plan Peace Program," *Post War World*, December 15, 1943, 1.

30. "North Dakota Reports Results of Forums" and "Johnstown Churches Educate for Peace," *Post War World*, April 15, 1944, 3.

31. Van Kirk, "Christian Mission Prepares Ground for Church Action."

32. Quoted in Preston, *Sword of the Spirit*, 395. On the activities of local councils of churches during the 1940s, see "City Council of Churches Records, 1909–1970," Burke Library, Union Theological Seminary, Columbia University Libraries, New York.

33. "Northern Baptist Crusade Planned," *Post War World*, February 15, 1944, 1; "Northern Baptist Crusade Launched," *Post War World*, April 15, 1944, 1.

34. On the historical memory of the Congregationalists, see Margaret Bendroth, *The Last Puritans: Mainline Protestants and the Power of the Past* (Chapel Hill: University of North Carolina Press, 2015).

35. "World Order Compact Signed on May 21 by Congregationalists," *Post War World*, June 15, 1944, 1. On the lobbying efforts of the Congregationalists' Washington Office, see Mark N. Wilhelm, "The Washington Office of the Congregational Christian Churches and the Search for a Public Theology" (PhD diss., Union Theological Seminary, New York, 2003).

36. "Congregationalists Start Campaign for World Order," *Post War World*, April 15, 1944, 1.

37. "World Order Studied by Lutheran Women," *Post War World*, April 15, 1944, 1; "Lutherans Study Post War Problems," *Post War World*, June 15, 1944, 3.

38. "Presbyterians U.S.A. Plan World Order Movement," *Post War World*, October 16, 1944, 3 (italics in original); "World Order Studied at Montreat Seminar," *Post War World*, October 16, 1944, 1.

39. "The Coming Peace," *Post War World*, October 16, 1944, 4.

40. Quoted in Robert Moats Miller, *Bishop G. Bromley Oxnam: Paladin of Liberal Protestantism* (Nashville, TN: Abingdon Press, 1990), 280.

41. Divine, *Second Chance*, 161.

42. Sarah E. Igo, *The Averaged American: Surveys, Citizens, and the Making of a Mass Public* (Cambridge, MA: Harvard University Press, 2007).

43. On the origins of Christian republicanism, see Mark A. Noll, *America's God: From Jonathan Edwards to Abraham Lincoln* (Oxford: Oxford University Press, 2002).

44. Miller, *G. Bromley Oxnam*, 280–86; "Religion: Methodist Crusade," *Time*, November 22, 1943, 43; Nurser, *For All Peoples*, 70–71.

45. Vera Micheles Dean, "Politics and Human Welfare," *Methodist Woman*, April 1943, 5–7; Thelma Stevens, "Church Activities: Demobilization Challenges the Church," *Methodist Woman*, October 1944, 20–22 (italics in original).

46. On Protestant women as "subordinated insiders" within the Protestant establishment, see Virginia Lieson Brereton, "United and Slighted: Women as Subordinated Insiders," in *Between the Times: The Travail of the Protestant Establishment in America 1900–1960*, ed. William R. Hutchison (New York: Cambridge University Press, 1989), 143–67. On ecumenical Protestant women's politics more broadly, see Lillian Calles Barger, "'Pray to God, She Will Hear Us': Women Reimagining Religion and Politics in the 1970s," in *The Religious Left in Modern America: Doorkeepers of a Radical Faith*, ed. Doug Rossinow, Leilah Danielson, and Marian Miller (New York: Palgrave MacMillan, 2008), 211–31; Margaret Bendroth, "Women, Politics, and Religion," in *Religion and American Politics*, ed. Mark Noll, 2nd ed. (New York: Oxford University Press, 2007); Ann Braude, ed., *Transforming the Faiths of Our Fathers: Women Who Changed American Religion* (New York: Palgrave Macmillan, 2004); Ann Braude, "A Religious Feminist—Who Can Find Her? Historiographical Challenges from the National Organization for Women," *Journal of Religion* 84, no. 4 (2004): 555–72; Bettye Collier-Thomas, *Jesus, Jobs, and Justice: African American Women and Religion* (Philadelphia, PA: Temple University Press, 2014); Susan Hartmann, "Expanding Feminism's Field and Focus: Activism in the National Council of Churches in the 1960s and Beyond," in

Women and Twentieth-Century Protestantism ed. Margaret Bendroth and Virginia Brereton (Champaign-Urbana: University of Illinois Press, 2005), 49–69; Melinda M. Johnson, "Building Bridges: Church Women United and Social Reform Work Across the Mid-Twentieth Century" (PhD diss., University of Kentucky, 2015); Natalie Maxson, *Journey for Justice: The Story of Women in the World Council of Churches* (Geneva: WCC Publications, 2013); Nancy Marie Robertson, *Christian Sisterhood, Race Relations, and the YWCA, 1906–46* (Champaign-Urbana: University of Illinois Press, 2007); Judith Weisenfeld, *African American Women and Christian Activism: New York's Black YWCA, 1905–1945* (Cambridge, MA: Harvard University Press, 1997); Martha Lee Wiggins and Rosemary Skinner Keller, "United Church Women: 'A Constant Drip of Water Will Wear a Hole in Iron': The Ecumenical Struggle of Church Women to Unite Across Race and Shape the Civil Rights Century" (PhD diss., Union Theological Seminary, 2006).

47. Jacquelyn Hall and Bob Hall, "Interview with Thelma Stevens," February 13, 1972, Interview G-0058, Southern Oral History Program Collection (#4007), University of North Carolina, Chapel Hill; Thelma Stevens, *Legacy for the Future: The History of Christian Social Relations in the Women's Division of Christian Service, 1940–1968* (Cincinnati: United Methodist Church, 1978), 11–23. See also Glenda Elizabeth Gilmore, *Defying Dixie: The Radical Roots of Civil Rights, 1919–1950* (New York: W. W. Norton, 2008), 416.

48. Stevens, *Legacy for the Future*, 32–33.

49. Nancy L. Wright, "A Study Experience at Mount Sequoyah," *Methodist Woman*, October 1942, 18–19; Stevens, *Legacy for the Future*, 28, 32.

50. Thelma Stevens, "Departmental Suggestions: The Larger Community," *Methodist Woman*, July 1943, 16–17. On the limits of racial liberalism, see Mark Brilliant, *The Color of America Has Changed: How Racial Diversity Shaped Civil Rights Reform, 1941–1978* (New York: Oxford University Press, 2010).

51. Mrs. Helen B. Bourne, "Education and Cultivation: The Church and America's Peoples," *Methodist Woman*, August 1943, 23–24.

52. Louis Adamic, *From Many Lands* (New York: Harper & Brothers, 1940); Carey McWilliams, *Brothers Under the Skin* (Boston: Little, Brown & Co., 1943).

53. Bourne, "Education and Cultivation."

54. "November Eleven World Community Day," *Methodist Woman*, October 1943, 3.

55. "D.C. Church Groups Will Join Nation-Wide Peace Program," *Washington Post*, November 7, 1943, 10.

56. "Women Vote 58–1 for Peace Union," *New York Times*, November 28, 1943, 32.

57. Thelma Stevens, "World Community Day—What Can We Do?," *Methodist Woman*, November 1943, 18–19.

58. Thelma Stevens, "Christian Social Relations in the Crusade," *Methodist Woman*, November 1944, 12–13.

59. Thelma Stevens, "Demobilization Challenges the Church," *Methodist Woman*, October 1944, 20–22; Helen B. Bourne, "Christians and a New World Economy," *Methodist Woman*, 24. On the triumph of rights-based liberalism, see Alan Brinkley, *The End of Reform: New Deal Liberalism in Recession and War* (New York: Alfred A. Knopf, 1995), 10.

60. Thelma Stevens, "Department of Christian Social Relations and Local Church Activities," *Methodist Woman*, November 1944, 23–24, 28 (italics in original); Franklin Roosevelt's Annual Address to Congress—the "Four Freedoms," Franklin D. Roosevelt Presidential Library and Museum, http://docs.fdrlibrary.marist.edu/od4frees.html.

61. Stevens, "Department of Christian Social Relations."

62. Stevens, *Legacy for the Future*, 41.

63. Stevens, "Department of Christian Social Relations."

64. Bendroth, "Women, Politics, and Religion"; Brereton, "United and Slighted."

65. Stevens, *Legacy for the Future*, 32.

66. Thomas Keehn and Kenneth Underwood, "Protestants in Political Action," *Social Action*, June 15, 1950, 5–39; "Council for Social Action, Congregational Christian Churches, Action on National Legislation," Folder LC-4, Box 4, Series 8, Congregational Christian Churches Council for Social Action Records, Congregational Library and Archives, Boston, MA (hereafter, CSA Papers); Benson Y. Landis, "Report from Washington Office Committee," Folder 17, Box 1, FCC Papers; Mark N. Wilhelm, "The Washington Office of the Congregational Christian Churches and the Search for a Public Theology" (PhD diss., Union Theological Seminary, 2003). On the precursors to the 1940s lobbying groups, see Luke Eugene Ebersole, *Church Lobbying in the Nation's Capital* (New York: Mcmillan, 1951). On early Catholic efforts at lobbying, see Douglas J. Slawson, *The Foundation and First Decade of the National Catholic Welfare Council* (Washington, DC: Catholic University of America Press, 1992).

67. John Evans, "Need Church in Politics, Pastor Asserts," *Chicago Tribune*, June 22, 1946, 13.

68. Ibid.

69. "Document A, Council for Social Action, Congregational Christian Churches, Action on National Legislation," LC-4, Box 3, Series 8, CSA Papers.

70. Divine, *Second Chance*, 227.

71. Ibid., 230–31.

72. On the early criticism of the United Nations, see Mark Mazower, *No Enchanted Palace: The End of Empire and the Ideological Origins of the United Nations* (Princeton, NJ: Princeton University Press, 2009).

73. Quoted in Divine, *Second Chance*, 216.

74. Edward Stettinius, Memorandum to the President, December 5, 1944, Box 131, Dumbarton Oaks Conference, October 1944–1945, Series 1: Safe File, Franklin D. Roosevelt, Papers as President: The President's Secretary's File, 1933–1945, Franklin D. Roosevelt Presidential Library & Museum, Hyde Park, NY.

75. "Minutes of the first meeting of the Committee on Arrangements for the Second National Study Conference on the Churches and a Just and Durable Peace," May 24, 1944, and May 31, 1944, Folder 1, Box 28, FCC Papers.

76. Walter W. Van Kirk to William Ernest Hocking, October 31, 1944, Item 1931, Folder 1, Carton 8, MS Am 2375, William Ernest Hocking Correspondence, Houghton Library, Harvard University, Cambridge, MA (hereafter, WEH Correspondence).

77. "MINUTES of the First Meeting of the Pre-Cleveland Commission I," October 9, 1944, Folder 21, Box 27, FCC Papers.

78. "MINUTES of the Second Meeting of the Pre-Cleveland Commission I," November 6, 1944, Folder 21, Box 27, FCC Papers.

79. Reinhold Niebuhr, "An Analysis and Criticism of the Dumbarton Oaks Agreement," Folder 22, Box 27, FCC Papers.

80. Ibid.

81. William Ernest Hocking to Walter W. Van Kirk, November 1, 1944, p. 2, Carton 8, WEH Correspondence.

82. O. Frederick Nolde, "Religious Liberty," Folder 22, Box 27, FCC Papers.

83. Nurser, *For All Peoples*, 41–42.

84. Gene Zubovich, "William Ernest Hocking and the Liberal Protestant Origins of Human Rights," in *Christianity and Human Rights Reconsidered*, ed. Sarah Shortall and Daniel Steinmetz-Jenkins (Cambridge: Cambridge University Press, 2020), 139–57.

85. William Ernest Hocking to Charles Malik, August 3, 1947, Folder 12, Box 20, Charles Habib Malik Papers, Library of Congress, Washington, DC. The most extensive account of the relationship between Hocking and Malik can be found in Linde Lindkvist, *Religious Freedom and the Universal Declaration of Human Rights* (Cambridge: Cambridge University Press, 2017), 52–55, 87–88.

86. Robert Moats Miller, *Harry Emerson Fosdick: Preacher, Pastor, Prophet* (New York: Oxford University Press, 1985), 52.

87. Gene Zubovich, "American Protestants and the Era of Anti-Racist Human Rights," *Journal of the History of Ideas* 79, no. 3 (September 20, 2018): 427–43.

88. *The Christian Mission in the Light of Race Conflict: Report of the Jerusalem Meeting of the International Missionary Council, March 24th—April 8th, 1928* (London: University of Oxford Press, 1928), 217–18, 237.

89. *1942 Christmas Message of Pope Pius XII* (Washington, DC: National Catholic Welfare Conference, 1943), 15.

90. "Sheen Says Man Is Being Crucified," *New York Times*, March 7, 1938, 11.

91. For a Protestant critique of Catholic conceptions of human rights, see W. E. Garrison, "Democratic Rights in the Roman Catholic Tradition," *Church History* 15, no. 3 (September 1946): 195–219.

92. On American Catholic ambivalence toward human rights in the World War II era, see John T. McGreevy, *Catholicism and American Freedom: A History* (New York: W.W. Norton, 2003), 200–203. For the Vatican's views, see Giuliana Chamedes, *A Twentieth-Century Crusade: The Vatican's Battle to Remake Christian Europe* (Cambridge, MA: Harvard University Press, 2019), 170–72, 237–45. See also Moyn, *Christian Human Rights*, 25–100. On Jewish understandings of human rights in an international perspective, see James Loeffler, *Rooted Cosmopolitans: Jews and Human Rights in the Twentieth Century* (New Haven, CT: Yale University Press, 2018).

93. "Summary of Consensus of Agreement, World Order Conference, Detroit, November 6, 1944," Folder 21, Box 27, FCC Papers.

94. "Summary of Consensus Agreement, World Order Conference, Indiana, PA, November 21, 1944," Folder 21, Box 27, FCC Papers.

95. "Summary of Consensus Agreement, World Order Conference, Philadelphia, November 16, 1944," Folder 21, Box 27, FCC Papers.

96. "Tentative Draft Report of Pre-Cleveland Commission on the Current International Situation," not dated, Folder 22, Box 27, FCC Papers.

97. For the wording of the nine amendments, see Richard M. Fagley, "The Cleveland Recommendations and the United Nations Charter," June 13, 1945, Folder 4, Box 28, FCC Papers.

98. "The Churches and World Order," *Christian Century*, February 7, 1945, 176.

99. "Foreign Relations," *Time*, January 20, 1945, 22.

100. "Tentative Draft Report of Pre-Cleveland Commission."

101. "The National Study Conference of the Churches and a Just and Durable Peace, Preliminary Documents, Memorandum III, What Shall the Churches Now Do?," n.d., 5–6, Folder 4, Box 28, FCC Papers.

102. James Tuttle to Walter Van Kirk, February 15, 1945, and Van Kirk to Tuttle, March 9, 1945, Folder 2, Box 28, FCC Papers.

103. "The Cleveland Conference," *Michigan Christian Advocate*, February 1, 1945, 3.

104. A. J. Muste to William Earnest Hocking, April 16, 1945, Folder 1943, Carton 8, WEH Correspondence.

105. William Ernest Hocking to A. J. Muste, April 18, 1945, Folder 1943, Carton 8, WEH Correspondence. See also draft, in same folder, William Ernest Hocking to A. J. Muste, April 18, 1945 [hand-written note on top-right corner].

106. On Nolde, see Nurser, *For All Peoples*.

107. Nurser, *For All Peoples*, xi.

108. On the Protestant establishment's relationship to the Soviet Union, see Gene Zubovich, "The Protestant Search for 'the Universal Christian Community' Between Decolonization and Communism," *Religions* 8, no. 2 (2017): 17.

109. Nurser, *For All Peoples*, 113.

110. Ibid., 113–17.

111. "Minutes of the Twenty-Sixth Meeting of the United States Delegation, Held at San Francisco, Wednesday, May 2, 1945, 5:30 p.m.," in *Foreign Relations of the United States: Diplomatic Papers, 1945*, vol. 1, *General: The United Nations* (Washington, DC: United States Government Printing Office, 1967), 533.

112. Heather A. Warren, *Theologians of a New World Order: Reinhold Niebuhr and the Christian Realists, 1920–1948* (New York: Oxford University Press, 1997), 106–8; Edward L. Parsons, "Report from San Francisco," *Christianity and Crisis*, June 11, 1945, 1–3.

113. Preston, *Sword of the Spirit*, 409; Warren, *Theologians of a New World Order*, 106–7.

114. "Minutes of the Tenth Meeting of the United States Delegation, Held at Washington, Monday, April 16, 1945, 9 a.m.," in *Foreign Relations of the United States: Diplomatic Papers, 1945*, vol. 1, *General: The United Nations*, 308–9.

115. Ronald Pruessen, *John Foster Dulles: The Road to Power* (New York: Free Press, 1982), 250.

116. Ibid., 251; "Minutes of the Fifty-First Meeting of the United States Delegation, Held at San Francisco, Wednesday, May 23, 1945, 9 a.m.," in *Foreign Relations of the United States: Diplomatic Papers, 1945*, vol. 1, *General: The United Nations*, 855.

117. Carol Anderson, *Eyes Off the Prize: The United Nations and the African American Struggle for Human Rights, 1944–1955* (New York: Cambridge University Press, 2003).

118. "The Federal Council and Internationalism," *United Evangelical Action*, February 1943, 1–3.

119. Ibid.

120. "The San Francisco Charter," *United Evangelical Action*, August 1, 1945, 13. The article emphasized the primacy of religious conversion over political action by quoting Galatians 2:21: "If righteousness is come by the law Christ is dead in vain."

121. Carl F. H. Henry, *The Uneasy Conscience of Modern Fundamentalism* (Grand Rapids, MI: William B. Eerdmans, 1947), 20.

122. K. Healan Gaston, *Imagining Judeo-Christian America: Religion, Secularism, and the Redefinition of Democracy* (Chicago: University of Chicago Press, 2019); Kevin Michael Schultz, *Tri-Faith America: How Catholics and Jews Held Postwar America to Its Protestant Promise* (Oxford: Oxford University Press, 2011).

123. Samuel McCrea Cavert to G. Bromley Oxnam, May 21, 1946, Folder 8, Box 16, FCC Papers.

124. Roswell P. Barnes to John G. Winant, May 22, 1946, Folder 22, Box 67, FCC Papers. Nolde's work at the Paris conference is summarized in "The Churches and the United Nations: Chronology of Proceedings," Folder 22, Box 67, FCC Papers.

125. Letters between Merrill and Nolde, quoted in Nurser, 160–61.

126. "The Universal Declaration of Human Rights," United Nations, https://www.un.org /en/about-us/universal-declaration-of-human-rights, accessed May 12, 2021.

127. Preston, *Sword of the Spirit*, 390.

Chapter 4

1. "The Church and Race Relations," pamphlet (New York: Federal Council of Churches, 1946), 5.

2. On ecumenical Protestant mobilization against anti-Japanese racism, see Anne M. Blankenship, *Christianity, Social Justice, and the Japanese American Incarceration During World War II* (Chapel Hill: University of North Carolina Press, 2016); Sarah Marie Griffith, *The Fight for Asian American Civil Rights: Liberal Protestant Activism, 1900–1950* (Urbana: University of Illinois Press, 2018); David A. Hollinger, *Protestants Abroad: How Missionaries Tried to Change the World but Changed America* (Princeton, NJ: Princeton University Press, 2017), 139–62; Robert Shaffer, "Cracks in the Consensus: Defending the Rights of Japanese Americans During World War II," *Radical History Review* 72 (1998): 84–120.

3. The most thorough account of ecumenical Protestant mobilization against anti-Black racism is James F. Findlay Jr., *The Church People in the Struggle: The National Council of Churches and the Black Freedom Movement, 1950–1970* (New York: Oxford University Press, 1997).

4. Griffith, *Fight for Asian American Civil Rights*; Nicholas T. Pruitt, *Open Hearts, Closed Doors: Immigration Reform and the Waning of Mainline Protestantism* (New York: New York University Press, 2021), 49–53.

5. On the role of Protestant missionaries in anti-racist movements in the middle decades of the twentieth century, see Hollinger, *Protestants Abroad*.

6. Shaffer, "Cracks in the Consensus."

7. The former missionaries relied on pre-existing network of well-connected figures with links to Japan, including Chicago Theological Seminary president Albert Palmer, John R. Mott, Luman J. Shafer, and Edmund D. Soper.

8. Robert Shaffer, "Galen Merriam Fisher," in *Densho Encyclopedia*, http://encyclopedia .densho.org/, accessed November 21, 2012.

9. Sarah Griffith, "'Where We Can Battle for the Lord and Japan': The Development of Liberal Protestant Antiracism before World War II," *Journal of American History* 100, no. 2 (September 2013): 429–53.

10. See biographical note to the Harry Lees Kingman Papers, 1921–1975, BANC MSS 76/173 c, Bancroft Library, University of California, Berkeley.

11. Ruth Kingman Interview, *The Earl Warren Oral History Project*, Japanese-American Relocation Reviewed, vol. 2, The Internment, Regional Oral History Office, Bancroft Library, University of California, Berkeley, 1–6.

12. Rebecca Ann Hodges, "Christian Citizenship and the Foreign Work of the YMCA" (PhD diss., University of California, Berkeley, 2017).

13. Galen Fisher to Rev. John M. Yamazaki, October 25, 1941, Documents 1: MS60 A 1, Fisher, Galen Merriam, 1873–1955: Correspondence, October 1941/"Removed from David P. Barrows Papers," C-B 1005 Bancroft Library, Berkeley (hereafter, Fisher Correspondence).

14. Richard Drinnon, *Keeper of Concentration Camps: Dillon S. Myer and American Racism* (Berkeley: University of California Press, 1987); Cherstin Lyon, *Prisons and Patriots: Japanese American Wartime Citizenship, Civil Disobedience, and Historical Memory* (Philadelphia: Temple University Press, 2011); Greg Robinson, *A Tragedy of Democracy: Japanese Confinement in North America* (New York: Columbia University Press, 2009); Greg Robinson, *By Order of the President : FDR and the Internment of Japanese Americans* (Cambridge, MA: Harvard University Press, 2001).

15. Peter Richardson, *American Prophet: The Life and Work of Carey McWilliams* (Ann Arbor: University of Michigan Press, 2005), 106–8.

16. Quoted in Blankenship, *Christianity, Social Justice*, 33.

17. "Minutes," pp. 41–42, Folder 12, Box 1, RG 18, Federal Council of Churches Papers, Presbyterian Historical Society, Philadelphia, PA (hereafter, FCC Papers). This criticism of Roosevelt's policy was inspired by Fisher, who had regularly fed information to the Federal Council during the war and whose reports became the basis of the organization's resolutions on internment. See Roswell Barnes to Galen Fisher, October 15, 1941, Documents 1: MS60 A 1, Fisher Correspondence.

18. "A Statement/Berkeley Fellowship of Churches and the First Congregational Church of Berkeley to Japanese Friends and Fellow Americans," Pacific Coast Committee on American Principles and Fair Play Records, 1940–1951, Folder 5, Carton 2, BANC MSS C-A 171, Bancroft Library, Berkeley (hereafter, Fair Play Records).

19. "Hitlerism Threatens the California Japanese," *Christian Century*, March 11, 1942, 309. The journal also argued that the anti-Mexican Zoot Suit riots and anti-Black racism were extensions of the fascist mobilization against Japanese Americans. See "Portent of Storm," *Christian Century*, June 23, 1943, 735–36.

20. On the central role of *Christianity and Crisis* in the development of a Protestant Left, see Mark Hulsether, *Building a Protestant Left: "Christianity and Crisis" Magazine, 1941–1993* (Knoxville: University of Tennessee Press, 1999).

21. "The Evacuation of Japanese Citizens," *Christianity and Crisis*, May 18, 1942, 2–5.

22. On the sharply different attitudes toward Myers, see Homer L. Morris to Caleb Foote, May 10, 1945, Folder 31; Caleb Foote to Nevin Sayre, April 14, 1945, Folder 5, Carton 2, Fair Play Records.

23. Joseph Kip Kosek, *Acts of Conscience: Christian Nonviolence and Modern American Democracy* (New York: Columbia University Press, 2009), 176–77.

24. A sum of $375 per month was granted for this work. See Dwight J. Bradley, "Report upon the Work of the Council for Social Action in Behalf of American Japanese. Season 1942–1943," RR-7, Council for Social Action Papers, Congregational Library, Boston, MA (hereafter, CSA Papers).

25. "Draft Proposal for Placing Japanese Families in Interior States," April 3, 1942, signed by Robert Inglis, John C. Bennett, Donald Gaylord, Galen M. Fisher, Folder 5, Carton 2, Fair Play Records.

26. Togo Tanaka to Ruth W. Kingman, November 2, 1944, Folder 31, Carton 2, Fair Play Records.

27. Blankenship, *Christianity, Social Justice*, 71.

28. "Statement of Dr. Roswell P. Barnes at Hearing on H.R. 2768," May 28, 1947, Folder 3, Box 12, FCC Papers.

29. Pruitt, *Open Hearts, Closed Doors*, 108–17, 153–61, 168–80, quotes at 157 and 165.

30. "Draft Proposal for Placing Japanese Families in Interior States," April 3, 1942, Folder 5, Carton 2; Northern California Council of Churches to the members of the Inter-Racial Commission, February 5, 1945, Folder 5, Carton 2; Togo Tanaka to Ruth W. Kingman, November 2, 1944, Folder 31, Carton 2; "Minutes and Findings of the Meeting of the Protestant Church Commission for Japanese Service," January 11–12, 1945, Folder 6, Carton 3; "Joint Conference On Future of Japanese Church Work, Resettlement, and Return," April 24–26, 1945, Folder 6, Carton 3, Fair Play Records.

31. "A Nisei Layman's Views on Church Integration," Folder 6, Carton 3, Fair Play Records.

32. Ray Gibbons to Rev. Z. Okayama, May 25, 1944, RR-7, CSA Papers.

33. Kosek, Acts of Conscience, 183.

34. Executive Committee Minutes, 1940, p. 11, Folder 11, Box 1, FCC Papers.

35. Buell Gallagher to Eugene Link, undated [June 1942], Eugene P. Link Papers, 1907–1993 (APAP-025), M. E. Grenander Department of Special Collections and Archives, University at Albany, SUNY, Albany, NY.

36. "A Statement to the President," Executive Committee of the Fraternal Council of Negro Churches, February 17, 1942, Folder 12, Box 1, FCC Papers.

37. Executive Committee minutes, 1942, p. 50, Folder 12, Box 1, FCC Papers.

38. Ibid.

39. Walter W. Van Kirk, A Christian Global Strategy (Chicago: Willett, Clark & Co., 1945), 75–80.

40. Rachel K. McDowell, "Churches to Mark Conference Gains," New York Times, June 23, 1945, 11.

41. Minutes of Administrative Committee, Department of Race Relations, November 21, 1941, Folder 1, Box 56, FCC Papers.

42. Ibid.

43. Minutes of Administrative Committee, Department of Race Relations, February 4, 1942, Folder 1, Box 56, FCC Papers.

44. Ibid.

45. Memorandum on Post-War Interracial and Intercultural Relations, February 3, 1942, Folder 1, Box 56, FCC Papers.

46. Executive Committee Minutes, 1942, pp. 26–28, Folder 12, Box 1, FCC Papers.

47. Quoted in Barbara Dianne Savage, Your Spirits Walk Beside Us: The Politics of Black Religion (Cambridge, MA: Belknap Press of Harvard University Press, 2008), 55.

48. On Benjamin E. Mays, see Lawrence Edward Carter, ed., Walking Integrity: Benjamin Elijah Mays, Mentor to Martin Luther King Jr. (Macon, GA: Mercer University Press, 1998); Randall Jelks, Benjamin Elijah Mays: Schoolmaster of the Movement, A Biography (Chapel Hill: University of North Carolina, 2012); Benjamin E. Mays, Born to Rebel: An Autobiography (Athens: University of Georgia Press, 2003). On Channing H. Tobias, see Nina Mjagkij, Light in the Darkness: African Americans and the YMCA, 1852–1946 (Lexington: University of Kentucky Press, 2003); O. Joyce Smith, "Channing H. Tobias: An Educational Change Agent in Race Relations, 1940–1960" (PhD diss., Loyola University, 1993); "Channing Tobias of N.A.A.C.P. Dead," New York Times, November 6, 1961, 37. On George E. Haynes, see Daniel Perlman, "Stirring the White Conscience: The Life of George Edmund Haynes" (PhD diss., New York University, 1972); Samuel Kelton Roberts, "Crucible for a Vision: The Work of George Edmund Haynes and the Commission on Race Relations, 1922–1947" (PhD diss., Columbia University, 1974); Ronald C. White Jr., Liberty and Justice for All: Racial Reform

and the Social Gospel, 1877–1925 (Louisville, KY: Westminster John Knox Press, 1990), 249–60.

49. For more on southern activism of this generation, see John Egerton, *Speak Now Against the Day: The Generation Before the Civil Rights Movement in the South* (Chapel Hill: University of North Carolina Press, 1995).

50. The initial group consisted of Will W. Alexander (chairman), Bradford S. Abernethy (director), Louis Adamic, Theodore F. Adams, Eugene M. Austin, Eugene Barnett, Noble Y. Beall, William Y. Bell, Fred L. Brownlee, Ralph J. Bunche, Henry Sloane Coffin, Clark W. Cummings, Dorothy Canfield Fisher, Shelby M. Harrison, George E. Haynes, Paul B. Kern, Benjamin E. Mays, Howard Odum, Liston Pope, Homer P. Rainey, J. McDowell Richards, Benton Rhodes, William Scarlett, David H. Sims, Thelma Stevens, Anson Phelps Stokes, John Thomas, Dorothy Tilly, Channing H. Tobias, Henry St. George Tucker, W. J. Walls, Forrester B. Washington, Luther A. Weigle, and Charles H. Wesley.

51. "Rev. Bradford S. Abernethy Joins Staff of Commission to Study the Bases of a Just and Durable Peace," Federal Council of Churches Press Release, August 19, 1941; Interview with David Abernethy, June 2012. Both in author's possession.

52. "Summary" [undated], Folder 21, Box 56, FCC Papers.

53. Loescher's research for the commission was later published as Frank Loescher, *The Protestant Church and the Negro: A Pattern of Segregation* (1948; repr., Westport, CT: Negro Universities Press, 1971), 15.

54. Daniel Crowe, *Prophets of Rage: The Black Freedom Struggle in San Francisco, 1945–1969* (New York: Garland Publishing, 2000), 16–20, 29, 38–39. On the East Bay during World War II, see Marilynn S. Johnson, *The Second Gold Rush: Oakland and the East Bay in World War II* (Berkeley: University of California Press, 1993).

55. Michael Emerson and Rodney Woo, *People of the Dream: Multiracial Congregations in the United States* (Princeton, NJ: Princeton University Press, 2006), 20. On interracial churches in the 1940s, see Homer A. Jack, "The Emergence of the Interracial Church," *Social Action* (1947): 31–38. On Thurman, see Paul Harvey, *Howard Thurman and the Disinherited: A Religious Biography* (Grand Rapids, MI: Wm. B. Eerdmans Publishing Co., 2020).

56. "All Races Join in Interracial Church on Coast," *Chicago Defender*, November 25, 1944, 8.

57. Buell G. Gallagher, *Color and Conscience: The Irrepressible Conflict* (New York: Harper & Brothers, 1946), 230.

58. Jack, "The Emergence of the Interracial Church."

59. Minutes, Commission on Church and Minority Peoples, April 21, 1944, Folder 20, Box 56, FCC Papers.

60. Ibid.

61. On segregated religious institutions giving rise to Black leadership, see Thomas Sugrue, *Sweet Land of Liberty: The Forgotten Struggle for Civil Rights in the North* (New York: Random House, 2008), chap. 1.

62. Savage, *Your Spirits Walk Beside Us*, 2; Curtis J. Evans, *The Burden of Black Religion* (New York: Oxford University Press, 2008).

63. "Top Churchmen Assail Segregation in Religion," *Chicago Defender*, December 23, 1944, 2; "Open-Door Church Asked," *New York Times*, December 16, 1944, 30.

64. See the pencil marks on the document "Suggested Procedures/Tentative draft of Section III of proposed statement by the Commission. For discussion at Princeton," Folder 1, Box 57, FCC Papers.

65. Liston Pope, "Revised List of Suggested Procedures," Folder 1, Box 57, FCC Papers.

66. Ibid.

67. Minutes, Commission on Church and Minority Peoples, May 8–10, 1945, pg. 3, Folder 20, Box 57, FCC Papers.

68. "Some Guiding Christian Affirmations," prepared by the Commission on the Church and Minority Peoples, p. 153, Folder 15, Box 1, FCC Papers.

69. Ibid.

70. Bishop William Scarlett, "A Statement of Christian Principles," Folder 1, Box 51, FCC Papers.

71. George Haynes to Roswell P. Barnes, "Memorandum," November 19, 1945, Folder 14, Box 57, FCC Papers. Underlining in original. See also "Memorandum to Bishop Oxnam," November 19, 1945, Folder 14, Box 57, FCC Papers.

72. "Council Actions at Columbus," *Federal Council Bulletin*, April 1946, 9–13, quote at 9.

73. Ibid., 10.

74. Mays, *Born to Rebel*, 223–24.

75. "Memorandum on Community Tensions," Folder 14, Box 54, FCC Papers.

76. "U.N.O. City Location Delayed Until January," *Los Angeles Times*, December 18, 1945, 5. See also George Padmore, "Race Bias Knocks Dixie Out of Contest for UNO Site," *Chicago Defender*, January 12, 1946, 4.

77. On the UN building, and the relationship between World War II–era internationalism and the built environment in New York City, see Samuel Zipp, *Manhattan Projects: The Rise and Fall of Urban Renewal in Cold War New York* (New York: Oxford University Press, 2012).

78. "The Church and Race Relations."

79. Oral history interview with Will Winton Alexander, 1952, Columbia Center for Oral History, Rare Books and Manuscript Library, Butler Library, Columbia University, New York, NY, 721–23.

80. Ibid.

81. Ibid.

82. "The Church and Race Relations."

83. "Biggest Church Body in America Rips Jim Crow," *Chicago Defender*, March 16, 1946, 1.

84. "Protestants Close Ranks," *Christian Century*, March 20, 1946, 360–61.

85. For the deleted text, which was crossed out, see "Memorandum on Community Tensions," p. 7, Folder 14, Box 57, FCC Papers. For the second draft with Haynes's handwritten note, see same title and folder with the words "Old—P7 deleted finally" on top-right corner of first page. On the history of interracial marriage, see Peggy Pascoe, *What Comes Naturally: Miscegenation Law and the Making of Race in America* (New York: Oxford University Press, 2010).

86. "The Church and Race Relations," 6–7.

87. For a step-by-step account of the clinical approach to racism, see George E. Haynes, "The Interracial Clinic," *Journal of Negro Education* 14, no. 2 (Spring 1945): 262–67. On human relations, see Leah N. Gordon, *From Power to Prejudice: The Rise of Racial Individualism in Midcentury America* (Chicago: University of Chicago Press, 2015), 66–75.

88. George E. Haynes, "Clinical Methods in Interracial and Intercultural Relations," *Journal of Educational Sociology* 19, no. 5 (January 1946): 316–25, esp. 318–20.

89. Haynes, "The Interracial Clinic," 262.

90. For the significance of the California Federation in postwar California history, see Mark Brilliant, *The Color of America Has Changed: How Racial Diversity Shaped Civil Rights Reform in California, 1941–1978* (New York: Oxford University Press, 2012), chap. 1.

91. The YMCA and YWCA did not publicly affirm the Federal Council's leadership on the issue of segregation when they not only denounced segregation but also desegregated their national bureaucracy. But the timing of the desegregation proclamation and the participation of YMCA and YWCA leaders in the Commission on Church and Minority Peoples, including Tobias and Eugene Barnett, makes clear the influence of the Federal Council's initiative.

92. George E. Haynes, *Africa: Continent of the Future* (New York: The Association Press, 1950).

93. On ecumenical Protestant programs to send students to the Global South, see Ada J. Focer, "Frontier Internship in Mission, 1961–1974: Young Christians Abroad in a Post-Colonial and Cold War World" (PhD diss., Boston University, 2016).

Chapter 5

1. On anti-racist readings of human rights in the United States, see Carol Anderson, *Eyes off the Prize: The United Nations and the African American Struggle for Human Rights* (New York: Cambridge University Press, 2003); Mark Philip Bradley, *The World Reimagined: Americans and Human Rights in the Twentieth Century* (Chicago: University of Chicago Press, 2016), chap. 4. On views of human rights among anti-colonial activists in Africa, see Bonny Ibhawoh, "Testing the Atlantic Charter: Linking Anticolonialism, Self-Determination and Universal Human Rights," *International Journal of Human Rights* 18, nos. 7–8 (2014): 842–60; Meredith Terretta, "'We Had Been Fooled into Thinking That the UN Watches over the Entire World': Human Rights, UN Trust Territories, and Africa's Decolonization," *Human Rights Quarterly* 34, no. 2 (May 2012): 329–60. Much of the literature on human rights in the 1940s highlights priorities other than anti-racism. See Elizabeth Borgwardt, *A New Deal for the World: America's Vision for Human Rights* (Cambridge, MA: Harvard University Press, 2007); Mary Ann Glendon, *A World Made New: Eleanor Roosevelt and the Universal Declaration of Human Rights* (New York: Random House, 2001); Paul Gordon Lauren, *The Evolution of International Human Rights: Visions Seen* (Philadelphia: University of Pennsylvania Press, 2003); Samuel Moyn, *Christian Human Rights* (Philadelphia: University of Pennsylvania Press, 2015); John Nurser, *For All Peoples and All Nations: The Ecumenical Church and Human Rights* (Washington, DC: Georgetown University Press, 2005). On the anthropologists' position, see The Executive Board, American Anthropological Association, "Statement on Human Rights," *American Anthropologist* 49, no. 4 (October–December 1947): 539–43.

2. On the anti-racist understanding of human rights in the 1960s, see Steven L. B. Jensen, *The Making of International Human Rights: The 1960s, Decolonization, and the Reconstruction of Global Values* (New York: Cambridge University Press, 2017). On the influence of the civil rights movement on human rights in the 1960s, see Sarah B. Snyder, *From Selma to Moscow: How Human Rights Activists Transformed U.S. Foreign Policy* (New York: Columbia University Press, 2018).

3. John W. Dower, *War Without Mercy: Race and Power in the Pacific War* (New York: Pantheon Books, 1986).

4. "Prime Minister Churchill's Speech," *New York Times*, November 11, 1942, 4.

5. "Record of Washington Meeting: College of Preachers, Washington Cathedral," Commission on Church and Minority Peoples, December 18–19, 1945, p. 3, Folder 20, Box 56, RG 18, Federal Council of Churches Papers, Presbyterian Historical Society, Philadelphia, PA (hereafter, FCC Papers); Edmund D. Soper, "Seminar on New Race Issues: Finding to be presented at Conference on Christian Bases of World Order, March 10, 1943," Folder 21, Box 8, Edmund D. Soper Papers, the United Library, Garrett-Evangelical/Seabury-Western Seminaries, Evanston, IL (hereafter, Soper Papers); Buell G. Gallagher, *Color and Conscience: The Irrepressible Conflict* (New York: Harper & Brothers, 1946), 63, 65–66.

6. Lothrop Stoddard, *The Rising Tide of Color Against White World-Supremacy* (New York: Scribner, 1920), 9.

7. Elazar Barkan, *The Retreat of Scientific Racism: Changing Concepts of Race in Britain and the United States Between the World Wars* (New York: Cambridge University Press, 1992), 81.

8. Stuart Svonkin, *Jews Against Prejudice : American Jews and the Fight for Civil Liberties* (New York: Columbia University Press, 1997).

9. Peggy Pascoe, *What Comes Naturally: Miscegenation Law and the Making of Race in America* (New York: Oxford University Press, 2010), 207–23.

10. John T. McGreevy, *Parish Boundaries: The Catholic Encounter with Race in the Twentieth-Century Urban North* (Chicago: University of Chicago Press, 1998).

11. Gerald H. Gamm, *Urban Exodus: Why the Jews Left Boston and the Catholics Stayed* (Cambridge, MA: Harvard University Press, 1999).

12. Frank Samuel Loescher, *The Protestant Church and the Negro: A Pattern of Segregation* (New York: Association Press, 1948).

13. Gunner Myrdal, *An American Dilemma: The Negro Problem and Modern Democracy* (New York: Harper and Brothers, 1944).

14. Ibid., 8.

15. David W. Southern, *Gunnar Myrdal and Black-White Relations: The Use and Abuse of An America Dilemma, 1944–1969* (Chapel Hill: University of North Carolina Press, 1987); Walter A. Jackson, *Gunnar Myrdal and America's Conscience: Social Engineering & Racial Liberalism, 1938–1987* (Chapel Hill: University of North Carolina Press, 1990).

16. Edmund Davison Soper, *The Religions of Mankind* (New York: Abingdon Press, 1921); Edmund Davison Soper, *The Philosophy of the Christian World Mission* (New York: Abingdon-Cokesbury Press, 1943).

17. David A. Hollinger describes this phenomenon as "missionary cosmopolitanism." See David A. Hollinger, *Protestants Abroad: How Missionaries Tried to Change the World but Changed America* (Princeton, NJ: Princeton University Press, 2017).

18. Edmund Davison Soper, *Racism: A World Issue* (New York: Abingdon-Cokesbury Press, 1947), 7. Participants in a follow-up conference included Dr. Lowell B. Hazzard, Dr. W.W. Sweet, Dr. Charles S. Braden, Dr. Murray Leiffer, E.D.S. [?], C.S.B. [Charles S. Bennett?], Dr. Paul Hutchinson, Dr. E. Burns Martin, Dr. Phillips Brooks Smith, Rev. M. W. Clair, Jr., Dr. Morgan Williams, Mrs. Olin Clarke Jones, Mr. and Mrs. Soper, Dr. Frank Herron Smith, Dr. L.R. Eckardt, Dr. Charles R. Goff, and Dr. Lynn J. Dadcliffe. There were also several others whose names were not listed. See "General Subjects of Delaware Conference," Folder 21, Box 8, Soper Papers.

19. Edmund D. Soper, "Seminar on New Race Issues," March 10, 1943, Folder 21, Box 8, Soper Papers.

20. Ibid. The call for a "Pacific Charter" was a featured in Wendell L. Wilkie, *One World* (New York: Simon & Schuster, 1943).

21. Soper, "Seminar on New Race Issues."

22. Soper, *Racism*, 7–11.

23. The breadth and systematic character of the book was unique. The study of the role of racism in world affairs was not new. See, for example, W.E.B. Du Bois, *The World and Africa: An Inquiry into the Part Which Africa Has Played in World History* (New York: Viking Press, 1947).

24. Gallagher, *Color and Conscience*, 13.

25. Myrdal drew on Gallagher's earlier writings and cited Gallagher's 1934 book *American Caste and the Negro College* respectfully in his study. Gunner Myrdal, *An American Dilemma: The Negro Problem and Modern Democracy* (1944; repr., New York: Harper & Row, 1962), 1377.

26. See Jackson, *Gunnar Myrdal and America's Conscience*.

27. Gallagher, *Color and Conscience*, 3.

28. Ibid., 98.

29. For a discussion of both the possibilities and limits of Cold War discourses on race, see Mary Dudziak, *Cold War Civil Rights: Race and the Image of American Democracy* (Princeton, NJ: Princeton University Press, 2000).

30. On the close relationship between international affairs and anti-racist activism in the Cold War era, see Azza Salama Layton, *International Politics and Civil Rights Policies in the United States, 1941–1960* (New York: Cambridge University Press, 2000); Thomas Borstelmann, *The Cold War and the Color Line: American Race Relations in the Global Arena* (Cambridge, MA: Harvard University Press, 2001); Dudziak, *Cold War Civil Rights*; Jonathan Rosenberg, *How Far the Promised Land? World Affairs and the American Civil Rights Movement from the First World War to Vietnam* (Princeton, NJ: Princeton University Press, 2006); Nikhil Pal Singh, *Black Is a Country: Race and the Unfinished Struggle for Democracy* (Cambridge, MA: Harvard University Press, 2004); Penny M. Von Eschen, *Race Against Empire: Black Americans and Anticolonialism, 1937–1957* (Ithaca, NY: Cornell University Press, 1997).

31. C. Vann Woodward, *The Strange Career of Jim Crow* (New York: Oxford University Press, 1955).

32. Frank Tannenbaum, *Slave and Citizen* (1946; repr., Boston: Beacon Press, 1992).

33. Ibid., 97.

34. Ibid., 115.

35. Tannenbaum's book has been continuously in print since 1946 and continues to be assigned in graduate history courses. On the enduring legacy of the book, and what it misses about race in Brazil, see Alejandro de la Fuente, "From Slaves to Citizens? Tannenbaum and the Debates on Slavery, Emancipation, and Race Relations in Latin America," *International Labor and Working-Class History* 77 (Spring 2010): 154–73.

36. Soper, *Racism*, 173.

37. Arnold Toynbee, *A Study of History*, vol. 6 (London: Oxford University Press, 1939).

38. Galen Fisher, "Racism and the World Outreach of Church and Nation," April 1945, Folder 1, Box 57, FCC Papers.

39. Toynbee is cited several times in *Racism*, yet Soper "had not felt that this dictum was sufficiently well supported to call attention to it," according to a participant in a discussion of the manuscript. See Wynn C. Fairfield to Rev. George F. Ketcham, November 12, 1945, Folder 1, Box 57, FCC Papers. Buell Gallagher praised the Toynbee thesis but also criticized some of its implications. See Gallagher, *Color and Conscience*, 55.

40. Soper, *Racism*, 175.

41. Ibid., 179.

42. Ibid., 182.

43. Ibid., 72–73.

44. Yuri Slezkine, *The Jewish Century* (Princeton, NJ: Princeton University Press, 2004).

45. Yuri Slezkine, "The USSR as a Communal Apartment, or How a Socialist State Promoted Ethnic Particularism," *Slavic Review* 53, no. 2 (1994): 414–52, quote at 415.

46. Francine Hirsch, *Empire of Nations: Ethnographic Knowledge and the Making of the Soviet Union* (Ithaca, NY: Cornell University Press, 2005), 14.

47. Terry Martin, *Affirmative Action Empire: Nations and Nationalism in the Soviet Union, 1923–1939* (Ithaca, NY: Cornell University Press, 2001).

48. Soper, *Racism*, 80.

49. Gallagher, *Color and Conscience*, 183.

50. Ibid., 184.

51. Soper, *Racism*, 80–81.

52. Ibid., 81.

53. Ibid., 84.

54. Ibid.

55. Gallagher, *Color and Conscience*, 188–89. Eugene Barnett, the YMCA head who authored its pronouncement that desegregated the national hierarchy in 1946, made similar observations, noting that "an influential section of labor, together with the USSR, have gone much further than the Church in dealing with the problem of race." See "Record of Washington Meeting."

56. Buell G. Gallagher to Walter White, July 16, 1944, Frames 785–787, Reel 7; and Walter White to Buell Gallagher, July 20, 1944, Frames 781–782, Reel 7, Papers of the NAACP, Supplement to Part 16, Board of Directors File, 1966–1970, [microform], ed. John H. Bracey Jr. and August Meier, University Publications of America, Bethesda, MD.

57. Fisher, "Racism and the World Outreach of Church and Nation," 15.

58. See, for example, Emily Conroy-Krutz, *Christian Imperialism: Converting the World in the Early American Republic* (Ithaca, NY: Cornell University Press, 2015); Tisa Joy Wenger, *Religious Freedom: The Contested History of an American Ideal* (Chapel Hill: University of North Carolina Press, 2017). On the complicated relationship of Christianity and imperialism in the twentieth century, see Melani McAlister, *The Kingdom of God Has No Borders: A Global History of American Evangelicals* (New York: Oxford University Press, 2018); Brian Stanley, *Christianity in the Twentieth Century: A World History* (Princeton, NJ: Princeton University Press, 2018), chaps. 2 and 9.

59. Headnote in W. E. B. Du Bois, *Color and Democracy: Colonies and Peace* (New York: Harcourt, Brace and Company, 1945), 123.

60. Ibid. See also Borstelmann, *The Cold War and the Color Line*, 41. Du Bois had previously been a sharp critic of American missionaries. In 1900, he railed against Christian missionaries at the first Pan-African Congress in London: "Let not the cloak of Christian

missionary enterprise be allowed in the future as so often in the past, to hide the ruthless economic exploitation and political downfall of less developed nations, whose chief fault has been reliance on the plighted faith of the Christian church." Quoted in Edward J. Blum, *W.E.B. Du Bois: American Prophet* (Philadelphia: University of Pennsylvania Press, 2009), 122.

61. Du Bois, *Color and Democracy*, 131.

62. Carol Anderson, *Bourgeois Radicals: The NAACP and the Struggle for Colonial Liberation, 1941–1960* (New York: Cambridge University Press, 2015), 84–132.

63. Soper, *Racism*, 276.

64. On India-US comparisons, see Sarah Azaransky, *This Worldwide Struggle: Religion and the International Roots of the Civil Rights Movement* (New York: Oxford University Press, 2017); Daniel Immerwahr, "Caste or Colony? Indianizing Race in the United States," *Modern Intellectual History* 4 (2007): 275–301; Nico Slate, *Colored Cosmopolitanism: The Shared Struggle for Freedom in the United States and India* (Cambridge, MA: Harvard University Press, 2017).

65. Gallagher, *Color and Conscience*, 174.

66. *Berkeley Daily Gazette*, May 28, 1948, 11.

67. *Berkeley Daily Gazette*, May 20, 1948; *Berkeley Daily Gazette*, May 27, 1948; Harland E. Hogue, *Christian Seed in Western Soil: Pacific School of Religion Through a Century* (Berkeley, CA: Pacific School of Religion, 1965), 138–39.

68. Buell G. Gallagher, "The Honor of a Certain Aim," *Christian Century*, December 22, 1948, 1393–96.

69. For the discussion of racial inclusion that preceded the Cincinnati meeting, see Memorandum to J. Oscar Lee and Roswell P. Barnes, October 1, 1948, Folder 13, Box 57, FCC Papers.

70. The commission consisted of Channing Tobias, Roland Bainton, Homer P. Rainey, Will W. Alexander, Lillian K. Hatford, Norman J. Padelford, Nelson Cruikshank, Shelby Harrison, Liston Pope, Dorothy Height, John H. Alexander, W.G. Mather (chairman), Wynn Fairfield, L. K. Anderson, Frederick Nolde, and Charles W. Seaver.

71. "The Churches and Human Rights: An Official Statement adopted by the Federal Council of Churches of Christ in America," December 1948, pp. 4–6, Folder 16, Box 57, FCC Papers.

72. Ibid.

73. George Dugan, "End of Racial Segregation Asked by Churches' Council," *New York Times*, December 4, 1948, 1; Martha J. Hall, "Protestant Council Indorses Complete End of Segregation," *Washington Post*, December 4, 1948, 1; "Church Leaders Visit Truman, Approve Civil Rights," *Chicago Defender*, December 25, 1948, 4.

74. John M. Alexander to Rev. Beverly M. Boyd, November 18, 1948, Folder 13, Box 57, FCC Papers.

75. Ibid.

76. "Council Action on Human Rights Gets Chief Public Notice: Goal to Ban Segregation Is Reaffirmed by Leadership," *Presbyterian Outlook*, December 13, 1948, 1.

77. Hall, "Protestant Council Indorses Complete End of Segregation," 1.

78. John M. Alexander, "Comments on the Council's Statement," *Presbyterian Outlook*, December 13, 1948, 7–8.

79. Loescher, *The Protestant Church and the Negro*, 45.

80. Martin Luther King Jr., "Letter from Birmingham Jail," *Christian Century*, June 12, 1963, 770.

81. Jane Dailey, "Sex, Segregation, and the Sacred After Brown," *Journal of American History* 91, no. 1 (June 2004): 119–44. The hierarchical bureaucracy of the Federal Council of Churches suppressed grassroots racist theology in national conversations among ecumenical leaders, who disregarded grassroots discourse until the 1954 *Brown v. Board* decision made it impossible to ignore. In addition, several large southern denominations and fundamentalist denominations were not members of the Federal Council, which further limited the appearance of theological racism among ecumenical Protestant leaders. Denominational histories also confirm that leaders of southern denominations were more liberal on racial matters than their constituencies. The Southern Baptist Convention, which was the largest southern denomination and was unaffiliated with the Federal Council, endorsed the *Brown v. Board* decision, even though it was deeply unpopular with churchgoers. See Alan Scot Willis, *All According to God's Plan: Southern Baptist Missions and Race, 1945–1970* (Lexington: University Press of Kentucky, 2005); Mark Newman, *Getting Right with God: Southern Baptists and Desegregation, 1945–1995* (Tuscaloosa: University of Alabama Press, 2001).

82. Leah N. Gordon, *From Power to Prejudice: The Rise of Racial Individualism in Midcentury America* (Chicago: University of Chicago Press, 2015).

83. For an example of how human rights permeated the ecumenical Protestant milieu, see Dorothy Canfield Fisher, *A Fair World for All: The Meaning of the Declaration of Human Rights* (New York: McGraw-Hill Book Co., 1952), esp. 83–87. This children's book printed for a wide audience by a popular author casually dismisses scientific racism, undermines claims of racial differences, and argues for the unity of mankind.

84. Dudziak, *Cold War Civil Rights*.

Chapter 6

1. Winston Churchill, "Churchill's 'Iron Curtain' Speech, 'Sinews of Peace,'" March 5, 1946, Wilson Center Digital Archive, https://digitalarchive.wilsoncenter.org/document/116180, accessed July 7, 2020.

2. Ibid.

3. "Crowd of 35,000 Greets President and Churchill in Columbus," *Columbus Dispatch*, March 6, 1946, 6A; Robert W. Potter, "Churchmen Called by Truman to Save World from Ruin," *New York Times*, March 7, 1946, 1; "Protestants Close Ranks," *Christian Century*, March 20, 1946, 360–61.

4. On the Cold War as an ideological project, see Anders Stephanson, "Cold War Degree Zero," in *Uncertain Empire: American History and the Idea of the Cold War*, ed. Joel Isaac and Duncan Bell (New York: Oxford University Press, 2012), 19–50. On the role of ideology in the global Cold War, see Odd Arne Westad, *The Global Cold War: Third World Interventions and the Making of Our Times* (New York: Cambridge University Press, 2005).

5. "Atomic Warfare and the Christian Faith," March 6, 1946, Folder 16, Box 2, RG 18, Federal Council of Churches Papers, Presbyterian Historical Society, Philadelphia, PA (hereafter, FCC Papers). On the atomic bomb in American popular imagination, see Paul Boyer, *By the Bomb's Early Light: American Thought and Culture at the Dawn of the Atomic Age* (New York: Pantheon, 1985).

6. "Protestants Close Ranks," 360–61.

7. Ibid.

8. Charter of the United Nations, https://www.un.org/en/charter-united-nations/, accessed July 7, 2020.

9. Mark Mazower, *No Enchanted Palace: The End of Empire and the Ideological Origins of the United Nations* (Princeton, NJ: Princeton University Press, 2009), 8.

10. Ibid., 7. On Protestant criticism of the United Nations, see Chapter 3 of this volume.

11. Senator Bricker quoted in Stewart Patrick, *The Sovereignty Wars: Reconciling America with the World* (Washington, DC: Brookings Institution Press, 2017), 127. Poll results in Alfred O. Hero, *American Religious Groups View Foreign Policy: Trends in Rank-and-File Opinion, 1937–1969* (Durham, NC: Duke University Press, 1973), 512.

12. "Council Actions at Columbus," *Federal Council Bulletin*, April 1946, 9–13, quotes at 9.

13. Ibid.

14. Ibid.

15. William Inboden, *Religion and American Foreign Policy, 1945–1960: The Soul of Containment* (Cambridge: Cambridge University Press, 2010), 34.

16. Churchill, "Sinews of Peace."

17. "Protestants Close Ranks," 360; "The Church and Race Relations: An Official Statement approved by the Federal Council of the Churches of Christ in America at a Special Meeting, Columbus, Ohio, March 5–7, 1946," pamphlet, Folder 14, Box 57, FCC Papers. For more on this statement, see Chapter 4 of this volume.

18. "Council Actions at Columbus," *Federal Council Bulletin*, April 1946, 12.

19. George C. Marshall Jr., "Remarks by the Secretary of State at Harvard University on June 5, 1947," https://www.marshallfoundation.org/library/wp-content/uploads/sites/16/2014/06/Marshall_Plan_Speech_Complete.pdf, accessed October 2, 2018.

20. Walter LaFeber, *The American Age: U.S. Foreign Policy at Home and Abroad*, vol. 2, 2nd ed. (New York: W. W. Norton, 1994), 480. On the American ecumenical Protestant reconstruction of religious institutions in Germany, see James D. Strasburg, "God's Marshall Plan: Transatlantic Christianity and the Quest for Godly Global Order, 1910–1963" (PhD diss., Notre Dame University, 2018), 167–295.

21. "The Churches and the European Recovery Program: Appendix C," n.d., Folder 20, Box 1, FCC Papers.

22. See Walter LaFeber, *America, Russia, and the Cold War, 1945–2006*, 10th ed. (Boston: McGraw-Hill, 2008).

23. "The Churches and the European Recovery Program."

24. "President Harry S. Truman's Address Before a Joint Session of Congress," March 12, 1947, Avalon Project, Yale Law School, http://avalon.law.yale.edu/20th_century/trudoc.asp, accessed October 2, 2018.

25. Executive Committee Minutes, p. 26, Folder 18, Box 1, FCC Papers.

26. Ibid. For the Federal Council's evaluation of the United Nations and its role circa 1947, see "United Nations," Appendix D, p. 20, Folder 18, Box 1, FCC Papers.

27. "American-Soviet Relations," 1946, Folder 17, Box 1, FCC Papers. See also "Statement on Soviet-American Relations (Confidential)," Folder 17, Box 1, FCC Papers.

28. George A. Coe, letter to the editor, *Christian Century*, April 13, 1949, 467.

29. "American-Soviet Relations."

30. Ibid.

31. Ibid., 10–11.

32. Ibid., 13.

33. G. Bromley Oxnam, "Must We Fight Russia?," *Christian Herald*, December 1947, 6. Italics in original.

34. Ibid., 7.

35. Ibid.

36. Ibid.

37. Inboden, *Religion and American Foreign Policy*, 54.

38. "The Cleveland Conference," *Christian Century*, March 2, 1949, 263–64.

39. James A. Craine to Walter W. Van Kirk, July 5, 1948, Folder 21, Box 37, FCC Papers.

40. "Churchmen Argue on Atlantic Pact," *New York Times*, March 10, 1949, 4.

41. Ibid.

42. "The Third National Study Conference on the Church and World Order: Message and Findings," April 1946, p. 6, Folder 20, Box 37, FCC Papers.

43. "Today and Tomorrow: Mr. Dulles on Scandinavia," *Washington Post*, March 10, 1949, 11.

44. "Dulles' Talk Angers Acheson," *Washington Post*, March 21, 1949, B15.

45. "Christians & World Order," *Time*, March 14, 1949, 65–66; "Churchmen & the Pact," *Time* March 21, 1949, 67–68.

46. "Churchmen & the Pact," *Time*, March 21, 1949, 67–68; "Cleveland Strikes Out!," *Christian Century*, March 23, 1949, 359–60. For Dulles's brief response and the response of the journal's editors, see "Correspondence," *Christian Century*, April 13, 1949, 467.

47. "A Message to the Churches" can be found in "The Third National Study Conference on the Church and World Order: Message and Findings," 1949, Folder 20, Box 37, FCC Papers. It was also published as a pamphlet.

48. "Third National Study Conference on the Churches and World Order: Message and Findings," April 1949, pp. 7–10, Folder 20, Box 37, FCC Papers.

49. Reinhold Niebuhr, *The Irony of American History* (New York: Charles Scribner's Sons, 1952).

50. The literature on Niebuhr is too large to list here. On his criticism of US policy during the Cold War, see Richard Wightman Fox, *Reinhold Niebuhr: A Biography* (New York: Pantheon Books, 1985).

51. Unsigned editorials for the *Christian Century* were written by a variety of individuals listed on the journal's masthead and sometimes by committee, making it difficult to determine authorship. I would like to thank Elesha Coffman for this insight on the editorial process at the journal. See also Elesha J. Coffman, *The Christian Century and the Rise of the Protestant Mainline* (New York: Oxford University Press, 2013).

52. "Cleveland Strikes Out!," *Christian Century*, March 23, 1949, 359–60.

53. Ibid. Charles F. Boss, the longtime head of the Methodists' foreign policy arm, echoed the *Christian Century*'s complaints in a letter he wrote directly to the Cleveland conference organizers. "Those in attendance who have been interested in the field over the years were prepared to go beyond the rather cautious statements of the top-level leaders," Boss wrote. See Charles F. Boss to Richard Fagley, July 27, 1949, Folder 20, Box 37, FCC Papers.

54. "Churchmen & the Pact," 67–68.

55. On US economic power in post–World War II Europe, see Victoria De Grazia, *Irresistible Empire: America's Advance Through Twentieth-Century Europe* (Cambridge, MA:

Belknap Press of Harvard University Press, 2005); Reinhold Wagnleitner, *Coca-Colonization and the Cold War: The Cultural Mission of the United States in Austria After the Second World War* (Chapel Hill: University of North Carolina Press, 1994).

56. Andrew Preston, "Peripheral Visions: American Mainline Protestants and the Global Cold War," *Cold War History* 13, no. 1 (2013): 112.

57. On the connections of the "China hands" to the missionary movement, see David A. Hollinger, *Protestants Abroad: How Missionaries Tried to Change the World but Changed America* (Princeton, NJ: Princeton University Press, 2017), 163–86.

58. John Foster Dulles to Mr. Joe J. Mickle, January 20, 1943, Folder 19, Box 163, Group 3, Series IA, Kenneth Scott Latourette Papers, Yale University (hereafter, KSL Papers). This folder contains much of the material on Latourette's involvement with the State Department and a group of ecumenical Protestant experts on the Far East in the first half of the 1940s. Among the people Latourette corresponded with during the war was Joseph R. Ballantine, director of the Office of Far Eastern Affairs in the State Department during the years 1944–45, and a special assistant to the secretary of state during 1945–47. Ballantine was born in India to Congregationalist missionary parents, and the missionary connection may be part of the reason why Ballantine took time to personally and thoroughly respond to position papers Latourette had written and sent to him.

59. Hollinger, *Protestants Abroad*, 235–37.

60. Kenneth Scott Latourette, "Background For Understanding the Current Situation in China, Final Revision," January 1, 1949, Folder 17, Box 37, FCC Papers.

61. Ibid.

62. Henry P. Van Dusen to Walter W. Van Kirk, January 31, 1949, Folder titled "Van Dusen, Henry Pitney 1937–1949," Box 117, Group 3, Series I, KSL Papers.

63. Henry P. Van Dusen to Walter W. Van Kirk, February 8, 1949, Folder 17, Box 37, FCC Papers. See also Walter W. Van Kirk to Henry P. Van Dusen, February 4, 1949, Folder 17, Box 37, FCC Papers.

64. Quoted in Preston, "Peripheral Visions," 128. See also Inboden, *Religion and American Foreign Policy*, 180.

65. *The Churches and American Policy in the Far East* (New York: Federal Council of Churches, 1949), copy in Folder 24, Box 63, FCC Papers.

66. Ibid., 4–5.

67. Arthur N. Feraru, "Public Opinion Polls on China," *Far Eastern Survey*, July 12, 1950, 130–32.

68. Quoted in John Mackay Metzger, *The Hand and the Road: The Life and Times of John A. Mackay* (Louisville, KY: Westminster John Knox Press, 2010), 286.

69. "Recognize Red China, Mission Leaders Ask," *New York Times*, April 29, 1950, 10.

70. John Mackay, "Stand on China Explained," *New York Times*, August 28, 1950, 16.

71. Ibid.

72. Executive Committee Minutes, p. 50, Folder 3, Box 2, FCC Papers.

73. Stephen J. Whitfield, *The Culture of the Cold War* (Baltimore, MD: Johns Hopkins University Press, 1991), 92–97.

74. J. B. Matthews and R. E. Shallcross, *Partners in Plunder: The Cost of Business Dictatorship* (New York: Covici Friede Publishers, 1935), 327–42.

75. Robert Griffith, *The Politics of Fear: Joseph R. McCarthy and the Senate*, 2nd ed. (Amherst: University of Massachusetts Press, 1987), 227–28. Yasuhiro Katagiri, *Black Freedom,*

White Resistance, and Red Menace: Civil Rights and Anticommunism in the Jim Crow South (Baton Rouge: Louisiana State University Press, 2014), 36–40.

76. On the *American Mercury* in the 1950s, see David Austin Walsh, "The Right-Wing Popular Front: The Far Right and American Conservatism in the 1950s," *Journal of American History* 107, no. 3 (September 2020): 411–32.

77. J. B. Matthews, "Reds and Our Churches," *American Mercury*, July 1953, 3.

78. Griffith, *The Politics of Fear*, 230–31.

79. C. P. Trussell, "Eisenhower Scores Attack on Clergy; M'Carthy Aid Out," *New York Times*, July 10, 1953, 1.

80. Griffith, *The Politics of Fear*, 232–33. For a full account of Matthews's activities during the civil rights movement, see Katagiri, *Black Freedom*.

81. Griffith, *The Politics of Fear*, 233.

82. For the testimony, see "Testimony of Bishop G. Bromley Oxnam: Hearing Before the Committee on Un-American Activities House of Representatives," 83rd Cong., 1st sess., 1953 (Washington: Committee on Un-American Activities, 1954), 3585–850.

83. Thomas Ferris, "The Christian Beacon," in *The Conservative Press in Twentieth-Century America*, ed. Ronald Lora and William Henry Longton (Westport, CT: Greenwood Press, 1999), 143. See also Carl McIntire, *G. Bromley Oxnam: Prophet of Marx* (Collingwood, NJ: Christian Beacon Press, 1953).

84. "Testimony of Bishop G. Bromley Oxnam," 3725–26.

85. Ibid., 3735.

86. Richard M. Fried, *Nightmare in Red: The McCarthy Era in Perspective* (New York: Oxford University Press, 1990), 173; Angela M. Lahr, *Millennial Dreams and Apocalyptic Nightmares: The Cold War Origins of Political Evangelicalism* (New York: Oxford University Press), 47.

87. "Cleric Repudiates Matthews Charge," *New York Times*, July 12, 1953, 29.

88. John A. Mackay, *A Letter to Presbyterians Concerning the Present Situation in Our Country and in the World*, (Philadelphia: Office of the General Assembly, 1953), 3.

89. Ibid.

90. Ibid., 6.

91. Ibid., 7.

92. Ibid. The quote came from Isaiah 1:18, KJV.

93. See, for example, the front-page coverage in the *New York Times*: George Dugan, "Presbyterians Warn on Methods Used Here in Fight on Communism," *New York Times*, November 3, 1953, 1. The newspaper also published the statement in the same issue, on page 20.

94. Mackay, *Letter to Presbyterians*, 6.

95. T. C. Chao, "Red Peiping After Six Months," *Christian Century*, September 14, 1949, 1067. See also Yongtao Chen, ed., *The Chinese Christology of T. C. Chao* (Boston: Brill, 2017); Winfried Glüer, *Christliche Theologie in China: T. C. Chao 1918–1956* (Gütersloh: Gütersloher Verlagshaus Mohn, 1979); Daniel Hoi Hui, *A Study of T. C. Chao's Christology in the Social Context of China (1920–1949)* (Bern: Peter Lang, 2017).

96. M. Richard Shaull, *Encounter with Revolution* (New York: Association Press, 1955).

97. On Shaull, the Student Volunteer Movement, and the emergence of the New Left, see Gene Zubovich, "U.S. Protestants and the International Origins of the 1960s Democratic Revolution," *Diplomatic History* 45, no. 1 (January 2021): 28–49.

98. William Ernest Hocking, *Re-Thinking Mission: A Laymen's Inquiry After One Hundred Years* (New York: Harper, 1932), 240–42.

99. [No author listed], *The Message and Decisions of Oxford on Church, Community and State* (Chicago: Universal Christian Council, [n.d.]), 35–37.

100. Shaull, *Encounter with Revolution*, 6–7. Italics in original.

101. On the centrality of consumerism in Cold War conceptions of US citizenship, see Lizabeth Cohen, *A Consumer's Republic: The Politics of Mass Consumption in Postwar America* (New York: Knopf, 2003).

102. Shaull, *Encounter with Revolution*, 50–51, 52.

103. Ibid., 52–54.

104. Ibid., 3.

105. Ibid., 44–45.

106. "Mackay Asks Visit by Press to China," *New York Times*, January 21, 1957, 43.

107. "A Church Mission to China Is Urged," *New York Times*, December 11, 1956, 9.

108. A thorough account of the Russia trip can be found in "Russia Trip, 1956," Folder 558, Box 27, Group 67, Series 111, Henry Knox Sherrill Papers, Yale Divinity Library Archives and Manuscripts, New Haven, CT. On the Hungary trip, see "World Council of Churches Central Committee meeting—Hungary," Folder 559, ibid.

109. Carl Henry, "NCC Conference Urges Recognition of Red China," *Christianity Today*, December 8, 1958, 25.

110. For the perspective of John C. Bennett, who was one of the architects of the call for recognition, see "Transcript of a Recorded Interview with John Coleman Bennett," May 13, 1965, the John Foster Dulles Oral History Project, Princeton University Library, Princeton, NJ. The juxtaposition of the resolution and Dulles's speech was reported widely. Two attempts were made to revise the draft at the conference, both of which attempted to weaken the call for recognition, but both attempts had not met the 25 percent threshold to register a printed dissent on the final statement. This threshold was a precedent established in previous conferences.

111. "A Message to the Churches in the United States of America Adopted by the Fifth World Order Study Conference," p. 7, Folder 18, Box 1, Series 5, John C. Bennett Papers, Burke Library Archives, Union Theological Seminary, New York, NY (hereafter, Bennett Papers). The text of the China section was reprinted as "Text of China Statement," *New York Times*, November 22, 1958, 8.

112. John C. Bennett to Rev. Gilbert Bakes, January 20, 1959, Folder 5, Box 1, Series 1A, Bennett Papers.

113. Henry P. Van Dusen to Henry R. Luce, February 16, 1959, Folder 18, Box 1, Series 5, Bennett Papers.

114. On the emergence of *Christianity Today*, see Chapter 7 in this volume.

115. John Wicklein, "Poling Condemns Bid to Red China," *New York Times*, November 23, 1958, 30.

116. "Dulles Is Cool to Advice of Churchmen on China," *New York Times*, November 27, 1958, 18.

117. Henry, "NCC Conference Urges Recognition of Red China," 27.

118. "NCC World Order Policy Softens on Red China," editorial, *Christianity Today*, December 22, 1958, 23.

119. Ibid., 28, 32.

120. The questionnaire, which was printed in the journal and asked for voluntary responses, asked whether *Christianity Today* readers agreed or disagreed with 1) "U.S. recognition of Red China" and 2) "U.N. admission of Red China." Printed in *Christianity Today*, December 22, 1958, 23.

121. "The NCC General Board and Protestant Commitments," editorial, *Christianity Today*, March 2, 1959, 22.

122. "NCC World Order Policy Softens on Red China"; "The NCC General Board and Protestant Commitments"; "NCC Sidesteps Action on Cleveland Report," *Christianity Today*, March 16, 1959, 25–26; "Ecumenical Free Speech and the Misrepresented Majority," *Christianity Today*, March 30, 1959, 22.

123. "The NCC General Board and Protestant Commitments." On the repudiation of the China resolution by a Brethren group, see "Group Rejects Recognition of Red China," *Los Angeles Times*, July 4, 1959, B2.

124. Ibid.

125. F. F., "American Baptists Support U.S. Red China Policy," *Christianity Today*, June 22, 1959, 27.

126. George Dugan, "Southern Church Bars Aid to China," *New York Times*, April 28, 1959, 71. A minority report of the Southern Presbyterians accused the National Council of having "fought the defense programs of the United States through the years, even when war and destruction were threatening. . . . They have greatly influenced the advance of socialism and its accompanying inflation; they have sought to curb and abolish the [House] Committee on Un-American Activities; they have created class and racial strife and discord and they have opposed the free enterprise system and advocated collectivism." Ibid.

127. Jill K. Gill, *Embattled Ecumenism: The National Council of Churches, the Vietnam War and the Trial of the Protestant Left* (DeKalb: Northern Illinois University Press, 2011).

Chapter 7

1. There is evidence that clergy were empowered by ecumenical denominations whose national leadership issued forceful public pronouncements. In such instances, clergy were more likely to share the political positions of national leaders (and less likely to share the views of churchgoers) and were more inclined to broadcast their stances on controversial issues to their church's members. See Charles Y. Glock and Benjamin B. Ringer, "Church Policy and the Attitudes of Ministers and Parishioners on Social Issues," *American Sociological Review* 21, no. 20 (April 1956): 148–56.

2. On the scholarship that emphasizes the importance of ecumenical Protestant activism against segregation in the 1960s but minimizes it in the 1940s and 1950s, see James F. Findlay, *Church People in the Struggle: The National Council of Churches and the Black Freedom Movement, 1950–1970* (New York: Oxford University Press, 1993); Mark Hulsether, *Building a Protestant Left: "Christianity and Crisis" Magazine, 1941–1993* (Knoxville: University of Tennessee Press, 1999). Ecumenical Protestantism warrants little mention, for example, in Kevin Michael Kruse and Stephen G. N. Tuck, *Fog of War: The Second World War and the Civil Rights Movement* (New York: Oxford University Press, 2012). On the difficulties of incorporating religion into the narrative of twentieth century US history, see Jon Butler, "Jack-in-the-Box Faith: The Religion Problem in Modern American History," *Journal of American History* 90, no. 4 (2004): 1357–78, https://doi.org/10.2307/3660356.

3. Alain Locke, "Reason and Race: A Review of the Literature of the Negro for 1946," *Phylon* 8, no. 1 (1947): 27.

4. *To Secure These Rights: The Report of Harry S Truman's Committee on Civil Rights*, ed. Steven F. Lawson (Boston: Bedford/St. Martin's Press, 2004), 12–20.

5. On the Commission on Church and Minority Peoples and for Tobias's biography, see Chapter 3 of this volume.

6. Jacquelyn Dowd Hall, *Revolt Against Chivalry: Jessie Daniel Ames and the Women's Campaign Against Lynching* (New York: Columbia University Press, 1979); Alice G. Knotts, *Fellowship of Love: Methodist Women Changing American Racial Attitudes, 1920–1968* (Nashville, TN: Kingswood Books, 1996); Edith Holbrook Riehm, "Dorothy Tilly and the Fellowship of the Concerned," in *Throwing Off the Cloak of Privilege: White Southern Women Activists in the Civil Rights Era*, ed. Gail S. Murray (Gainesville: University Press of Florida, 2004), 23–48.

7. Two other commission participants had connections to ecumenical Protestant institutions. Boris Shishkin, who represented the American Federation of Labor, actively cooperated with the Federal Council's Department of Church and Economic Life. One of the staff members for the commission had worked for the YWCA.

8. *To Secure These Rights*, 59. See Gunnar Myrdal and Arnold M. Rose, *The Negro in America: The Condensed Version of Gunnar Myrdal's "An American Dilemma"* (New York: Harper & Row, 1964).

9. Thomas J. Sugrue, *Sweet Land of Liberty: The Forgotten Struggle for Civil Rights in the North* (New York: Random House, 2008), 99–100.

10. *To Secure These Rights*, 111.

11. Ibid.

12. Ibid., 26–27.

13. One of the best accounts of Sherrill's conservative instincts are recalled in "The Reminiscences of Francis B. Sayre, Jr.," *Bishop Henry Knox Sherrill Project*, 1983, Columbia Center for Oral History, Columbia University, New York, NY. See also Sherrill's autobiography, Henry Knox Sherrill, *Among Friends: An Autobiography* (New York: Little Brown, 1962).

14. "Minutes," pp. 93–94, Folder 20, Box 1, RG 18, Federal Council of Churches Papers, Presbyterian Historical Society, Philadelphia, PA (hereafter, FCC Papers).

15. Wolfgang Saxon, "James Oscar Lee, 85, Educator and Worker on Race Relations," *New York Times*, June 16, 1995, 25.

16. On the "Vermont Plan," see A. Ritchie Low and Galen R. Weaver, *The "Vermont Plan": Interracial Visitation* (New York: Committee on Church and Race of the Congregational Christian Churches, n.d.)

17. An amicus curiae brief in the Takahashi case was submitted jointly by the Home Missions Council of North America, the Council for Social Action of the Congregational Christian Churches, the Council for Social Progress of the Northern Baptist Convention, and the Human Relations Commission of the Protestant Council of the City of New York. "Brief for Amici Curiae," 1947, Folder 15, Box 61, FCC Papers. For the *Shelley* brief, see "Supreme Court of the United States," 1947, ibid.

18. "Digest of the Proceedings, Retreat of Denominational and Interdenominational Secretaries on Social Action, Held May 28–29, 1948," Folder 21, Box 60, FCC Papers.

19. Ibid. On Height's cohort of African American women activists, see Bettye Collier-Thomas, *Jesus, Jobs, and Justice: African American Women and Religion* (Philadelphia, PA:

Temple University Press, 2014); and Julie A. Gallagher, *Black Women and Politics in New York City* (Urbana: University of Illinois Press, 2012). For the YMCA and YWCA as organizations that empowered African American activism in the North, see Sugrue, *Sweet Land of Liberty*.

20. Annual Reports and Meetings, 1945–1955 [Los Angeles], Folders 8–10, Box 3; Bulletins and Newsletters, 1947–1962 [Los Angeles], Folders 11–12, Box 3; Annual Reports and Meetings, 1945–1953 [San Francisco], Folder 17, Box 5, City Councils of Churches Records, 1909–1970, Burke Library Archives, Union Theological Seminary, New York, NY.

21. "Digest of the Proceedings."

22. On Protestant lobbying groups, see Chapter 3 of this volume.

23. Philip Hamburger, *Separation of Church and State* (Cambridge, MA: Harvard University Press, 2004), 454–78; Kathleen A. Holscher, *Religious Lessons: Catholic Sisters and the Captured Schools Crisis in New Mexico* (New York: Oxford University Press, 2012), 114–17, 154–65; John T. McGreevy, *Catholicism and American Freedom: A History* (New York: W.W. Norton, 2003).

24. Mrs. Harper Sibley to Senator Henry Cabot Lodge Jr., June 17, 1948, Folder 20, Box 56, FCC Papers.

25. "Memorandum," J. Oscar Lee to Boyd, Johnson, and Van Kirk, April 23, 1948, Folder 13, Box 57, FCC Papers.

26. Richard M. Fagley to Ray Gibbons, August 9, 1948, Folder 21, Box 37, FCC Papers.

27. Joseph Kip Kosek, *Acts of Conscience: Christian Nonviolence and Modern American Democracy* (New York: Columbia University Press, 2009).

28. George M. Houser to J. Oscar Lee, June 23, 1947, Folder 15, Box 57, FCC Papers.

29. Olyve L. Jeter to George M. Houser, June 25, 1947, Folder 15, Box 57, FCC Papers.

30. George M. Houser to Olyve L. Jeter, June 28, 1947, Folder 15, Box 57, FCC Papers.

31. The Journey of Reconciliation included members of socialist organizations, the Workers Defense League and the Southern Workers Defense League. Roswell P. Barnes thought the that the Journey of Reconciliation was "interesting" and "significant." See handwritten note on "Journey of Reconciliation, A Report by George M. Houser and Bayard Rustin," Folder 16, Box 57, FCC Papers.

32. J. Oscar Lee to George M. Houser, July 3, 1947, Folder 15, Box 57, FCC Papers.

33. August Meier and Elliot Rudwick, *CORE: A Study in the Civil Rights Movement, 1942–1968* (New York: Oxford University Press, 1973); Kosek, *Acts of Conscience*.

34. Galen Weaver to J. Oscar Lee, January 12, 1949, Folder 15, Box 61, FCC Papers.

35. Marian Wynn Perry to J. Oscar Lee, February 23, 1949; "Memorandum," J. Oscar Lee to Samuel McCrea Cavert, February 28, 1949, Folder 15, Box 61, FCC Papers.

36. "Memorandum," J. Oscar Lee to Samuel McCrea Cavert, February 28, 1949. A copy of the brief submitted to the Supreme Court can be found under "Appendix B," Folder 6, Box 56, FCC Papers.

37. "Appendix B, Motion for Leave to File Brief Amicus Curiae," Folder 6, Box 56, FCC Papers. By referencing emancipation and by calling segregation "a survival, and in its operation, a perpetuation, of the caste system," the brief also reflected the historical sensibility of Buell Gallagher. On the historical analysis of racism and segregation, see Chapter 5 in this volume.

38. "Minutes," p. 22, Folder 1, Box 2; "Report of Advisory Committee to the Executive Committee, May 17, 1949," Folder 15, Box 61; "Resolution on Filing a Brief of Amicus Curiae," Folder 15, Box 61, FCC Papers.

39. "Memorandum," F. E. Johnson to Samuel McCrea Cavert, March 17, 1948, Folder 4, Box 12, FCC Papers.

40. Ibid.

41. "Memorandum," J. Oscar Lee and Thomas C. Allen to Samuel McCrea Cavert, May 11, 1949, Folder 17, Box 12, FCC Papers.

42. "Report of Advisory Committee to the Executive Committee, May 17, 1949," Folder 15, Box 61, FCC Papers.

43. "Appendix B, Motion For Leave to File Brief Amicus Curiae," p. 2.

44. "Common welfare—federal council," press release draft, Folder 17, Box 61, FCC Papers.

45. Edward Hughes Pruden to Thomas C. Allen, October 21, 1949; Thomas C. Allen to Edward H. Pruden, October 25, 1949, Folder 17, Box 61, FCC Papers.

46. J. Waties Waring to Samuel McCrea Cavert, January 6, 1950, Folder 18, Box 61, FCC Papers; Findlay, *Church People in the Struggle*, 16–17.

47. Jane Dailey, "The Theology of Massive Resistance," in *Massive Resistance: Sothern Opposition to the Second Reconstruction*, ed. Clive Webb (Oxford: Oxford University Press, 2005), 156.

48. J. McDowell Richards, "Explanation," *Presbyterian Outlook*, December 19, 1949, 4.

49. "Agrees That Segregation Is Un-Christian," *Presbyterian Outlook*, March 6, 1950, 6.

50. On the connection between resistance to segregation among Protestant churches and the modern conservative movement, see Joseph Crespino, *In Search of Another Country: Mississippi and the Conservative Counterrevolution* (Princeton, NJ: Princeton University Press, 2007).

51. "Attorney General of Texas Challenges Segregation Brief," *Presbyterian Outlook*, January 16, 1950, 1; "Challenges Federal Council Anti-Segregation Brief," *Religious News Service*, December 30, 1949, clipping in Folder 17, Box 61, FCC Papers.

52. "Past Usefulness," *News*, February 25, 1950, clipping in Folder 18, Box 61, FCC Papers.

53. "Talladega's First Methodist Secedes," *Birmingham News*, December 8, 1949, 1.

54. Samuel McCrea Cavert to Bishop Clare Purcell, December 19, 1949, Folder 18, Box 61, FCC Papers.

55. "Resolution Adopted by the Quarterly Conference of Ashbury Memorial Methodist Church," Folder 18, Box 61, FCC Papers.

56. Findlay, *Church People in the Struggle*, 14–15.

57. Brown v. Board of Education of Topeka, 347 U.S. 483 (1954).

58. Virginia Brereton, "United and Slighted: Women as Subordinated Insiders," in *Between the Times: The Travail of the Protestant Establishment in America, 1900–1960*, ed. William R. Hutchison (New York: Cambridge University Press, 1989), 143–67.

59. "The School Decision," *Christian Century*, June 2, 1954, 662; "A Summary of Resolutions of the National Council of Churches, 1950–1961," p. 23, Folder 2, Box 1, Series 1A, National Council of Churches Records, 1948–1973, Burke Library Archives, Union Theological Seminary, New York (hereafter, NCC Papers).

60. "The School Decision," *Christian Century*, June 2, 1954, 662.

61. Ibid., 663.

62. Niebuhr also praised the *Plessy v. Ferguson* decision as "a very good doctrine for its day" because it avoided prompting a "revolt" by southerners. Reinhold Niebuhr, "The Supreme Court on Segregation in the Schools," *Christianity and Crisis*, June 14, 1954, 75–77.

63. John C. Bennett, untitled editorial, *Christianity and Crisis*, June 28, 1954, 83.

64. "Editorial," *Christian Century*, June 16, 1954, 732; Mark Newman, *Getting Right with God: Southern Baptists and Desegregation, 1945–1995* (Tuscaloosa: University of Alabama Press, 2001); Alan Scot Willis, *All According to God's Plan: Southern Baptist Missions and Race, 1945–1970* (Lexington: University Press of Kentucky, 2005), 105–6. For a corrective to Willis's claim that "Christian" attitudes were synonymous with progressive views on race, see Jane Dailey, "Sex, Segregation, and the Sacred After Brown," *Journal of American History* 91, no. 1 (2004): 119–44, https://doi.org/10.2307/3659617.

65. Max Gilstrap, "Covering the World Council," *Christian Science Monitor*, August 27, 1954, 18; "World Peace Called Goal of Churches," *Washington Post*, August 17, 1954, 1.

66. Benjamin Mays, "The Church Will Be Challenged at Evanston," *Christianity and Crisis*, August 9, 1954, 106–8.

67. George Daniels, "WCC Approves Mays' Plan for Brotherhood," *Chicago Defender*, September 11, 1954, 1.

68. *The Evanston Report: Second Assembly of the World Council of Churches, 1954*, ed. W. A. Visser 't Hooft (New York: Harper & Brothers, 1955), 156–57.

69. Ibid., 155.

70. Albert Barnett, "Five Outstanding Impressions of Recent World Council of Churches," *Chicago Defender*, September 18, 1954, 4; *Evanston Report*, 157.

71. Quoted in Chesly Manly, "Segregation Is a Scandal, World Council Told," *Chicago Tribune*, August 22, 1954, 8; George Dugan, "Bias In Churches Held False Trend: Negro Leaders Tells Session at Evanston Segregation Is Modern Development," *New York Times*, August 22, 1954, 66.

72. "World Leaders Appeal for Church Integration," *Chicago Defender*, August 28, 1954, 4; "Our Opinions: The World Council of Churches," *Chicago Defender*, September 4, 1954, 11.

73. Rufus Burrow Jr., *God and Human Dignity: The Personalism, Theology, and Ethics of Martin Luther King, Jr.* (Notre Dame, IN: University of Notre Dame Press, 1992); Taylor Branch, *Parting the Waters: America in the King Years, 1954–63* (New York: Simon & Schuster, 1989); David J. Garrow, *Bearing the Cross: Martin Luther King, Jr., and the Southern Christian Leadership Conference* (New York: W. Morrow, 1986); Thomas F. Jackson, *From Civil Rights to Human Rights: Martin Luther King, Jr., and the Struggle for Economic Justice* (Philadelphia: University of Pennsylvania Press, 2007).

74. Kelly Baker, *Gospel According to the Klan: The KKK's Appeal to Protestant America, 1915–1930* (Lawrence: University Press of Kansas, 2011); Linda Gordon, *The Second Coming of the KKK: The Ku Klux Klan of the 1920s and the American Political Tradition* (New York: Liveright, 2017).

75. "Inaugural Address of Governor George Wallace," January 14, 1963, https://digital.archives.alabama.gov/digital/collection/voices/id/2952, accessed May 17, 2021.

76. Quoted in Findlay, *Church People in the Struggle*, 21.

77. Ibid., 22–24.

78. Quoted in Mary Dudziak, *Cold War Civil Rights: Race and the Image of American Democracy* (Princeton, NJ: Princeton University Press, 2001), 132.

79. Dwight D. Eisenhower, "Federal Court Orders Must Be Upheld," Little Rock Speech, September 24, 1957, https://usa.usembassy.de/etexts/speeches/rhetoric/ikefeder.htm, accessed September 7, 2018.

80. Karen Anderson, *Little Rock: Race and Resistance at Central High School* (Princeton, NJ: Princeton University Press, 2009). John A. Kirk, *Beyond Little Rock: The Origins and Legacies of the Central High Crisis* (Fayetteville: University of Arkansas Press, 2007).

81. Findlay, *Church People in the Struggle*, 23.

82. "First meeting of C.S.A. Committee on Racial and Cultural Relations," October 30, 1952, RR-1, Congregational Council for Social Action Papers, Congregational Library, Boston, MA (hereafter, CSA Papers). See also Galen R. Weaver, "Annual Report for 1953," RR-2, CSA Papers; "Council for Social Action and Commission on Christian Social Action, Committee on Racial Integration," January 6, 1956, p. 6, RR-1, CSA Papers.

83. Mrs. E. A. Albright, quoted in meeting notes of the "Council for Social Action and Commission on Christian Social Action Committee on Racial Integration," January 6, 1956, RR-1, CSA Papers. See also "Our Segregated Churches in the Segregated Southeast Convention," RR-4, CSA Papers.

84. Robert G. Geoffroy to Galen R. Weaver, November 23, 1955, RR-4, CSA Papers.

85. "Our Segregated Churches in the Segregated Southeast Convention," p. 14.

86. Ibid.

87. "A Summary of Resolutions of the National Council of Churches," p. 23, Folder 2, Box 1, NCC Papers; "Council for Social Action and Commission on Christian Social Action, Committee on Racial Integration," January 6, 1956, p. 2, RR-1, CSA Papers.

88. Carolyn Renée Dupont, *Mississippi Praying: Southern White Evangelicals and the Civil Rights Movement, 1945–1975* (New York: New York University Press, 2013), 97–103, quote at 103.

89. For an outline of the program, see "Minutes of the Joint Committee on Race Relations," November 2, 1956, RR-1, CSA Papers. See also Folders 6–7, Box 58, Council for Social Action of the Congregational Christian Churches, 1949–1958, Fund for the Republic Records, Public Policy Papers, Department of Rare Books and Special Collections, Princeton University Library, Princeton, NJ.

90. "Report of Galen R. Weaver for 1956," pp. 3–4, RR-2, CSA Papers.

91. "Summary Report for the Committee on Race Relations, Oct. 16, 1957, by Dorothy E. Hampton," RR-4, CSA Papers.

92. Doug Rossinow, *The Politics of Authenticity: Liberalism, Christianity, and the New Left in America* (New York: Columbia University Press, 1998), 6.

93. *motive*, November 1955.

94. M. Richard Shaull, *Encounter with Revolution* (New York: Association Press, 1955). For a thorough discussion of Shaull and his book, see Chapter 6 of this volume.

95. Jeremi Suri, *Power and Protest: Global Revolution and the Rise of Detente* (Cambridge, MA: Harvard University Press, 2005).

96. Shaull, *Encounter with Revolution*, 8.

97. C. Wright Mills, *White Collar: The American Middle Classes* (New York: Oxford University Press, 1952); David Riesman, Nathan Glazer, and Reuel Denney, *The Lonely Crowd: A Study of the Changing American Character* (New Haven, CT: Yale University Press, 1950); William H. Whyte, *The Organization Man* (New York: Simon & Schuster, 1956).

98. David E. Durham, "Revolution and Reconciliation," *motive*, November 1955, 45.

99. Cherian Thomas et al. to the Steering Committee, December 29, 1951, Folder 7252, Box 635, SVM-GP42, Student Volunteer Movement Papers, Yale Divinity Library Special Collections, New Haven, CT (hereafter, SVM Papers); Tracey K. Jones Jr. to Bayard Rustin, January 16, 1952, Folder 2759, Box 636, SVM Papers.

100. "West Held a Seed of Global Revolt," *New York Times*, December 29, 1955, 4.

101. Stanley Rowland Jr., "Apartheid Issue Put to Students," *New York Times*, December 30, 1955, 12; "West Held a Seed of Global Revolt," 4.

102. Stanley Rowland Jr., "Southern Youths Back Integration," *New York Times*, January 1, 1956, 42.

103. Rossinow, *The Politics of Authenticity*, 111.

104. It also showcased students' new interests in theologians with anti-fascist credentials, like those of the president of the World's Student Christian Federation, Philippe Maury, who worked in the French underground during World War II. Students attending the Athens, Ohio, meeting read his book in preparation for the meeting. Philippe Maury, *Politics and Evangelism* (New York: Doubleday, 1959).

105. Martin Luther King Jr., Speech to the 18th Ecumenical Student Conference on the Christian World Mission in Athens, Ohio, December 30, 1959, Folder 7298, Box 639, SVM Papers.

106. UPI teletype, untitled [Athens, Ohio, byline], December 28, 1959; "3600 Youths Attend Parley on OU Campus," *Wilmington News-Journal*, clippings in Ecumenical Student Conferences on the Christian World Mission Records, Collection UA00410, 18th Conference, 1959–1960, Ohio University, Athens, OH; "Students Buck Bias to Attend Christian Meet," *Chicago Defender*, December 29, 1959, 3.

107. Quoted in Sara M. Evans, *Journeys That Opened Up the World: Women, Student Christian Movements, and Social Justice, 1955–1975* (New Brunswick, NJ: Rutgers University Press, 2003), 17.

108. "A Summary of Resolutions of the National Council of Churches, 1950–1961," p. 24, Folder 2, Box 1, Series 1A, NCC Papers.

109. "YWCA National Board Backs Sin-In Objective," *Chicago Defender*, April 23, 1960, 9.

110. George Dugan, "Sit-Ins Supported in Church Report," *New York Times*, May 25, 1960, 27; "Episcopalian Church Backs 'Sit-in' Move in South," *Washington Post*, April 2, 1960, A14; "Methodists Praise Student Sit-In Drive: Vow to End All Racial Barriers," *Chicago Defender*, May 9, 1960, A2.

111. "Cleric Urges Snub of Sit-In Laws: Asks Challenge of White Man's Rules," *Chicago Defender*, June 18, 1960, 21.

112. "Meeting at the II General Assembly of the National Student Christian Federation," Folder 584, Box 45, RG 247, National Student Christian Federation Papers, Yale Divinity School Special Collections, New Haven, CT.

113. Melani McAlister, *The Kingdom of God Has No Borders: A Global History of American Evangelicals* (New York: Oxford University Press, 2018), 11–12.

114. "Meeting at the II General Assembly of the National Student Christian Federation."

115. Other accounts of Protestant student radicalization stress the exposure of liberal Protestant student groups to existentialism. See Rossinow, *Politics of Authenticity*.

116. "Dr. Blake Among 283 Held in Racial Rally in Maryland," *New York Times*, July 5, 1963, 1; "High Churchmen Are Arrested in March," *Chicago Defender*, July 6, 1963, 1; Victoria W. Wolcott, *Race, Riots, and Roller Coasters: the Struggle over Segregated Recreation in America* (Philadelphia: University of Pennsylvania Press, 2012), 183–86.

117. "High Churchmen Are Arrested in March," 1.

118. On the polling data demonstrating the clergy-laity gap, see Jill K. Gill, *Embattled Ecumenism: The National Council of Churches, the Vietnam War and the Trial of the Protestant Left* (DeKalb: Northern Illinois University Press, 2011), 162. On lay opposition to civil rights, see Findlay, *Church People in the Struggle*.

119. Molly Worthen, *Apostles of Reason: The Crisis of Authority in American Evangelicalism* (New York: Oxford University Press, 2014), 135–37.

120. Curtis J. Evans, "A Politics of Conversion," in *Billy Graham: American Pilgrim*, ed. Andrew Finstuen, Grant Wacker, and Anne Blue Wills (New York: Oxford University Press, 2017), 154.

121. Quoted in Worthen, *Apostles of Reason*, 137.

122. Aaron Griffith, *God's Law and Order: The Politics of Punishment in Evangelical America* (Cambridge, MA: Harvard University Press, 2020).

123. On the persistence of racism in evangelical communities, see Anthea Butler, *White Evangelical Racism: The Politics of Morality in America* (Chapel Hill: University of North Carolina Press, 2021).

124. Collier-Thomas, *Jesus, Jobs, and Justice*, 420–22; Jennifer Scanlon, *Until There Is Justice: The Life of Anna Arnold Hedgeman* (New York: Oxford University Press, 2016).

125. Findlay, *Church People in the Struggle*, 61.

126. Ibid., 57. For a full account of lobbying for the Civil Rights Act, see 48–65.

127. "Excerpts from Addresses at Lincoln Memorial During Capital Civil Rights March," *New York Times*, August 29, 1963, 21.

128. Collier-Thomas, *Jesus, Jobs, and Justice*, 420–22.

129. Claude E. Welch, "Mobilizing Morality: The World Council of Churches and Its Program to Combat Racism, 1969–1994," *Human Rights Quarterly* 23, no. 4 (2001): 875–77.

130. Findlay, *Church People in the Struggle*, 206, 212.

131. Robert D. Putnam and David E. Campbell, *American Grace: How Religion Divides and Unites Us* (New York: Simon & Schuster, 2012).

132. For an overview of evangelicals and Black-white relations, see Michael O. Emerson and Christian Smith, *Divided by Faith: Evangelical Religion and the Problem of Race in America* (Oxford: Oxford University Press, 2000).

Chapter 8

1. "Text of Report on 'The Church and Disorder of Society,'" *New York Times*, September 3, 1948, 11.

2. Jonathan P. Herzog, *The Spiritual-Industrial Complex: America's Religious Battle Against Communism in the Early Cold War* (New York: Oxford University Press, 2011); Kevin M. Kruse, *One Nation Under God: How Corporate America Invented Christian America* (New York: Basic Books, 2015). On the parallels between the postwar political-economic advocacy by American liberals and British Labour leaders, which downplays the differences between the New Deal and European welfare states, see Ilnyun Kim, "The Party of Reform in the Doldrums: The Convergence of Anglo-American Political Progressivism," *Modern Intellectual History*, FirstView, 1–24, https://doi.org/10.1017/S1479244320000104. See also Ira Katznelson, *Fear Itself: The New Deal and the Origins of Our Time* (New York: Liveright, 2013); Daniel T. Rodgers, *Atlantic Crossings: Social Politics in a Progressive Age* (Cambridge, MA: Belknap Press of Harvard University Press, 1998).

3. George D. Kelsey, "The Challenge of Our Economic Culture to the Churches," Folder 7262, Box 636, SVM-GP42, Student Volunteer Movement for Foreign Missions Records, Yale Divinity Library and Archives, New Haven, CT.

4. Quoted in David M. Henkin and Rebecca M. McLennan, *Becoming America: A History for the 21st Century* (New York: McGraw-Hill Education, 2015), 758.

5. Darren Dochuk, *From Bible Belt to Sunbelt: Plain-Folk Religion, Grassroots Politics, and the Rise of Evangelical Conservatism* (New York: W.W. Norton, 2012).

6. Johnson's most important work on personality is Frederick Ernest Johnson, *The Social Gospel and Personal Religion: Are They in Conflict?* (New York: Federal Council of the Churches, 1922).

7. Minutes of the Executive Committee of the Federal Council of Churches, p. 126, Folder 15, Box 1, RG 18, Federal Council of Churches Papers, Presbyterian Historical Society, Philadelphia, PA (hereafter, FCC Papers).

8. John C. Bennett, *Christian Ethics and Social Policy* (New York: Charles Scribner's Sons, 1946), 77–81.

9. Ibid., 81.

10. On postwar intellectuals' debates over the issues of freedom and social control, see Richard H. Pells, *The Liberal Mind in a Conservative Age: American Intellectuals in the 1940s and 1950s* (New York: Harper & Row, 1985), 141–46.

11. Kruse, *One Nation Under God*, 13. Christian libertarians preferred the language of "individual personality" and "individual rights" to "human persons" and "human rights."

12. Quoted in ibid. On libertarian thought more broadly, see Angus Burgin, *The Great Persuasion: Reinventing Free Markets Since the Depression* (Cambridge, MA: Harvard University Press, 2012).

13. "Christianity and the Economic Order, Study No. 4, Non-Profit Incentives in Our Economic Life," *Information Service*, November 23, 1946, 1–8.

14. Ibid.

15. "Christianity and the Economic Order, Study No. 2, Labor-Management Relations," *Information Service*, June 29, 1946, 1–8.

16. Ibid.

17. The request for the conference came from the Northern Presbyterian representatives at the Federal Council. See Robert W. Potter, "Talks Today Link Church, Economics," *New York Times*, February 18, 1947, 28. On the conference participants, see David E. Thomas, "Questionnaire Study of the Pittsburgh Conference on the Church and Economic Life," Folder 15, Box 63, FCC Papers.

18. "Christianity and the Economic Order, More from the Critics," *Information Service*, January 25, 1947, 5.

19. "Opening Address of Charles P. Taft," February 18, 1947, pg. 1, Folder 14, Box 63, FCC Papers.

20. Joseph B. Treaster, "Charles P. Taft, Former Mayor of Cincinnati," *New York Times*, June 25, 1983, 14.

21. "Church Conference Set to Study Economic Life," *Religious News Service*, February 4, 1947. Perkins was unable to attend the conference, but she did attend the follow-up conference in Detroit in 1950.

22. For a list of all the participants in the Pittsburgh conference, see "Committee on Report" and "Roster of Delegates," both in Folder 14, Box 63, FCC Papers.

23. *Report of the National Study Conference on the Church and Economic Life, Pittsburgh, Pennsylvania, February 18–20, 1947* (New York: Federal Council of Churches, 1947), p. 5, Folder 14, Box 63, FCC Papers; "Church Study Group Opposes Laissez-Faire Doctrine," *Religious News Service*, February 20, 1947, 1. The condemnation of Smith was written by Harvey Seifert, professor of social ethics at USC's School of Religion; Howard Coonley, past president

of the National Association of Manufacturers; and Robert W. Searle, secretary of the Protestant Council of New York.

24. "Church Parley Neatly Ducks Closed Shop," *Chicago Daily Tribune*, February 20, 1947, 23; Robert W. Potter, "Church Group Asks a Fight on Poverty," *New York Times*, February 20, 1947, 27.

25. Potter, "Church Group Asks a Fight on Poverty," 27. See also Harold E. Fey, "Protestant Leaders Discuss Church and Economic Order," *Christian Century*, March 5, 1947, 308, 317–19.

26. *Report of the National Study Conference on the Church and Economic Life*, Pittsburgh, 9.

27. "Church Study Group Opposes Laissez-Faire Doctrine," *Religious News Service*, February 20, 1947, 2.

28. *Report of the National Study Conference on the Church and Economic Life*, Pittsburgh, 2, 8–11.

29. Ibid., 19.

30. See, for example, "The Church and Capital: New England Religious and Lay Leaders Examine Free Enterprise, Reach Some Interesting Conclusions Concerning the American Way of Life," *Trends in Church, Education and Industry Cooperation*, October, 1949, 5–7. On the mixed results of NAM's campaigns to forge ties with religious groups in the 1940s, see Elizabeth A. Fones-Wolf, *Selling Free Enterprise: The Business Assault on Labor and Liberalism, 1945–60* (Urbana: University of Illinois Press, 1994), 220–22. Kevin Kruse concludes that the efforts of Christian libertarians were more effective at promoting public religiosity than at influencing economic policy. See Kruse, *One Nation Under God*.

31. *Report of the National Study Conference on the Church and Economic Life*, Pittsburgh, 17–18.

32. "Christianity and the Economic Order, Study No. 10," *Information Service*, May 13, 1948, 1–8. There was little consistency in the use of "upper," "middle," and "lower" classes, both in terms of how these categories were conceived as well as how the information about class was collected. Some polls relied on pollsters' observations of the household belongings during interviews, while others used different factors, such as the type of employment. In this era, income was rarely a determining factor of class status. Note also that statistics on voting patterns excluded the vast majority of African Americans, who were disenfranchised in the 1940s.

33. "Christianity and the Economic Order, Study No. 10," 1–8.

34. "Church Parley Says Monopoly Is 'Intolerable,'" *Chicago Daily Tribune*, February 21, 1947, 15. For postconference reactions in the press, see Walter George Muelder, "The Pittsburgh Conference," *Christianity and Crisis*, March 17, 1947, 3–6; "Editorial Notes," *Christianity and Crisis*, March 17, 1947, 2; Potter, "Church Group Asks a Fight on Poverty," 27; Fey, "Protestant Leaders Discuss Church and Economic Order," 308, 317–19. Coverage was largely absent from the journals targeting women. *The Methodist Woman* and *Church Woman*, both of which gave tremendous publicity to conferences sponsored by the Dulles Commission, were silent on the Pittsburgh meeting. The discussion of economics in those journals focused on racial justice, consumption, and household economics.

35. [Rev. Paul Silas Heath] to John C. Bennett, March 24, 1947; John C. Bennett to Rev. Paul Silas Heath, March 27, 1947, Folder 15, Box 63, FCC Papers.

36. Muelder, "The Pittsburgh Conference," 3–6.

37. *Report of the National Study Conference on the Church and Economic Life, Pitts-burgh*, 19.

38. "Memorandum," Samuel McCrea Cavert to Roswell Barnes, February 26, 1947, Folder 17, Box 63, FCC Papers. E. R. Bowen, a proponent of cooperatives who had attended the Pitts-burgh conference, lobbied G. Bromley Oxnam to expand the Industrial Division. See E. R. Bowen to Charles P. Taft, April 14, 1947, Folder 17, Box 63, FCC Papers. See also Cameron Hall to Liston Pope, April 3, 1947, Folder 171, Box 11, Series I, Group 49, Liston Pope Papers, Yale Divinity School Library and Archives, New Haven, CT (hereafter, Pope Papers).

39. On a detailed institutional history of the department, see Howard M. Mills, "The De-partment of the Church and Economic Life of the National Council of Churches, 1947–1966: A Critical Analysis" (PhD diss., Union Theological Seminary, 1970).

40. "Report of Cameron P. Hall," p. 2, Folder 1, Box 63, FCC Papers.

41. Reuther, Shishkin, and Cruikshank attended department meetings regularly. See, for example, "Minutes of the Meeting in Philadelphia, Pa., October 2–4, 1947," Folder 21, Box 63, FCC Papers. Cruikshank, who served as a Methodist minister before joining the AFL, is widely credited for playing a major role in extending Social Security to cover disability in 1956, and for Medicare in 1965.

42. James Myers to Cameron Hall, May 26, 1947, Folder 21, Box 63, FCC Papers. On My-ers's activities during the 1930s on behalf of labor, see Elizabeth Fones-Wolf and Ken Fones-Wolf, "Lending a Hand to Labor: James Myers and the Federal Council of Churches, 1926–1947," *Church History* 68, no. 1 (March 1999): 62–86.

43. Originally, two dozen follow-up conferences had been planned, but by 1950 thirty had been held, including many "repeat" conferences. Mills, "The Department of the Church and Economic Life," 141.

44. "Report to Informal Meeting on March 24 [1947]," Folder 15, Box 63, FCC Papers.

45. "Report of Cameron P. Hall," pp. 1–2, Folder 1, Box 63, FCC Papers; Cameron P. Hall to Liston Pope, October 1, 1947, Folder 171, Box 11, Series I, Pope Papers.

46. Dochuk, *From Bible Belt to Sunbelt*; Michelle M. Nickerson and Darren Dochuk, eds., *Sunbelt Rising: The Politics of Place, Space, and Region* (Philadelphia: University of Pennsyl-vania Press, 2011).

47. T. C. Chao, "Red Peiping After Six Months," *Christian Century*, September 14, 1949, 1067.

48. The most thorough account of the shift in Dulles's thinking remains Mark G. Tou-louse, *The Transformation of John Foster Dulles: From Prophet of Realism to Priest of Nation-alism* (Macon, GA: Mercer University Press, 1985), 196–200. See also Andrew Preston, *Sword of the Spirit, Shield of Faith* (New York: Alfred A. Knopf, 2012), 450–59.

49. Quoted in Toulouse, *The Transformation of John Foster Dulles*, 198.

50. "Text of Dulles' Address to Assembly of Council of Churches," *New York Times*, Au-gust 25, 1948, 4.

51. "Warns Against Division," *New York Times*, August 25, 1948, 4.

52. Toulouse, *The Transformation of John Foster Dulles*, 198.

53. "Church Council Closes Doors For Discussion of Communism," *Washington Post*, August 26, 1948, 1.

54. Rev. John Evans, "World Council Hears 2 Views of Reds," *New York Times*, August 25, 1948, 24.

55. "Text of Report on 'The Church and Disorder of Society,'" 11.

56. Pells, *The Liberal Mind in a Conservative Age.*

57. *The Responsible Society: "Christian Action in Society,"* pamphlet (New York: World Council of Churches, 1949), 7.

58. Ibid.

59. Kevin Mattson, *When America Was Great: The Fighting Faith of Liberalism in Post-War America* (New York: Taylor & Francis, 2005).

60. Arthur Meier Schlesinger, *The Vital Center: The Politics of Freedom* (Boston: Houghton Mifflin, 1949), 3–5.

61. *The Responsible Society,* 10–11. On the anti-secularism of the World Council, see Udi Greenberg, "Protestants, Decolonization, and European Integration, 1885–1961," *Journal of Modern History* 89, no. 2 (June 2017): 314–54; Justin Reynolds, "Against the World: International Protestantism and the Ecumenical Movement Between Secularization and Politics, 1900–1952" (PhD diss., Columbia University, 2016); Samuel Moyn, *Christian Human Rights* (Philadelphia: University of Pennsylvania Press, 2015). On anti-secularism among American ecumenical Protestants, see K. Healan Gaston, *Imagining Judeo-Christian America: Religion, Secularism, and the Redefinition of Democracy* (Chicago: University of Chicago Press, 2019).

62. "Bewilderment at Amsterdam," *Los Angeles Times,* September 5, 1948, A4.

63. Ibid.; George Dugan, "Church Council Eases Criticism of Capitalism in Final Session," *New York Times,* September 5, 1948, 1, 28. Sockman quoted in "Clergymen Report on World Council," *New York Times,* September 22, 1948, 5.

64. Uncle Eversley to John, September 13, 1948, Folder 11, Box 2, Series 5, John Coleman Bennett Papers, Burke Library Archives, Union Theological Seminary, New York, NY (hereafter, Bennett Papers).

65. John C. Bennett to Uncle Eversley, September 22, 1948, Folder 11, Box 2, Series 5, Bennett Papers.

66. Cameron P. Hall, "Confidential Memorandum," Folder 5, Box 63, FCC Papers; Thomas F. Peterson, "Highlights of the Detroit Study Conference on the Church and Economic Life," Folder 5, Box 63, FCC Papers; Rev. Franklin D. Elmer Jr., ". . . and nobody walked out!," *Kiwanis Magazine,* copy in Folder 5, Box 63, FCC Papers. Stanley High's article "Methodism's Pink Fringe," published in *Reader's Digest,* is discussed in Chapter 9 in this volume.

67. Nelson Lichtenstein, *The Most Dangerous Man in Detroit: Walter Reuther and the Fate of American Labor* (New York: Basic Books, 1995), 8.

68. Peterson, "Highlights of the Detroit Study Conference."

69. William Johnson, "The Middle Way, the Middle Truth, and the Middle Life," *Faith and Freedom: The Monthly Journal of Spiritual Mobilization* 1, no. 5 (April 1950): 5–6; Peterson, "Highlights of the Detroit Study Conference"; Walter W. Ruch, "Reuther Proposes Economic Parley," *New York Times,* February 17, 1950, 25.

70. Kim, "The Party of Reform in the Doldrums."

71. "Group Urges Taxing to Cut Inequalities," *Washington Post,* February 18, 1950, 11.

72. George S. Benson to Cameron P. Hall, July 17, 1950, Folder 5, Box 63, FCC Papers. For the statement Benson was responding to, see "Taxation and Income Distribution: Passages from Eminent and Authoritative Sources" in the same folder.

73. Dochuk, *From Bible Belt to Sunbelt,* 60–66, 112–14.

74. Hall, "Confidential Memorandum."

75. Reinhold Niebuhr, "The National Study Conference on Church and Economic Life," *Christianity and Crisis,* March 6, 1950, 22–23.

76. Ted F. Silvey to Cameron Hall, n.d., Folder 5, Box 63, FCC Papers.

77. Elmer, ". . . and nobody walked out!"; Harold E. Fey, "The Detroit Conference," *Christian Century*, March 1, 1950, 264–65; Cameron P. Hall to Roy C. Blough, April 11, 1950, Folder 15, Box 64, FCC Papers; "Protestants Urge Christian Policy," *Los Angeles Times*, February 19, 1950, 14; Johnson, "The Middle Way," 9. On the "middle way" thinking of the era, see Pells, *The Liberal Mind in a Conservative Age*, 135–39, 141–42.

78. "Churchmen Ask Study of Atom Bomb Problem," *Chicago Tribune*, February 20, 1950, 5; Walter W. Ruch, "Restraint Asked in Economic Rule," *New York Times*, February 20, 1950, 2.

79. William Beveridge, *Social Insurance and Allied Services* (London: H. M. Stationery Office, 1942).

80. James T. Sparrow, *Warfare State: World War II Americans and the Age of Big Government* (New York: Oxford University Press, 2011), 242–47.

Chapter 9

1. Recent historiography of the Christian Right has emphasized its religious roots in the anti–New Deal mobilization of the 1930s, especially among fundamentalists. Scholars have also emphasized the tenuousness of the formation of the religious Right, with coalitions—especially between evangelicals, Catholics, and Mormons—often warring among themselves. This chapter emphasizes opposition to the political economy of ecumenical Protestants and the clergy-laity gap as key dynamics of the formation of the Christian Right. On the Christian Right's origins in the 1930s, see Kevin M. Kruse, *One Nation Under God: How Corporate America Invented Christian America* (New York: Basic Books, 2015), chap. 1; Matthew Avery Sutton, "Was FDR the Antichrist? The Birth of Fundamentalist Antiliberalism in a Global Age," *Journal of American History* 98, no. 4 (2012): 1052–74. See also the classic work, Leo P. Ribuffo, *The Old Christian Right: The Protestant Far Right from the Great Depression to the Cold War* (Philadelphia: Temple University Press, 1983). On the tenuousness of the Christian Right coalition, see especially Neil J. Young, *We Gather Together: The Religious Right and the Problem of Interfaith Politics* (New York: Oxford University Press, 2016). Young emphasizes the opposition to ecumenical Protestants as the most important backdrop to the rise of the Christian Right. "The emergence of the Religious Right was not a brilliant political strategy of compromise and coalition-building hatched on the eve of a history-altering election," he writes. "Rather, it was the latest iteration of a religious debate that had gone on for decades, sparked by the ecumenical contentions of mainline Protestantism rather than by secular liberal political victories" (5).

2. Historians have largely raised these questions about church-state relations and American democracy in the context of "Judeo-Christian" pluralism rather than the clergy-laity gap. See K. Healan Gaston, *Imagining Judeo-Christian America: Religion, Secularism, and the Redefinition of Democracy* (Chicago: University of Chicago Press, 2019); Kevin Michael Schultz, *Tri-Faith America: How Catholics and Jews Held Postwar America to Its Protestant Promise* (Oxford: Oxford University Press, 2011); Ronit Y. Stahl, *Enlisting Faith: How the Military Chaplaincy Shaped Religion and State in Modern America* (Cambridge, MA: Harvard University Press, 2017).

3. John T. Flynn, *The Road Ahead: America's Creeping Revolution* (New York: Distributed by the Committee for Constitutional Government by special arrangement with Devin-Adair, 1949).

4. This chapter emphasizes the internal dynamics of ecumenical Protestant institutions as a key factor in the shaping of Protestant economic thought in the postwar United States.

Many accounts of postwar liberal debates on the economy leave out the important contributions of ecumenical Protestants. Others highlight Reinhold Niebuhr as a singular figure. See Kevin Mattson, *When America Was Great: The Fighting Faith of Liberalism in Post-War America* (New York: Taylor & Francis, 2005). See also Timothy Stanley and Jonathan Bell, *Making Sense of American Liberalism* (Urbana: University of Illinois Press, 2012).

5. On Christian libertarianism, which was especially prevalent among Congregationalists, see Kruse, *One Nation Under God*, 3–34. See also Margaret Lamberts Bendroth, *The Last Puritans: Mainline Protestants and the Power of the Past* (Chapel Hill: University of North Carolina Press, 2015).

6. "The Most Important Contemporary Area for Social Action," Folder 4, Box 25, General Council Records, Congregational Library, Boston, MA (hereafter, GCR).

7. G. Bromley Oxnam, *Labor and Tomorrow's World* (New York: Abingdon-Cokesbury Press, 1944), 149.

8. Quoted in Kruse, *One Nation Under God*, 38.

9. Douglas Horton to James E. Walter, February 12, 1943, Folder 4, Box 25, GCR.

10. Oxnam, *Labor and Tomorrow's World*, 24, 32. On Oxnam's views of the Soviet Union, see Chapter 1 of this volume.

11. On Oxnam's anti-Catholicism, see Robert Moats Miller, *Bishop G. Bromley Oxnam: Paladin of Liberal Protestantism* (Nashville, TN: Abingdon Press, 1990), 398–446. Horton was friendlier with Catholics and saw cooperation with the Catholic Church as an extension of his ecumenism. See Theodore Louis Trost, *Douglas Horton and the Ecumenical Impulse in American Religion* (Cambridge, MA: Harvard University Press, 2002), 158–71.

12. "The Most Important Contemporary Area for Social Action," Folder 4, Box 25, GCR.

13. On the "laity" as an identity category, see Chapter 1 of this volume.

14. Quoted in Elesha J. Coffman, *The Christian Century and the Rise of the Protestant Mainline* (New York: Oxford University Press, 2013), 162–63.

15. "The Most Important Contemporary Area for Social Action," Folder 4, Box 25, GCR.

16. Oxnam, *Labor and Tomorrow's World*, 111.

17. Douglas Horton to James E. Walter, February 12, 1943, Folder 4, Box 25, GCR.

18. Oxnam, *Labor and Tomorrow's World*, 102, 139, 142–43, 146.

19. On the use of the "laymen" label by conservative women activists and its gendered implications, see Michelle M. Nickerson, *Mothers of Conservatism: Women and the Postwar Right* (Princeton, NJ: Princeton University Press, 2012), 79–82.

20. See, for example, Darren Dochuk, *Anointed with Oil: How Christianity and Crude Made Modern America* (New York, NY: Basic Books, 2019).

21. On the information-gathering apparatus created by fundamentalists and their corporate allies to monitor the Federal Council of Churches, see Michael J. McVicar, "Apostles of Deceit: Ecumenism, Fundamentalism, Surveillance, and the Contested Loyalties of Protestant Clergy during the Cold War," in *The FBI and Religion: Faith and National Security Before and After 9/11*, ed. Sylvester A. Johnson and Steven Weitzman (Berkeley: University of California Press, 2017), 85–107.

22. John E. Moser, *Right Turn: John T. Flynn and the Transformation of American Liberalism* (New York: New York University Press, 2005), 7.

23. Ibid., 94–95.

24. Ibid., 2, 196.

25. Flynn, *The Road Ahead*, 1, 9.

26. Ibid., 108.

27. Italics added by Flynn. Quoted in ibid., 113. See John C. Bennett, *Christianity and Communism* (New York: Association Press, 1948).

28. Flynn, *The Road Ahead*, 113.

29. Ibid., 119. The National Association of Evangelicals, formed in 1942, was not well known beyond evangelical circles in 1949 and therefore went unmentioned in Flynn's book.

30. Harry Truman, "Special Message to the Congress Recommending a Comprehensive Health Program," November 19, 1945, The American Presidency Project, https://www .presidency.ucsb.edu/documents/special-message-the-congress-recommending -comprehensive-health-program, accessed May 20, 2021.

31. Moser, *Right Turn*, 177–78; Flynn, *The Road Ahead*, 206; Ralph W. Gwinn to Rev. Cameron P. Hall, December 21, 1949, Folder 5, Box 63, RG 18, Federal Council of Churches Papers, Presbyterian Historical Society, Philadelphia, PA.

32. Roswell P. Barnes, *Forces Disrupting the Churches* (New York: The Federal Council of the Churches of Christ in America, 1944), 3–4.

33. "Memorandum by John C. Bennett on John T. Flynn's attack on him in *The Road Ahead*," Folder 5, Box 2, Series 5, John C. Bennett Papers, Union Theological Seminary, New York, NY.

34. *The Truth About the Federal Council of Churches* (New York: The Federal Council of Churches, 1950).

35. "Memorandum by John C. Bennett."

36. Ibid.

37. On the profit motive resolution, see Chapter 1 of this volume.

38. Cyrus Ransom Pangborn, "Free Churches and Social Change: A Critical Study of the Council for Social Action of the Congregational Christian Churches of the United States" (PhD diss., Columbia University, 1951), 50–53. For a sampling of the council's political activities, see "Action on National Legislation, 82nd Congress," "Council for Social Action Congregational Christian Churches Action on National Legislation," and "History of Legislative Department, Council for Social Action," LC-4, Council for Social Action Papers, Congregational Library, Boston, MA.

39. Italicized words appear in bold type in original. Walter H. Judd to Chester I. Bernard, September 29, 1953, appended to the "Report of the Board of Review of the Activities of the Council for Social Action," in "Council for Social Action. League to Uphold Congregational Principles," Box 112, GCR.

40. Committee Opposing Congregational Political Action, *They're Using Our Church* (Minneapolis: Committee Opposing Congregational Political Action, n.d.), Folder 5, Box 241, Walter Judd Papers, Hoover Institution Library and Archives, Stanford, CA (hereafter, Judd Papers).

41. On progressivism and volunteerism, see the discussion of Herbert Hoover in David M. Kennedy, *Freedom from Fear: The American People in Depression and War, 1929–1945* (New York: Oxford University Press, 1999), 70–103.

42. Russell J. Clinchy, "A Statement Presented to the Study Commission of the Council for Social Action—April 1951," Folder 5, Box 241, Judd Papers. On anti-secular reactions to the New Deal in a southern context, see Alison Collis Greene, *No Depression in Heaven: The Great Depression, the New Deal, and the Transformation of Religion in the Delta* (New York: Oxford University Press, 2015).

43. Buell G. Gallagher, "Welfare Work: Ally or Alternative," in *The Church and Organized Movements*, ed. Randolph Crump Miller (New York: Harper, 1946), 125–28.

44. John C. Bennett, "A Statement Presented to the Study Commission of the Council for Social Action—April 1951," Folder 5, Box 241, Judd Papers.

45. Advocates of the Council for Social Action were Albert B. Coe, Buell G. Gallagher, and Samuel C. Kincheloe. Critics of the council were Walter H. Judd, Thomas G. Long, and Gideon Seymour. The neutral members were Chester I. Barnard (president of the Rockefeller Foundation and member of the Department of Church and Economic Life and the Department of International Justice and Goodwill), Eugene E. Barnett (YMCA leader), and Frank W. Pierce (Standard Oil of New Jersey, and member of the National Lay Committee of the National Council of Churches).

46. "Report of the Board of Review of the Activities of the Council for Social Action," Box 112, GCR.

47. Walter H. Judd to Chester I. Bernard, September 29, 1953, in "Council for Social Action. League to Uphold Congregational Principles," Box 112, GCR.

48. Billy Graham to Walter Judd, July 18, 1950, Folder 6, Box 30, Judd Papers.

49. J. William T. Youngs, *The Congregationalists* (New York: Greenwood Press, 1990), chap. 10.

50. Walter H. Judd to Fred Hoskins, April 20, 1957, Folder 4, Box 241, Judd Papers.

51. See various files in Folder 4, Box 241, Judd Papers.

52. For an overview, see Jeanne Gayle Knepper, "Thy Kingdom Come: The Methodist Federation for Social Service and Human Rights, 1907–1948" (PhD diss., Iliff School of Theology and the University of Denver, 1996).

53. Ibid., 192–98.

54. "Negro Heads Methodist Church Federation for the First Time," *Los Angeles Sentinel*, January 8, 1948, 6. For biographical details of Brooks's life, see "Brooks, Robert Nathaniel," in *Encyclopedia of African American Religions*, ed. Larry G. Murphy, J. Gordon Melton, and Gary L. Ward (New York: Routledge, 2011), 117. On the educational and institutional trajectories of African American leaders like Brooks, see Chapter 4 in this volume.

55. "Feng's Accusation," *South China Morning Post*, December 29, 1947, 12.

56. "Methodists Scout a Communist Link," *New York Times*, December 30, 1947, 18.

57. "Methodist Bishop of Texas Smears Group Brooks Heads," *Afro-American*, January 17, 1948; "Revoking of Prize to Reporter Urged," *New York Times*, February 5, 1948, 21.

58. Yasuhiro Katagiri, *Black Freedom, White Resistance, and Red Menace: Civil Rights and Anticommunism in the Jim Crow South* (Baton Rouge: Louisiana State University Press, 2014), 27.

59. "Church Blasts Press Fallacy," *Chicago Defender*, February 21, 1948, 3.

60. On the 1948 meeting, see "Report Concerning 'Unofficial' Organizations Associated with the Methodist Church and Resolution," 2136-3-6:01, General Conference 1948 (D2002-005), Records of the Methodist Federation for Social Action, United Methodist Archives, Drew University.

61. Katagiri, *Black Freedom, White Resistance, and Red Menace*.

62. Ibid., 27–29.

63. Ibid., 31–32.

64. Knepper, "Thy Kingdom Come," 199–200; *Review of the Methodist Federation For Social Action, Formerly the Methodist Federation for Social Service*, February 17, 1952 (Washington, DC: Committee on Un-American Activities, U.S. House of Representatives, 1952),

6–21; "Church Urged to Disown Unit with 'Red Ideas,'" *Chicago Tribune*, November 4, 1951, 42; Kenneth Dole, "Social Action Official Raps Circuit Riders," November 14, 1951, *Washington Post*, B10.

65. On Pew, see Dochuk, *Anointed with Oil*.

66. On the National Lay Committee as a power struggle between the ecumenical and evangelical factions of American Protestantism, see Henry J. Pratt, *The Liberalization of American Protestantism: A Case Study in Complex Organizations* (Detroit: Wayne State University Press, 1972), 84–104; Eckard Vance Toy Jr., "The National Committee and the National Council of Churches: A Case Study of Protestants in Conflict," *American Quarterly* 21 (Summer 1969): 190–209. On the National Lay Committee as a contest between labor and capital, see Elizabeth A. Fones-Wolf, *Selling Free Enterprise: The Business Assault on Labor and Liberalism, 1945–60* (Urbana: University of Illinois Press, 1994), 218–45.

67. Quoted Fones-Wolf, *Selling Free Enterprise*, 238.

68. Ibid., 237–39.

69. Ibid., 244–45.

70. Ibid., 242–43.

71. William Inboden, *Religion and American Foreign Policy, 1945–1960: The Soul of Containment* (New York: Cambridge University Press, 2008), 81–84.

72. Molly Worthen, *Apostles of Reason: The Crisis of Authority in American Evangelicalism* (New York: Oxford University Press, 2016), 62, 66.

73. "Christian Criticism and Labor's Big Stick," *Christianity Today*, December 10, 1956, 23–25.

74. Dochuk, *Anointed with Oil*; Kruse, *One Nation Under God*; Bethany Moreton, *To Serve God and Wal-Mart: The Making of Christian Free Enterprise* (Cambridge, MA: Harvard University Press, 2009).

75. *The Christian Conscience and an Economy of Abundance* (New York: National Council of the Churches of Christ in the U.S.A., 1956), 5.

76. John Kenneth Galbraith, *The Affluent Society* (Boston: Houghton Mifflin, 1958), 2–3.

77. Michael Harrington, *The Other America: Poverty in the United States* (New York: Macmillan, 1962), 1.

78. *The Christian Conscience and an Economy of Abundance*.

79. *American Abundance: Possibilities and Problems from the Perspective of the Christian Conscience: Message and Reports* (New York: National Council of the Churches, 1956), 17.

80. Ibid., 7.

81. Ibid., 8–9.

82. Samuel Moyn, *Not Enough: Human Rights in an Unequal World* (Cambridge, MA: Belknap Press of Harvard University Press, 2018), 2–6.

83. *Harvest of Shame*, produced by David Lowe (New York: Columbia Broadcasting System, 1960), videocassette.

84. Lyndon B. Johnson, Michigan Commencement Address (Great Society Speech), May 22, 1964, American Rhetoric: Top 100 Speeches, https://www.americanrhetoric.com/speeches/lbjthegreatsociety.htm, accessed December 12, 2018.

Epilogue

1. Ray Holton and Marc Schogol, "Theologian, Wife Saw Only Suffering Left So They Decided It Was 'Time to Go,'" *Boston Globe*, March 2, 1975, 22; Marjorie Hyer, "Colleague Explains Cleric's Suicide Try," *Washington Post*, April 4, 1975, C5.

2. Harvey G. Cox, "The 'New Breed' in American Churches: Sources of Social Activism in American Religion," *Daedalus* 96, no. 1 (1967): 135–50, Alinsky quote at 138–39.

3. Darril Hudson, "The World Council of Churches and Racism in Southern Africa," *International Journal* 34, no. 3 (Summer 1979): 475–500; Claude E. Welch Jr., "Mobilizing Morality: The World Council of Churches and Its Program to Combat Racism, 1969–1994," *Human Rights Quarterly* 23, no. 4 (November 2001): 863–910. On Blake at the Baltimore amusement park, see Victoria W. Wolcott, *Race, Riots, and Roller Coasters: The Struggle over Segregated Recreation in America* (Philadelphia: University of Pennsylvania Press, 2012), 183–86.

4. Steven L. B. Jensen, *The Making of International Human Rights: The 1960s, Decolonization, and the Reconstruction of Global Values* (New York: Cambridge University Press, 2017). See also Bonny Ibhawoh, "Testing the Atlantic Charter: Linking Anticolonialism, Self-Determination and Universal Human Rights," *International Journal of Human Rights* 18, nos. 7–8 (2014): 842–60; Meredith Terretta, "'We Had Been Fooled into Thinking That the UN Watches over the Entire World': Human Rights, UN Trust Territories, and Africa's Decolonization," *Human Rights Quarterly* 34, no. 2 (2012): 329–60.

5. Mary L. Dudziak, *Cold War Civil Rights: Race and the Image of American Democracy* (Princeton, NJ: Princeton University Press, 2000).

6. Carol Anderson, *Eyes off the Prize: The United Nations and the African American Struggle for Human Rights, 1944–1955* (New York: Cambridge University Press, 2003); Carol Anderson, *Bourgeois Radicals: The NAACP and the Struggle for Colonial Liberation, 1941–1960* (New York: Cambridge University Press, 2015); Thomas F. Jackson, *From Civil Rights to Human Rights: Martin Luther King, Jr., and the Struggle for Economic Justice* (Philadelphia: University of Pennsylvania Press, 2007); Dudziak, *Cold War Civil Rights*.

7. Samuel Moyn, *The Last Utopia: Human Rights in History* (Cambridge, MA: Belknap Press of Harvard University Press, 2010), 129–33; Sarah B. Snyder, *From Selma to Moscow: How Human Rights Activists Transformed U.S. Foreign Policy* (New York: Columbia University Press, 2018), 99, 120–21.

8. Mark Philip Bradley, *The World Reimagined: Americans and Human Rights in the Twentieth Century* (New York: Cambridge University Press, 2016), 3.

9. On post-Protestants, see N. J. Demerath, "Cultural Victory and Organizational Defeat in the Paradoxical Decline of Liberal Protestantism," *Journal for the Scientific Study of Religion* 34, no. 4 (1995): 458–69; Matthew Hedstrom, *The Rise of Liberal Religion: Book Culture and American Spirituality in the Twentieth Century* (New York: Oxford University Press, 2012); David A. Hollinger, *After Cloven Tongues of Fire: Protestant Liberalism in Modern American History* (Princeton, NJ: Princeton University Press, 2013).

10. See, for example, Justin Reynolds, "Against the World: International Protestantism and the Ecumenical Movement Between Secularization and Politics, 1900–1952" (PhD diss., Columbia University, 2016), 345–408.

11. American Friends Service Committee, *Speak Truth to Power: A Quaker Search for an Alternative to Violence; A Study of International Conflict* ([Philadelphia]: American Friends Service Committee, 1955).

12. James F. Findlay, *Church People in the Struggle: The National Council of Churches and the Black Freedom Movement, 1950–1970* (New York: Oxford University Press, 1993), 203–4.

13. "Youth Sit-In at Church Conference," *South China Morning Post*, July 20, 1968, 16.

14. Jill K. Gill, *Embattled Ecumenism: The National Council of Churches, the Vietnam War, and the Trials of the Protestant Left* (DeKalb: Northern Illinois University Press, 2011), 162.

15. Sam Hodges, "Diverse Leaders' Group Offers Separation Plan," *UM News*, January 3, 2020, https://www.umnews.org/en/news/diverse-leaders-group-offers-separation-plan; Kristin Kobes Du Mez, *Jesus and John Wayne: How White Evangelicals Corrupted a Faith and Fractured a Nation* (New York: Liveright, 2021); R. Marie Griffith, *Moral Combat: How Sex Divided American Christians and Fractured American Politics* (New York: Basic Books, 2017); Anthony Michael Petro, *After the Wrath of God: AIDS, Sexuality, and American Religion* (New York: Oxford University Press, 2015); Robert O. Self, *All in the Family: The Realignment of American Democracy since the 1960s* (New York: Hill & Wang, 2012).

16. See, for example, Lily Geismer, "More Than Megachurches: Liberal Religion and Politics in the Suburbs," in *Faithful Republic: Religion and Politics in Modern America*, ed. Andrew Preston, Bruce J. Schulman, and Julian E. Zelizer (Philadelphia: University of Pennsylvania Press, 2015), 117–30.

17. Robert D. Putnam and David E. Campbell, *American Grace: How Religion Divides and Unites Us* (New York: Simon & Schuster, 2010); Robert Wuthnow, *The Restructuring of American Religion: Society and Faith Since World War II* (Princeton, NJ: Princeton University Press, 1988). The role of gender in the demographic decline of Christianity in the 1960s is most thoroughly interrogated in the British context. See Callum G. Brown, *The Death of Christian Britain: Understanding Secularisation, 1800–2000*, 2nd ed. (New York: Routledge, 2009).

18. Elesha J. Coffman, *The Christian Century and the Rise of the Protestant Mainline* (New York: Oxford University Press, 2013), 5.

19. Reliable data for the mid-century are hard to find, but a common estimate of about 30 percent in 1970 is cited here: Ed Stetzer, "If It Doesn't Stem Its Decline, Mainline Protestantism Has Just 23 Easters Left," *Washington Post*, April 28, 2017, https://www.washingtonpost.com/news/acts-of-faith/wp/2017/04/28/if-it-doesnt-stem-its-decline-mainline-protestantism-has-just-23-easters-left/. On the 2007 and 2014 statistics, see Michael Lipka, "Mainline Protestants Make Up Shrinking Number of U.S. Adults," May 18, 2015, Pew Research Center, http://www.pewresearch.org/fact-tank/2015/05/18/mainline-protestants-make-up-shrinking-number-of-u-s-adults/.

20. Wade Clark Roof and William McKinney, *American Mainline Religion: Its Changing Shape and Future* (New Brunswick, NJ: Rutgers University Press, 1987), 152.

21. "Mainline Protestants," Religious Landscape Study, Pew Research Center, https://www.pewforum.org/religious-landscape-study/religious-tradition/mainline-protestant/, accessed May 20, 2021.

22. On the politics of institutional funding, see Jill K. Gill, "The Politics of Ecumenical Disunity: The Troubled Marriage of Church World Service and the National Council of Churches," *Religion and American Culture* 14, no. 2 (2004): 175–212.

23. Bobby Chris Alexander, *Televangelism Reconsidered: Ritual in the Search for Human Community* (Atlanta, GA: Scholars Press, 1994); Razelle Frankl, *Televangelism: The Marketing of Popular Religion* (Carbondale: Southern Illinois University Press, 1987); Shayne Lee, *Holy Mavericks: Evangelical Innovators and the Spiritual Marketplace* (New York: University Press, 2009); R. Laurence Moore, *Selling God: American Religion in the Marketplace of Culture* (New York: Oxford University Press, 1994); Daniel Vaca, *Evangelicals Incorporated: Books and the Business of Religion in America* (Cambridge, MA: Harvard University Press, 2019); James Wellman, *High on God: How Megachurches Won the Heart of America* (New York: Oxford University Press, 2020).

24. For a nuanced reading of evangelicals and South African apartheid through a foreign policy lens, see Lauren Frances Turek, *To Bring the Good News to All Nations: Evangelical Influence on Human Rights and U.S. Foreign Relations* (Ithaca, NY: Cornell University Press, 2020), 151–80.

25. Recent scholarship on evangelicals has demonstrated their long relationship with conservatism. See, for example, Darren Dochuk, *From Bible Belt to Sunbelt: Plain-Folk Religion, Grassroots Politics, and the Rise of Evangelical Conservatism* (New York: W.W. Norton, 2012); Du Mez, *Jesus and John Wayne*; Matthew Avery Sutton, *American Apocalypse: A History of Modern Evangelicalism* (Cambridge, MA: Belknap Press of Harvard University Press, 2017); Molly Worthen, *Apostles of Reason: The Crisis of Authority in American Evangelicalism* (New York: Oxford University Press, 2016). For an account that disputes these findings, see David William Bebbington, George M. Marsden, and Mark A. Noll, *Evangelicals: Who They Have Been, Are Now, and Could Be* (Grand Rapids, MI: Eerdmans, 2019). Scholars have also noted that the opposition among fundamentalists to ecumenical Protestants had predated the 1940s, with substantial hostility to the social gospel and ecumenism dating back to at least the 1910s. The mid-twentieth-century period has been highlighted here because it was a key moment for the institutionalization of that hostility.

26. See Jefferson Cowie, *Stayin' Alive: The 1970s and the Last Days of the Working Class* (New York: New Press, 2010).

27. James T. Kloppenberg, *Reading Obama: Dreams, Hope, and the American Political Tradition* (Princeton, NJ: Princeton University Press, 2012), 198–209; Kristin Du Mez, "Can Hillary Clinton's Faith Help Her Lead a Fractured Nation?," *Religion and Politics*, July 25, 2016, https://religionandpolitics.org/2016/07/25/can-clintons-faith-help-her-lead-a-fractured-nation/.

28. For an overview of the contemporary religious Left, see Jack Jenkins, *American Prophets: The Religious Roots of Progressive Politics and the Ongoing Fight for the Soul of the Country* (New York: Harper Collins, 2020); R. Marie Griffith and Melani McAlister, eds., *Religion and Politics in the Contemporary United States* (Baltimore, MD: Johns Hopkins University Press, 2008).

INDEX

Page numbers in italics refer to figures.

ACKNOWLEDGMENTS

Finishing a book during a pandemic, at a moment when so many of us are cut off from our family, friends, and colleagues, is a stark reminder of just how indebted I am to the multitude of people who have helped make writing this book possible. I am deeply grateful to the historians, archivists, administrators, research assistants, and students without whom I could not have written this book.

This book began at the University of California, Berkeley, where generous colleagues patiently listened to nascent ideas and carefully read early drafts. They include Jennifer L. Allen, Ross Astoria, Christopher Church, Maggie Elmore, Hannah Farber, Lynne Gerber, Alice Goff, Rebecca Hodges, Daniel Immerwahr, George Lazopolous, James Lin, Damon Mayrl, Natalie Mendoza, Gabriel Milner, Pablo Palomino, Terence Renaud, Caroline Ritter, Tim Ruckle, Tehila Sasson, Brandon Schechter, German Vergara, and Albert Wu. I am also grateful for the mentorship I received from Mark Brilliant, John Connelly, Brian DeLay, Robin Einhorn, Victoria Frede, Nils Gilman, Kerwin Klein, Waldo Martin, Mark Peterson, Daniel Sargent, Jonathan Sheehan, and Sarah Song. Richard Hutson took a personal interest in my work and gave me plenty of thoughtful feedback. Richard Cándida Smith has not only helped me see this project through with helpful commentary and words of encouragement, but he is also more responsible than anyone else for my decision to become a historian. I am especially grateful to David A. Hollinger, whose professionalism, devotion to intellectual rigor, and commitment to the historical community has been my model for what it means to be an academic and to dedicate one's life to scholarly pursuits.

Much of this manuscript was written at the John C. Danforth Center on Religion and Politics at Washington University in St. Louis. I had the privilege of working with Fannie Bialek, Christine Croxall, John Inazu, Moshe Kornfeld, Dana Logan, Laurie Maffly-Kipp, Lerone Martin, Mark Valeri, and Abram Van Engen, all of whom read portions of this book. I am especially grateful to R. Marie Griffith and Leigh Eric Schmidt for their continued support. I gratefully acknowledge financial support for the publication of this book from the John C. Danforth Center on Religion and Politics.

Colleagues at the University of Toronto and Mississippi State University were thoughtful interlocutors and gave helpful feedback on my work. At U of T, I was delighted to have discussed my work with Cindy Ewing, Pamela Klassen, Néstor Medina, Emily Nacol, William Nelson, Ronald Pruessen, Timothy Sayle, Barton Scott, Anna Su, Luis van Isschot, Lynne Viola, and Robert Vipond. I am especially grateful to Phyllis Airhart, who invited me to Emmanuel College, and to Nicholas Sammond, who invited me to join the Centre for the Study of the United States. Nic, along with Kevin O'Neill at the Centre for Diaspora and Transnational Studies, give me opportunities to present my work in progress. I am also grateful to the many wonderful scholars and friends in the greater Toronto area, including Margaret Boittin, Maxime Dagenais, Miguel de Figueiredo, Heidi Matthews, Emily Nacol, William Nelson, Anna Su, and Lilia Topouzova. At Mississippi State University, I would like to thank Stephanie Freeman, Andrew Lang, Davide Orsini, Morgan J. Robinson, Courtney Thompson, and Joseph Thompson for reading parts of my book.

This book was completed at the University at Buffalo, SUNY. All of my colleagues have been welcoming and supportive, but special thanks are due to Susan Cahn, Sasha Pack, Erik Seeman, Kristin Stapleton, Tamara Thornton, and Victoria Wolcott for carefully reading my manuscript and for invaluable advice. I gratefully acknowledge financial support for the publication of this book from the Julian Park Fund of the College of Arts and Sciences at the University at Buffalo, SUNY.

I am lucky to be part of an international community of historians who have helped me along the way. Many folks have offered me thoughtful commentary and good advice over the years, including Claire Rydell Arcenas, Margaret Bendroth, Venus Bivar, Anne Blankenship, Elizabeth Borgwardt, Jennifer Burns, Peter Cajka, Gordon H. Chang, Darren Dochuk, Alexandre Dubé, Mark Edwards, Ada Focer, Andrea Friedman, Healan Gaston, Kathryn Gin Lum, Leah Gordon, Udi Greenberg, Ian Hall, Paul Harvey, Matthew Hedstrom, Daniel Hummel, Steven Jensen, Christine Johnson, Natalie Johnson, Peter Kastor, Gale Kenny, David Kirkpatrick, Amy Kittelstrom, Linde Lindkvist, Rachel Lindsey, Melani McAlister, Natalie Mendoza, Jennifer Miller, David Mislin, Kate Moran, Samuel Moyn, Christopher Nichols, Veronica Paredes, Nicholas Pruitt, Justin Reynolds, Or Rosenboim, Timothy Schenk, Victoria Smolkin, Sarah Snyder, Ronit Stahl, Tiffany Stanley, Daniel Steinmetz-Jenkins, Chris Suh, David Swartz, Michael Thompson, Lauren Turek, Laura Westhoff, and Caroline Winterer. Amanda Peery helped edit the introduction and Amy Fallas helped me track down important documents. I thank Daniel Bessner for reading the Introduction and Alison Greene and Matthew Sutton for reading the book's Epilogue.

This book would not have been possible without the tireless work of archivists and librarians. I am thankful for the dedicated staff of the Bancroft Library at the University of California, Berkeley; the Hoover Institution Special Collections at Stanford University; the Houghton Library at Harvard University; the Library of Congress; Special Collections at Ohio State University; the Oral History Research Office at Columbia University; the Stuart A. Rose Manuscript, Archives, and Rare Book Library at Emory University; the United Library at Garrett-Evangelical Seminary; and the Yale Divinity Library. I owe special thanks to Nancy J. Taylor at the Presbyterian Historical Society and Margaret Bendroth at the Congregational Library for their extended help. Frances Bristol and Brian Shetler at the Methodist Archives at Drew University and Betty Bolden at Union Theological Seminary helped me through the disruptions to my research created by Hurricane Sandy. Dolores Colon, Allison Davis, Frances Lyons, Jeffrey Monseau, Sarah Patton, and Charlene Peacock helped me track down images during the COVID outbreak, when travel was impossible.

The staff at the University of Pennsylvania Press were the model of professionalism. Bob Lockhart shepherded this book with wisdom and patience, for which I am grateful. I would also like to thank the series editors, including Jennifer Ratner-Rosenhagen, Joel Isaac, and Samuel Moyn, for their invaluable advice, and especially Angus Burgin, who was a thoughtful reader of my work and devoted much of his time to improving the manuscript. I greatly appreciate the helpful feedback on the manuscript by Andrew Preston and the anonymous reader.

Friends and family have supported me throughout this process. I am grateful to have the lifelong friendships of Gary, Ian, John, and Michael. I am lucky to have in my life Mary, Steve, Anne, Jonathan, Michael, Jen, Dave, Andrea, Faina, Mikhail, Abram, and Galina. I greatly miss the company of Janet and Roman. No words can fully acknowledge my debt to Katherine, to whom this book is dedicated.